THE STATE OF ACCESS

INNOVATIVE GOVERNANCE IN THE 21ST CENTURY

GOWHER RIZVI
Series editor

This is the third volume in a series that examines important issues of governance, public policy, and administration, highlighting innovative practices and original research worldwide. All titles in the series will be copublished by the Brookings Institution Press and the Ash Institute for Democratic Governance and Innovation, housed at Harvard University's John F. Kennedy School of Government.

Decentralizing Governance: Emerging Concepts and Practices,
G. Shabbir Cheema and Dennis A. Rondinelli, eds. (2007)

Innovations in Government: Research, Recognition, and Replication
Sandford Borins, ed. (2008)

Unlocking the Power of Networks: Keys to High-Performance Government
Stephen Goldsmith and Donald F. Kettl, eds. (forthcoming, 2009)

THE STATE OF ACCESS

Success and Failure of Democracies to Create Equal Opportunities

JORRIT DE JONG
GOWHER RIZVI

editors

ASH INSTITUTE FOR DEMOCRATIC GOVERNANCE AND INNOVATION
John F. Kennedy School of Government
Harvard University

BROOKINGS INSTITUTION PRESS
Washington, D.C.

Copyright © 2008

ASH INSTITUTE FOR DEMOCRATIC GOVERNANCE AND INNOVATION
HARVARD UNIVERSITY

Library of Congress Cataloging-in-Publication data
The state of access : success and failure of democracies to create equal opportunities / Jorrit de Jong, Gowher Rizvi, editors.
   p.   cm. — (Innovative governance in the 21st century)
   Includes bibliographical references and index.
   Summary: "A comparative, cross-disciplinary exploration of the ways in which democratic institutions fail or succeed to create the equal opportunities that they have promised to deliver to the people they serve"—Provided by publisher.
   ISBN 978-0-8157-7501-0 (pbk. : alk. paper)
   1. Equality.   2. Democracy.   3. Economic history.   4. Social justice.   I. Jong, Jorrit de.   II. Rizvi, Gowher.   III. Title.   IV. Series.
   JC575.S75 2008
   320.01'1—dc22   2008038065

9 8 7 6 5 4 3 2 1
The paper used in this publication meets minimum requirements of the American National Standard for Information Sciences—Permanence of Paper for Printed Library Materials: ANSI Z39.48-1992.

Typeset in Adobe Garamond

Composition by R. Lynn Rivenbark
Macon, Georgia

Contents

Where, after all, do universal human rights begin? In small places, close to home—so close and so small that they cannot be seen on any map of the world. Yet they are the world of the individual person: the neighborhood he lives in; the school or college he attends; the factory, farm, or office where he works. Such are the places where every man, woman, and child seeks equal justice, equal opportunity, and equal dignity without discrimination. Unless these rights have meaning there, they have little meaning anywhere. Without concerted citizen action to uphold them so close to home, we shall look in vain for progress in the larger world.

—ELEANOR ROOSEVELT
March 27, 1958, United Nations, New York
(see www.udhr.net/index.php/eleanor-roosevelt)

Preface

This book is about gaps between principle and practice in democratic governance. It is an attempt to explore the ways in which democratic institutions around the world fail or succeed to create the equal opportunities that they have promised to deliver on behalf of society. Ideally, rights, rules, and regulations guarantee equal access to democratic processes, public services, and justice. Reality routinely disappoints: policymaking processes in democracies are sometimes opaque and exclusionary. Dominant stakeholders' interests often prevail in consultative rounds and fine-tuning of laws after they have been passed. Once laws are enacted, it is generally left to executive agencies to determine the practice of policy, the precise shape of which may determine who has easy access to benefits and services and who doesn't. Even in participatory democracies, weaker voices do not always have the opportunity to influence policy implementation. Devolved decisionmaking is supposed to bring the policymaking process closer to the people, but it often puts power in the hands of powerful local forces. Minority rights are not necessarily guaranteed nor enforced once power is decentralized.

Another problem with exclusionary decisionmaking processes is that they can short-circuit adequate assessment of people's needs. If citizens are not even consulted in the policymaking process, how can policymakers be sure they are meeting their constituents' real needs? Flawed democratic processes lead to flawed public services and flawed rules and regulations. And flawed services and regulations lead to undesirable societal outcomes. Access to democratic processes is therefore an important condition to ensure equal opportunities and access to public services.

Public services are typically administered through standardized and formalized bureaucracies. Although public organizations generally work for the common good, the inherent constraints exerted by legal frameworks, established power dynamics, and scarce resources limit their ability to create value for citizens. Bureaucracies, faced with inadequate funding, tend to develop rationing strategies. They may discourage even those who are entitled to services from applying for them, not by means of policy restrictions but by means of excessively complicated procedures. When officials have a large amount of discretionary authority, their decisions may be arbitrary and may disadvantage certain groups. In cases where discretionary power is minimal, on the other hand, street-level service providers may be unable to respond adequately to client need; excessive attention to the rules may not allow for special circumstances or equitable treatment. Although management concepts such as Total Quality Management and New Public Management have recognized the vast inefficiencies intrinsic to malfunctioning public organizations, not much emphasis has been placed on the fact that underperforming bureaucracies also create large *inequities*. Efficacy and efficiency are important principles in public administration, but when they are divorced from democratic values such as equality and equity, they reduce government to its business function, neglecting its role as the guarantor of social justice.

Democratic rights have meaning only if an individual can exercise them. Entitlements to public services and benefits are only useful insofar as a citizen may claim them. Legal rights are only real protections when an individual can rely on enforcement. Transparent and fair judicial institutions can only guarantee people's rights when all citizens have adequate access to the legal system. If legal assistance is critical for a fair trial, but is too expensive for low-income individuals, social injustice is likely to be reproduced in the courts. If there are insufficient funds to incentivize and oversee pro bono litigation, "equal rights under the law" becomes empty rhetoric rather than actual practice.

Malfunctioning institutions of democratic governance not only have an adverse effect on distributive justice but also undermine procedural justice. Lack of access should therefore concern theorists and practitioners on both the right and left of the political spectrum. Those supporting a minimalist democratic model of statehood still maintain that government should secure basic political and property rights. Liberal egalitarians invest in properly functioning institutions because they promote distributive justice. Those advocating equality of outcomes share a stake in identifying mechanisms of exclusion and disentitlement.

In this volume we hope to serve all practitioners regardless of political and ideological inclination. No matter how much or how little we condone state intervention in society's workings, as individuals invested in democracy we can agree that we want our institutions to work as they are supposed to work—effectively,

efficiently, and equitably. Obviously, we can disagree about the amount of effort
we can afford to spend on that or the extent to which the state is responsible for
this. The bottom line, however, is that democracies seeking social justice—however we define it and however much we are willing to invest in it—need strong,
responsive, and accountable institutions because, regardless of the ideological and
political choices concerning state intervention, equal access is a fundamental
modern value. In chapter 1 we examine the concept of "equal access" in greater
depth and in relation to related concepts such as "fair treatment" and "equal
opportunity."

The access paradox bedeviling democracies without responsive or accountable
institutions is that it is precisely the citizens who most depend on public services
who are often least able to access them. Typically, those who are well off have
more options in life. Because they are wealthier, more mobile, better educated,
and have better networks, they are able to obtain or regain access to services that
are denied to the less privileged. Thus, lack of access is generally first and most
noticeable among the least advantaged groups in society, who often suffer from a
convergence of disabilities that impede access: poor health, little or no education,
and social marginalization. Clearly, those who are dependent on external assistance or on fair law enforcement suffer the most when such assistance or enforcement underperforms or is simply unavailable. Weaker groups in society are more
vulnerable than the privileged to excessive bureaucracy and tangled procedures for
redressing wrongs, and they suffer from them more often, more directly, and with
greater consequences.

The chapters in this volume typically start with an assessment of the obstacles
facing specific disadvantaged groups in society vis-à-vis certain public services or
social benefits. Each chapter has as its point of departure the social outcomes of
particular institutions, policies, procedures, and group behavior. The question is
always: How can the inequalities or inequities that we find in practice be
explained in the context of promises of equal opportunity offered by a state's constitution, laws, policies, or operating procedures? Each chapter then describes
mechanisms that have systematically disadvantaged or excluded certain groups or
individuals. An analysis of the shortcomings of democratic institutions and public organizations leads to suggestions for improvement and the implications of
various solutions. In these discussions, we also examine the roles and responsibilities that citizens themselves—individually, in organized groups, or as a community at large—need to play in order to obtain better access to services.

We hope that this volume leads to a deeper understanding of the mechanisms
of exclusion in place even in democratic societies and helps develop strategies for
inclusion through improved access for citizens. Fortunately, there are many examples of innovative approaches and high-performing institutions that have the
democratic value of equal access at the heart of their missions. Unless individuals
across society receive equal opportunities to realize their potential, democracy as

a whole cannot achieve its larger purpose of guaranteeing social justice for its citizens. The evidence and insights provided by this book are intended as modest
contributions to the identification and removal of impediments to that ideal.

This book is the result of a collaborative effort of a diverse international group
of scholars, who have been drawn together from a range of fields: political science,
public administration, economics, law, development studies, management and
organizational theory, sociology, history, and philosophy. They share a common
desire to understand the nature of exclusion and to develop remedies for
improved access. In an effort to achieve these goals, all of them have had to look
beyond the boundaries of their respective disciplines and have engaged in workshop and conference discussions, a process that has produced a work that is more
than the sum of its parts. Those interested in following and joining this interdisciplinary research and teaching project on improving access can visit the website
www.improvingaccess.org.

We are indebted to many people who helped us shape this book. First and
foremost, we are grateful to the contributors, who were willing to get a new perspective on their own work by viewing it through the lens of access. We also want
to thank our wonderful colleagues and the distinguished members of the advisory
committee of the Harvard Kennedy School's Ash Institute for Democratic Governance and Innovation. In particular, we want to thank Tony Saich, Marty
Mauzy, Bruce Jackan, Susan Valaskovic, Carla Chrisfield, Jason Pryde, and Andre
Rolle. They have supported us in many ways. Our colleagues from the Center for
Government Studies at Leiden University have also been very dedicated and
resourceful in their support of the project: Anja van der Wal, Albert Jan Kruiter,
Floor van Dijk, Janine van Niel, Constant Hijzen, Johannes Taal, and Jouke de
Vries. Joeri van den Steenhoven, Lobke van der Meulen, and Carolien Bok at the
Knowledge Land Foundation (Nederland Kennisland) have also been unfailingly
encouraging. We are very grateful to Mark Moore, Arre Zuurmond, Bina Agarwal, Irwin Turbitt, and Sanderijn Cels for their comments on portions of the
manuscript. Peter Kasbergen deserves much praise for his help in preparing the
workshops and the manuscript. Jessica Crewe has provided us with excellent edi-
torial assistance. We thank our editors at Brookings, Chris Kelaher, Janet Walker,
and Katherine Scott for their guidance and Susan Woollen for help with the
cover. Finally we would like to thank our families for all they are: Agnese Barolo,
Maya Barolo-Rizvi, Sanderijn Cels, and Dante de Jong. We promise to be more
accessible, now that the book is finished!

This volume stands at the beginning, not the end, of this research project. It
is our hope that the perspectives offered here will open up new areas for exploration and debate. To this end we welcome feedback and suggestions through our
website, www.improvingaccess.org.

PART I

Access and the State

1

The Castle and the Village: The Many Faces of Limited Access

JORRIT DE JONG AND GOWHER RIZVI

Access Denied

No author in world literature has done more to give shape to the nightmarish challenges posed to access by modern bureaucracies than Franz Kafka. In his novel *The Castle*, "K.," a land surveyor, arrives in a village ruled by a castle on a hill (see Kafka 1998). He is under the impression that he is to report for duty to a castle authority. As a result of a bureaucratic mix-up in communications between the castle officials and the villagers, K. is stuck in the village at the foot of the hill and fails to gain access to the authorities. The villagers, who hold the castle officials in high regard, elaborately justify the rules and procedures to K. The more K. learns about the castle, its officials, and the way they relate to the village and its inhabitants, the less he understands his own position. The Byzantine codes and formalities governing the exchanges between castle and village seem to have only one purpose: to exclude K. from the castle. Not only is there no way for him to reach the castle, but there is also no way for him to leave the village. The villagers tolerate him, but his tireless struggle to clarify his place there only emphasizes his quasi-legal status. Given K.'s belief that he had been summoned for an assignment by the authorities, he remains convinced that he has not only a right but also a duty to go to the castle! How can a bureaucracy operate in direct opposition to its own stated purposes? How can a rule-driven institution be so unaccountable? And how can the "obedient subordinates" in the village wield so much power to act in their own self-interest? But because everyone seems to find the castle bureaucracy flawless, it is K. himself who seems to be the problematic element.

The original German title of *The Castle, Das Schloss,* is ambiguous because *Schloss* means both "castle" and "lock." This double meaning is typical of the way authority manifests itself in the book. The seemingly legal-rational administration on the hill has the appearance of a well-organized state, but in practice it becomes an obscure and incompetent bureaucracy that remains closed to outsiders.[1] Interestingly, the villagers are completely insensitive to the castle's opacity and inefficiency. It takes an outsider like K. to question the status quo. K does not *fit in*. As a result of his otherness (he comes from outside the village, has an unfamiliar profession, and claims to have a special assignment), he is marginalized and seen as an obnoxious, demanding pain in the neck. The burden of proof is put on K., not on the bureaucracy, to demonstrate he has the right to enter. K. receives scarcely any explanation of what recourse he has to gain access to the castle and its rulers. The arbitrariness of the officials' behavior and the fundamental uncertainty it creates on K.'s part would be a stunning violation by any standard of administrative law.

On the other hand, the villagers themselves are not particularly helpful. They have their own agendas, opinions, and ways of dealing with K. Some help him (but only for their own advantage), some deliberately misdirect him, and others remain utterly indifferent to his situation. One thing is clear: no one has a real interest in helping K. gain access to the castle. It is certainly possible that it is not the castle itself that denies K. access to the authorities it houses, but rather the village and its inhabitants. They use institutional procedures as an excuse while in fact employing their own informational advantages, social networks, and discretionary powers to secure their interests. Perhaps the castle's authorities do not even know that K. is trying to reach them . . .

Defining Access: Matching Rights and Capacities

The subject of this book is the concept of access. We understand access as

> . . . the match between societal commitment and institutional capacity to deliver rights and services and people's capacity to benefit from those rights and services.

This definition is a bold attempt to develop an approach to institutions of democratic governance that recognizes hidden mechanisms generating inequitable outcomes such that some citizens are excluded from access. These exclusionary systems may be hidden in more than one way: First, in the sense that potential

---

1. This is just one possible interpretation of the tale's core meaning, and is not necessarily what Kafka intended to illustrate with the novel or its title. As a matter of fact, the meaning of the novel has been the subject of quite a lot discussion. For an overview, see http://en.wikipedia.org/wiki/The_Castle_%28 novel%29.

beneficiaries do not know how or why they are being denied access to certain services and goods (think of the land surveyor K.). They may also be obscured in the sense that the institutions themselves remain unaware of the discrepancies between de jure and de facto equality of access (think of the castle authorities). Finally, the mechanisms of access may be kept from the public eye; people may be very well aware of inequitable access but they may lack the power and the motivation to do something about it (like most of Kafka's villagers).

In our definition the distinction between "societal commitment" and "institutional capacity" on the one hand (taking into account the various constraints and dynamics of democratic institutions) and "people's capacity" on the other hand (taking into account the real capabilities with which nature and heritage have provided them) enables us to examine (mis)matches between the two. When full access is understood as a perfect match and lack of access as a complete mismatch, the scope of our definition covers a broad range of situations in between. Although this approach remains neutral to causes, reasons, and motivations behind various instances of impeded access, its focus on rights leaves it not neutral to consequences of impeded access. At the heart of this book is our definition of rights as *enforceable* rights and entitlements as *enforceable* entitlements. "Access" is nothing less than the means by which individual rights become (or fail to become) practice in real-life encounters between people and institutions. For it is exactly in these encounters that the democratic values of equity, equality, and social justice have meaning.

Furthermore, we must distinguish between societal commitment and institutional capacity. In some societies, equality of opportunity may be a widely shared ideal that institutional capacity is insufficient to realize. Conversely, social obstacles may prevent the equity of access that a community's institutions have the ability to deliver. Our definition acknowledges the tension between societal commitment and institutional capacity in order to remain aware of the forces that limit access in broader social terms. This distinction becomes relevant in chapters 4, 10, and especially 6. Finally, our definition explicitly emphasizes that it takes two to tango: it is not just failing states that cause a lack of access. People's capacity to benefit from their rights and claim their entitlements is an equally important variable, which we will explore in many ways. As we shall see, neither problems with access nor solutions to improve access originate at just one side of the equation. The equitable implementation of societal commitments through democratic institutions requires work on both sides of the mismatch.

Access to What?

Citizens living in democracies all over the world require access to a vast range of facilities on a daily basis: food, clean water, sanitation, electricity, and transportation, to name just a few. Businesses can't survive without access to markets, financial services, and telecommunications. Communities suffer when access to health care, education, and protection against crime and violence is inadequate. In societies with higher living standards, social safety nets have been established by the state. Those who are chronically ill, unemployed, or otherwise disadvantaged are often entitled to social services and public benefits. Adequate access to these social security provisions should prevent the people who need these services from becoming marginalized and relatively deprived.

The provision of these goods and services is usually administered through intermediary organizations. In the case of public goods, the government itself may be a direct provider, or it may outsource implementation to other parties within a given legal framework or management contract (Goldsmith and Eggers 2004). In many countries, water, electricity, transportation, education, and health care are considered public goods, but the actual providers are private sector organizations, operating in relation to the government with certain mandates concerning price, quality of service, and accessibility. If the government provides goods or services itself, it may do so directly or via semi-autonomous executive agencies or lower levels of government. It may also choose to resort to alternative delivery mechanisms, such as vouchers (Trebilcock and Daniels 2005). In both cases the delivery mechanism is the medium between a citizen (client) and a good or service. In order to have access to the good, the citizen needs to have access to the intermediary. For example, in order to have access to electricity, one needs to register with a power company. In order to receive unemployment benefits, one needs to apply at the social benefits office. In order to be treated in a hospital, one needs to be enrolled in an insurance scheme. Thus, in practice, access to certain goods means access to the organizations, programs, or schemes administering said goods. Even though equal access to certain services may have been politically mandated, equal access to the organizations and procedures can turn out to be a completely different thing. Much depends on the capacity of intermediary providers to design and manage equitable processes and procedures (Ensor and others 2002; Cook and others 1999; Jacobs and Price 2006; Valdez and others 1993; Tate and Quesnel 1995).

This holds true not only for rights to goods and services but also for rights that protect people from the government or from each other (Rhode 2004). Even with minimal government intervention, the protection of basic political and social liberties is dependent on the state's capacity to enforce these rights. And the capacity to enforce these rights depends ultimately on publicly financed intermediary organizations, such as the police, the army, inspectors of all kinds, and the justice system. This means that even if we do not want to expand the social compact beyond the protection of basic rights, we still need to pay for the administration of the enforcement of these rights (Holmes and Sunstein 1999). Quality of enforcement is variable. Let us imagine a state that promises only to protect citizens from foreign enemies and from violation of their property rights, but that cannot adequately fund the agencies responsible for these tasks. In this case, enforcement officials would have to make serious choices about whom to protect first, what to protect them from, and how. Access to safety and security, which according to policy is the mainstay of government service provision, would still turn out not to be equal for everyone. Again the institutional capacity to realize rights is determined by intermediary organizations that shape encounters between government and citizens.

The more rights people expect, as to both goods and services and government protection, the higher the costs of service delivery and law enforcement. The higher the costs, the more likely taxes will increase. If a government's population is largely poor, its ability to extract taxes is low. In this case, either the general quality of service delivery is low but everybody has equal access to what there is, or the availability of goods is better but fewer citizens can access state benefits. These inequalities may be completely random if the scarce resources are allocated by lottery. More realistically, inequalities in receiving services, goods, or protection will be related to preexisting social inequalities that determine access to intermediary organizations. Those with better contacts, better education, better endowments, and so on are more likely to gain access to the government's delivery systems and to benefit from protection by the state.

Even in situations when citizens enjoy many rights and the state has plentiful resources, individuals do not necessarily have the opportunity to claim the full range of their entitlements. Financial resources may be in place, but specific goods or services may be unavailable for shorter or longer periods of time (for example, think of shortages of certain crops, clean water, and teachers or medical personnel). Professionals and officials may be arbitrary, discriminatory, or corrupt in distributing public goods, and the quality of these services may not meet the expectations of the citizens.

In all such cases, it becomes very important for citizens to have access to mechanisms for making their needs known (Hirschmann 1970; Cheema 2005; Shah 2005). In early stages of the policymaking process, this means the ability to express demands, either individually or through organized interest and advocacy groups. During policy execution, procedures of appeal and redress may provide access to accountability. If citizens feel that they have been treated unfairly by the government or its intermediaries, they should be able to seek redress by filing a complaint, by appealing court decisions, or simply by applying directly to the authorities.

The executive branch alone cannot guarantee access to services. The legislative branch and the judicial branch play major parts in the establishment of equal access to public goods. If weaker voices are not heard in the process of designing laws and regulations, and if stronger stakeholders dominate the agenda, the needs of the disadvantaged are likely to remain unmet in the resulting policy. Not surprisingly, projects designed for the benefit of the poor in developing countries are often monopolized by those in power with access to the

government. If those disadvantaged by a government do not have proper channels of recourse, their problems will remain unsolved and their situations unrec-
ognized, and unjust administrative systems will remain unchanged. That is why
access to public services is closely linked to, and in fact inseparable from, access
to mechanisms of accountability. (In a later section, "Faces of Access," we discuss
the "chain of access" in more depth.)

Access as Social Justice

Equal access touches on the concept of social justice. It is a norm of equal opportunity across different areas of life: politics, economy, social services, justice, and
more. As a normative conception of equal opportunity, equal access distinguishes itself from broader liberal theories of social justice in the sense that it is
both more specific than these theories and is applicable to a wider domain. Equal
access is more specific in the sense that it focuses on implementation, on the
practice of democratic institutions vis-à-vis their beneficiaries. Most theories
focus the institutions per se, or on policy in general. Equal access also covers
a wider domain than most theories of justice in the sense that the concept does
not relate merely to distributions of income and wealth, nor to membership in
political and social entities, but to a wide range of areas of life in which people
desire to participate. Our theory of access is concerned with the specific mechanisms of exclusion and inclusion that occur in a wide variety of realms within
democratic societies.

Nevertheless, in developing these ideas we were informed and guided by the
ideas of theorists of social justice who were concerned with broader questions of
political, economic, and social justice. We do not intend to cover their ideas here
in depth, because we would not do justice to the subject. However, to elaborate our
central concept, access, we want to highlight some of the most important notions
that have guided our thinking about equal access as a conception of justice.

Justice as Fairness

The conception of "justice as fairness" propounded by the American philosopher
John Rawls has arguably been the most influential formulation of social justice for
practitioners and scholars of democratic governance. Rawls was concerned with
the design of a just "basic structure" of society as expressed through its fundamental institutions, such as the constitution, markets, and courts. These institutions are responsible for the delivery of rights and obligations and the (re)distri-
bution of socioeconomic goods. Rawls holds that in a well-ordered society, these
institutions are to be guided by two underlying principles of justice:

—Principle 1: "Each person has the same indefeasible claim to a fully adequate
scheme of basic liberties, which scheme is compatible with the same scheme of
liberties for all."

—Principle 2: Social and economic inequalities are to satisfy two conditions.[2] First, they are to be attached to offices and positions open to all under conditions of fair equality and opportunity. Second, according to the "difference principle," [these inequalities] are to be to the greatest benefit of the least advantaged members of society (Rawls 2001, 42).

Rawls's first principle protects the liberal freedoms of conscience, expression, association, and related political rights. In order to make sure that these rights are indeed meaningful options for anyone, regardless of background, status, or wealth, the second principle protects fair equality of opportunity. This means that inequalities are only acceptable if people with comparable talent and motivation have similar chances to improve their lives. The second condition of the second principle (the difference principle) offers a criterion to evaluate institutional or policy options in terms of the effect they have on the weakest groups in society.

As we mentioned earlier, Rawls's theory applies to the basic structure of societies. Our theory of access has a modest goal and indeed a different domain of application. What we derive from Rawls's theory is the structure of his argument: for rights to make sense to everyone, one needs to take into account their capacity to benefit from those rights. Rawls calls for a redistribution of income and wealth in order to ensure fair equality of opportunity. We refrain from engaging in that particular (socioeconomic) discussion in this book. Instead, we focus on other mechanisms that keep people from exercising the rights as intended in Rawls's first principle, that have to do more with the practice than with the policies of democratic states. Even if a society manages to design and implement institutions that meet Rawls's conception of justice, it needs to make sure that they keep functioning according to intent and design. What happens on the ground is often invisible to the public eye. Institutions that may appear just and offices that may seem open to anyone may in fact—unintentionally and unbeknownst to officials—have an exclusionary effect on certain groups or individuals. Consequently, the structure of Rawls's argument rather than its domain of application is of the highest relevance for our analysis of equal access.

Equality of Opportunity

Another concept that needs further elaboration as we refine our approach to access is that of equality of opportunity. John Roemer (1998) has distinguished between two more or less implicit conceptions of equality of opportunity that are prevalent today in Western democracies. The first may be characterized as "leveling the playing field among individuals who compete for positions." The second may be called the "nondiscrimination principle," which states that in the competition for positions in society, all individuals who possess the attributes relevant

2. Rawls means that inequalities are only morally acceptable if and only if they occur under the two conditions that he proposes.

for performance of the duties of the position in question be included in the pool of eligible candidates (1–2). Although these principles are clearly related and both are part of the same larger scheme of social justice, in practice the first principle leads to quite different policies than the second. If a state resolves to level the playing field for children from different groups in society to compete equitably in the labor market, it will probably have to invest in education, neighborhood infrastructure, and possibly in training and economic assistance for parents to better support their children. If, on the other hand, state service providers decide to favor the second principle, they may resort to affirmative action policies, antidiscrimination laws, and perhaps reservation requirements in public institutions and private sector organizations.[3] Roemer's analysis of the consequences of choosing between these two principles, even though they are both social-justice goals, demonstrates not only that the *societal commitment* to equality of opportunity matters, but also that *institutions* play a crucial role in final outcomes.

It is important to note that our concept of equal access does not, like Roemers two conceptions of equal opportunity, apply to the vast range of policy options available to governments. Obviously, both conceptions of equal opportunity (leveling playing fields and nondiscrimination) may result in equal access, because certain policies compensate for inequalities and certain rules demand equal treatment. For example, children of ethnic minorities may be admitted to certain schools because the government has established a quota or enforces nondiscrimination regulation. As a result, these children have more equal access to education. In this book we are particularly interested in a narrower conception of equal opportunity that applies to the capacity of the state to live up to its own promises with respect to all of the entitlement holders. To stay with our example: the government may have an affirmative action plan in place, but are all of the eligible candidates equally able to apply for a scholarship? There may be antidiscrimination legislation, but how competent, biased, and accountable is the government with regard to the enforcement of these rules? In other words, real access, as we conceive it, is realized when policies aimed at creating equality of opportunity are adequately implemented and successfully result in the desired outcomes.

Responsibility and Capability

A third major question is to what extent societies and their institutions can and should be concerned about all possible and actual inequalities. Ronald Dworkin (2000) has proposed that distributive justice should focus on the principles of equal importance and special responsibility (5):

3. Reservation is a form of affirmative action whereby a percentage of positions in public institutions (and sometimes private sector organizations) are reserved for socially backward classes of citizens, who are generally underrepresented in these positions.

It is important, from an objective point of view, that human lives . . . be successful rather than wasted, and this is equally important, from that objective point of view, for each human life. . . . Though we must all recognize the equal objective importance of the success of a human life, one person has a special and final responsibility for that success: the person whose life it is.

The premise of this book is very much in line with Dworkin's statement. It articulates both the social values of responsibility and solidarity and the modern idea that individuals have their own responsibilities to themselves, and should not only indulge in obtaining entitlements. Dworkin's formulation is generic, and it is difficult to disagree with such a generic formulation. Although Dworkin applies his ideas to many different concrete cases in his own work, the central idea remains that values should find expression in institutions that will finally work to create situations in which equality of resources, as Dworkin calls it, becomes a reality.

Again, we are reluctant to engage in the debate about criteria for distributive justice, because we pursue a conception of equal access that is not fully compatible with Dworkin's broader egalitarian ideas. However, the ideas articulated in Dworkin's theory of justice resonate in our narrower definition of equal access; the juxtaposition of concern for each human life on the part of the collective and personal responsibility on the part of the individual is reflected in our formulation of societal commitment and institutional capacity on the one hand and people's capacity on the other hand. It *is* important for democratic governments to make sure that every citizen has an equal opportunity to benefit from her entitlements. And it *is* important that individuals take responsibility and make an effort to participate in society. One way to view our endeavor here is to see it as an examination of conditions under which both collective and individual are practically able to do their part.

Real Freedoms

Amartya Sen's notion of the removal of "unfreedoms" underlies our specific conception of *access*. Sen (1999) argues that development is in fact a process of "expanding the real freedoms that people enjoy" (3). That process, aimed at detecting actual rather than theoretical injustice, is impossible without an empirical orientation. It is not the design of institutions that determines whether outcomes are just or not; rather, unjust outcomes raise questions about the functioning of institutions, regardless of design. Empirical research on actual inequalities may help us orchestrate a meaningful and informed debate about access as justice. The empirical research and critical analysis in this book mainly focuses on three questions (Baker and others 2004):

1. What are the central, significant patterns of inequality in societies?
2. How can those patterns be explained?
3. What is the role of policies and institutions in the persistence of inequality?

Controlling Access: The Exercise of Power

We have been reluctant to include power in our definition of access. As mentioned earlier, we prefer to analyze our subject from a rights-based perspective, leaving open the question of whether a mismatch between people and institutions is a consequence of deliberate action—the unjust exercise of power. We have used the term "capacity" with respect to people and institutions. Capacity, however, does imply power, given that the properties and capabilities that define someone's (or something's) capacity to pursue goals are basically his, her, or its collection of powers (Ghani 1995). The fact that we prefer the word "capacity" to "power" reflects the conviction that not all instances of impeded access are a result of the concerted exercise of power by some over others. Having said that, we would be immensely naïve not to acknowledge the ways in which power is exercised through mechanisms of access and exclusion. After all, access is about the distribution of resources and opportunities, and since these are often scarce, and people are often needy or greedy, the stakes in controlling access to resources are likely to be high.

Power: A Closer Look

So what does power mean and what does it look like? According to the political theorist Robert Dahl (1957, 80), "A has power over B to the extent that he can get B to do something that B would not otherwise do." This operational definition had been in use for some time when Peter Bachrach and Morton S. Baratz (1962) published their widely acclaimed article "Two Faces of Power." They argued that decisionmaking is only one way to use power and that behavior is only one kind of evidence of the exertion of power. One face of power, its overt exercise, is easily recognized. The other face is a bit more obscure and is characterized by nondecisionmaking—when those in authority can prevent certain issues from being put on the agenda through their social, economic, institutional, and political clout. In so doing, they manage to win conflicts over policy preferences or social grievances by avoiding them entirely. In a famous critique, Stephen Lukes (1974) went even further, finding their two-faces approach too behavioral and too focused on decisionmaking or lack thereof. Lukes looks at the exercise of control over the political agenda not necessarily through observable decisions or lack of them but through "latent conflict." He refuses, in the end, to define interests merely as policy preferences or grievances or, in other words, as subjective interests. His point is that people can have interests of which they are unaware because those in power are able to shape the perception of what is possible, acceptable, and desirable for their citizens.

We can apply all three formulations usefully to the phenomenon of impeded access in democratic societies, but not necessarily to the policymaking process alone. Whereas the discussed theories focus on the exercise of power through

agenda setting, policy formation, and political (non)decisions, we shift our attention of the practical functioning of institutions and to the implementation and
execution of policies. Throughout this book we will discuss the exercise of power
in its various manifestations. Lukes's conception of "latent conflict" is of particular interest to us, as we seek to reveal the *hidden* mechanisms of exclusion. However, the fact that these mechanisms are hidden does not necessarily mean that
malignant forces overtly exercise their power over vulnerable people. The mechanisms impeding access are often much less straightforward.

In a response to his critics, Lukes concludes that his original conception of
power is not fully adequate. He argues instead that the concept of power is rela-
tional rather than propositional, meaning that it can only be analyzed in terms of
power relations between actors and not as capacities that can be attributed to
actors individually. He also states that binary power relations and simplistic
assumptions about dependencies are not satisfactory as explanations of the many
ways in which power manifests itself. We very much agree with him here. Power
is obviously an important explanatory concept in access analyses, but it leads us
to an undesirable choice: either we modestly and tentatively stipulate manifestations of power but fail to grasp the phenomenon in its entire complexity, or we
develop an intricate and sophisticated analytical framework but fail to see anything other than the exercise of power.

We choose not to choose. First, as we mentioned before, we must take into
account that not everything that impedes access is an exercise of power. Without
being naïve, we do want to keep open the option that impeded access can be a
result of lack of awareness and accidental negligence by people with the best
intentions. The examples of innovations and successful remedies to improve
access that we have found all over the world show us that even without political
pressure or popular demand, institutions have worked to fix their access problems. Once made aware of institutionalized impediments to access and their solutions, politicians, appointed officials, and civil servants have proactively restored
equity in service-delivery systems, in mechanisms of voice and accountability,
and in institutions of justice in numerous cases. We want to acknowledge the
efforts of well-intentioned bureaucrats and politicians all over the world, who
work for the benefit of all. At the same time, we must remain highly attentive to
the exclusionary powers that be.

Sources of Power

One way of remaining attentive to the exercise of power is to pay attention to
sources of power. By focusing on the *means* through which access is gained, maintained, and controlled, we escape from the multivariate minefield to which dis-
secting the anatomy of power relations would lead us. The highly interesting
article "Theory of Access" by Jesse Ribot and Nancy Lee Peluso (2003) provides
us with a range of means through which access can be gained, maintained, and

controlled. According to Ribot and Peluso, "Access is about all possible means by which a person is able to benefit from things" (154). They clearly distinguish between "rights," which may or may not lead to actual benefits, and "access," which means that there are actually mechanisms in place to derive tangible benefits from those rights. Interestingly, they make a distinction between legal access and illegal access: the former indicates that there exists a legal entitlement to public resources; the latter, that there exists no such right. In both cases, the means through which people acquire access are largely similar: sources of power. Ribot and Peluso identify the following sources of power (which they call structural mechanisms of access): technology, capital, markets, labor opportunities, authority, social relations, and social identities. All of these enable individuals to access resources, whether they are entitled to do so or not. In our discussion we will confine ourselves primarily to situations in which people are indeed entitled to benefits, or protection, but lack the means to enforce their privileges. In many chapters in this volume (particularly in chapters 5, 7, and 12), the configuration of sources of power is discussed in more detail.

The concept "sources of power" is closely linked to the concept of empowerment, which dominates many of the remedies to improve access that are presented in this book. Empowerment does not tap into the idea of actors exercising *power over* other actors. Instead, it focuses on *generating the power to* do something. To empower people means to provide them with the sources of power (information, skills, authority, and so on) so that they can benefit from resources. In this sense, the concept of empowerment is complementary to the concept of institutional development. Institutional development (in the context of this book) means strategies to improve an institution's capacity to deliver citizens' rights and services, whereas empowerment refers to mechanisms that increase citizens' capacity to benefit from these rights and services.

Faces of Access[4]

The provision of goods and services and the enforcement of rights, as we have discussed, is administered through intermediary institutions. Although these institutions are sometimes private sector or voluntary sector organizations, they operate nonetheless within a public sector framework. This means that to a certain extent the agencies and their managers and professionals operate within a rule-bound system under a political or constitutional-legal mandate. The typical form such organizations adopt is that of the bureaucracy. The most salient constituting principles of a bureaucracy are: (1) formalization, (2) standardization, (3) hierarchy, (4) specialization, and (5) expertise (Weber 1972). These

4. This section draws on the working paper by J. de Jong, "Faces of Access," posted on www.improving access.org.

principles should guarantee that policies are executed without interference from factors other than the rightful application of law. Bureaucratic forms of organization are by no means to be found only in the public sector; private sector organizations have also found bureaucracy to be a rational, efficient, and controllable organizational form.

Bureaucracy in the pejorative sense of the term is obviously a phenomenon almost everybody loves to hate—remember Kafka! (Howard 1994; Kettl and Fesler 2005; Barzelay 1992; Osborne and Plastrik 1997). Bureaucracies and bureaucrats have become notorious for inflexibility, ignorance, and slowness. Typical symptoms of malfunctioning bureaucracy include difficult forms to fill out, long lines to stand in, and unfriendly staff. These nuisances are not just uncomfortable facts of modern life—they affect the relationship between the citizen and the state in a fundamental way by determining the level of trust people have in government (Peters 1995, 239–40). They thereby affect the perception of the legitimacy of the state. The volume of so-called red tape determines the manner in which a citizen does or does not deal with government (Nye and others 1997). It also influences who benefits from public resources and who does not (Social and Cultural Planning Office 2003). The more time or money a procedure takes, the more people who have time or money benefit; the more complex a procedure is, the more intelligent or savvy people benefit; the more tailored a procedure is to the average citizen, the more people fitting that profile will benefit.

To get a better understanding of the mechanisms that lead to these inequitable practices and the subsequent limitation of access, we first turn to a discussion of four relevant dimensions of a political-administrative system: bureaucrat behavior, agency performance, network dynamics, and contextual factors.

Bureaucrat Behavior

In his groundbreaking work *Street-Level Bureaucracy,* Michael Lipsky (1980) analyzes in depth how bureaucratic organizations operate and why. The conditions that determine the work context of bureaucrats operating in agencies, including conflicting or ambiguous goals, limited resources, fixed means and tools, performance measures, client expectations and behavior, lead to embedded mechanisms that appear to be contrary to the policy goals these public officials are supposed to achieve. Lipsky reserves a key role for the so-called street-level bureaucrats, those civil servants who work in frontline jobs and have direct contacts with clients. Given the relatively high amount of discretionary power they have at their disposal to make specific judgments and decisions on individual cases and the autonomy they enjoy relative to their agencies, Michael Lipsky argues that street-level bureaucrats are in effect policymakers. Their individual behavior adds up to agency behavior and de facto policy (Lipsky 1980, 13; see also chapter 6, this volume).

The constraints that shape the work of civil servants lead to certain patterns of practice that Lipsky describes as rationing services. First of all, the idea that demand for (free) public services will always exceed supply makes agencies devise ways to ration goods. There are several ways to deal with this (Lipsky 1980, 88–104):

—*Imposing costs of services on clients.* Costs can be expressed in time and in money. They can be explicit, but also embedded in application procedures. The invisible costs that clients have to pay to obtain certain services can decrease the demand.

—*Withholding information.* Agencies and individuals can decide in which way, to what extent, and to whom they make information available. Knowledge about availability of services, eligibility criteria, and application procedures is highly dependent on the available information.

—*Psychological strategies.* The act of applying for services can be either very discreet or highly embarrassing for clients. Psychological thresholds can be built into intake interviews, control mechanisms, or general attitudes of frontline workers. Clients may withdraw because they do not want to be subjected to perceived indignities.

—*Queuing.* A common way of rationing is to create waiting lists or waiting lines. The idea of first come, first serve seems fair and logical, but does not take into account that the costs of waiting for some are higher than for others, that some are in higher need of service than others, and that some have fewer alternatives than others.

—*Categorization.* Not everyone is equally entitled to public services. Although eligibility for entitlements is usually a political decision, people-processing bureaucracies have two important practical tasks: first, to develop an appropriate set of categories by means of which clients will be processed, and, second, to map clients in terms of their qualifying or disqualifying characteristics. This authority sometimes leads to *cream skimming*: giving priority to those clients who are most likely to succeed in terms of bureaucratic success criteria.

—*Worker bias.* Discretionary powers of street-level bureaucrats allow them to make decisions influenced by prejudice and personal values and beliefs. Moral judgments rather than professional assessment might induce a bias in their work, resulting in unequal chances for certain client groups.

These mechanisms (more elaborately described and analyzed in Lipsky 1980; Prottas 1979) might give the impression that government agencies and the civil servants working in them are malignant and not interested in best serving their clients or the public interest. In fact, these patterns of practice can go either way: discretionary powers can just as easily favor the disadvantaged as the advantaged. And the aggregate effect of decisions by some street-level bureaucrats can be balanced by the decisions of others. Still, one thing is clear: equitable treatment for individual clients is not guaranteed. This applies not only to service delivery but also, possibly more so, to law enforcement by regulatory agencies. The nature of the contacts between citizens and law enforcement officers is usually not characterized by customer orientation but rather by compelling citizens to contribute to public purposes. Mark Moore (1995, 37) characterizes these contacts as "obliga-tion encounters." The role of regulators in the context of enforcement is much more focused on preventing and correcting deviant behavior, and is therefore by definition very much rule-oriented. Consideration for particular individual cir-cumstances, or for equity, for that matter, is considerably less prominent in their task orientations.

Malcolm Sparrow (2000) points out that regulators must adopt a broader vocabulary so that they think in terms not only of "customers" but also of stake-holders, citizens, obligatees, objects or targets of enforcement, beneficiaries, tax-payers, and society itself. "They must contemplate the broader public purposes that their missions encompass and the numerous individual sacrifices necessary to deliver them," he writes (63). Achieving these missions is clearly a complicated task, requiring many smaller and bigger decisions that can have major impacts on the lives of citizens. Because the complexity of the task demands higher levels of autonomy and more discretionary power for individual bureaucrats, it also leaves room for agents to let personal beliefs, values, and judgments influence their deci-sions. Given the fact that regulators, like case workers and other frontline public servants, have the most frequent and immediate contacts with citizens, the pat-terns of practice of street-level bureaucrats exert a major influence on access to public resources.

Agency Performance

On the agency level, other mechanisms play their part. Executive bodies with a cer-tain level of autonomy tend to develop a will of their own. These organizations are under continuous pressure to perform as they are faced with juridical and budget-ary constraints, close scrutiny by the media, and high expectations from politicians and the public (Wilson 1989). Depending on specific performance measures, institutional focuses and behavior may vary, but in the end it is the agencies them-selves that have the best information about what is happening when they work with citizens. It is a curious situation that agencies' political masters often depend on the agencies' own figures for oversight. These organizations may use rationing tactics, risk-averse behavior, and budget-maximizing strategies to act in their own interest rather than in the interest of the population they are supposed to serve. The privatization of public services that has occurred in many countries over the past couple of decades has led to the creation of semi-autonomous bodies per-forming tasks for the government. These agencies were believed to perform more effectively and efficiently if placed at a relative distance from the political arena and subjected to market incentives (Pollitt and others 2004), but one question that has hardly been asked in the discourse of privatization, liberalization, and deconcen-tration of government agencies is, What is the impact of agencies' relative auton-omy on access? The Organization for Economic Cooperation and Development and the World Bank (2006) have conducted interesting surveys and case studies into accessibility and equity of social services under neoliberal policy regimes, but the specific role of agencies as mediators of those policies has largely remained unexplored.

Although it is hardly possible to assert general truths about an organizational form that takes so many different shapes in different countries and policy areas, it is important to realize that structures, strategies, tactics, and culture on the agency level are another major factor determining the chances that certain groups will be prevented from enjoying their entitlements.

System Dynamics

The complex triangulated relations among citizens, government agencies, and the street-level bureaucrats that represent them provide opportunities for different levels of analysis that are relevant for the examination of exclusionary mechanisms in policy fields. Another level that is less distinct, but perhaps all the more relevant, is that of governance arrangements. Here we leave the clear-cut boundaries of one organizational entity and enter the sometimes rather diffuse realm of interorganizational networks, regulated markets, and voluntary initiatives. Many if not most policy fields long ago abandoned the idea that the delivery of public services or the protection of public goods is the sole responsibility of governments. The most adequate arrangement for financing, producing, and controlling public tasks involves a constellation of actors from public, private, and voluntary sectors that coproduce governance and concerted action. Advocates such as Goldsmith and Eggers (2004) and Kamarck (2007) have hailed networked government as the wave of the future. Yet there is a caveat: networked governance may excel in efficiency and effectiveness, but the question of accountability is less easily answered than in traditional forms of government.

Even if the state remains responsible for defining tasks and regulating markets, the more networked providers there are, the more room there is for confusion over allocation of resources and over assigning responsibility. The complexity increases when the interests of network actors only overlap partially. All actors in a network can share an interest in delivering one particular service efficiently and effectively, but beyond that, their interests may diverge: a voluntary organization might only have local or community-related interests, a private sector company only sectoral interests, and a governmental organization just jurisdictional interests. Although hybrid networks have enormous potential to be responsive to the needs of citizens, chances are that cooperation and commitment only extend to the defined goal and target group. These agencies may have no interest in cooperating with one another to innovate beyond set tasks, to explore connections with other policy areas, or to consider societal impact of social programming (Bogdanor 2005).

Another problem that frequently occurs in governance arrangements is the problem of collective responsibility and organizational autonomy. Network partners may agree on collective goals and joint interests, but they often fail to work out the details of such cooperation. Sometimes this is the result of neglect or poor management, but often network partners are hesitant to give up too much autonomy in favor of the network as a whole. They want to keep their own databases, intake procedures, help desks, and planning and control mechanisms in place. This can lead to serious flaws in terms of customer orientation. For example, in the case of social welfare policy in large cities, people in serious need of money, treatment, or guidance can slip through the cracks because networked service providers all think that some other agency should be assisting them. If a difficult case makes it into the system, the individual may be shunted from one organization to another because no one knows what to do, and no single agency wants to take responsibility. Of course, a well-functioning, responsible, and responsive network is far from unthinkable, but as streamlining and communication demand increasing institutional focus, the risk of reduced accessibility is relatively high.

Contextual Factors

This book focuses on the role that states, through processes of (coproduced) democratic governance, play in creating equal opportunities. It is logical, therefore, to identify and explore the different levels at which (and forms through which) states operate. We have discussed three levels of analysis that refer to the state in its various manifestations: bureaucrat behavior, agency performance, and system dynamics. These levels of analysis represent the *institutional capacity* that the state, on behalf of society, employs to deliver rights and services. The other variable in our access definition is *people's capacity* to benefit from these rights and services. People's capacity to access democratic processes, public services, the economy, and justice is influenced by several factors. Some of those factors appear to be individual, such as intelligence, social skills, personal effort, and motivation. On the other hand, individual intelligence, skills, and performance are developed in a physical environment and a social context that may either help or impede, encourage or discourage the individual. Cultural, social, and religious norms may allow women to attend school or accept a job, or not. All over the world, ethnicity, caste, and race are still important defining characteristics of people, and minority groups are often discriminated against, either overtly or covertly. There are, of course, constitutions and laws in many countries that make discrimination illegal. Some countries, such as India, even have official and significant affirmative action policies. Still, most social interaction takes place beyond the influence of the constitution and the state. Women may have a right to vote or get elected, but if their men successfully "persuade" them to stay away from politics, they are effectively excluded. Minority groups may have the right not to be discriminated against in the labor market, but if employers prefer candidates of "equal competency" from their own ethnic group, minorities are effectively marginalized.

The social and cultural environment, combined with the effect of market forces, constitutes the context in which individuals develop and use their capabilities. Their capacity to benefit from rights and services depends to a large extent on their immediate families, neighbors, colleagues, employers, and fellow citizens. The fact that contextual factors are to an extent beyond the control of the state does neither mean that the state can or should be more active, nor that it should leave things as they are. It just means that when looking at the issue of access, it is important to take into account what sociocultural and socioeconomic factors impact people's capacity to benefit from their rights. An analysis that lacks this dimension and only focuses on institutional capacity is likely to miss out on important explanations for lack of access. More important, it is likely to miss out on potential solutions.

Access Analysis: A Framework

Here we are as we began this chapter, outside the castle in Kafka's story and trying to get in. We see, from a citizen's perspective, that these several levels of analysis we have discussed do not particularly make sense. K. is simply on the outside of something he does not understand. He cannot discern, from the outside, whether it is the street-level bureaucrats, the strategy of the castle as organization, or poor communication between the village and the castle that leaves him excluded and uncertain. Or is it just that the villagers do not like him or his "strange" behavior? All he knows is that he has no access, and he does not know how to go about getting it. He feels powerless, confused, and marginalized. The interesting thing about the story, and the reason it is such an extraordinary metaphor for what happens in public administration all around the world, is that *nobody* seems to really know what exactly causes the lack of access, either outside or inside the system. Exclusion is not always a straightforward process. On the contrary, lack of access may be the result of many interacting mechanisms at many different levels.

To better understand what these mechanisms are, how they manifest themselves, and how they interrelate, we need to look at inequalities in access in a more systematic way. We propose a framework that includes the four levels of analysis that we have discussed: bureaucrat behavior, agency performance, system dynamics, and contextual factors. Each level has its particular unit of analysis, scope of influence (or realm), and typical sources of power that control access. The bureaucrat-agency-system-context, or BASC, framework is a lens that enables us to dissect situations in which access is impeded (see table 1-1). In the concluding chapter we use this framework to discuss the findings of all the chapters in this book, looking for differences, similarities, and patterns of exclusion. This same BASC framework provides us with a means of organizing innovative solutions and recommendations with regard to improving access.

Table 1-1. *The BASC (Bureaucrat-Agency-System-Context) Framework*

Level of analysis	Unit of analysis	Scope of influence	Main sources of power
Bureaucrat	Individuals	Administrative discretion	Information, decisions
Agency	Organizations	Relative autonomy	Resources, procedures, (legal) authority
System	Institutional arrangements	Coordinated institutional activity, networks	Policy agendas, delivery systems, advocacy coalitions
Context	Social and economic forces	Human interaction	Norms, group membership, informal hierarchy, performance, behavior, incentives, sanctions, mobilization, and organization

Source: Authors.

Applying the Access Framework: The Chain of Access

Now that we have defined our basic concepts, elaborated the theoretical underpinnings of the access perspective, and sharpened our conceptual lens, we turn to presenting the subsections of this book: access to political decisionmaking (part II), access to the economy (part III), access to public services (part IV), access to accountable government (part V), and access to justice (part VI). These subsections constitute closely linked domains that form a chain of access.

Access to Political Decisionmaking

When President Abraham Lincoln, in his Gettysburg Address, defended the struggle for "government of the people, by the people, and for the people," the United States was still a long way from achieving the ideal of equal democratic rights. Some argue that this ideal never has been realized. Others may argue that it never will be. In any case, the conviction that "all men are created equal" hardly ever translates into really equal treatment. Mere institutions and equitable delivery mechanisms can never be enough to ensure that all citizens have equal opportunities to enjoy their rights and to achieve the goods and services to which they are entitled. Government for the people is only as good as the people defining what it should deliver and how. Thus, access to politics is a first prerequisite to improved access to rights.

Government by the people is of course an intrinsically democratic value understood here to mean the variety of ways individuals can participate in governance, either directly or through mechanisms of representation. Thus, voting rights have been a key issue in many campaigns for minority rights. Being able and allowed to cast a vote constitutes an important part of what we mean by democratic citizenship (de Jong 2008). But government by the people far exceeds the right to participate in elections. Democratic processes are also indispensable mechanisms on every level to identify needs, problems, conflicts, values, solutions, ideas, and resources. From village group meetings in rural areas to general national elections and everything in between, the democratic process is not only about choosing between candidates and policy options but also about exploring the concerns and expressing the will of the electorate. In this sense, good government *for* the people is dependent on good government *by* the people.

Obviously, many democratic processes do not live up to these ideals. Elections may be unfair or nontransparent, voters may be disenfranchised, representation mechanisms may be flawed, and so on and so forth. Democracy, as a form of social organization, has never been and will never be perfect and undisputed, and we do not argue that it is or will be. Nevertheless, there are degrees of imperfection, and we do argue that although democracy may never be perfect, it will certainly fail to come close to living up to its promise if access to its decisionmaking processes is limited. The democratic ideal that citizen involvement contributes to both the self-actualization of democratic communities and more comprehensive articulation of the needs and demands of citizens depends on the unfettered access to democracy's institutions for all members of society.

Central to the ideal of people's participation in development, however diverse and contested its definition and scope, is inclusiveness—the inclusion, in decisionmaking, of those most affected by the proposed intervention. Bina Agarwal, in chapter 2, on "participatory exclusions," examines how women are excluded from decisionmaking in community forestry groups in India. In the context of natural resource management (be it forests or water), devolving greater power to village communities is now widely accepted as an institutional imperative by governments, international agencies, and nongovernmental organizations. Rural community forestry groups (CFGs) represent one of the most widespread and rapidly expanding attempts at participative development. Ostensibly set up to operate on principles of cooperation, CFGs are meant to involve and to benefit all sections of the community. Yet despite these stated egalitarian aims, Agarwal shows that those in power can still effectively exclude significant social sectors, such as women. These "participatory exclusions" (that is, exclusions within seemingly participatory institutions) stem from systemic factors and can in turn unfavorably affect both equity and institutional efficiency. Drawing on South Asian experience in addition to Agarwal's own extensive fieldwork among such groups in India and Nepal, Agarwal analyzes the nature of such exclusions, their outcomes, and ways these results can be improved. She argues that participation is particularly determined by rules, norms, and perceptions, in addition to the endowments and attributes of those affected. These factors can disadvantage women, both separately and communally. Women's ability to alter these norms will depend on their bargaining power vis-à-vis the state, the community, and the family.

Exclusionary processes also take place at other levels of participation. Susan Rose-Ackerman (chapter 3) discusses the problems associated with access to government policymaking on the national level in eastern Europe. Lobbyists and pressure groups have been able to influence environmental policymaking in Hungary, but the weaker voices have not been able to weigh in on the consultative process. She points out that formal hearing procedures and consultative rounds tend to work to the advantage of groups that have already established themselves as discussion partners in the policymaking process. Getting a seat at the table is very much the result of long-term lobbying and a strong organizing capacity, and a seat at said table generally endows stakeholders with more opportunities to further advance their agendas. Creating better opportunities for weaker voices to develop lobbying capacity involves more than just making consultative processes more accessible. Rose-Ackerman argues that a vital civil society requires adequate and stimulating legal and financial arrangements. If organizing citizens around issues that concern them is hard to accomplish legally, or is difficult to afford for common people, formal access to the table does not have much meaning. If it is relatively easy to engage in politics, citizens are more likely to organize themselves. Governments will also benefit from improving access: policies are more likely to gain legitimacy if they are the result of a broader deliberative process, and they are more likely to be effective if more people, interests, and ideas have been mobilized to create them.

Access to the Economy

Today, very few people disagree with the view that markets are an essential institution for welfare growth in societies. Nevertheless, there is much discussion as to when, where, and how to employ market mechanisms. The free trade of goods and services in general may not be contested, but in many specific situations, dilemmas emerge. When one considers international trade agreements negotiated to stimulate economic activity as well as to protect specific national and economic interests via various types of trade barriers, one might conclude that we hardly have a free market economy in the world at all. Trade barriers typically disadvantage the weaker states and their economies. Farmers in sub-Saharan Africa and Latin America, who are not able to compete on the world market to sell their sugar and coffee because Western countries subsidize their own farmers or establish import restrictions, would very much favor a more liberalized world economy. At the same time, if free market policies are promoted without the necessary conditions under which they will actually produce market efficiency (for example, transparency, information, and access), globalization has devastating effects on local economies. In such cases, people depend on their governments to deal with market failures (Stiglitz 2002).

The lack of government intervention in and regulation of market economies may indeed exclude people from economic participation in many ways. Discrimination based on ethnicity or race or gender may exclude people from the labor market, even though they have a formal right to work. Price agreements and cartel formation may push smaller parties out of the marketplace. Free markets do not equal economic freedom, and regulated economies do not necessarily limit or improve access. Government interventions to create level playing fields and deal with market failures are crucial to ensure economic freedom. As Amartya Sen notes in *Development as Freedom* (1999, 3): "Development requires the removal of major sources of unfreedom: poverty as well as tyranny, poor economic opportunities as well as intolerance or overactivity of repressive states." Sen defines his notion of instrumental freedoms and, more specifically, economic facilities as "the opportunities that individuals respectively enjoy to utilize economic resources for the purpose of consumption, production, or exchange" (38–39). Democratic governments willing to fulfill the full potential of the least advantaged members of the societies they serve share an interest in improving and possibly even guaranteeing access to economic facilities.

Access to the economy starts with the right to enter the market as an entrepreneur. In many countries there are very few restrictions with respect to the basic right to entrepreneurship, but there are many specific licenses that business owners need to obtain before they can officially open their doors for trade. Business licensing can be extremely inhibitive, especially in developing countries (de Soto 1989). According to the World Bank's annual *Doing Business* reports (World Bank 2005, 2006), an important reason why access to the formal economy is so difficult is that the gatekeepers who monitor licensing for entrepreneurs make part of their income out of bribes. Every obligatory encounter of an actual or potential business owner with the government is an opportunity for a gatekeeper bureaucrat to ask for a bribe. There are very few incentives for bureaucrats to change this practice. Given the expense, there are also very few incentives for business owners to enter a formal economy. Hernando de Soto (2000) has pointed out that the poor would be much richer if only they were be able to become part of the formal economy, because without the legal documents that prove ownership of a small business, it is very hard to get a mortgage, attract investors, or borrow money. Therefore, limited access to government licensing also limits economic opportunities and social mobility for poor families. This is the case not only for developing countries but also for certain social groups in postindustrial countries, as de Jong and Kasbergen point out in chapter 4 of this volume.

Non-Western immigrants in urban areas are often entrepreneurs by necessity, not by choice. For many immigrants the only way to make a living and secure a sustainable income is to start a business; it is easiest in the food sector, yet the food sector is a highly regulated branch of the economy. Although in many Western countries deregulation and regulatory reform have been high on the agenda for the past couple of decades, immigrant entrepreneurs have scarcely benefited from these policies. De Jong and Kasbergen argue that most attempts at regulatory reform have focused on macro-level strategies from an economic point of view and have neglected the micro-level economy operating in urban neighborhoods. Reform agendas that could really be of benefit to these "entrepreneurs by necessity" would have to focus on the social economic contexts of the target groups. The role of the government in improving access to the formal economy may be not only that of rule maker and enforcer but also that of facilitator and manager of compliance.

One other very important precondition for successful entrepreneurship is possession of or access to capital. It is always easier for rich people to borrow money than for poor people. The reason is simple: it is assumed that rich people are more likely to repay the loan and poor people are more likely to default. There is another reason: for financial institutions such as banks it is simply not worth the transaction costs to deal with small loans. The micro-finance revolution, led by Muhammad Yunus of the Grameen Bank and Fazle Abed of BRAC (originally, the Bangladesh Rural Advancement Committee), has shown that the default rate is actually extremely low among poor populations. Access to financing, although not a sufficient condition to escape from structural deprivation, is the first step in a long chain of small steps toward improvement of the economic status of families and communities. Guy Stuart points out, in chapter 5, that there is another important explanation for the success of microfinance institutions (MFIs): the very manner in which the delivery mechanism works is itself an innovation. Typical MFIs involve groups (often of women) within communities that identify needs, administer loans, and manage risk. The group as a whole becomes responsible for loan repayment, even though loans are given to individuals in the group. Stuart argues that the true genius of successful microfinance institutions lies in their having invented a way to accommodate local needs on a large scale, through a postbureaucratic delivery mechanism. Because of this mechanism, millions of people who were previously denied access to financial services have gained access to the economy. Financial services for the poor are not a guarantee of success, but at least they create more equal opportunities for people to improve the lives of their families.

Access to Public Services

The faces of limited access are perhaps most visible in the delivery of public services. Nitpicking bureaucratic behavior, flawed agency performance, poor coordination between agencies and sectors, and lack of responsiveness to local contexts and changing circumstances are obstacles with which citizens the world over are all too familiar. This is often problematic because public services are typically delivered by a monopolist government. For many public services, such as health care, education, or welfare, there is no other provider within the reach of common people. Although initiatives for privatization and, more important, the introduction of competition to public service delivery have been attempts to provide citizens with customer choice, many people remain dependent on the government service provider assigned to them. Given this necessity, it is all the more important that state service providers function well in terms of effectiveness, efficiency, and accessibility. One explanation for the fact that public organizations do not always particularly exemplify these ideals is that they are rule-bound organizations, subject to a politicized environment. The popular assumption is that bureaucracies are inherently rigid organizations that must be responsive to their political masters rather than to the communities they serve. Fortunately, many innovations in government have proved over the past decades that this assumption is based on a false dichotomy. Public managers all over the world have shown that public service delivery can be both customer friendly and accountable, both effective and obedient, both efficient and respectful of administrative law (Altshuler and Behn 1997; Bogdanor 2005; Borins 1998; Moore 1995; Shah 2005; United Nations 2007; Sparrow 2000).

Despite this potential for efficiency and good service, politicians and taxpayers hardly ever let public organizations off the hook: if they are underperforming they are criticized by everyone, and if they do better than expected, they will be the first to face budget cuts. Michael Lipsky points out, in chapter 6, that this phenomenon is a symptom of broader trends in Western societies. According to Lipsky, in a political and social climate that favors the general shrinking of the welfare state, public managers faced with budget cuts have to make decisions that are bound to affect the accessibility of public services. When funding falls short of public demand, rationing strategies become inevitable. Strategies more in line with the social compact—that is, with acts of solidarity involving individuals' paying tax money for services from which they themselves may never benefit— would involve more serious attempts at innovation. Finally, Lipsky argues that the process of limiting access to public benefits should be at least as transparent as the process of creating public benefits.

Information and communication technology has enabled public managers to improve many of the processes of public service delivery. Customized communication strategies and transactions via the Internet or e-mail are among government's new repertoire of tools. Data mining and information exchange have also enabled agencies to detect fraud and abuse of public benefits. In chapter 7, Arre Zuurmond shows that this same information technology can be extended to enable agencies to detect the non-use of public benefits (also called non-take-up). Comparing data from different agencies may lead to the identification of eligible nonrecipients who are not taking advantage of public services such as welfare, Medicare, or child support. Zuurmond asks to what extent managers and agencies should feel responsible for the delivery of services to those who are not asking for them. Evidence from Belgium and the United Kingdom suggests that many eligible nonrecipients are less-educated, low-income citizens who are often afraid of encounters with the government. Some of these people live in social environments that lead them to fundamentally distrust authorities. They perceive the government as being against them rather than helping them. Again, we can see that contextual factors such as popular perceptions in society determine to a large extent the ability that people have to enjoy their rights. Another explanation is that people are simply not aware of their rights and entitlements. In the United States, for example, each year billions of dollars in tax refunds remain unclaimed by taxpayers (Files 2006).[5] More proactive strategies of service delivery may be able to counter this waste of opportunity.

The least advantaged members of society are generally the most dependent on public services. They typically find themselves in situations where multiple problems collide: joblessness, financial problems, health problems, and others. If public services are available to these people at all, they are not likely to have much effect because they only address a part of the overall problems facing these individuals. People at the bottom of society may have much potential for improvement, but if their context is not taken into account, the cycle of poverty is hard to break. To give an example, if a single mother is provided with a job, but not with day care for her children, the solution is not sustainable. If children are sent to school free of charge, but no replacement income is guaranteed for their labor, parents may not be able to feed them when they come home. In Western societies, Albert-Jan Kruiter and de Jong write in chapter 8, social services for the people at the bottom of society often show the negative effects of a similar lack of context orientation. Despite political mandates, financial resources, and extensive organizational capacity, the service-delivery system suffers from fragmentation and bureaucratization. Social workers, police officers, teachers, and nurses all feel constricted by rules and regulations governing their ability to help the disadvantaged. Kruiter and de Jong argue that despite general developments in society and in delivery systems that have added to the complexity of their work, public servants still can exercise a fair amount of discretion to take action custom-tailored to particular clients with particular problems. Unfortunately, evidence from the Netherlands shows that frontline workers may make up their own rules to avoid the responsibility that comes with exercising discretion. These rules may provide the professional with a sense of protection, but they seriously inhibit an agency's capacity to assist social service clients adequately. Strategies to improve access in this field would involve not deregulation but rather a reform of management strategies to empower frontline professionals to be more effective on behalf of clients.

5. J. Files, "Washington: Deadline to Collect 2002 Tax Refunds," *New York Times*, February 22, 2006.

Access to Accountable Government

In the previous section we discussed strategies to improve the accessibility of public services from an institutional or managerial perspective. However, as we discussed earlier, institutions and managers have limited knowledge of the outside world. They do not see problems the same way or to the same extent that citizens do. They also do not necessarily know if their policies and interventions actually work. They need feedback, which they can get via procedures that allow citizens to voice complaints and hold governments accountable for their performance or lack thereof. It is important for every government and public organization to have accountability mechanisms in place. The ultimate accountability mechanisms in democracies are, obviously, periodic elections: citizens can vote to reelect executive leaders with which they are content, or they can vote for other candidates if they are looking for change. But the time between elections is usually considerable, and the issues on the candidates' electoral agendas are usually much bigger and more abstract than those day-to-day issues that citizens face. Having access to the government to voice complaints and to pressure it to do a better job is thus an essential feature of responsive governance.

The 311 systems in place in many American cities—whereby one easy-to-remember telephone number, 311, is used for all questions and complaints citizens may have—have become a symbol of accessible and responsive local government. The potential of the 311 systems has not yet been plumbed, however. Although many cities have acquired the technologies and call centers required for the service, very few have managed to utilize the data from the vast number of telephone calls to reinvent their organizations. One can deal with questions and complaints by answering the former and solving the latter, but this will not structurally improve the quality of the organization or prevent similar problems from recurring. Another, more effective, way of improving local service delivery is to analyze patterns of information requests and complaints to develop recommendations for structural improvement.

Effective accountability mechanisms are not just channels to air frustration or help desks for the citizen, but rather, they are fundamental elements of a learning organization. Alexander Schellong introduces the term "citizen relationship management" in chapter 9. Adapted from "customer relation management" in the private sector, CiRM systems such as the one in Miami-Dade County are advanced information and communication systems that facilitate two-way communication between government and its citizen, while at the same time detecting patterns and informing policy divisions. By using multiple channels such as physical city hall counters, Internet sites, email, and telephone centers, Miami has been able to make the system accessible for many different groups of citizens. The more accessible the system, the more effective the policy information becomes. According to Schellong, the key to a successful implementation of the system is openness to organizational realignment. Adaptiveness to signals from citizens must be a widely shared value throughout the organization.

Over the last two decades, many strategies to improve government accountability to citizens have been proposed. An absence of mechanisms holding governments accountable for service delivery, especially in developing countries, has become a nagging problem. According to Anwar Shah (see chapter 10), the roots of the problem lie in the fact that many of the approaches tried have not taken into account the complexity of the task environment in these countries. In developing countries public managers' scope for action is usually impaired by a combination of limited operational capacity, insufficient funds, a difficult and politicized authorizing environment, and immense challenges in terms of the creation of public value. Focusing on only one of these elements is not likely to be successful. Shah argues that in order to hold governments accountable for access to services, mechanisms should be tailored to the local configuration of these elements, while putting citizens at the center of all policymaking decisions. Empowering citizens to act as principals rather than imposing external assistance or replicated management concepts from the developed world ensures context-specific and citizen-focused governance. Evidence from both developed and developing countries show that "citizen charters" are among the most successful tools to implement the concept of citizen-centered governance, but the potential for innovation in accountability mechanisms, especially with respect to access, is far from exhausted. After all, most accountability mechanisms work best for those who already have access to government. The big challenge is to give outsiders a voice. A. O. Hirschman (1970), in a classic study of responses to decline and poor performance of organizations, identifies three options for individuals (customers, clients, organization members) to deal with their dissatisfaction: "exit" (stop buying, leaving the organization), "voice" (staying, but expressing dissatisfaction to authorities) and "loyalty"(exercising neither option). But the people we write about in this book may not even have these options. Those who are not 'in' obviously have no exit option to exercise. Those who are not heard, have no voice option vis-à-vis the powers that be. The people we refer to are still looking for the option of "entry" into markets, hospitals, schools, courts, social groups, and democratic processes. The challenge, therefore, is to create mechanisms that mobilize and amplify the messages of outsiders in order to identify those who are left behind, and to reduce the barriers that limit their ability to participate in the areas that are important for their well being.

Access to Justice

The modern legal foundation for the right to access to justice can be found in international treaties such as the European Convention on Human Rights (Article 6) and the International Convention on Civil and Political Rights (Article 14). This codification of access to justice signifies that "the right to court" is a fundamental right much like freedom of speech and freedom of religion. As with so many human rights, however, there is a gap between the ideal of access and the reality of practice. Several problems with access to justice emerge from practice. The first is perhaps the most obvious: some citizens do not know their rights and cannot afford legal aid to advocate on their behalf. A second challenge is complexity of adjudication: legal proceedings are lengthy and costly. The third problem is fairness of access when the people involved in legal proceedings are not voluntary participants, as in the case of criminal prosecutions. Each of these obstacles to access to justice requires its own solution.[6]

In chapter 11, on access to justice in the United States, Deborah Rhode analyzes the various obstacles that low-income individuals face in both criminal and civil cases. According to Rhode, the systems of legal aid and pro bono litigation are both seriously flawed. There are perverse incentives for lawyers that disadvantage the client's interests. Moreover, attorneys are not held accountable for their performance in a transparent manner, so even if legal assistance is available in theory, in practice, working-class and underclass citizens do not have equal opportunities to represent themselves in court. Strategies to improve access to justice must include more substantial funding for legal representation, governance mechanisms to ensure quality and account for malpractice, and alternative forms of dispute resolution that empower people to solve problems among themselves instead of taking cases to court.

In the developing world, the neglect of the legal needs of the common people is widespread. The Commission on Legal Empowerment of the Poor, a high-level commission of the United Nations, was set up in 2006. The jumping-off point of the commission was the observation that, around the world, for the poorest and most disadvantaged groups in society the majority of their social, economic, and even political transactions and interactions occur in what is called the informal sector, also called the informal economy or the "extralegal sector"—meaning these transactions are outside the rule and the protections of the law. The work of the commission clearly showed how access to justice is related to access to the economy: individuals who don't have legal documents, licenses, or land titles cannot engage in informal economic traffic. Also, if their property rights are violated, they cannot take the case to court, and if they are charged with an offense, whether they are innocent or not, the chances that they will be able to defend themselves against parties that do have proper legal assistance are not very high (United Nations 2008).

Drawing on case studies from Africa, Maaike de Langen and Maurits Barendrecht show in chapter 12 that there are some obstacles even more inhibitive and harder for poor people to overcome than the most obvious barriers, which are

---

6. A. Brenninkmeijer, "Introduction to the Panel on Access to Justice," paper presented at the conference "Improving Access," The Hague, November 7, 2007 (see www.improvingaccess.org).

geographic, financial, and educational disadvantages. Widespread corruption among underpaid lower-level officers has led to the phenomenon of "gatekeepers" in the justice system who demand payment of bribes in return for access to judicial buildings and procedures, adding an invisible cost to the legal expenses of the poor. In addition to that, cultural norms of communities often stigmatize the court system as something external to the community. People may be kept from seeking justice in court by their own community members, because to do so would be seen as an insult to customary dispute resolution. De Langen and Barendrecht conclude with an examination of the shortcomings of institutions of justice themselves in developing countries. Dysfunctional agencies and a dearth of laws and regulations guiding the practice of law (called secondary laws) mean that entering the justice system is hardly a guarantee that justice will be done fairly and equitably. Rather than overhauling the legal system and its institutions from the top down, however, the authors argue that a more promising approach is to focus on legal needs, alternative forms of justice, the introduction of paralegals (lay practitioners of law), and closer cooperation with civil society organizations.

To return to *The Castle,* the land surveyor K. and the authorities at the castle have only one thing in common: they have limited knowledge of the nature and impact of all the mechanisms that keep K. from accessing the castle. Obviously, if one could combine both perspectives, the puzzle might be easier to solve. But that is the key to the problem: the twain shall never meet. This is the paradox of access: in order to fully understand the hidden mechanisms that exclude people, we need to have access to their experiences. Unless we listen carefully to those who experience inequalities in their lives, we are likely to remain subject to the fallacies of the institutional perspective. Methodologically, resolving this conundrum requires a blended research approach: empirical observations and grounded theory contrasted with institutional and organizational analysis. Only then will researchers be more likely to reveal obstacles in the long chain of access. It is our hope that this book will contribute to an awareness of those impediments and to forceful analytical and practical efforts to remove them.

References

Altshuler, A., and R. Behn. 1997. *Innovation in American Government: Challenges, Opportunities, Dilemmas.* Brookings.
Bachrach, P., and M. S. Baratz. 1962. "Two Faces of Power." *American Political Science Review* 56, no. 4: 947–52.
Baker, J., K. Lynch, S. Cantillon, and J. Walsh. 2004. *Equality: From Theory to Action.* New York: Palgrave Macmillan.
Barzelay, M. 1992. *Breaking through Bureaucracy: A New Vision for Managing in Government.* University of California Press.

Bogdanor, V., ed. 2005. *Joined-Up government*. Oxford University Press.

Borins, S. 1998. *Innovating with Integrity: How Local Heroes Are Transforming American Government*. Georgetown University Press.

Cook C. A. L., K. L. Selig, B. J. Wedge, and E. A. Gohn-Baube. 1999. "Access Barriers and the Use of Prenatal Care by Low-Income, Inner-City Women." *Social Work* 44, no. 2 (March): 129–39.

Cheema, G. 2005. *Building Democratic Institutions. Governance Reform in Developing Countries*. Bloomfield, Conn.: Kumarian Press.

Dahl, R. A. 1957. "The Concept of Power." *Behavioral Science* 2: 201–15.

de Jong, J. 2008. "Trends and Challenges in Election Monitoring." *Innovations: Technology, Governance, Globalization* 3, no. 2: 159–64.

de Soto, H. 1989. *The Other Path*. New York: Harper & Row.

———. 2000. *The Mystery of Capital: Why Capitalism Triumphs in the West and Fails Everywhere Else*. New York: Basic Books.

Dworkin, R. 2000. *Sovereign Virtue: The Theory and Practice of Equality*. Harvard University Press.

Ensor, T., and others. 2002. "Do Essential Service Packages Benefit the Poor? Preliminary Evidence from Bangladesh." *Health Policy and Planning* 17, no. 3: 247–56.

Ghani, A. 1995. "Production and Reproduction of Property as a Bundle of Powers: Afghanistan 1771–1901." Draft discussion paper. Yale University, Agrarian Studies Program.

Goldsmith, S., and W. Eggers. 2004. *Governing by Network: The New Shape of the Public Sector*. Brookings.

Hirschman, A. O. 1970. *Exit, Voice, Loyalty: Responses to Decline in Firms, Organizations, and States*. Harvard University Press.

Holmes, S., and C. R. Sunstein. 1999. *The Cost of Rights: Why Liberty Depends on Taxes*. New York: Norton.

Howard, P. K. 1994. *The Death of Common Sense: How Law Is Suffocating America*. New York: Random House.

Jacobs, B., and N. Price. 2006. "Improving Access for the Poorest to Public Sector Health Services: Insights from Kirivong Operational Health District in Cambodia." *Health Policy and Planning* 21, no. 1: 27–39.

Kafka, Franz. 1928/1998. *The Castle*. Translated by Mark Harman. New York: Schocken Books.

Kamarck, E. C. 2007. *The End of Government . . . as We Know It: Making Public Policy Work*. Boulder: Lynne Rienner.

Kettl, D., and J. Fesler. 2005. *The Politics of the Administrative Process*. Washington: CQ Press.

Lipsky, M. 1980. *Street-Level Bureaucracy*. New York: Russell Sage Foundation.

———. 1984. "Bureaucratic Disentitlement." *Social Service Review* 58: 3–27.

Lukes, S. 1974. *Power: A Radical View*. London: Macmillan.

Moore, M. 1995. *Creating Public Value: Strategic Management in Government*. Harvard University Press.

Nye Jr., J., P. D. Zelikow, and D. King. 1997. *Why People Don't Trust Government*. Harvard University Press.

Organization for Economic Cooperation and Development and the World Bank. 2006. *Liberalization and Universal Access to Basic Services: Telecommunications, Water and Sanitation, Financial Services and Electricity*. Paris: OECD Publications.

Osborne, D., and P. Plastrik. 1997. *Banishing Bureaucracy: The Five Strategies for Reinventing Government*. Reading, Mass.: Addison-Wesley.

Peters, B. G. 1995. *The Politics of Bureaucracy*. New York: Longman.

Pollitt, C., C. Talbot, J. Caulfield, and A. Smullen. 2004. *Agencies: How Governments Do Things through Semi-Autonomous Organizations*. London: Palgrave Macmillan.

Prottas, J. M. 1979. *People-Processing. The Street-Level Bureaucrat in Public-Service Bureaucracies*. Toronto: Lexington Books.

Rawls, J. 2001. *Justice as Fairness: A Restatement*. Belknap Press/Harvard University Press.

Rhode, D. 2004. *Access to Justice*. Oxford University Press.

Ribot, J. C., and N. L. Peluso. 2003. "A Theory of Access." *Rural Sociology* 68, no. 2: 153–81.

Roemer, John. 1998. *Equality of Opportunity*. Harvard University Press.

Social and Cultural Planning Office. 2003. *Benefits from Public Benefits*. [In Dutch.] The Hague.

Sen, A. 1999. *Development as Freedom*. New York: Anchor Books.

Shah, A., ed. 2005. *Public Services Delivery*. Washington: World Bank.

Sparrow, M. 2000. *The Regulatory Craft: Controlling Risks, Solving Problems and Managing Compliance*. Brookings.

Stiglitz, Joseph. 2002. *Globalization and Its Discontents*. New York: Norton.

Tate, E., and L. Quesnel. 1995. "Accessibility of Municipal Services for Ethnocultural Populations in Toronto and Montreal." *Canadian Public Administration* 38, no. 3: 325–51.

Trebilcock, M., and R. Daniels. 2005. *Rethinking the Welfare State*. New York: Routledge.

United Nations. 2007. *Innovations in Governance and Public Administration. Replicating what works*. New York: United Nations Press.

———. 2008. *Making the Law Work for Everyone: Report of the Commission on Legal Empowerment of the Poor*. New York: United Nations Press.

Valdez, R. B., A. Giachello, H. Rodrigueztrias, P. Gomez, and C. Delarocha. 1993. "Improving Access to Health Care in Latino Communities." *Public Health Reports* 108, no. 5: 534–39.

Weber, Max. 1972. *Wirtschaft und Gesellschaft: Grundriß der verstehenden Soziologie*. [Economy and society: Foundations in interpretive sociology.] Tübingen: Mohr.

Wilson, J. Q. 1989. *Bureaucracy: What Government Agencies Do and Why They Do It*. New York: Basic Books.

World Bank. 2005. *Doing Business in 2005*. Washington: World Bank Group.

———. 2006. *Equity and Development: World Development Report*. Washington: World Bank Group.

PART II

Access to Political Decisionmaking

2

Toward Participatory Inclusion: A Gender Analysis of Community Forestry in South Asia

BINA AGARWAL

Central to the idea of people's participation in development, however
diverse and contested its definition and scope, is inclusiveness—the inclusion in decisionmaking of those most affected by the proposed intervention.
There is also an emerging consensus that effective governance requires people's
involvement not just as individuals but also as a collectivity, such as a village
community. We are thus seeing an increasing emphasis on community participation through group formation in all forms of development interventions and
local governance initiatives. Indeed, for managing natural resources such as
forests and water, devolving greater power to village communities is now widely
accepted as an institutional imperative by governments, international agencies,
as well as nongovernmental organizations (NGOs). Rural community forestry
groups (CFGs) represent one of the most widespread and rapidly expanding
forms of participative development initiatives. They also represent one of the

This is a modified and updated version of a paper that appeared earlier under the title "The Hidden
Side of Group Behaviour: A Gender Analysis of Community Forestry Groups in South Asia," in Heyer,
Stewart, and Thorp (2002). The current version also reports the results, in summary form, of my analysis of the data I collected primarily from 2000 to 2001. Part of this analysis was undertaken in 2006 when
I was a research fellow at the Ash Institute at Harvard University's Kennedy School of Government. I am
most grateful to Gowher Rizwi, director of the Ash Institute at that time, for his warm hospitality and
stimulating conversations. I also thank Jorrit de Jong and the participants of the two workshops held at
the Ash Institute in 2006 and 2007 on the theme of this book for their responses to the ideas presented
in my paper.

fastest-growing forms of collective action around a public good—forests—in the developing world.

Set up to operate on principles of cooperation, CFGs are intended to involve and benefit all sections of the community, but in practice they can exclude significant sections, such as women, from their decisionmaking processes, with potentially adverse effects both on equity of benefit sharing and efficiency of forest conservation. Improving the condition of a degraded forest, for instance, requires forest closure (restricting forest use), which can range from a complete ban on the entry of people and animals into the protected site to allowing limited extraction of selected items such as firewood and fodder. Excluding people from decisionmaking means excluding them from having a say in the formulation of forest use rules as well as from contributing to forest improvement. These "participatory exclusions"—exclusions within seemingly participatory institutions—are unlikely to get rectified simply with the passage of time, since they stem from systemic factors and can, in turn, unfavorably affect both equity and institutional efficiency.

In this chapter I draw on South Asian experience and my extensive fieldwork among CFGs in India and Nepal to analyze the nature of such exclusions and their unfavorable outcomes. I also analyze the potential benefits from greater inclusion. Where relevant, I discuss the interplay of class and caste with gender in defining outcomes for different categories of women. I also outline a conceptual framework that can illuminate what underlies participatory exclusions, and how we could move toward greater inclusion.

I argue here that participation is determined especially by rules, norms, and perceptions, in addition to the endowments and attributes of those affected. These factors—both separately and interactively—can critically disadvantage women by undermining their access to public goods such as forests and to the institutions governing them, such as CFGs. Women's ability to overcome these disadvantages and enhance their access, I argue, will depend on their bargaining power vis-à-vis the State, the community, and the family. The likely determinants of women's bargaining power in these three arenas are spelled out. Although the context here is community forestry, examined from a gender perspective, the conceptual framework would also have relevance for understanding social and economic exclusions in other contexts.

The chapter is based largely on the field visits and interviews I undertook during 1998 and 1999 in eighty-seven community forestry sites across five states of India (Gujarat, Karnataka, Madhya Pradesh, Orissa, and the Uttar Pradesh hills) and two districts (Kaski and Dang) of Nepal.[1] Information was obtained mostly through unstructured interviews with villagers—at times with women and men in separate groups, at other times with both sexes jointly—in addition to indi-

1. In India, the term "state" relates to the biggest administrative divisions within the country and is not to be confused with "the State," used throughout in the political economy sense of the word. In Nepal, the biggest administrative divisions are districts. In India, districts are smaller divisions within states.

vidual interviews with key informants, especially office holders in the community forestry groups. These data are supplemented by initial results from a systematic field survey I undertook from 2000 to 2001 in India and Nepal, and an earlier field visit in 1995.[2]

Background

In rural South Asia, forests and village commons have always been important sources of basic necessities and supplementary livelihoods, providing villagers with firewood, fodder, small timber, and various nontimber products. Especially for the poor and for women, who own little private land, they have been critical for survival. In the 1980s, for instance, in India's semi-arid regions, the landless and land-poor procured over 90 percent of their firewood and satisfied 69 to 89 percent of their grazing needs from common pool resources (Jodha 1986). At that time, firewood alone provided 65 to 67 percent of total domestic energy in the hills and desert areas of India and over 90 percent in Nepal (Agarwal 1987). This situation remained largely unchanged even into the early 1990s, when community forestry programs were formally launched in both countries. Firewood was then still the single most important source—and for many the only source— of rural domestic energy in South Asia, and was still largely gathered, not bought. In 1992–93, 62 percent of rural India's domestic energy came from firewood.[3] In most Indian states, over 80 percent of rural households used some firewood as domestic fuel, and (on an all-India average) only about 15 percent of it was purchased (Natrajan 1995).

Over time, however, people's ability to fulfill their needs had been eroding with the decline in communal resources, owing both to degradation of the resource and to shifts in property rights away from communities to the State and to individuals. The push toward community forest management represented a small but notable reversal in these processes of statization and privatization, toward a reestablishment of greater community control over forests and village commons. Indeed, community forestry groups (CFGs) have been mushrooming in South Asia.[4]

In India, these CFGs include the following types:

—State-initiated groups formed under the Joint Forest Management (JFM) program launched in 1990, in which village communities and the government share the responsibilities and benefits of regenerating degraded local forests.

2. I refer to these field visits at various points in the chapter to provide supportive evidence, indicating in which year I made the visit. The field notes from those field visits are in my personal archives.

3. Data from the early 1990s for India and 2001 for Nepal show that 92 percent of rural domestic energy in India (Natrajan 1995) and 99 percent in Nepal (Government of Nepal 2001) comes from unprocessed biofuels such as firewood, crop waste, and cattle dung, of which firewood is the most important.

4. I use CFG as a general term to cover all types of community forestry groups in both India and Nepal.

—Self-initiated groups, started autonomously by a village council, youth club, or village elder; these are concentrated mainly in Bihar and Orissa (in eastern India).

—Groups with a mixed history, such as the *van panchayats,* or forest councils, in the state of Uttarakhand (earlier a part of Uttar Pradesh), initiated by the British in the 1930s. Some of these have survived or been revived by NGOs.

JFM groups are the most widespread, both geographically and in terms of the forest area they account for. To date, virtually all Indian states have passed JFM resolutions, which grant participating villagers access to most nontimber forest products and to 25 to 50 percent (varying by state) of any mature timber harvested. There were approximately 84,000 JFM groups in the early 2000s, covering 17.3 million hectares,[5] or 25 percent of the 76.5 million hectares administered as forest land, and involving 8.4 million participants (Bahuguna and others 2004). In addition, there are a few thousand groups of the other types.

Nepal's community forestry program, launched in 1993, is largely State-initiated. Here the State transfers even good forest to a set of identified users who form a forest-user group and are entitled to all of the forest benefits.[6] Around 2006, there were about 14,000 forest-user groups (also called here community forest groups or CFGs) involving 1.6 million households and covering 1.18 million hectares, or 20.3 percent of the country's 5.8 million hectares of forestland (Government of Nepal 2007). In both India and Nepal, NGOs can act as intermediaries in group formation and functioning.

Unlike the old systems of communal resource management, which usually recognized the usufruct rights of all village residents, the new CFGs represent a more formalized system of rights. Typically these rights are based either on membership (as in the State-initiated groups), or on rules specified by selected (often self-selected) community members, as in the self-initiated groups. In other words, membership or some other formal system is replacing village citizenship as the defining criterion for establishing rights in the commons.

This raises some critical questions: How are the CFGs performing in terms of participation, equity, and efficiency from the perspective of women, especially the poor? Are the emerging systems of rights in communal property inclusive and equitable, or are they replicating the patterns of elite- and male-centeredness that characterize rights in private land? The next section focuses on these issues.

Gendered Outcomes: Participation, Equity, and Efficiency

Many CFGs have had notable success in forest regeneration. Often all that is involved to achieve this result is to restrict the entry of people and animals and to

---

5. 1 hectare = 2.47 acres.

6. The government, however, retains the right to reclaim any forests seen to be mismanaged by the forest-user group.

ensure protection through a guard or village patrol group, or both. In some cases tree planting is also done to fill in gaps. Even with simple protection measures, natural revival is often rapid if the rootstock is intact. Within five to seven years, many of the severely degraded tracts in semi-arid India have become covered with young trees, and areas that were degrading but had some vegetation left show encouraging signs of regeneration. Indeed, in most ecological zones CFG initiatives show beneficial results, and in a number of cases incomes and employment have also increased,[7] seasonal out-migration has fallen,[8] the land's carrying capacity has improved, and biodiversity has been enhanced.[9] Some villages have even received awards for conservation.[10]

Viewed from a gender perspective, however, and especially the perspective of poor women, these results look less impressive on several important counts: effective participation, equity in the sharing of costs and benefits, and efficiency in functioning.

Participation

In both India and Nepal, the State-initiated groups typically have a two-tier organizational structure, consisting of a general body (GB) with members drawn from the whole village and an executive committee (EC) of some nine to fifteen persons. Typically the GB meets once or twice a year and the EC meets about once a month. Both bodies interactively define the rules for forest use and benefit sharing, the structure of fines for rules violation, the method of protection (such as guards, patrol groups), and so on. Which categories of persons have a voice in the GB and the EC bears critically on how well these organizations function, and who gains or loses from them.

Women's effective participation in CFG decisionmaking would require not only that they become members of the group (the GB or the EC) but also that they attend and speak up at group meetings, and can ensure that decisions are in their interest at least some of the time. Such participation is important both in and of itself, as an indicator of democratic institutional functioning, and for its effects on cost and benefit sharing and on efficiency. To what extent do women in general, and poor women in particular, participate in this way?

PARTICIPATION IN MANAGEMENT. In most JFM groups women constitute less than 10 percent of the general body;[11] they are typically absent in the self-

7. See, for example, Raju, Vaghela, and Raju (1993), Kant, Singh, and Singh (1991), and Society for Promotion of Wastelands Development (1998)

8. See Viegas and Menon (1993) and Chopra and Gulati (1997).

9. See Raju, Vaghela, and Raju (1993) and Arul and Poffenberget (1990). I also observed this during my field visits in 1995 and 1998–99.

10. Shah and Shah (1995) and my field observations in 1998–99.

11. See Roy, Mukerjee, and Chatterjee (1992); Guhathakurta and Bhatia (1992); Narain (1994).

initiated groups,[12] and are virtually absent in the *van panchayats*.[13] Their presence in Nepal's CFGs is similarly sparse (Dahal 1994, 78).

In India, the eligibility criteria for membership in the JFM general body and the EC vary by state (for details, see Agarwal 2001). Eight of the twenty-two states for which information is so far available restrict GB membership to only one person per household. This is almost always the male household head. In eight other states, as a result of amendments in the initial orders, both spouses, or one man and one woman, can now be members, but this still excludes other household adults. Only three states have opened membership to all village adults. In the self-initiated autonomous CFGs, the customary exclusion of women from village decisionmaking bodies has been replicated. In Nepal's CFGs, again, the household is the unit of membership, and in male-headed households it is the man's name that is entered in the membership list (Seeley 1996).

Without being GB members, women usually hear little about what transpires at meetings. Many women complain about this:

> Our husbands don't tell us about meetings. They simply say they have a meeting and go when the watchman brings around the notice for the meeting. (Woman to author, five-village cluster, Orissa, 1998)

> When we ask them what happened at the meeting, they say: What will you gain by knowing? (Women to author, five-village cluster, Orissa, 1998)

> Typically men don't tell their wives what happens in meetings. Even if there is a dispute about something, they don't tell us; nor do they volunteer information about other matters. (Women to author, Kheripada village, Gujarat, 1999).

Women's representation in the ECs is also typically low, although there is some variation by region and context. In a study of twenty JFM groups in West Bengal (east India), 60 percent had no women serving on the EC, and only 8 percent of the 180 EC members were women. Landless families, too, are little represented (Sarin 1998). In many states, JFM resolutions now require the inclusion of women in the EC, ranging from a minimum of two members to one-third of the membership. I found, however, that many CFGs deviated from the minimum; also the women so included were rarely chosen by other women as their representatives. Sometimes male EC members chose the women to fill the mandatory slots. In Nepal, similarly, women have only a nominal presence in the ECs. Those who join are often poorly informed about the activities of their CFG, and in the early years some are even unaware that they are EC members (Upadhyay and Jeddere-Fisher

---

12. See Kant, Singh, and Singh (1991) and Singh and Kumar (1993).

13. See, Sharma and Sinha (1993) and Tata Energy Research Institute (1995). In the TERI study, out of the fifty *van panchayats* examined only nine had any women members.

1998; Moffatt 1998). In both countries, there is a better prospect of women being seen as potential representatives when the names are proposed in the GB and decided by consensus (my field observations in 1998–99).

Whether from a lack of awareness or other constraints (discussed later in this chapter), only a small percentage of the women who are GB or EC members usually attend the meetings of these bodies. Those who attend rarely speak up, and if they do speak, they say their opinions are given little weight: "Men don't listen, except perhaps one or two. They feel they should be the spokespersons" (woman to author, Garbe Kuna CFG, Kaski district, Nepal, 1998); "What is the point of going to meetings. We would only sit silently" (women to author, Panasa Diha village, Orissa, 1998); "I attend *van panchayat* meetings, but I only sign, I don't say much. Or I say I agree" (woman *van panchayat* member to author, Sallarautela village, Uttar Pradesh hills).

Having a voice in the EC is important, since this is the site for discussions and decisions on many critical aspects of CFG functioning. As matters stand, women are not party to many crucial decisions. An analysis of JFM decisionmaking in five Gujarat villages revealed that all major decisions on forest protection, use, distribution of wood and grass, and future planning were made by men. The only joint decisions with women were those concerning tree nurseries (Joshi 1998). Women are also often left out of the CFG teams that go on "exposure" visits to other sites, that is visits to learn from the experience of other groups, or that receive technical training in new silviculture practices.

Although there are some contrasting examples of all-women CFGs and mixed CFGs (that is CFGs with both men and women on the EC) with a high female presence, these remain atypical. All-women CFGs are found especially where there is high male out-migration (as in the Uttar Pradesh hills in India), or where there has been a prior history of women's groups being formed for some development activity by a local NGO or an international donor (as in parts of both Nepal and India).[14] Occasionally women initiate an all-women's group themselves. There are no consolidated figures for India on the number of such groups, but in Nepal, in 2000, such CFGs constituted only 3.8 percent of all CFGs and controlled 1.1 percent of all CFG land.[15] Half of the all-women CFGs have 10 hectares or less of forest land, and virtually none have over 50 hectares. Typically the land they have is quite degraded. In contrast, mixed CFGs commonly control a few hundred hectares, often of good natural forest. Similarly, mixed groups with a high female presence (say, 30 percent or even 50 percent women in the GB or EC) are found only in selected pockets of Nepal and India (Narain 1994; Viegas and Menon 1993; my field observations in 1998–99).

14. See Mukerjee and Roy (1993); Correa (1997); Adhikari and others (1991); Mansingh (1991); Regmi (1989); Singh and Burra (1993); Raju (1997). I also observed this during my field visits in 1998–99 and 2000–01.

15. Calculated from figures given in Government of Nepal (2000).

PARTICIPATION IN PROTECTION. Despite their limited presence as formal members, many women play an active role in forest protection. In formal terms, the bounded forest area is usually protected either by employing a guard, with CFG members contributing the wage, or by forming a patrol group from among member households, or a combination of the two, in addition to keeping an informal lookout as they go about their daily tasks. Of the eighty-seven sites I visited, 45 percent were protected by a male guard and 18 percent by an all-male patrol. Only a small percentage of patrols were constituted by both women and men or by women alone, and there was a rare female guard. Occasionally, there are shifts from all-women to all-men patrols, and vice versa.

More commonly, women patrol informally. In some villages of Gujarat and the Uttar Pradesh hills they have formed separate informal protection groups parallel to men's because they feel men's formal patrolling is ineffective. Women's informal vigilance improves protection in important ways. In most villages I visited, women told me that they had apprehended intruders both from other villages and from their own, and that when they caught women intruders they sought to dissuade them from breaking the rules. Women also join in firefighting, and in several instances their alertness alone saved the forest.

Thus, although most women are excluded from CFG membership and management, many women contribute notably to protection efforts, indicating their stake in forest regeneration.

Equity

Women's limited involvement in the decisionmaking process has implications for both equity and efficiency. How equitable are the CFGs in the sharing of costs and benefits?

COST BEARING. The costs of forest closure are broadly of two types: those associated with protection and management and those associated with forgoing forest use (see table 2-1). The former usually include membership fees, the forest guard's pay, the opportunity cost of time spent in patrolling, and so on. These types of costs are borne largely by men. The costs of forgoing forest use include the opportunity cost of time spent in finding alternative sites for essential items such as firewood and fodder, other costs associated with firewood shortages, the loss of livelihoods dependent on the sale or use of forest products beyond subsistence needs, and so on. Such costs fall largely on women.

Consider the firewood-related effects of forest closure in more detail. Firewood is an everyday need, and obtaining it is mainly women's responsibility, while obtaining small timber that is needed occasionally for agricultural implements, for example, is mainly men's responsibility. Typically, when forest protection begins, all human and animal entry into the protected site is banned, especially in the semi-arid regions. Where the land was barren anyway, this causes no extra hardship. But

Table 2-1. *Main Direct Costs and Benefits of Forest Closure, by Gender*[a]

Mainly affecting women	*Mainly affecting men*
Costs	
• Firewood shortages (more time and energy expended in collection and cooking; adverse health effects; fines if caught stealing firewood)	• Membership fee
	• Patrolling time; guard's pay
	• Fodder shortages (must purchase)
• Fodder shortages (more time and energy expended in collection)	• Loss of source for small timber
	• Erosion of some livelihoods, for example, fuel shortage for black-
• Increased time in stall-feeding animals	smiths using woodfuel in furnaces
• Informal patrolling time	
• Erosion of some livelihoods, for example, firewood sellers, NTFP collectors[a]	
• Higher (late-entry) membership fee	
Benefits	
• Firewood supply available for a few weeks, if forest is opened	• Availability of small timber (if extraction allowed)
• Fodder supply available for a few weeks, if forest is opened	• Housebuilding timber (if extraction allowed)
• Nontimber forest products available seasonally[b]	• Cash (if distributed) from sale of forest products
	• Use of collective fund

Source: Author's compilation.

a. This is a broad outline of the main direct costs and benefits. Each of these need not apply to every CFG. There may also be some indirect costs and benefits. For instance, a greater supply of firewood indirectly benefits the whole family.

b. These include fruits, flowers, berries, wild vegetables, herbs, and similar items, which are collected primarily by women.

where women could earlier fulfill at least part of their firewood needs from the protected area, after closure they are forced to travel to neighboring sites, involving additional time, energy, and—where the neighbors are also protecting—the risk of being caught and fined (Sarin 1995, Agarwal 1997a, and my field observations during 1998–99). As a result, in the early years of JFM, Sarin (1995) noted that in some protected sites in Gujarat and West Bengal, women's collection time for a headload of firewood had increased from one or two hours to four or five hours, and journeys of half a kilometer had lengthened to eight or nine. In many households, women were also compelled to take their daughters along, and they spent several extra hours a day to collect the same quantity of firewood (Shah and Shah 1995). Over time this could negatively affect the girls' education. When neighboring villages, too, started protecting their forests, many women faced severe shortages. Most sought to make do with the limited amounts available from trees on their home fields, supplemented by inferior fuels such as crop waste that have worse health effects due to excessive smoke. But the landless often did not have even this option and were compelled to continue collecting clandestinely, risking fines and reprimands from guards or patrol groups if they were caught.

Such gendered consequences were widespread, causing considerable resentment among the women. For example, in Pingot village, Gujarat, women, when asked about an award for environmental conservation that had been conferred on the village, responded with bitterness: "What forest? We used to go [there] to pick fuelwood, but ever since the men have started protecting it they don't even allow us to look at it!" (Shah and Shah 1995, 80).

We might have expected this picture to change after several years of protection. In fact, in most places the shortages persist. Of the eighty-seven CFGs I visited in 1998–99, firewood was available in eighty. Of these, forty-five, or 60 percent, still had a ban on firewood collection, with twenty-one not opening the forest at all and twenty-four opening it for a few days annually for drywood collection or cutback and cleaning operations. The remaining CFGs allowed some collection, usually only of fallen twigs and branches. Such exceptions were more common in parts of Orissa, Karnataka, and Madhya Pradesh, where CFGs had thicker forests and more lenient rules for firewood collection by members; here women reported they were better off than before, even if not self-sufficient in firewood. Typically, however, even after years of protection, women reported a persistence of firewood shortages in most of the villages I visited in Gujarat, the Uttar Pradesh hills, Karnataka, parts of Madhya Pradesh bordering Gujarat, and in the Kaski and Dang districts of Nepal.

The following statements by women I interviewed illustrate experiences that are common among poor women: "We go in the morning and only return in the evening. Since the end of the rainy season, we have been going every day. I go myself and so does my daughter. Earlier, too, there was a shortage but not as acute" (woman EC member to author, Kangod village, Karnataka, 1998); "It is women who need the forest, they need firewood to cook. . . . Men preach to women about not cutting trees, but what can women do? They cannot cook food without firewood and they cannot collect firewood from other places" (group discussion with women in Kabhre Palanchok, Nepal, cited in Hobley 1996, 147).

Usually women from both middle peasant and poor peasant households report firewood shortages, since even the former seldom purchase firewood or have enough private trees for self-sufficiency. Where possible, as noted, women have substituted other fuels. A few were able to switch to biogas (this was usually where there was an effective NGO program in the area), but for most households gas or kerosene were not real options, hence the women had to use inferior fuels such as crop waste, twigs, dung (although many preferred to keep the dung for manure), and even dry leaves. These fuels need more time to ignite and tending to keep alight, thus adding to cooking time and preventing women from simultaneously attending to other work. In some areas women economize on fuel by forgoing a winter fire for space heating, even in subzero temperatures, or by not heating bathwater in winter or heating it only for husbands.

Most important, the substitute fuels generate even more smoke than firewood, with seriously negative health effects in poorly ventilated conditions. According to estimates by Smith, Agarwal, and Dave (1983), even cooking with firewood on an open stove leads to the daily inhalation of a large amount of benzo(a)pyrene equivalent to smoking twenty packs of cigarettes a day. This increases women's risk of cancer, tuberculosis, and various respiratory ailments (Center for Science and Environment 2001). Overall, women are found to face 50 percent greater risk of mortality than men resulting from acute respiratory infections associated with smoky fuels, and several thousand infants die each year in India from such infections (Goldemberg and others 2004; Misra, Smith, and Retherford 2005). Dung and crop waste are much worse offenders on this count than firewood. And even with firewood, some of the species that women are allowed to collect generate more smoke than the so-called timber species, which they are not allowed to touch.

Women of landless or land-poor households lack even the option of using crop waste or dung, since they have no land or trees of their own and few cattle.[16] Indeed, forest closures have forced many poorer families to reduce their animal stocks because of fodder shortages, which in turn reduces dung supply. As a poor woman in the Uttar Pradesh hills told me, "We don't know in the morning if we will be able to cook at night." Another added, "Our *bahus* [daughters-in-law] have to undertake a full day's journey to get a basket of grass and some firewood from the reserve forest."[17] Her daughter-in-law chimed in, "But even in the reserve forest you can be caught by the forest guard. I paid twenty rupees as a fine to retrieve my axe, and all I was doing was cutting a fallen log." In a Nepal village in Kaski district, a group of poor women told me, "We go at night. . . . Other women have gas and stoves, but we are poor, so we have to steal." Often they get caught and are fined.

Is this cost unavoidable—a necessary price to pay for sustainable forest regeneration? Existing evidence suggests otherwise. A study of twelve villages, all with CFGs, in three Indian states, undertaken by a network of ecologists, social scientists, and NGOs, is indicative (Ravindranath, Murali, and Malhotra 2000; see also Agarwal 2006). On the basis of information on the annual woody biomass regenerated in the protected forests, and the annual firewood extracted and needed, and assuming that 50 percent of the biomass regenerated per year could be extracted sustainably, the study found that in ten of the twelve villages extractions were far below this conservative extractable limit, and in the remaining two, extraction was still below the total biomass produced per year. If more were extracted, as is possible to do sustainably, several of the villages would have no

16. See also Jodha (1986) on differences between landed and land-poor rural households in India on the extent to which they depend on the commons for firewood and fodder.

17. Reserve forests are directly under government control; no grazing or extraction of forest produce is normally permitted in them.

firewood shortages and the rest would have less acute shortages. Such extraction could be supplemented by other measures, such as establishing fuelwood plantations in part of the forest, promoting and maintaining workable biogas plants, and so on. The very low levels of extraction in cases such as these are due to strict closure regimes, enforced without women's acquiescence. In virtually none of these twelve villages was there even one woman on the EC.

Similarly, since grazing is usually banned, households with cattle have to procure fodder in other ways than gathering it in the forest in the form of grass or tree leaves. Since cattle care is usually women's responsibility, if the household cannot afford to buy fodder women have to spend additional time looking for other sites to procure some. Moreover, animals now have to be fed in their stalls, because they are no longer allowed to graze freely in the forest. In parts of Gujarat many women report an extra workload of two to three hours a day because of stall feeding alone. Where some of the better-off households have replaced their goats with stall-fed milk cattle, it has further increased women's labor.

In many places, therefore, the scarcities that women are experiencing, especially of firewood, appear to have less to do with aggregate availability or a lack of potential solutions than with women's limited bargaining power with the CFGs. Their problems are seen as individual and private rather than as warranting community attention.

BENEFIT SHARING. There are also gender inequities in benefit sharing. In some cases the benefits are not distributed at all. Among Orissa's self-initiated groups, a number of all-male youth clubs have completely banned forest entry to community members and have been selling the wood they obtain from thinning and cleaning operations, as well as other forest produce. In many cases, the quite substantial funds so obtained have been spent on an annual religious festival (my field observations in 1998), or on a clubhouse or club functions for their own group (Singh and Kumar 1993).

In other types of CFGs, the money is normally put in a collective fund to be used as the group deems fit. Women typically have little say in how it is used. Women in a CFG in Ghusra village, Dang district, Nepal, told me in 1998, "The money obtained from grass and firewood is deposited by them into their fund. We have not seen one penny of it. We buy grass, which is auctioned in bundles."

Where the CFGs distribute forest products in, say, the form of firewood or grass, as in some of the JFM groups, women of nonmember households usually receive none, since entitlements are typically linked to membership.[18] Often these

---

18. Membership is usually determined on the basis of more than one criterion, one of which is membership fees, which are more common in India than in Nepal. Another criterion, common among CFGs in both countries, is contributing toward the guard's pay or joining the village patrol.

are poor households whose members have to migrate for work, or are out all day on wage labor and cannot easily contribute to patrolling or to the guard's wages.

Even in member households, usually men alone can claim the benefits directly, either because only they are members, or because entitlements are on a household basis so that even if both spouses are members they get only one share. Of course, women can benefit indirectly in some degree if the benefits are in kind, such as firewood, or where member households continue to enjoy the right to collect dry wood or leaves from the protected area.[19] But where the CFGs distribute cash benefits, if money is given to men it does not guarantee equal sharing, or even any sharing, within the family. In fact, outside the context of forest management there is substantial evidence of men in poor households spending a significant part of their incomes on personal items such as tobacco and liquor, while women spend almost all of their incomes on basic household needs (for India see Mencher 1988, and Noponen 1991). This pattern is repeated in the context of CFGs. In many cases men are found to spend the money on gambling, liquor, or personal items (Guhathakurta and Bhatia 1992; my field observations, 1998–99).

Many women are aware that unless they receive a share from the CFG directly, rather than through male members, they may get nothing. When asked their views on this at a meeting of three JFM villages in West Bengal where both women and men were present, all the women wanted equal and separate shares for husbands and wives (Sarin 1995). Being members in their own right would be one way women could benefit directly, provided that the individual and not the household was the unit of entitlement.

Inequities also arise because people differ in their needs, or in their ability to contribute or to pay. Broadly, three types of principles can underlie the distribution of forest products: market-determined, contribution, and need. Although seemingly neutral, these distributive principles have notable gender and class implications. The market principle (or willingness to pay), embodied in practices such as the auctioning of grass to the highest bidder, tends to be both unequal *and* inequitable, since those who cannot afford to pay have to do without. Given that rural women, even in rich households, tend to have less access to financial resources than men, auctions tend to be both anti-poor and anti-women. Distribution according to contribution—by, say, giving each household that contributes to protection an equal number of grass bundles—would be equal but inequitable for those more dependent on the commons for grass, such as the poorer households, and women in general. Moreover, women's ability to contribute may be circumscribed. For instance, even if they wanted to join patrol duty, they may be prevented from doing so by social norms of seclusion. Only

19. See Kant, Singh, and Singh (1991); ISO-Swedforest (1993); Arul and Poffenberger (1990). I also observed this during my field visits in 1998–99.

where distribution embodies some concept of economic need, such as where poor women are given rights to an additional grass patch, would the distribution be relatively more equitable, in that those most in need would get more.

In my fieldwork I found that the most common criterion underlying distribution was contribution (membership fees, protection, and so on), with all contributing households having equal claims to the firewood or grass cut during the days when the forest was opened. However, there were also occasional cases of auctioning, such as the auctioning of grass in the Uttar Pradesh hills and in Nepal, and of other forest produce in Orissa. Economic need seldom guided distribution. Hence, for poor women, in particular, the outcome tended to prove inequitable.

In recent literature on collective action, questions of equity have been raised largely in terms of whether existing economic and social inequality affects the possibility of collective action and efficient institutional functioning (see, for example, Ostrom 1990; Bardhan 1993; Baland and Platteau 1996, 1999). There has been a relative neglect of whether or not the *outcomes* of collective action in terms of, say, cost and benefit sharing are equitable, and how those outcomes impinge on the sustainability of collective action. As previously argued, equity of outcome is important in itself for evaluating institutions governing the commons, quite apart from the links between equity and efficiency (and between participation and efficiency) that are elaborated below.

Efficiency

Women's lack of participation in CFG decisionmaking, and gender inequities in the sharing of costs and benefits from protection, can have a range of efficiency implications. Some initiatives may fail to take off at all; others may not sustain the gains; yet others may have a notable gap between realizable and actual gains (in terms of resource productivity and diversity, satisfying household needs, enhancing incomes, and so forth). Inefficiencies can stem from one or more of the following problems (see also Agarwal 2000a, 2000b).

First, in almost all the villages I visited there were at least some cases of rule violation, and at times this was a frequent occurrence.[20] Violations by men usually involve timber for self-use or sale, the latter in areas with commercially valuable trees. Violations by women typically involve firewood. Where a CFG bans collection without consulting women or addressing their difficulties, many women are under great pressure to break the rules, given their daily need for firewood. Sometimes, women in situations of acute need enter into persistent altercations with the guards. In one Gujarat village the guard threatened to resign as a result. Only then did the EC address the issue and agree to open the forest for

---

20. Shah and Shah (1995), Singh and Kumar (1993), and Agarwal (1997a). I also observed this during my field visits in 1998–99).

a few days annually. In Agrawal's study (1999) of a *van panchayat* village, women constituted 70 to 80 percent of reported offenders between 1951 and 1991; many of them belonged to poor and low-caste households.

A second source of inefficiency is inadequate information sharing with women. Information about the rules (especially membership rules), conflicts encountered, and other aspects of forest management does not always reach women (my field observations during 1998–99). Similarly, male forest officials seldom consult women or seek their feedback when preparing micro-plans for forest development. Some women hear about the plans through their husbands, others not at all (Guhathakurta and Bhatia 1992). Such communication problems can prove particularly acute in regions of high male out-migration, since the women who are left behind tend to get excluded from the largely male channels of communication.

Third, inefficiencies can arise if the male guard or patrol fails to notice resource depletion. During my 1995 field visit to Gujarat, a women's informal patrol in Machipada village took me to the protected site and, pointing out the illegal cuttings that the men had missed, told me, "Men don't check carefully for illegal cuttings. Women keep a more careful lookout." My subsequent fieldwork in 1998–99 revealed similar differences in several other field sites. This gender difference arises in part because women, as the main and most frequent collectors of forest products, are more familiar with the forest than men.

A fourth and related point is that there are problems in catching transgressors. In virtually all the regions I visited, all-male patrols or male guards were unable to deal effectively with women intruders because they risked being charged with sexual harassment or molestation. Threats to this effect were not uncommon when nonmember women or women from neighboring villages were caught. In some incidents, women and their families had even registered false police cases against patrol members or beaten them up. Equally, however, women on their own find it difficult to do night patrolling or to confront aggressive male intruders. By all accounts, the most efficient solution appears to be a patrol team consisting of both sexes. Recognizing this, in some regions male patrollers have included some village women in their patrol, but this is atypical.

When women voluntarily set up informal patrols, even where there is a male guard or patrol, the efficiency of protection can improve notably. In their study of twelve *van panchayats*, Sharma and Sinha (1993) found that the four councils that could be deemed "robust" all had active women's associations. However, insofar as women's groups are typically informal, they lack the authority to punish offenders, who still have to be reported to the formal (typically all-male) committees. This separation of authority and responsibility introduces inefficiencies in functioning. For instance, sometimes male EC members fail to mete out punishments to the culprits women catch, causing women to abandon their efforts. I found several such cases in Karnataka, Gujarat, and the Uttar Pradesh hills. Also, when women catch intruders, they are seldom party to discussions or decisions on appropriate penalties.

Fifth, a related issue is that efficient functioning requires effective methods of conflict resolution. This is made difficult with women's virtual exclusion from the formal committees, especially where the conflict involves women, as is not infrequently the case with firewood-related intrusions.

A sixth form of inefficiency stems from CFGs taking little account of women's knowledge of plants and species when preparing plans for forest regeneration. Women and men are often privy to different types of knowledge as a result of the differences in the tasks they perform and in their spatial domains. Women as the main fuel and fodder collectors can often better explain the attributes of trees than men (Pandey 1990) and can identify a large number of trees, shrubs, and grasses in the vicinity of fields and pastures (Chen 1993). In general, women are better informed about the local environment in which they gather and collect, and men about species found in distant areas (Gaul 1994). Women's systematic exclusion from decisionmaking and management of new planting programs is thus likely to have negative efficiency implications, by failing to tap women's knowledge of diverse species for enhancing biodiversity.

A seventh form of inefficiency can arise from ignoring possible gender differences in preferences regarding when grass should be cut or which trees should be planted. I found that in the rare cases when women were consulted, they often came up with alternative, more suitable suggestions on when the forest should be opened for forest produce collection. Women are also known usually to prefer trees that have more domestic use value, as for fuel and fodder, whereas men more typically opt for trees that bring in cash (see, for example, Brara 1987 and Hobley 1996). The exceptions are cases where fuel and fodder are ample, in which case women too might prefer commercially valuable species (Chen 1993). Women's greater involvement in forest planning would thus better fulfill household needs and so also increase their commitment to the CFG initiative.

Basically, when examined from a gender perspective, it is clear that the CFGs are violating many of the conditions deemed by several scholars to be necessary for building enduring institutions for managing common-pool resources. This includes conditions such as ensuring that those affected by the rules participate in framing and modifying the rules; that the rules be kept simple and fair; that there be effective mechanisms for monitoring the resource and resolving conflicts; and so on (see especially Ostrom 1990 and Baland and Platteau 1996).

Forests might regenerate despite women's low involvement in CFGs, but some of the CFGs might not be sustainable and others might produce less than their potential benefits. Improving women's participation and equity is thus important both in itself and because it can be complementary to, rather than (as often assumed) in conflict with, efficient institutional functioning.

What Determines Gendered Outcomes?

The gender-related efficiency outcomes just discussed are in large part *secondary* in nature, stemming from women's low participation in the CFGs and from inequities in the rules of forest use, benefit sharing, and so forth. Efficiency outcomes are therefore not discussed separately in the section below. Rather I focus on what underlies women's low participation and the consequent inequities in cost and benefit sharing.

Factors Affecting Women's Participation in CFGs

In broad terms, the degree of participation and the distribution of costs and benefits can be seen to depend especially on rules, norms, perceptions, the woman's individual endowments and attributes, and her household's endowments and attributes (which define where the family falls within the structural hierarchies of class, caste, and so on).

RULES. In formal CFGs, such as the JFM groups in India or the forest-user groups in Nepal, rules determine membership in the GB or the EC. As noted earlier, where the rule restricts membership to only one person per household, it is the male household head who tends to join. The rule that allows one man and one woman per household to join is somewhat more inclusive, but full inclusiveness would require all adults to be allowed to join. This is rare.

In addition to the rules themselves, a lack of awareness of the rules or of changes in them can also constrain women's participation. In West Bengal, for instance, a study of nineteen CFGs showed that even four years after the state order was amended to allow women's inclusion, barely two-fifths of the members knew of the change (Raju 1997).

Among the self-initiated groups, which lack formal membership rules, long-standing conventions that traditionally excluded women from public decision-making forums also deny women entry into the CFGs.

SOCIAL NORMS. Even when membership rules are favorable and women join CFGs, they seldom attend or speak up at meetings because social norms place strictures on their visibility, mobility, and behavior. These norms, whether internalized by women or imposed on them by threat of gossip, reprimand, or even violence, impinge directly on women's autonomy and ability to participate effectively in CFGs dominated by men.[21]

Some communities have quite strict female seclusion norms. But more pervasive is the subtle gendering of physical space and social behavior. For instance, norms often dictate a gender segregation of public space. Women of "good character" are expected to avoid village spaces where men congregate, such as tea stalls and the market place (Agarwal 1994). For older women, the restriction is generally less but

21. See also Stewart's (1996) more general discussion on the function of norms in hierarchical contexts.

never fully absent. As a result, many women feel uncomfortable going to CFG meetings unless explicitly invited by the men:

> The meetings are considered for men only. Women are never called. The men attend and their opinions or consent are taken as representative of the whole family—it is understood. (Woman in a *van panchayat* village, Uttar Pradesh hills, cited in Britt 1993, 148)

> Rural women and men can't sit together. But we convey our decisions to them. (Man to author, Chattipur village, Orissa, 1998)

The gender division of labor is another pernicious norm. The fact that women bear the main responsibility of childcare and housework, in addition to the load of agricultural work, cattle care, and so on, makes for high work burdens and logistical constraints. This seriously restricts women's ability to attend lengthy meetings held at inconvenient times. As some women in Barde village, Karnataka state, south India, told me in 1998, "There are problems in attending meetings since we need to cook and serve the evening meal. The meeting is long. We also have to feed the cattle." Men are usually reluctant to share not just domestic tasks and childcare but even care of cattle. Most women in the *van panchayat* villages Mansingh (1991) studied told her that they did not have time to "sit around for [the] four hours that it took to have a meeting in the middle of the day." As a result women's attendance decreased over time.

Norms also reduce women's participation by creating subtle gender hierarchies, such as by requiring women to sit on the floor while husbands and older men sit on cots, or requiring women to sit at the back of the meeting space where they are less visible and less able to raise a point effectively. Moreover, where senior male family members are present, women either do not attend meetings, or do not oppose men publicly. The hierarchy that marks "respectful" behavior in the family also marks community gatherings (see also Raju 1997).

SOCIAL PERCEPTIONS. Incorrect perceptions regarding women's abilities impinge on men's willingness to include women in the CFGs. Men often view women's involvement in CFGs as serving no useful purpose and tend to downplay women's potential contributions. Some men's direct responses to questions are indicative:

> There is no advantage in having women in the EC. We have been told by the forest officials that we must have two women in the committee, that is why we have included them. (Male to author, Pathari village, Karnataka)

> Women can't make any helpful suggestions. (Man to author, Arjunpur village, Orissa, 1998)

> Women are illiterate. If they come to meetings, we men might as well stay at home. (EC chairman to author, Ghusra village, Dang district, Nepal, 1998)

In some cases, I found that the men who were decrying my interviewing the women on the grounds that they were illiterate were themselves illiterate!

ENTRENCHED TERRITORIAL CLAIMS. Men oppose women's inclusion much more strongly once their own claims are entrenched. Thus, where CFGs start out with only male members, or where men feel they have a prior claim to the land, they resist new claimants. Some young men in Basapur village, Karnataka state, reacted to the idea of including women in CFGs as follows: "Women have DWARCA, they have savings groups, why don't you leave the CFGs to us men?" (my field visit in 1998).[22] Men in Asundriya village, Gujarat, strongly opposed NGO attempts to increase women's CFG membership, arguing, "Why do we need women? What we are doing is okay" (my field visit in 1999). In Kudamunda village, Orissa, when I asked the women who wanted their own separate patch for protection why they needed one, they responded, "If we have our own forest, we would not need to ask the men each time for a bit of wood. They are not willing to give us even a patch to protect. Why would they be willing to give us a whole tree if we asked?"

PERSONAL ENDOWMENTS AND ATTRIBUTES. Women's lesser access to personal property or to political connections reduces the weight of their opinions. In addition, limited experience in public interaction undermines their effectiveness in public forums. Some of these disadvantages can partly be overcome if the women are older or married or have leadership qualities and have the self-confidence to speak up (Narain 1994; Britt 1993; my field observations in1998–99).

HOUSEHOLD ENDOWMENTS AND ATTRIBUTES. Factors such as the class and caste position of the woman's household are likely to matter if the village is multi-caste and is dominated by the upper caste, or where the CFG is constituted of several villages, each if which is homogeneous in itself but is hierarchically placed in relation to other villages in the CFG (my field observations in 1998–99; see also Sarin 1998 and Hobley 1996). But the caste factor works in complex ways. On the one hand, being low caste and poor can adversely affect a person's ability to bargain for a better deal within a predominantly upper-caste community; and even low-caste men (like women in general) often hesitate to speak up at meetings in such contexts. On the other hand, low-caste women are less subject than upper-caste women to norms of seclusion, restricted mobility, and soft speech. Hence if present in large enough numbers, they would be more likely to speak up in meetings, as I found to be the case in my 2000–01 research (discussed in the next section).

Factors Affecting Distributional Equity

Similar but not identical factors affect gender-inequitable outcomes in terms of costs and benefits. The principal factor underlying gender differences in cost sharing appears to be social norms governing the gender division of labor. As already

---

22. DWACRA—Development of Women and Children in Rural Areas—is an antipoverty program of the Indian government. One part of the program provides women's groups with subsidized loans for income-generating activities.

discussed, women's primary responsibility for collecting firewood and fodder means that women bear the bulk of the costs of forgoing forest use.

Benefit sharing is likely to be affected especially by five types of factors. First, there are the rules regarding entitlements to benefits. Here both entry rules and distribution rules matter. As noted earlier, access to some types of benefits is linked to membership. However, even if both spouses are members, the woman may not get a separate or additional share if the CFG has decided that the household rather than the individual will be the unit of distribution. In recent years, this has in fact proved to be a bottleneck in inducting women members in parts of Gujarat, where women are demanding shares on an individual basis as a condition for their becoming CFG members, especially since the CFGs also ask for higher membership fees from those joining late. Hence, although women's low participation in CFG decisionmaking affects equity of outcomes through the distribution rules, inequitable distribution rules can in turn restrict women's participation.

Second, the principles (willingness to pay, contribution, or need) underlying distribution affect equity of benefit sharing. At present (as noted earlier), contribution is the dominant criterion underlying distribution rules in most CFGs, whereby all those contributing get equal access to the resource or equal amounts of firewood and fodder when they are distributed. Auctions are undertaken in some cases, and distribution by economic need is rare.

Third, perceptions about need, contribution, and deservedness matter. Even if there were to be a shift from contribution to need as the defining principle, whether or not women get a better deal can still depend on whether they are *perceived* as deserving more (Agarwal 1997b; Sen 1990). There can be and often is a divergence between what a person actually contributes, needs, or is able to do and perceptions about her or his contributions, needs, and abilities. Thus, women's contribution to household income is often undervalued, both by family members and by those implementing development programs, because of the "invisible" nature of many household tasks that rural women perform. These tasks—such as collecting firewood and fodder, stall-feeding animals, storing and processing grain—are often economically invisible because they usually do not bring in cash, and tasks done within the home are also rendered physically invisible. Hence, women's contributions would be better recognized if women were *seen* to be participating in forest management and would thus be better placed to claim benefits equal to men's.

Fourth, whether or not the outcome is equitable depends on pre-existing personal endowments and attributes. Since women as a gender (even if not all women as individuals) have fewer private economic endowments, CFG shares given only to male members typically result in inequitable outcomes for women in both rich and poor households. Again, women's personal attributes such as age and marital status can affect intra-household distribution by influencing perceptions about deservedness.

Fifth, as we have noted, how acutely women are affected by forest closure or short-ages is influenced by their household's economic endowments and social attributes, in particular by their household's class, caste, and ethnicity. In some respects, how-ever, this can work in both directions. For instance, although women in upper-caste households that own land and animals can get some fuel and fodder from private assets, they are also likely to face greater social constraints on their mobility, which would limit their options with respect to alternative collection sites. In any event, when it comes to fuel, the class difference may not be substantial (unless we are speaking of those able to afford cooking gas), since many women even of middle peasant households have to depend mostly on what they themselves can gather.

Improving Outcomes: The Bargaining Framework

In what ways can these factors be acted upon to improve outcomes? Some factors that obstruct women's well-being antedate the community forestry programs and have deep economic and social roots. The programs could either lead to the obsta-cles' becoming further entrenched or provide an opportunity for undermining them. Other factors, such as CFG rules, are part of institutional functioning. Both types of factors are constituted at several levels. For example, rules are broadly made at two levels, the State and the community. Membership criteria under JFM are determined at the State level, but such issues as whether forest closure should be total or partial, or in what ways different forest products should be distributed, are determined largely by the community. And social norms, social perceptions, and endowments are constituted and contested at all levels—within the State, the community, the family, and various institutions of civil society, including NGOs.

Bargaining: Some Conceptual Issues

A promising analytical framework for examining the possibilities for change on all these counts is that of bargaining (Agarwal 1997b). Women's ability to change rules, norms, perceptions, and endowments in a gender-progressive direction would depend on their bargaining power—with the State, the community, and the family, as the case may be. What would affect women's ability to bargain effectively in these three arenas?

THE STATE. The State can be seen as an arena of bargaining at multiple levels. For instance, the State may formulate gender-progressive laws at the highest level, but it could face resistance in implementation from the local bureaucracy. Or some departments or ministries (such as women's ministries) may pursue gender-progressive policies within an overall gender-retrogressive State structure. Likewise, there are often some gender-progressive individuals within State departments who play key positive roles, typically but not only in response to demands made by inter-est groups (see Sanyal 1991; Agarwal 1994). In other words, the State is an arena of contestation between parties, such as policymaking vs. policy-implementing bodies, and between different regional elements of the State structure with varying commitments to gender equality.

The State might respond positively to demands by gender-progressive groups and NGOs because such groups could build up political pressure through, say, the support of opposition parties or the media, with implications for voting patterns; or because of pressure from international aid agencies; or because the State recognizes the inefficacy both of market mechanisms and of its own machinery in implementing essential development programs. In India, the State's attempts since the mid-1980s to enlist NGO support for various development projects, including community forestry, reflects this recognition.

We would expect women's bargaining strength with the State to depend on a complex set of factors, such as whether they function as a group or as individuals and what the cohesiveness and strength of the group is. The bargaining power of such a group is likely to be higher, the larger and more unified it is; the greater the political weight carried by the castes of which it is composed; the greater its command over economic resources; the more support it gets from NGOs, the media, academics, and international donors; and the more State officials are influenced by gender-progressive norms and perceptions.

THE COMMUNITY. Implicit or explicit bargaining can occur between an individual (or a subset of individuals) and the community, over the rules and norms governing economic resource use or social behavior, and over the enforcement of those rules and norms. Noncompliance with CFG rules could be seen as a form of implicit bargaining.

Like women's bargaining power with the State, women's bargaining power within the community would be enhanced if they had support from external agents such as NGOs and the State. Group cohesiveness and strength is also important. For instance, an individual woman breaking seclusion norms could easily be penalized by others' casting aspersions on her character. Such reprisals are less possible if a group of women decides to transgress the norms (see also Agarwal 1994).

In addition, in a multicaste or class-heterogeneous village we would expect women's bargaining power to depend on the socioeconomic composition of their group and their ability to command funds. For instance, in the sharing of communal resources, the negotiating strength of low-caste or poor peasant women, even if they formed a group, is likely to be weaker than that of high-caste or rich peasant women whose caste or class as a whole commands greater power in the village.

THE FAMILY. The third major arena of bargaining is the family. Intrafamily bargaining for a more equitable sharing of benefits or tasks or for greater freedom to participate publicly is perhaps the most complex aspect of bargaining (spelled out in Agarwal 1994, 1997b). Broadly, four types of factors are likely to impinge on a woman's bargaining power in the home: her personal endowments and attributes (educational level, whether or not she earns an income, property ownership, age, marital status); her ability to draw upon extra-household support from friends, relatives, women's groups in the village, gender-progressive NGOs outside the village, and the State; social norms, which might define who gets what or who does what within the household; and social perceptions about deservedness.

ALL ARENAS. Some of the common determinants of bargaining power in all three arenas are support from external agents, social norms and perceptions, and group strength. Norms, perceptions, and group strength require some elaboration.

Social norms can affect bargaining power in both direct and indirect ways. For instance, norms that restrict women's presence in public spaces directly reduce women's ability to bargain for rule changes within CFGs, but they may also do so indirectly by reducing women's ability to build contacts with NGOs or State officials. Social norms can also influence how bargaining is conducted: covertly or overtly, aggressively or quietly. In cultures or contexts where social norms stifle explicit voice, women may be pushed into using covert forms of contestation within the family, such as persistent complaining or withdrawing into silence (Agarwal 1994). Moreover, attempts to change social norms can themselves constitute a bargaining process (Agarwal 1997b).

Social perceptions can affect women's bargaining power insofar as women's contributions and abilities diverge from perceptions about their contributions and abilities. As noted, much of what women do is rendered invisible and is therefore undervalued by both families and communities. To the extent that women internalize these perceptions, they can self-restrict their range of options or what they seek to change and bargain over. Hence, to enhance women's bargaining power, a necessary step would be to change women's own perceptions about their potential options and abilities, as well as the perceptions of their families, the community, and the State regarding their abilities and the legitimacy of their claims.

Group strength can prove to be a critical factor at all levels and in all forms of bargaining (including over social norms and perceptions). Here village women's group strength derives not merely from the number of women who would like a change in rules and norms but also from their willingness to act collectively in their common interest, an interest predicated on gender. In other words, it depends on whether gender is a basis of group identity, over and above the possible divisiveness of caste or class. The creation of such group identity will thus need to be part of the process of improving outcomes for women.

Bargaining: Actual Experiences

Let us now consider the actual experience of some groups in their attempts to improve women's participation and distributional equity in CFGs. These experiences illustrate some, albeit not all, of the key elements of the bargaining framework just described.

THE STATE. Experience in the Joint Forest Management program indicates that successfully bargaining with the State for changing the initial rules of entry is not very difficult. Pressure from external agents such as gender-progressive

NGOs and key individuals has led a number of Indian states to make JFM membership rules more women-inclusive. Village women did not have to explicitly bargain for changes because the women's movement in South Asia had brought about a sufficient shift in perceptions regarding gender inequalities to make such issues easier to resolve with the State, through outside intervention. In this context, village women started from a position of some bargaining strength.

THE COMMUNITY. Bargaining with the community to ensure that more women-inclusive membership rules are implemented and to increase women's effective voice in CFGs has proved more difficult. On the positive side, some of the gender-progressive NGOs, forest officials, and donors have used their bargaining power with the community to bring about changes that favor women, sometimes on their own initiative, at other times when village women approached them.

For instance, some Indian NGOs have made a high proportion of female membership in mixed groups a condition for forming the groups. In Gujarat, one NGO now insists, when starting new CFGs, that 50 percent of members be women. Similarly, some state-level officials in India have increased women's membership in mixed groups by stipulating that there should be at least 30 percent women in the general body, or have sought to increase women's presence in GB meetings by refusing to start meetings unless the men also invite the women (Viegas and Menon 1993; Sarin 1998). Similarly, in the cause of distributional equity, the staff of a Gujarat-based NGO took up women's complaints about firewood shortages at a CFG meeting. This resulted in a shift from total closure of the forest to its opening up for a few days annually.

For a larger and sustained impact, however, active input is required from women themselves, both through an enhanced presence in the ECs, which are the principal decisionmaking bodies, and not simply in the GBs, and through active participation in the process of decisionmaking by attending meetings and speaking up at them.

Left to themselves, women have typically relied on covert forms of bargaining to change distributional rules, such as simply ignoring closure rules, challenging the authority of the patrol group or guard who catches them, persistently complaining, and so on. In some instances, this had led village committees to open the forest for short spells. However, complaining or breaking rules, with the attendant risk of being caught and fined, are seldom the most effective ways of changing the rules. For effective change, women are likely to need more formal involvement in rule making and the bargaining power to ensure changes in their favor. Actual experience on the ground suggests that a prerequisite for bringing this about is often the presence of a critical mass of women. This can give women more voice in mixed forums and help them challenge restrictive social norms and perceptions. My recent empirical research (discussed in the next section) also provides substantial support for this.

THE FAMILY. Bargaining within the family is in many ways a much more complex issue to tackle than bargaining with the community, and few rural NGOs directly intervene in intra-household relations. Forming all-women CFGs or even women's savings groups can have indirect positive effects. For instance, during my field visits I found several cases where a women's group had supported individual women in their negotiations with husbands, or where joining a group had improved women's situations at home:

> There are one or two men who objected to their wives' attending our meetings, and said you can't go. But when our women's association came to their aid, the men let their wives go. (Women to author in Almavadi village, Gujarat, 1998)

> My husband feels I contribute financially, take up employment, obtain credit for the home. This increases his respect for me. (Woman to author in Almavadi village, Gujarat, 1998)

In other words, group strength and women's visible contributions can help weaken restrictive social norms and improve a man's view of his wife's deservedness, although some norms, such as the gender division of domestic work, are particularly rigid and difficult to change.

The issue of group strength has been much debated in recent years in the context of quotas for women and the question of "critical mass." It has been argued that women need to constitute a minimum percentage—a critical mass—within public decisionmaking bodies before they can be effective. Although substantial support exists for the idea that women's proportional strength matters, much of the discussion is focused on whether it affects women's ability to influence policies, rather then whether it can affect the very process of women's participation. There is also little empirical testing to identify what proportion would be effective. More generally, too, there is little empirical examination of the impact of the gender composition of a group on its decisionmaking and functioning. In the next section I present a summary of some results from my recent research on these aspects.[23]

Effect of Women's Proportional Strength: Recent Empirical Evidence

Does having more women in a decisionmaking body make a difference to their participation and the outcomes of institutional functioning? I tested this through an econometric analysis of primary data collected from 2000 to 2002 through

---

23. Based on my fieldwork in Gujarat state (India) and Nepal in 2000–01, as mentioned earlier. Results are taken from my draft book manuscript (Agarwal, forthcoming).

systematic fieldwork in sixty-five CFGs located in three districts of Gujarat (west India) and seventy CFGs located in three districts of Nepal.[24] I do indeed find that the higher the percentage of women in the ECs the greater is women's effective participation in decisionmaking and access to forest products such as firewood (taken as a measure of distributional equity), and the better is forest regeneration (taken as a measure of efficiency).

EFFECTIVE PARTICIPATION. The higher the percentage of women in the EC, the more likely it is that women will attend meetings, speak up at them, and take up leadership positions—that is, hold office. Village women themselves stress that the presence of more women will give them voice:

> If we were in a majority we would speak in the meeting. (EC women in a CFG in Baglung, Nepal, 2000)

> The presence of more women will give us support and confidence. It makes a difference when there are other women in meetings. (EC women in a village in Panchmahals, Gujarat, 2000)

But how large a percentage do women need to be effective? Is a minimum threshold of female presence necessary? In my analysis I find threshold effects on some counts. For instance, in both Gujarat and Nepal, the threshold for women's participation as measured by the female attendance rate (the average proportion of EC women attending a meeting)[25] is found to lie in the range 25 to 33 percent women on the EC. For speaking up it is not possible to identify a threshold effect, since not every woman who attends needs to speak up, even if she is able to. I do find, however, that for both Gujarat and Nepal the probability of at least one woman speaking up (as versus none speaking up) is significantly more if we move from ECs with less than 25 percent women to ECs with 33 percent or more women, although the proportion of meetings where no woman spoke up is notably lower in Nepal than in Gujarat. Moreover, in the case of Nepal, women are significantly more likely to be office bearers if they constitute 33 percent or more of the EC. In Gujarat, virtually no women are found to be holding office, irrespective of the EC's gender composition, indicating that simply increasing women's presence in the EC is not a sufficient condition to overcome the glass ceiling effect in all social contexts.

The difference between the Gujarat and Nepal sites, especially in terms of women speaking up and being office bearers, appears to be due to differences in

---

24. A few sample CFGs had to be replaced by some in a fourth adjacent district, when those in one of the selected districts became inaccessible, as a result of security problems in Nepal during the period of the survey.

25. Female attendance rate for CFG A $= \frac{1}{n} \sum_{i=1}^{n} \frac{w_i}{w}$, where w_i = number of EC women attending the ith meeting (i = 1, 2…n); w = number of EC women in CFG A; n = number of meetings held in CFG A. As an illustration, if CFG A has 3 women in the EC and there are 4 meetings, each attended by 2, 3, 1, and 0 EC women, the female attendance rate would be 0.5.

social norms in the two regions. In the Gujarat sample, although the majority of women belong to tribal populations where female seclusion is not emphasized, the ideology of seclusion and female modesty has been growing, influenced by a local religious reform movement and by upper-caste Hindu communities. The geographic location of my Nepal sites in the middle hills makes for less restrictive social norms, even among the upper-caste population, and certainly among the ethnic groups that are widespread in the area. This suggests that although women's effectiveness is clearly enhanced by the presence of more women, enabling social norms also matter.

One-third has become the popularly accepted percentage in arguments about how much female presence is needed for effectiveness in the context of legislatures or other public bodies such as village councils. My results broadly support this popularly emphasized proportion, although they also show that there is a somewhat wider range—somewhere between a quarter and a third women—linked with effective participation.

Women's class position also matters; in particular, the inclusion of *landless* women in the EC is important. I found in the case of Gujarat that women are more likely to attend and speak up in EC meetings where a high percentage of them come from landless households. Women from such households are less constrained by social norms and face firewood shortages in greater measure, compelling them to speak up. This alerts us to the importance of representation by disadvantaged women, and not simply by any women, in community institutions.

Some feminist scholars have argued that relative socioeconomic equality is a necessary condition for the disadvantaged to participate effectively (for example, Fraser 1990). My analysis suggests otherwise. Poor, low-caste women, especially if present in sufficient numbers, or with prior exposure to women's empowerment programs, can be more outspoken and effective in public forums than women from well-off households, since the former are less constrained by social status considerations and have a higher personal stake in the outcomes of decisions because of their greater dependence on forests.

EFFECT OF WOMEN'S PARTICIPATION ON FOREST CONDITION (EFFICIENCY OUTCOMES). The EC's gender composition also makes a difference to resource conservation. In Gujarat, CFGs with more than the mandatory two women in their EC tend to show greater improvement in forest condition than those with two women or less, and in Nepal the same is true of all-women CFGs relative to other (mixed plus a few all-male) CFGs. There are many reasons for this. Involving women in EC decisions tends to enlarge the pool of villagers with responsibility for and commitment to resource conservation. Even if the rules that the EC eventually makes impose personal hardship on the women committee members, if they are part of the decisionmaking process they are more likely to follow the rules themselves, as well as persuade other women to do so. Dissemination of information about the rules and about the need for conservation also improves, since women EC members can reach a much wider cross-section of people than can be reached only through male committee members. In addition, having more women on the EC enlarges the pool of those keeping an informal lookout for rule breakers. It also increases the chances of women's contributing their knowledge of plants and species and conveying their preferences when the micro-plans for forest development are being prepared or implemented. We thus need measures that can enhance women's presence in the governance institutions, not only because women's participation is of intrinsic importance but also because it can help better fulfill the conservation objectives of such institutions.

EFFECT ON FIREWOOD SHORTAGES (EQUITY OUTCOMES). In the Gujarat CFGs, those with a larger percentage of female EC members are found to be less likely to report firewood shortages. Women's voice, therefore, does count in getting the community to extract more from the protected area. However, the question of alternative fuels that are cleaner and less damaging for women and children's health than firewood and other unprocessed biofuels still remains to be addressed by the women representatives and their communities.

Toward Increasing Women's Proportionate Strength

We have seen that women's proportionate strength in the EC can have a beneficial effect on their participation, as well as on the efficiency and equity of outcomes. The question then is: How do we enhance women's presence in village institutions?

There is a growing consensus among gender-progressive NGOs and elements of the State apparatus that to increase women's presence in CFGs will require, as a first step, the formation of separate women's groups. Maya Devi, a Nepalese grassroots activist with long experience in group organizing, told me emphatically in 1998, "In mixed groups, when women speak, men make fun of them, so women need to learn to deal with this. . . . When women join a [separate] group they gradually lose their fear of making fools of themselves when speaking up. . . . Women need their own small groups. This is what I know from my twenty-two years of experience working with the government and NGOs."

There is less consensus, however, on what type of group this should be. Where all-women CFGs have been formed, many have done well in terms of protection and increasing women's self-confidence. However, so far, all-women CFGs (as noted earlier) have usually arisen in special circumstances and are still marginal in terms of numbers and area protected. Also, they cannot solve the problem of women's meager presence and lack of effective voice in the more typical all-male or mixed CFGs. For this, other kinds of efforts are needed. Toward this end, some rural NGOs have been forming all-women savings-and-credit groups, which, unlike CFGs, do not involve a resource over which there is a generalized community claim. In some regions, more multifunctional women's groups are also doing well.

Such separate women's groups, organized around savings or some other issue, have helped build women's self-confidence and experience in collective functioning and promoted a sense of collective identity. They have also increased women's ability to deal with government agencies, improved male perceptions about women's capabilities, and brought about some change in social norms that earlier confined women to the domestic space. The response below is fairly typical:

> Men used to shut us up and say we shouldn't speak. Women learned to speak up in a *sangathan* [group]. Earlier we couldn't speak up even at home. Now we can be more assertive and also go out. I am able to help other women gain confidence as well. (Woman leader to author, Vejpur village, Gujarat, 1999)

These experiences are not dissimilar to those of many other rural women's groups across South Asia, which also indicate that group strength, external agency support, and activities that enable women to make a visible contribution (especially in monetary terms) can alter social norms and perceptions and increase the social acceptance of women in public roles. But in many villages, separate women's savings groups have also sharpened gender segregation in collective functioning. Often women's savings groups are seen as "women's groups" and the CFGs as "men's groups." Also, separate women's savings groups do not adequately challenge unequal gender relations or noticeably change the dynamics of *mixed*-group functioning. In other words, forming separate women's groups may well be a necessary condition, but it is not a sufficient one for women's effective participation in the CFGs.

For effective integration, more concerted efforts appear necessary. In a few cases, NGOs working with both women and men have sought to integrate all-women savings groups with the CFG. For instance, India Development Service, an NGO in rural Karnataka, encourages women's savings groups to discuss CFG functioning, collect CFG membership dues, and persuade women to join the CFG. As a result, in several of its villages, some 80 to 90 percent of the women in the savings groups are now in the CFG general body.[26] Bringing this about, however, has taken many years of persistent effort and trust building between the NGO, the women, and the villagers.

An alternative approach—one yet to be tried, I believe—could be to form a women's subgroup within each mixed CFG. Such a subgroup could first meet separately to discuss women's specific forest-related concerns and then strategically place these concerns before the full CFG meeting. This could also enable female EC members to better represent women's interests within the CFG.

---

26. Personal communication in 1998 from Pratibha Mundergee, then a staff member of this NGO.

Finally, any group, including a CFG, is likely to be affected not only by its immediate locale but also by the wider context of structural and cultural inequalities within which it is located. For instance, both participation and distributional equity are affected by the preexisting inequalities predicated on the caste and class of women's households, as well as on gender. These inequalities are unlikely to decline substantially within the parameters of CFG functioning. For instance, greater participation in CFGs alone is unlikely to notably improve the economic endowment position of women vis- à-vis men or of the poor vis-à-vis the rich. Also, as long as gender inequality in economic endowments remains entrenched, women will remain in a considerably weaker bargaining position in the family relative to men (Agarwal 1994; 1997b). To change this, more wide-ranging measures to enhance the access of women and of poor and low-caste households in general to land or other assets are likely to be needed.

Conclusion

CFGs are a significant example of how new institutions of governance can take one of two paths: that of challenging embedded and hidden social inequalities such as those of gender and caste, or that of ignoring these preexisting inequalities and, in the process, further embedding them. The first path consciously seeks to enhance access and open new doors; the second implicitly continues to restrict access. We see examples of both types among the several thousand CFGs in existence in India and Nepal today, determined largely by the nature of external interventions. The majority of CFGs have been gender exclusionary rather than inclusionary. Although most have done quite well in regenerating forests (at least in the short term), they have been less successful in bringing about women's participation in decisionmaking, or in ensuring gender equity in the sharing of costs and benefits from forest protection. As a result, they have also failed to tap the full potential of the collective effort in terms of improvement in forest condition. My analysis shows that for more participatory, equitable, and efficient outcomes, we will need changes in factors such as rules, norms, perceptions, and the pre-existing structural inequalities in endowments and attributes of women's households and of women themselves.

As argued here, it is useful to conceptualize such change within a bargaining framework, and to act on the factors that will strengthen women's bargaining power with the State, the community, and the family. This has been achieved to some degree through the intervention of external agents, especially NGOs, which in some cases have acted both directly and indirectly—indirectly especially by forming separate women's savings groups at the village level to enhance women's self-confidence and collective strength. At the same time, the analysis cautions that such separate women's groups can also lead to greater gender segregation unless conscious steps are taken to integrate women's savings groups with mixed CFGs. An alternative or complementary approach would be to form women's subgroups within each CFG to strategically induct women's concerns into CFG decisionmaking. In either case, these are only a few steps among the many that will be needed to transform mixed CFGs into more accessible and gender-egalitarian institutions, and so bridge the gap between the vision and the practice of local environmental governance.

References

Adhikari, N., G. Yadav, S. B. Ray, and S. Kumar. 1991. "Process Documentation of Women's Involvement in Forest Management at Maheshpur, Ranchi." In *Managing the Village Commons: Proceedings of the National Workshop, Dec. 15–16, 1991, Indian Institute of Forest Management, Bhopal*, edited by R. Singh, 118–23. Bhopal, Madhya Pradesh: Indian Institute of Forest Management.

Agarwal, B. 1987. "Under the Cooking Pot: The Political Economy of the Domestic Fuel Crisis in Rural South Asia." *IDS Bulletin* 18, no. 1: 11–22.

———. 1994. *A Field of One's Own: Gender and Land Rights in South Asia*. Cambridge University Press.

———. 1997a. "Environmental Action, Gender Equity and Women's Participation." *Development and Change* 28, no. 1: 1–44.

———. 1997b. "Bargaining and Gender Relations: Within and beyond the Household." *Feminist Economics* 3, no. 1: 1–51.

———. 2000a. "Group Functioning and Community Forestry in South Asia: A Gender Analysis and Conceptual Framework." UNU Working Paper 172. Helsinki: United Nations University and the World Institute for Development Economics Research.

———. 2000b. "Conceptualizing Environmental Collective Action: Why Gender Matters." *Cambridge Journal of Economics* 24, no. 3: 283–310.

———. 2001. "Participatory Exclusions, Community Forestry and Gender." *World Development* 29, no. 10: 1623–48.

———. 2006. "Gender, Cooperation and Environmental Sustainability." In *Inequality, Cooperation, and Environmental Sustainability*, edited by J.-M. Baland, P. Bardhan, and S. Bowles, 274–313. Princeton University Press.

———. Forthcoming. *Gender and Green Governance*.

Agrawal, Arun. 1999. "State Formation in Community Spaces: Control over Forests in the Kumaon Himalaya, India." Paper prepared for presentation at the Workshop on Environmental Politics. University of California, Berkeley, April 30.

Arul, N. J., and M. Poffenberger. 1990. "FPC Case Studies." In *Forest Protection Committees in Gujarat: Joint Management Initiative*, edited by R. S. Pathan, N. J. Arul, and M. Poffenburger, 13–25. New Delhi: Ford Foundation.

Bahuguna, V. K., K. Mitra, D. Capistrano, and S. Saigal, eds. 2004. *Root to Canopy: Regenerating Forests through Community-State Partnerships*. Delhi: Winrock International and Commonwealth Forestry Association.

Baland, J. M., and J. P. Platteau. 1996. *Halting Degradation of Natural Resources: Is There a Role for Rural Communities?* Oxford: Clarendon Press.

———. 1999. "The Ambiguous Impact of Inequality on Local Resource Management." *World Development* 27, no. 5: 773–88.

Bardhan, P. 1993. "Analytics of the Institutions of Informal Cooperation in Rural Development." *World Development* 21, no. 4: 633–39.

Brara, R. 1987. "Shifting Sands: A Study of Rights in Common Pastures." Unpublished paper (mimeograph). Jaipur: Institute of Development Studies.

Britt, C. 1993. "Out of the Wood? Local Institutions and Community Forest Management in Two Central Himalayan Villages." Unpublished paper. Cornell University.

Center for Science and Environment. 2001. "Biomass: A Smoky Problem." Health and Environment Newsletter (Center for Science and Environment, Delhi) 1, no. 1: 6.

Chen, M. 1993. "Women and Wasteland Development in India: An Issue Paper." In *Women and Wasteland Development in India*, edited by A. Singh and N. Burra, 21–90. Delhi: Sage.

Chopra, K., and S. C. Gulati. 1997. "Environmental Degradation and Population Movements: The Role of Property Rights." *Environment and Resource Economics* 9: 383–408.

Correa, M. 1997. *Gender and Joint Forest Planning and Management: A Research Study in Uttara Kannada District, Karnataka.* Dharwad: India Development Service.

Dahal, D. R. 1994. *A Review of Forest User Groups: Case Studies from Eastern Nepal.* Kathmandu: International Center for Integrated Mountain Development.

Fraser, N. 1990. "Rethinking the Public Sphere: A Contribution to the Critique of Actually Existing Democracy." *Social Text* 25–26: 56–80.

Gaul, K. K. 1994. "Negotiated Positions and Shifting Terrains: Apprehension of Forest Resources in the Western Himalaya." Ph.D. dissertation. University of Massachusetts, Amherst, Department of Anthropology.

Goldemberg, J., T. B. Johansson, A. K. N. Reddy, and R. H. Williams. 2004. "A Global Clean Fuel Initiative." *Energy for Sustainable Development* 8, no. 3: 5–12.

Government of Nepal. 2000. *Forest User Group Statistics.* Kathmandu: Department of Forests, Community and Private Forestry Division.

———. 2001. *Population Monograph: Census of Nepal 2001.* Kathmandu: Central Bureau of Statistics.

———. 2007. *Forest User Group Statistics.* Kathmandu: Department of Forests, Community and Private Forestry Division.

Guhathakurta, P., and K. S. Bhatia. 1992. *A Case Study on Gender and Forest Resources in West Bengal.* Delhi: World Bank (June 16).

Heyer, J., F. Stewart, and R. Thorp, eds. 2002. *Group Behaviour and Development.* Oxford: Clarendon Press.

Hobley, M. 1996. *Participatory Forestry: The Process of Change in India and Nepal.* London: Overseas Development Institute.

ISO/Swedforest. 1993. *Forests, People and Protection: Case Studies of Voluntary Forest Protection by Communities in Orissa.* New Delhi: Swedish International Development Agency.

Jodha, N. S. 1986. "Common Property Resources and the Rural Poor." *Economic and Political Weekly* 21, no. 27: 1169–81.

Joshi, A. L. 1996. "Community Forestry in Nepal: 1978 to 2010." Paper presented at the Fifth Asia Forest Network Meeting. Surajkund, India, December 3–6, organized by the Asia Forest Network, with headquarters in the Philippines.

Joshi, S. 1998. *Report of the Workshop on JFM and Women.* Netrang, Gujarat: Agha Khan Rural Support Program (September 14).

Kant, S., N. M. Singh, and K. K. Singh. 1991. *Community-Based Forest Management Systems: Case Studies from Orissa.* Delhi: Swedish International Development Agency and ISO/Swedforest; Bhopal, Madhya Pradesh: Indian Institute of Forest Management.

Mansingh, O. 1991. "Community Organization and Ecological Restoration: An Analysis of Strategic Options for NGOs in Central Himalaya, with Particular Reference to the Community Forestry Program of the NGO Chirag." Master's dissertation. University of Sussex, AFRAS (School of African and Asian Studies).

Mencher, J. P. 1988. "Women's Work and Poverty: Contributions to Household Maintenance in Two Regions of South India." In *A Home Divided: Women and Income in the Third World*, edited by D. Dwyer and J. Bruce. Stanford University Press.

Misra, V., K. R. Smith, and V. Retherford. 2005. "Effects of Cooking Fuel and Environmental Tobacco Smoke on Acute Respiratory Infections in Young Indian Children." *Population and Environment* 26, no. 5: 375–96.

Moffatt, M. 1998. "A Gender Analysis of Community Forestry and Community Leasehold Forestry in Nepal with a Macro-Meso-Micro Framework." Master's dissertation. University of Manchester, Department of Economics and Social Studies.

Mukerjee, R., and S. B. Roy. 1993. "Influence of Social Institutions on Women's Participation in JFM: A Case Study from Sargarh, North Bengal." Working Paper 17. Calcutta: Indian Institute of Bio-Social Research and Development.

Narain, U. 1994. "Women's Involvement in Joint Forest Management: Analyzing the Issues." Draft paper. New Delhi: Ford Foundation (May 6).

Natrajan, I. 1995. "Trends in Firewood Consumption in Rural India." *Margin* 28, no. 1: 41–45.

Noponen, H. 1991. "The Dynamics of Work and Survival for Urban Poor: A Gender Analysis of Panel Data from Madras." *Development and Change* 22, no. 2: 233–60.

Ostrom, E. 1990. *Governing the Commons.* Cambridge University Press.

Pandey, S. 1990. "Women in Hattidunde Forest Management in Dhading District, Nepal." MPE Series 9. Kathmandu: International Center for Integrated Mountain Development, Mountain, Population, and Employment Division.

Raju, G., R. Vaghela, and M. S. Raju. 1993. *Development of People's Institutions for Management of Forests.* Ahemdabad, India: Vikram Sarabhai Center for Development Interaction.

Raju, M. 1997. *Seeking Niches in Forest Canopy: An Enquiry into Women's Participation.* Unpublished report (mimeograph). New Delhi: Ford Foundation.

Ravindranath, N. H., K. S. Murali, and K. C. Malhotra. 2000. *Joint Forest Management and Community Forestry in India: An Ecological and Institutional Assessment.* New Delhi: Oxford and IBH.

Regmi, S. C. 1989. "Female Participation in Forest Resource Management. A Case Study of a Women's Forest Committee in a Nepalese Village." Master's dissertation. Ateneo de Manila University.

Roy, S. B., R. Mukerjee, and M. Chatterjee. 1992. *Endogenous Development: Gender Role in Participatory Forest Management.* Calcutta: Indian Institute of Bio-Social Research and Development.

Sanyal, B. 1991. "Antagonistic Cooperation: A Caste Study of Non-Governmental Organizations', Government, and Donors' Relationships in Income-Generating Projects in Bangladesh." *World Development* 19, no. 10: 1367–79.

Sarin, M. 1995. "Regenerating India's Forest: Reconciling Gender Equity and Joint Forest Management." *IDS Bulletin* 26, no. 1: 83–91.

———. 1998. *Who Is Gaining? Who Is Losing? Gender and Equality Concerns in Joint Forest Management.* New Delhi: Society for Promotion of Wasteland Development.

Seeley, J. 1996. "Who Benefits from Participatory Forest Management?" *Banko Janakari* 6, no. 1: 38–39.

Sen, A. K. 1990. "Gender and Cooperative Conflicts." In *Persistent Inequalities: Women and World Development,* edited by I. Tinker, 123–49. Oxford University Press.

Shah, M. K., and P. Shah. 1995. "Gender, Environment and Livelihood Security: An Alternative Viewpoint from India." *IDS Bulletin* 26, no. 1: 75–82.

Sharma, A., and A. Sinha. 1993. "A Study of the Common Property Resources in the Project Area of the Central Himalaya Rural Action Group." Unpublished report (mimeograph). Bhopal, Madhya Pradesh: Indian Institute of Forest Management.

Singh, A., and N. Burra, eds. 1993. *Women and Wasteland Development in India.* New Delhi: Sage.

Singh, N., and K. Kumar. 1993. "Community Initiatives to Protect and Manage Forests in Balangir and Sambalpur Districts." Unpublished paper (mimeograph). New Delhi: Swedish International Development Corporation.

Smith, K. R., A. L. Agarwal, and R. M. Dave. 1983. "Air Pollution and Rural Fuels: Implications for Policy and Research." Honolulu: East-West Center, Resource Systems Institute.

Society for Promotion of Wastelands Development. 1998. *Joint Forest Management Update, 1997.* New Delhi.

Stewart, F. 1996. "Groups for Good or Ill." *Oxford Development Studies* 24, no. 1: 9–25.

Tata Energy Research Institute. 1995. "Community Participation in *Van Panchayats* of Kumaon Region of Uttar Pradesh." Paper No. 1, part I. New Delhi.

Upadhyay, S., and K. Jeddere-Fisher. 1998. "An Analysis of Community Forestry Characteristics in the Dhaulagiri Hills." Report N/NUKCFP/09. Kathmandu: Nepal-UK Community Forestry Project.

Viegas, P., and G. Menon. 1993. "Bringing Government and People Together: Forest Protection Committees of West Bengal—Role and Participation of Women." In *Women and Wasteland Development in India,* edited by A. Singh and N. Burra, 71–210. New Delhi: Sage.

3

Access to Government in Eastern Europe: Environmental Policymaking in Hungary

SUSAN ROSE-ACKERMAN

In a democracy, politicians and other policymakers are supposed to be account-able to voters.[1] But even in a direct democracy, not everyone will agree on the best policy. Even after dialogue and discussion, citizens may disagree about what to do, so that states need acceptable procedures to resolve conflicts. Voting rules are one way to make public choices, but they may leave some citizens in a sys-tematically disadvantaged position. The system may be fair in the technical sense of treating all voters equally, but substantively unfair if some are usually in the minority and seldom see their preferences prevail. Even if a policy is approved with no negative votes, it may have vastly disparate impacts on different groups of citizens and may lock in an unequal status quo.

Problems of unfairness and injustice multiply in real polities where direct democracy is not feasible. Elected officials enact laws, and political appointees, civil servants, and judges implement the law. Any of these actors may make choices that are biased against certain groups, particularly those with few resources or weak political organization. Even if officials seek to be fair and evenhanded in adminis-tering the law, they may not have the necessary information to assess the needs of the population. To help remedy both of these problems, citizens need to be able to

1. This chapter is based on Rose-Ackerman (2005), which includes fuller citations and information about interviews conducted in the fall and winter of 2002–03 in Hungary.

tell decisionmakers how they perceive public programs and to contribute their views on the benefits and costs of policies.

Of course, the relative advantages of those with wealth and political organization can never be completely overcome in a democracy, but states can take steps to strengthen the voices of ordinary citizens and groups not affiliated with political parties. There are two sides to such efforts. On the one hand, state institutions must be organized to listen to and respond to the concerns of citizens and organized groups. On the other hand, the state should facilitate the organization of advocacy groups without interfering with the very independence that makes them valuable aids to improving the fairness and accountability of state program implementation.

Achieving this type of citizen accountability presents a paradox. How can public bodies be responsive to the concerns of citizens, especially those from poor and disadvantaged groups, and yet remain insulated from improper influence? How can they perform both as competent experts and as democratically responsible policymakers? This tension is a fundamental one in the public law of all democratic systems, but it has particular salience as the new democracies of central and eastern Europe try to create well-functioning states that are accountable to their citizens. These countries inherited top-heavy bureaucratic governments that were viewed with hostility and distrust by their citizens (Elster, Offe, and Preuss 1998). During the first decade of the transition to democracy, not much emphasis was given to issues of popular control outside of the electoral process. I argue that the relative neglect of that aspect of democratic consolidation has been costly for countries making a transition from socialism and ought to receive greater emphasis as the transition proceeds. The costs I have in mind are not primarily economic; they are of two interrelated kinds. The first is an overall disillusionment and distrust of the state that can undermine the acceptability of democratic government to its citizens (Elster, Offe, and Preuss 1998; Howard 2003). The second is a lack of competence and fairness in carrying out public programs. In short, the problems for democratic functioning are not just popular attitudes toward government but also include the actual, concrete performance of the state in carrying out its day-to-day business of implementing the law.

What steps can countries take that want to broaden the voices heard by policymakers in government ministries and to enhance the accountability of government processes to citizens, including those at the bottom of the economic and social ladder? I discuss a two-sided strategy for enhancing the fairness and transparency of executive-branch policymaking. The first is an administrative process that is transparent and invites input from a wide range of interested individuals, not just preapproved "stakeholders." The integrity of that process would be subject to judicial oversight. The second includes measures to streamline the creation and funding of advocacy nonprofits and the provision of public funds in a neutral way not tied to the partisan composition of government. This two-pronged strategy is not a panacea. It will have no impact if citizens are apathetic or unwilling to organize to affect policy. However, it is a necessary precondition that can be part of a move toward the broader goal of more inclusive public policymaking.

This chapter is part of a larger project designed to assess and critique the institutions in central Europe that aim to create accountable and transparent governments.[2] I concentrate here on Hungary, one of the most successful of the transition economies and one of the countries that have recently joined the European Union (EU). In my book (Rose-Ackerman 2005) I also study the Polish case. Hungary and Poland are what Grzymała-Busse and Luong (2002) call "nearly consolidated democratic states." If these countries suffer from weaknesses in their participatory processes, one can expect that the less-advanced countries in the region will have even deeper problems.

The first section outlines a framework for the analysis of government accountability that shows how citizen participation fits into the overall structure. The second section outlines the policymaking process in Hungary. To illustrate the role of civil society organizations, the third section focuses on the case of environmental organizations in Hungary. I conclude with a discussion of the benefits and risks of participatory processes in present-day eastern Europe and include some suggestions for reform.

Government Accountability: Alternative Frameworks

An idealized model of parliamentary democracy stands behind many discussions of accountability. Under this framework, citizens vote for politicians who represent political parties, and a group of parties forms a government that promulgates policies after consultation with the partisan groups in the legislature. The resulting statutes are administered by an apolitical, professional bureaucracy as a technical, expert exercise that is not influenced by political considerations. In other words, politics and administration operate in separate spheres. The main constraint on self-seeking behavior by politicians is the threat of loss at the polls in the next round of elections. Bureaucrats are expected to operate according to technical, legal, and scientific criteria that provide the "right" answers. The civil service follows clear rules that require them to exercise little discretion, and officials treat everyone evenhandedly. Court review is available only to protect individual rights that might otherwise be ignored by bureaucrats focused on general administrative goals.

The basic limitation of this model is the assumption that the political control of the government can be carried out effectively by the parliament. Bureaucrats

2. That project is the Collegium Budapest project on Honesty and Trust: Theory and Experience in the Light of the Post-Socialist Transition. See Rose-Ackerman (2001a, 2001b, 2005), Kornai and Rose-Ackerman (2004), and Kornai, Rothstein, and Rose-Ackerman (2004).

and executive-branch officials perform political and policymaking tasks as they draft statutes and implement imprecise laws, and the governing coalition has little incentive to create independent oversight processes that could interfere with the exercise of its power. As a result, oversight is likely to be weak or partisan, especially for high-level executive policymaking. But elected representatives cannot solve all political or policy issues. Given this condition, democratic consolidation can be aided by oversight and participation from both political and apolitical bodies and groups other than political parties. There are four basic options.

The first option is to modify the pure parliamentary structure through the creation of independent agencies. The goal is the same as in the idealized model discussed above—the insulation of administration from politics. The second option, international treaties, imposes constraints on nation-states. These are not always unwelcome. In some cases, an incumbent government can benefit from tying its own hands through international commitments such as European Union access requirements. The third option is delegation to lower-level governments to bring government decisionmaking closer to the citizens.[3]

The fourth option is the creation of institutions that encourage public participation. It embraces, rather than deplores, public influence on national government decisions and is my focus here. The drafting and implementation of complex statutes raise political issues, and this option accepts these political concerns as valid extensions of democratic ideals. A basic problem of executive-branch organization is then the incorporation of these political concerns into policymaking without giving up the benefits of delegation by a democratically elected legislature. This perspective recognizes the objections to participation voiced by supporters of the idealized model, with their worries about bias and about the public's poor information and its short-term orientation. However, it sees a corresponding value in incorporating public input into government policymaking processes.

All legislatures pass laws that lack specificity and clarity, but the problem has been particularly acute in central and eastern Europe during the transition period. Legislatures have been described as "law factories"—producing many laws rapidly in areas where the parliamentarians are uninformed about the technical details. Thus, governments face a major task in putting these laws into force. State building in central and eastern Europe needs to confront the problem of competently administering statutory policies. The interaction between policymaking and citizens' participation in public affairs needs to be acknowledged. This requires institutions that permit participation while both limiting confusion or delay and avoiding capture by narrow interests.

---

3. These options are discussed in Rose-Ackerman (2005), where I argue that they are not a sufficient response to the need for policymaking accountability in the central government.

Public Participation in Hungary[4]

Public participation apart from elections is not well institutionalized in Hungary. Although Hungary has an administrative code and recognizes the need for reasoned decisionmaking within the government, no law requires the publication of draft rules or gives outsiders general participation rights. The government does make some draft rules available on the Internet and invites comments, but this practice is not universal and is not required by statute. If consultation occurs, it usually involves only a limited number of prespecified groups and individuals who are sent drafts or are consulted as members of official advisory bodies. Some statutes include requirements for participation, mostly by advisory committees. Formal hearings open to the public are uncommon, and even when they do take place, they appear to be of limited importance to the outcome.

Hungary has had a Freedom of Information Act since 1992, and it requires the publication of central government rules for implementing policy. However, the law requires neither written justifications nor publication of informal rules or resolutions—although in practice most are made public. The courts, including the Constitutional Court, although central to the overall consolidation of democracy, have been of little importance in opening up executive processes to participation and oversight by the general public.

The Constitution and the Law on Normative Acts

The Hungarian constitution recognizes the need to delegate tasks to the executive and consequently authorizes the issuance of decrees by the government, so long as they do not conflict with statutes or with higher-ranking legal norms. The Constitutional Court has upheld government policymaking authority but has limited the power of the executive in several ways. For example, in a case dealing with the regulation of abortion, the Court in 1991 held that it was unconstitutional to regulate fundamental rights through executive decrees. A statute was necessary (Sólyom and Brunner 2000, 178–99). However, the decision accepted the need to use executive decrees in many cases to avoid overburdening the parliament, such as in the regulation of air pollution or workplace health and safety.

A distinctive feature of the Hungarian legal system is the Law on Normative Acts, originally passed in 1987, at the end of the Socialist period, that specifies the procedures to be used for issuing decrees. The minister is responsible for promulgating the decree, but "citizens—directly or through their representative bodies—participate in the preparation and creation of legal regulations [that is, normative acts] affecting their daily life" (Article 19). Furthermore, prior to promulgating a decree, "jurisdictional bodies, social organizations, and interest representative

---

4. The material on Hungary is based on interviews carried out in 2002 and 2003. It does not reflect developments since that time. See Rose-Ackerman (2005) for details.

organs have to be involved in the preparation of draft legal regulations which affect either the interests represented and protected by them or their social relations" (Article 20). Unfortunately, the law does not create legally enforceable rights. The only possibility for judicial review would be to claim constitutional violations. However, the Constitutional Court has not been sympathetic to attempts to build consultation requirements into the constitution. In 2001 the Court held that consultation was not constitutionally required unless the groups to be consulted were explicitly listed in the statute.[5]

Advisory Councils

Instead of mandating open-ended public participation, a number of Hungarian laws call for the creation of advisory councils. These are permanent bodies with shifting individual membership that review a range of government proposals and sometimes initiate studies on their own.

For example, in the environmental area the government consults with the National Environmental Council (NEC), an advisory group that reviews all draft laws and rules that have an environmental impact (Hungarian National Environmental Council 2002). It consists of seven members representing the environmental movement, seven representing the scientific community, and seven from business. The members are chosen by each of the three groups acting independently.

In practice, the NEC has structural weaknesses that limit its effectiveness. Although the government is obligated to provide drafts to the council and give it time to respond, this does not always happen. Frequently, the time frame to respond is a week or two, even though the act specifies thirty days for the review of environmental assessments. More fundamentally, the NEC cannot be characterized as a public forum and is not equivalent to an open hearing process. Rather, the interests and the people consulted are defined ex ante, not issue by issue.

In other areas as well, advisory committees comment on draft laws and regulations and provide policy advice. These committees include representatives from interested state bodies, citizens' representative organizations, and scientists and professionals with expertise on the issue. The required participants are organizations of citizens or other interests such as business or the professions; individuals seldom get directly involved (Galligan, Langan, and Nicandrou 1998). For example, councils made up of representatives of groups that advocate for the handicapped, for the elderly, and for social issues advise the Ministry of Social, Health and Family Welfare. However, in many areas active client groups do not exist, so that clients are "represented" only by service providers. In the field of education,

5. Constitutional Court, Decision 10/2001. The Law on Normative Acts does not list specific groups.

formal consultation bodies exist both for higher education and for primary and secondary schooling. The National Regional Development Council (NRDC) advises the government on economic development issues in the Hungarian regions. Its official members are from the several ministries, seven regions, business, trade unions, and some counties. There is no obligation to include NGOs, but a representative of the National Society of Conservationists (NSC), an NGO umbrella group with eighty-six member groups, is invited to the meetings. It was also asked by the government to organize public hearings on the National Development Plan, but the NSC did this at the request of the government, not because there was a legal right to public hearings (Farkas 2002, 46–52).

Thus, a general pattern is repeated in a number of policy areas. An advisory council is set up that includes members who fulfill statutory criteria, but the selection of specific members is left to the organized groups. The ministry or the government must consult with the council, but is not subject to penalties if it fails to do so. Even when a council invites a representative from an NGO that specializes in the issue, this is not a legal requirement. The government decisionmakers are under no obligation to consult more broadly or to consider whether particular interests are poorly represented on the councils.

Legal Challenges

The constitution gives citizens the right to learn about and disseminate information of public interest. The 1992 Freedom of Information Act (FOIA), which also covers the protection of personal data from disclosure, codified this right; the Act on Environmental (statute number LIII/1995) also contains a freedom of information provision. Both acts can be used by anyone—there is no need to show a personal or legal interest in order to obtain information. According to the Environmental Management and Law Association (2002, 11–12), however, information is not always easily available. Nevertheless, many requests are filled. The Environmental Ministry's Office of Public Information handles 650 requests per month, and the total number of requests for information rises to about 1,000 if one includes other bodies that handle requests for environmental information (Environmental Management and Law Association 2002, 18–19).

Civil-society groups have tried to use FOIA requests to increase their influence by pushing for the disclosure of drafts prepared by the government or its various ministries. The act contains a restriction on what information can be obtained: "Unless otherwise provided by law, working documents and other data prepared for the authority's own use, or for the purpose of decision making, are not public within 30 years of their creation. Upon request, the head of the authority may permit access to these documents or data" (Article 19[5]). In 2000 a civic organization objected that some ministries sent drafts of decrees for comment but stipulated that the drafts could not be made public for thirty years. The organization complained that this effectively prevented local organizations from participating in a discussion of the drafts. László Majtényi, the first ombudsman for data protection and freedom of information, pointed out that some ministries treat drafts circulated to outsiders as exceptions under Article 19(5) while others do not. He argued that the line between public and private drafts needed to be clarified in light of the public interest in understanding and debating proposed rules and laws.[6]

Notice that the petitioning organization was not complaining about the denial of a request for information but instead asserted that the government had an obligation to make draft proposals public at the time that it sought comments from outside groups. A next step would be to claim that the government should not only provide information but also facilitate broad public consultation. Instead of relying only on advisory committees with fixed membership, it should also hold public hearings open to a wide range of participants.

In short, mechanisms for consultation exist in Hungary, especially in the area of environmental policy. They mostly take the form of consultation committees with an advisory role whose members are more or less independent. Overall, there are no general legal requirements governing notice, participation, and reasoned justification with respect to the government's strategic policymaking and the issuance of decrees and rules.

Conclusions

The Hungarian government faces serious challenges in developing more accountable policymaking procedures. The difficulties it faces fall into four categories: public knowledge, open processes, government justifications, and judicial review.

The government does not routinely publicize draft regulations and statutes when they are still under consideration. Hungary is moving toward broader Internet access for drafts, but many agencies still only circulate drafts to a select list of entities that are forbidden to circulate them further. Even when plans and drafts are made public, few laws require open-ended hearings or input from the public. Instead, consultation is limited to preselected advisory groups or a select group of insiders. The law does not require that the government provide written justifications for normative acts (regulations), and it seldom does so.

The Hungarian judiciary has not required much in the way of administrative process at the level of policymaking. Challenges to the administrative rule-making process are difficult to bring. Access to the Constitutional Court is open to all citizens who want to challenge the constitutionality of a law, but the court has been unsympathetic to claims concerning process unless the particular substantive statute includes clear procedural requirements. Furthermore, delays, high costs,

6. László Majtényi, interview with author, October 14, 2002.

and the small chance of winning discourage NGOs and other groups from undertaking lawsuits.

Thus, the basic process of establishing legal norms and decrees inside the government risks being either an insular exercise carried out by ministers and their top assistants or a cooperative process that involves a few outsiders serving on advisory committees or associated with the few groups with special access to the government. These procedures may work well in particular cases, but they make it difficult for those who are excluded from the process to do anything about it. They have no right to demand to be heard or to insist that the government defend its policies short of charging unconstitutionality.

Expanded requirements for notice, hearing, and justifications will mean nothing, however, unless private groups exist that care about the results. Thus, it is important to understand how organized civil society functions. This is a very broad topic, but in the next section I touch on some of the essential points with a study of advocacy-oriented environmental NGOs in Hungary.

The Role of Private Groups:
Advocacy-Oriented Environmental NGOs in Hungary

In central Europe, in addition to political parties, four different types of organizations play a role in policymaking and implementation. (1) "Jurisdictional" organizations. These are mostly self-governing local and regional governments, but the category includes other government ministries, regional bodies, or agencies that will be affected by the policy in question. Officials consult them mainly because they will play a role in implementing the policy. (2) Professional "chambers" for groups such as lawyers and doctors, where membership is mandatory for all members of the profession. These organizations have been created by statute to regulate their respective professions, and their implementing statutes frequently require that they be consulted on draft laws and regulations that concern them. In some cases they have authority to promulgate rules that bind their members.[7] (3) "Interest groups" or "social organizations" that represent the economic interests of particular groups (these English terms are somewhat misleading because their meanings are too broad and imprecise). Examples are labor unions, business associations, farmers' associations, and associations of pensioners. Sometimes the group itself drafts the rules that will govern its actions, subject to government approval. In other cases, they must be consulted if a draft law or regulation concerns them. (4) Civil organizations. These are nonprofit or civil-society groups representing interests that are poorly institutionalized and cannot draw on

---

7. In a 1997 case the Constitutional Court approved a statute that delegated regulation of the medical profession to the Hungarian Medical Association but limited its authority (Sólyom and Brunner 2000, 368).

membership dues to cover their budgetary needs. Many consultation processes are limited to the first three groups, but it is this fourth category of civil organizations that interests me here. Although economic and professional interests may be involved, civil-society groups have policy goals that affect a broad range of citizens who are not directly part of the group. Examples of such groups are those that focus on the environment, poverty, and human rights. Groups concerned with women, the disabled, the old, and disadvantaged minorities seek economic and social benefits for the groups they represent, but they also have broader goals and attract members who will not benefit personally.

To begin, I provide some summary information on the overall nonprofit civil-society sector in Hungary and on its small advocacy component. The role of nonprofits as advocates and gadflies varies by policy area and is in its infancy in central Europe. Hence, one also needs a more fine-grained sense of what advocacy organizations actually do and whom they claim to represent. To begin that exploration, I focus on one area where nonprofits are relatively well established: environmental protection organizations. My interviews with leading members of many of the most important Hungarian groups provide an instructive window into the strengths and weakness of nonprofit advocacy in transition.

Nonprofit Advocacy Organizations

In central Europe a diverse nonprofit sector is reemerging after a period of suppression, but only a few organizations are primarily engaged in policy advocacy, and, in general, they have few staff and limited funds. The overall nonprofit sector is small, accounting for 1.3 percent of employees in Hungary in 1995 compared with 7.8 percent in the United States and almost 5 percent in both France and Germany in 1998. The cash expenditures of the sector were 2.8 percent of GDP in Hungary, a high for the region, but far below the shares of 7.5 percent, 4 percent, and 4 percent for the United States, France, and Germany, respectively (Salamon and others 1999).

Private monetary donations are not the primary source of funding. The government operates in partnership with nonprofits in many sectors, and fees and charges are also a major source of revenue. In some fields, especially the advocacy areas that are my focus, much funding comes from foreign donors. In 2000 in Hungary the NGO sector received 34 percent of its funding from the state and 19 percent from private funds—with about one-third of the latter coming from foreign grants (Hungary, Central Statistical Office 2000, 2002).

A tax law permits filers to allot 1 percent of their tax bill to a Hungarian charity of their choice, but the government collects less than half of what could be given at no cost to the taxpayer. Most contributions are made to churches and to organizations that provide services, such as schools attended by the taxpayer's children (Kuti 2000). Adding together private donations and the 1 percent checkoff, between 2 and 3 percent of the sector's funding is the result of individual household choice (Hungary, Central Statistical Office 2000).

Advocacy organizations such as environmental and human rights organizations have characteristics that are similar to the sector as a whole. In 2000, government grants made up over 20 percent of the budget of the 1,019 environmental groups and 561 human rights groups in Hungary. Human rights groups received more than 50 percent of their funds from abroad, whereas environmental groups received only 10 percent from abroad, mainly because the sector includes a number of nonprofit businesses (Hungary, Central Statistical Office 2000). The external sources of funds were often critical to their establishment and survival. Unrelated business income accounted for 26 percent of total revenues of environmental groups. The groups whose members I interviewed raise funds via projects such as a recycling business, conference fees, and the sale of books and training materials. Domestic private donations and dues from individuals and business firms account for only a bit over 5 percent of income for both environmental and human rights groups. The 1 percent tax checkoff for charities provides less than 1 percent of these groups' revenue (Hungary, Central Statistical Office 2002, tables 93, 94).

To have staying power, advocacy organizations need professional staff and a budget with some stability. Only a small number of organizations appear to be in that category. Hence, on any given issue the group of organizations capable of monitoring government and participating in policymaking is likely to be small. In the environmental area in Hungary there are ten or twelve organizations in the top group, and twenty to twenty-five form the core of the movement. Even the most established organizations have a precarious financial existence because of the low level of private domestic donations from individuals and business.

Environmental Advocacy Organizations in Hungary

Environmental activism in Hungary began at the end of the Socialist period with small cores of activists who were able to mobilize large numbers of people to protest particular issues. Although these mobilizations continued into the democratic transition, newer groups focus their efforts less on demonstrating and more on affecting policy by means of technical and policy arguments (Pickvance and Gabor 2001).

A few NGOs date from the 1970s, but they had recreational and social purposes such as bird watching. Activists established environmental groups in larger numbers in the late eighties, when they were given space to operate by the rather progressive Communist leadership that took power in 1987. By the time of the regime change, in 1990, dozens of NGOs existed, partly because a law legalizing free associations was passed in 1989 (Harper 1999, 58–93; Pickvance 1998; Pickvance and Gabor 2001).

During the nineties large numbers of new groups formed, but most are small volunteer organizations with few funds. At present several more professional organizations play a key role in government policymaking processes. The most active are members of several specialized umbrella organizations dealing with issues such as air pollution, waste management, energy, and nature protection. The key members of most of these groups interacted for most of the transition period. They hold an annual National Gathering of Environmental and Nature Protection NGOs and are advised by the Environmental Management and Law Association (EMLA). Even these groups, however, depend on the energy of a few committed people, have few funds, and rely on grants that may be canceled after a few years (Kuti 2000, 29; Harper 1999, 43).

The types of problems dealt with by the groups range from local waste disposal problems to preventing construction of a major dam across the Danube to broad national issues such as air pollution. Case studies by Katy Pickvance (1998) and Pickvance and Gabor (2001) in the mid-nineties and my own interviews confirm that it is possible to establish nonpartisan NGOs that gain the attention of political bodies through a reputation both for expertise and for responding to genuine citizen concerns. Relations with public officials are sometimes rocky, but the groups' access to the media and public sympathy for their efforts have helped keep them in operation and given them some influence. Some politicians support these groups as a way to increase the salience of environmental issues inside government, and there is some movement of people back and forth between government and NGOs (Pickvance 1998, 150–55). But some groups distrust the state, limit their dealings with public officials, and claim to be "antipolitical" (Harper 1999).

In the environmental area the basic Hungarian environmental statute (LIII/1995) requires consultation with concerned groups, and an executive decree provides more specifics. The most detailed provisions are directed at participation in decisions about individual projects at the local level. Although legal provisions concerning participation in policymaking are vague and not judicially enforceable, international agreements also encourage participation. The Aarhus Convention of the United Nations Economic Commission for Europe was ratified by Hungary in 2001, and it requires strengthened democratic environmental governance (Rose-Ackerman and Halpaap 2002). The European Union requires the provision of information to the public and the preparation of environmental impact statements (Caddy 2000). Thus, in the environmental area relatively good opportunities for participation exist and may strengthen over time.

The problem may be not a lack of opportunities for participation so much as the thinness of the nonprofit advocacy sector, with its dependence on government and international funding and on the energy of a small number of unusually committed individuals. Nonprofits face three interlocked difficulties: problems of financial and human capacity, problems of credibility, and problems of effective access to the policymaking process. I summarize each in turn in the light of interviews I conducted in fall of 2002 with leading members of most of the major policy-oriented groups and umbrella organizations (see also Rose-Ackerman 2005). The groups are of five broad types:

1. A group in decline that was a key player in the transition from Socialism to democracy (Danube Circle)

2. A moderate membership-based group founded during the Socialist period (Birdlife Hungary)

3. A local branch of a moderate international environmental group (World Wildlife Fund–Hungary)

4. Umbrella groups with a subject-matter focus and professional staff (HuMuSz [the Waste Management Working Group], Energia Klub, the Clean Air Action Group, and the National Association of Conservationists)

5. Local groups with national visibility (Reflex, Green Future)

All the groups are funded about equally by the Hungarian government and by foreign foundations and public bodies and by small contributions from individuals and domestic businesses. Typically, neither membership fees nor the 1 percent tax checkoff is a major source of funds. Multinational firms with business in Hungary provide some project funding to a few groups. Some groups run related businesses that bring in considerable revenue. None appeared to have a sizable endowment.

Government funding comes from several grant programs administered by the Ministry of the Environment with nonprofit input and through project funds from various ministries, the government, and the parliament. The consequences of failing to receive government funds can be harsh. For example, Danube Circle is a well-known group that mobilized mass protests in the eighties to protest the Socialist government's plans to build a dam on the Danube (Jancar-Webster 1998, 71; Pickvance 1998; Pickvance and Gabor 2001). In the fall of 2002 it had no paid staff, a small membership base, and an annual budget of about 1.5 million Hungarian forints (under $6,000 in 2002 dollars), and it shared an office with an animal protection group. It failed to receive government funding for professional development in 2002, and to maintain its independence, it did not apply for funds from the Environment Ministry. It sees its mission as being a critical voice that provides competent technical assessments of policies and projects. Nevertheless, however independent its stance, it has limited impact simply because of lack of funds.

The other groups were all struggling financially, but none was in as weak a condition as Danube Circle, partly because they received government funds, on which they were heavily dependent. Despite the government monies, the funding picture that emerged from my interviews is not very secure. Domestic private donations from individuals provide only a tiny share of revenue, with the exception of Birdlife Hungary, the one membership organization in the group. Business support is generally weak as well and seems to be mostly project-based. Support

from abroad, both from official sources and from foundations, is critical for several groups but has no long-run staying power. Government support is likely to
grow in relative importance. Even if some public funds are given with no strings
attached, the ability of these groups to carry out independent advocacy activities
may be compromised. It appears that these groups must attract local private funds
if they are to survive into the future as strong voices for environmental causes.

A second concern for these groups is whether government officials have any
reason to take them seriously. The groups have followed two types of strategies.
The first is to develop sources of grassroots support and to educate people about
environmental problems. Access to the media is a key resource here and has been
used creatively by several groups. Second, the group can gain credibility through
the provision of expert opinions to public officials. Of course, the two overlap.
Expertise can help mobilize ordinary people, and a group's expert opinions may
be taken more seriously if it can point to a constituency of support and media
willing to publicize its positions.

The major environmental groups are not mass organizations. Most of them
work to mobilize public support for issues and seek publicity in the media to
increase the salience of issues. Only Birdlife Hungary is a mass membership
organization, with 6,000 members and numerous local chapters. The umbrella
groups—the National Society of Conservationists, the Clean Air Action Group,
Energia Klub, and the Waste Management Working Group—all have some member organizations that are locally based citizen groups. However, many of their
member organizations are very poorly institutionalized, and consultation with
policymakers mainly occurs through their Budapest offices.

A common pattern for a group that is an elite or an umbrella association is to
mobilize the public around an issue and to create events that are then covered by
the media. For example, Green Future was founded by scientists in 1989 to raise
awareness of the problem of hazardous pollutants in a mixed industrial-residential
district of Budapest. The group worked to help convince people of the seriousness
of the health problems they faced. Eventually the group attracted large numbers of
neighborhood residents to its meetings and held an open meeting to counter the
local government's closed meeting on the district's environmental problems.
Although the group tries to mobilize people around particular issues, it is not a
mass membership or client-based organization. It has twenty to thirty members, of
whom eight to ten are active. The alternative strategy of providing expert advice
and critiques of draft laws and regulations is the focus of the umbrella groups and
the Hungary chapter of the World Wildlife Fund, although they also sponsor public events and forums. WWF has enough resources to carry out original research
designed to put new issues on the parliament's and government's agendas.

A third concern is that the groups' relations with government are a function
both of background legal and political practice and of the shifting personalities in
key positions inside government at all levels. When a policy is under considera-

tion, a group will request a copy of the draft law or regulation. If the ministry stalls, the group can go to the media, and the threat of bad publicity has on some occasions been effective. HuMuSz described a well-staged media event in which they used a catapult to shoot waste paper at the front of the Environmental Ministry in a successful effort to embarrass the ministry and obtain a copy of a draft law dealing with waste and packaging (Rose-Ackerman 2005, 187).

If access to government is denied or if a government decision is contrary to a group's interests, one remedy is to go to the courts, either to force greater openness or to challenge decisions after they are made. This is not often a fruitful approach if government laws and norms are at stake. András Lukács, the president of the Clean Air Action Group, said that in principle it is possible to ask a court to order the Environmental Ministry to release a draft, but in practice this is not a realistic option.

Nevertheless, legal challenges are sometimes worthwhile. The Hungarian Environmental and Management Law Association (EMLA), founded in 1994, has brought over 350 cases and has assisted on many others.[8] In one eighteen-month period EMLA initiated 42 new cases and provided advice on 200 smaller cases. In its 2000–2001 annual report EMLA outlined its victories and losses as well as major outstanding cases. The cases appear mainly to be challenges to particular development projects or pollution from particular sources (Environmental and Management Law Association 2002, 5).

The environmental sector in Hungary has some relatively well-established nonprofits, including some with a history going back to before the change in regime. The Socialist regime neglected environmental issues. As a consequence, some pollution problems were particularly obvious to all, while other, more subtle sources of harm to humans and to wildlife were unknown. Environmentalism is associated with opposition to the previous regime and gains public support as a result, but the economic strains of the transition have made strong environmental protection seem like a luxury and have worked against costly environmental protection policies. Furthermore, sensible environmental policy requires participants in the debate to be informed about scientific and technical issues. The environmental groups are trying to be technically competent themselves and to involve ordinary people in protests and educational events, but these groups have been only partly successful—hardly surprising, given the difficulties of finding funding, motivating ordinary citizens, educating their own staff, and getting effective access to government processes that are themselves in flux. They use various strategies to work within the existing system of organized advisory committees and elite consultation and to mobilize public support and media coverage.

8. For more information on the Environmental Management and Law Association, see http://emla.hu/englishsite/index.shtml.

Developing Accountable Rule-Making Processes

The lack of participation opportunities within the executive branch complements the lack of organizational strength in the private nonprofit sector. If one accepts my claim that public participation in policymaking is a necessary aspect of democratic consolidation, then Hungary needs to take steps to improve this aspect of its system. My research on Poland led me to similar conclusions and suggests that the problem is a general one in the region. A two-pronged strategy is needed: a policy to encourage a more open and accountable process in the executive branch and a policy of supporting the creation and consolidation of independent nongovernmental advocacy organizations (Howard 2002).

The first prong includes the public posting of draft rules, open-ended requests for comments, and publicizing the justifications for new decrees or rules. The government or the relevant ministry is ultimately responsible for the legal measures that it undertakes, but it must be willing to hear alternative viewpoints and to explain why it has decided on a particular policy. Citizens should be able to challenge the resulting rule in court on the grounds that the process was not sufficiently open and inclusive or that the rule is inconsistent with the authorizing statute or the constitution. Existing advisory committees do help to generate and organize discussion, but they risk limiting participation to particular groups. Thus, the government should be open to input representing a broader range of interests and individuals.

Critics of broader participation, however, worry that ministries will be overwhelmed with trivial and uninformed comments that will simply delay decisionmaking. Of course, some delay is the necessary cost of greater openness, but ministries can manage public input with the creative use of their Web pages, time-limited comment periods, and other devices such as limits on the length of written submissions and time limits for oral presentations. The actual deliberative processes inside the agencies need not be public. Rather, decisions must be publicly justified, and relevant comments must be acknowledged and discussed. My proposal does not envisage a negotiation process in which the stakeholders hammer out a consensus rule. Rather, the ministry still represents the electoral coalition in control of the government and is guided by that coalition's policy platform but must be open to objections and information from the public.

Judicial review of administrative action is inadequate in Hungary and Poland. This is partly because the underlying statutes and constitutions provide no basis for review. However, even if new statutes were to specify limited grounds for review, it might not be effective unless the courts are reorganized. Hungary needs judges with more background in public law and might consider creating an Administrative Court, as in Poland. To avoid interference by judges in the operation of bureaucracies, the grounds for review need to be well specified by statute and limited to procedural violations and clear inconsistencies between rules and statutes or the constitution.

The second prong—strengthening the private nonprofit sector—requires both a strong legal framework for the creation and maintenance of civil-society organizations and the careful design of public subsidies. An important goal is to strengthen groups that operate independent of political parties and concentrate on a small set of issues, be they feminist causes, environmental issues, or burdensome business regulation. The available evidence suggests that wide imbalances exist among those groups reorganized out of old official groups, new groups with public or foreign foundation support, and a large fringe of small, poorly institutionalized groups with few financial resources. There is an urgent need to create an environment in which public participation can function well without officials seeing it as merely a nuisance to be contained and marginalized. Better administrative processes can give officials information about the costs and benefits of particular programs in both technical and political terms. The goal is to permit them to make more competent and politically acceptable decisions, not to have civil-society groups take over that function.

If government funds are used to support nonprofit advocacy groups, the support needs to be provided in a way that does not undermine the groups' independence. Matching funds based on membership numbers are one option, and tax checkoffs are another. However, even though 1 percent of an individual's taxes can be earmarked for charity in Hungary, only about one-half of the potential funds are earmarked. Another option is direct support for participation through grants to cover the marginal costs of informed participation. The government would have to disburse these funds without making judgments on any group's substantive positions. Hungary has a program of government grants in the environmental area that is largely controlled by NGO representatives themselves. This is one option, similar to peer review for research grants, but it assumes that the sector is well enough organized to take on this task.

The EU expects new member states to cooperate with nonprofits in a number of specific areas by creating "partnership groups" to carry out joint projects, but this mandate has proved difficult to implement. The problem is two-fold. First, the government has little incentive to strengthen the nonprofit advocacy sector, and second, the existing sector is full of small organizations with weak coordinating mechanisms. Some umbrella organizations have been created, so the EU process may be having an impact. Freedom House, a US-based NGO that has been active in democratic and market reform in central Europe, reports some attempts to organize networks of local groups and to set up umbrella organizations, and environmental groups meet annually to discuss strategy and common concerns (Karatnycky, Motyl, and Shor 1997, 180–82).

The thrust of EU policy has been toward collaborative processes where the stakeholders get together to find solutions. I am skeptical of this model, particularly in the context of central and eastern Europe. The weakness of individual groups limits the sector's ability to create hierarchical organizations that can effectively negotiate with their counterpart "interest groups" or "self-governing" bodies. Furthermore, such coordination could destroy the very diversity that is the hallmark of a vital civil society. Instead, governments need to recognize that some diffuse groups will never be as well organized as business associations, professional chambers, and labor unions, both because they do not have monolithic policy goals and because individuals may seek to get a free ride on the efforts of others, with the result that no one takes on organizational tasks. Expecting civil-society groups to be able to negotiate on an equal footing with labor unions and business and professional associations indicates a misunderstanding of the nature of civil society and underestimates the organizational problems of diffuse groups.

Some claim that the focus should be not on overcoming these problems but on strengthening political parties. But political parties are not a good substitute for independent civil-society organizations. Parties represent a conglomeration of interests and are focused on winning elections, not mastering the details of policy. The governing coalition supports broad statutory mandates that it then implements through the bureaucracy. In doing so, the executive must have the ultimate authority to issue decrees with the force of law. If it is to do this competently and responsibly, it needs to listen to organized groups and citizens who are informed about and concerned with particular policy areas. These groups need to be able to seek court review of any alleged irregularities in the process.

Although there may be some tradeoffs between the development of strong parties and the establishment of well-institutionalized nonparty groups, Hungary appears to have room for both. Too strong a move to incorporate independent groups under political party labels could produce a system of rotating elected cartels. In practice, Hungary has few formal requirements for civil-society participation in executive policymaking, and the current role and organization of independent nonprofits varies across policy areas, but the sector is overall rather weak. Better administrative processes can give officials information about the costs and benefits of particular programs in both technical and political terms. The goal is to permit them to make more competent and politically acceptable decisions. There seems no reason, in principle or in practice, why reforms could not increase effective public participation. To do this, rights to participation need to have legal status and to be open to judicial review, and organized groups need to be strengthened.

My argument in this chapter is essentially normative. I have outlined the administrative policymaking process in Hungary and argued that it is insufficiently democratic and is likely to disadvantage low-income and poorly organized groups. Even groups with an organizational presence, such as Hungarian environmental groups, may have little impact if their funds are inadequate for the lobbying tasks at hand. These claims raise the positive political science question of whether those in power would ever find it in their interest to create a more accountable administrative process. Comparing the administrative processes in Germany and the United States, I have argued that the more accountable U.S. process has a political basis in the divided governments frequently produced by the U.S. presidential system. Congress has an interest in controlling the bureaucracy in order to limit presidential power (Rose-Ackerman 1995; see also McCubbins, Noll, and Weingast 1987). In contrast, governments where a single coalition controls both the parliament and the executive have no such incentive, and this may explain the lack of broad-based participation rights in most parliamentary systems (Rose-Ackerman 1995). If this supposition is correct, Hungary and Poland are in a difficult situation, one where the low level of participation rights provides few incentives for organizations to develop the constituencies that could push for an expansion of such rights. One response would be for the EU to change its strategy in central Europe. Rather than pushing a corporatist agenda in countries with weak labor and civil-society groups, it might instead seek to foster the development of a more diverse and active collection of civil-society organizations not tied so closely to conventional categories such as labor unions, the professions, and business.

The problems of democratic consolidation in central Europe are the problems of countries that have democratic structures, secure borders, no organized violence, and a functioning private sector. They are not different in kind from the problems facing democracies that have much longer histories than the newer democracies in that region. The scale of the difficulties is larger for some issues, and the existing institutions in the public and the private sectors are fragile and untested, but none of these issues suggests an imminent breakdown of the state. Central Europe can learn from experiences elsewhere, from both success stories and obvious failures. Its politicians and policymakers can enter into a productive dialogue with those in wealthier, more established democracies as the region seeks ways to create more accountable government institutions that can garner popular support.

References

Caddy, J. 2000. "Implementation of EU Environmental Policy in Central European Applicant States: The case of EIA." In *Implementing EU Environmental Policy: New Directions and Old Problems,* edited by C. Knill and A. Lenschow, 197–221. Manchester University Press.

Elster, J., C. Offe, and U. Preuss. 1998. *Institutional Design in Post-Communist Societies: Rebuilding the Ship at Sea.* Cambridge University Press.

Environmental Management and Law Association. 2002. *Identified Legal, Institutional, and Practical Barriers to Public Access to Environmental Information to Support Public Involvement in Hungary for Danube Pollution Reduction Goals.* Budapest.

Farkas, I. 2002. "Hungarian Situation on Public Participation in Regional Development." In *Public Participation in Regional Development in Central Europe,* edited by P. Pelci, 57–67. Szentendre, Hungary: Regional Environmental Center.

Galligan, D. J., R. H. Langan, and C. S. Nicandrou. 1998. *Administrative Justice in the new European Democracies: Case Studies of Administrative Law and Process in Bulgaria, Estonia, Hungary, Poland, and Ukraine.* Budapest: Open Society Institute, Constitutional and Legal Policy Institute; and Oxford University, Center for Socio-Legal Studies.

Grzymała-Busse, A., and P. Jones Luong. 2002. "Reconceptualizing the State: Lessons from Post-Communism." *Politics and Society* 30: 529–54.

Harper, K. M. 1999. "From Green Dissidents to Green Skeptics: Environmental Activists and Post-Socialist Political Ecology in Hungary." Ph.D. dissertation. University of California, Santa Cruz, Department of Anthropology.

Howard, M. M. 2002. "The Weakness of Postcommunist Civil Society." *Journal of Democracy* 13: 157–69.

———. 2003. *The Weakness of Civil Society in Post-Communist Europe.* Cambridge University Press.

Hungarian National Environmental Council, Secretariat. 2002. *Hungarian National Environmental Council 2000–2001.* Budapest.

Hungary, Central Statistical Office (Központi Statisztikai Hivatal). 2000. *Környezetvédelmi Célú Nonprofit Szervezetek.* [Environmental Nonprofit Organizations]. Budapest.

———. 2002. *Nonprofit Szervezetek Magyarországon.* [Hungarian Nonprofit Organizations.] Budapest.

Jancar-Webster, B. 1998. "Environmental Movements and Social Change in the Transition Countries." *Environmental Politics* 7: 69–90.

Karatnycky, A., A. Motyl, and B. Shor. 1997. *Nations in Transit—1997: Civil Society, Democracy and Market in East Central Europe and the Newly Independent States.* New Brunswick, N.J.: Transaction.

Kornai, J., and S. Rose-Ackerman, eds. 2004. *Building a Trustworthy State in Post-Socialist Transition.* New York: Palgrave Macmillan.

Kornai, J., B. Rothstein, and S. Rose-Ackerman, eds. 2004. *Creating Social Trust in Post-Socialist Transition.* New York: Palgrave Macmillan.

Kuti, É. 2000. "1%: Forint Votes for Civil Society Organizations." Report. Budapest: Research Project on Nonprofit Organizations.

McCubbins, M., R. Noll, and B. Weingast. 1987. "Administrative Procedures as Instruments of Political Control." *Journal of Law, Economics & Organization* 3: 243–277.

Pickvance, K. 1998. *Democracy and Environmental Movements in Eastern Europe: A Comparative Study of Hungary and Russia.* Boulder, Colo.: Westview Press.

Pickvance, K., and L. Gabor. 2001. "Green Future—in Hungary." In *Pink, Purple, Green: Women's, Religious, Environmental and Gay/Lesbian movements in Central Europe Today,* edited by H. Flam, 104–111. Boulder, Colo.: East European Monographs.

Rose-Ackerman, S. 1995. *Controlling Environmental Policy: The Limits of Public Law in Germany and the United States.* Yale University Press.

———. 2001a. "Trust and Honesty in Post-Socialist Societies." *Kyklos* 54: 15–43.

———. 2001b. "Trust, Honesty, and Corruption: Reflections on the State-Building Process." *Archives Européennes de Sociologie* 42: 526–70.

————. 2005. *From Elections to Democracy: Building Accountable Government in Hungary and Poland.* Cambridge University Press.

Rose-Ackerman, S., and A. A. Halpaap. 2002. "The Aarhus Convention and the Politics of Process: The Political Economy of Procedural Environmental Rights." *Research in Law and Economics* 20: 27–64.

Salamon, L. M., H. K. Anheier, R. List, S. Toepler, S. Wójciech Sokolowski, and others. 1999. *Global Civil Society: Dimensions of the Nonprofit Sector.* Johns Hopkins University, Center of Civil Society Studies.

Sólyom, L., and G. Brunner, eds. 2000. *Constitutional Judiciary in a New Democracy: The Hungarian Constitutional Court.* University of Michigan Press.

PART III

Access to the Economy

4

Economic Entitlements: Facilitating Immigrant Entrepreneurship

JORRIT DE JONG AND PETER KASBERGEN

"The rules are killing me!" exclaims Tamer Akgün, sitting in his sandwich bar in the western part of Amsterdam. It has been two years since the Dutch entrepreneur of Turkish descent first decided to start a sandwich bar, and he has been largely unsuccessful. Although the shop is beautifully furnished, well equipped, and otherwise ready to welcome customers, the doors remain closed. Akgün has been forced to pay rent to his landlord while awaiting official permission to open his business, draining his bank accounts dry as he obtained the required licenses. As he sips his coffee while sitting amid his paperwork, Akgün makes no effort to conceal his frustration with the endless red tape, commenting, "I had to deal with ten, fifteen, maybe twenty different agencies. I stopped counting. I think I know more about the rules now than the government itself. They don't know their own rules, but they have the power. It is very complicated."[1]

The Economic Perspective: Removing Hurdles to Starting a Business

The governments of the European Union member countries, united in their commitment to the Lisbon Strategy, have placed entrepreneurship high on their agendas as they recover from recession but continue to lag behind other parts of the

1. Extract from a teaching case based on research in Huijboom and de Jong (2005).

world in productivity growth (European Commission 2003).[2] In keeping with this larger change, in recent years Dutch federal and local governments have recognized the vital importance of removing hurdles to starting a business (Cabinet of the Netherlands 2002, 2003, 2007). Prime Minister Jan-Peter Balkenende (2006) stated in 2006:

> Entrepreneurship is fully exploited in an open, tolerant society in which people know how to contact and approach each other. . . . It's not government's task to solve all problems; its task is to create room and possibilities for people with plans and ambitions. That is what this administration is working on. Reducing the number of rules and [the] administrative burden for entrepreneurs in the Netherlands and paying attention to education and innovation. This policy works. . . . Dutch entrepreneurs—among whom there are 60,000 entrepreneurs with a non-Western background—can face the future with confidence again.

Most efforts to keep political promises to the private sector have led to quantitative results. For example, the Dutch government prides itself on a reduction of the average administrative burden for private firms of almost 20 percent (Ministries of Finance and Economic Affairs 2007). The government has established institutions to monitor the reduction of administrative burdens (for example, ACTAL and IPAL), and these and similar reforms have led to higher rankings by the World Bank (2006).[3] The state has been particularly enthusiastic about supplying information and assistance to potential and startup entrepreneurs—businesspeople in respectively the pre-startup or startup phase of their planning. All levels of the Dutch government, local Chambers of Commerce, and semipublic intermediary organizations have created websites and organized seminars, training sessions, and trade fairs to reach these nascent and startup entrepreneurs. Given all these measures and assistance, why is the Turkish-Dutch sandwich bar owner having so many problems? In light of the political intentions and efforts just described, his case raises questions. If it is even slightly representative of the problems that entrepreneurs encounter, the reality differs significantly from the one that the prime minister painted, and the sandwich bar owner can scarcely face the future with confidence. How can his case be explained?

    If we look for answers in government reports on Dutch entrepreneurship, it is clear that the majority of entrepreneurs remain very far from praising the Dutch government for its regulatory policies. Several major representative bodies of large, medium-size, and small enterprises have claimed that the situation over the

---

2. The Lisbon Strategy is a strategy, set out by the European Council in Lisbon in March 2000, aimed at "making the European Union the most competitive economy in the world and achieving full employment by 2010." Available at http://europa.eu/scadplus/glossary/lisbon_strategy_en.htm.

3. ACTAL stands for Advisory Board on Administrative Burdens to the Dutch Government; IPAL stands for the Interdepartmental Division Responsible for the Alleviation of Administrative Burdens.

past few years has scarcely improved.[4] But if we dig deeper and look for more specific answers that directly refer to problems of small entrepreneurs of non-Western descent, we do not find them. Nascent entrepreneurs, a target group of numerous new programs, have yet to associate and so remain largely unheard.

The reason for the lack of answers can be found in the way entrepreneurship is currently analyzed. The effectiveness of the Netherlands' programs is weighed in terms of efficiency and effectiveness of means (that is, which websites, training methods, and meetings are the most productive?) using a one-dimensional economic perspective focusing on aggregate results for the national or local economy. From this perspective, policy programs are analyzed in order to establish their effectiveness. This perspective is based on two assumptions: that all individuals become entrepreneurs by choice and that the population of entrepreneurs is not very varied. There is no distinction made between groups of entrepreneurs, and therefore no distinction is made in possible problems they may encounter as a result of their non-Western background. The overall effect and efficiency are weighed, and the outcomes are neither specified nor differentiated.

We can continue to use this perspective. On the other hand, if we take a different point of departure for our examination of entrepreneurial climates, we may find other realities that may have quite divergent consequences for policy evaluation. If we assume that not all individuals become entrepreneurs by choice, but in some cases by necessity, do established reform agendas provide adequate support measures? If we accept the possibility of a highly varied population of entrepreneurs who may share little in common beyond the requirement to register at the local Chamber of Commerce, do regulatory frameworks accommodate this diversity?

The Social Perspective: Empowering Entrepreneurs

We propose that the economy is not merely a means to generate productivity growth, but that it is also a tool for people from all walks of life to develop themselves and their communities. The Turkish-Dutch sandwich bar owner could have risen out of his poor and uneducated background by running a successful enterprise. In fact, the failure of his enterprise is a missed opportunity not only for economic growth but also for personal development. Successful entrepreneurship can stimulate integration into society, whereas failure can drive would-be proprietors away from society. On top of that, a successful sandwich bar can have positive effects on neighborhood development; a shop with closed doors, full of graffiti, at

4. The Confederation of Netherlands Industry and Employers (known as VNO-NCW), "Entrepreneurs: This Is a Cabinet of Many Words and Little Action" (in Dutch), press release, June 14, 2007 (www.vno-ncw.nl/web/show/id=95652/dbcode=501/filetype=press [accessed June 29, 2008]); Organization for Small and Medium Businesses in the Netherlands (known as MKB), "Cabinet Fails to Reduce Regulatory Burdens" (in Dutch), press release, June 4, 2008 (www.mkb.nl/Nieuws/287.10602 [accessed June 29, 2008]).

an ignored corner of the street does not contribute to the well-being and the safety of the neighborhood's inhabitants.

From this perspective, government must do more than just "create room" for entrepreneurship by reducing the "number of rules," as the prime minister said. It also must actively remove barriers to entrepreneurship and actively encourage its citizens. Government needs to enforce economic rights and enhance the economic entitlements of the population. Reform should therefore be aimed at guaranteeing what Amartya Sen calls "instrumental freedoms" (Sen 1999, 38–39). Instrumental freedoms help to advance the capability of people to enjoy their formal rights. Simply allowing individuals the right to start a business does not give them sufficient means actually to begin one. To exercise one's rights as a prospective entrepreneur, one needs to have access to institutional freedoms such as a source of finance, access to licenses, fair and adequate law enforcement, and so on. Sen elaborates: "Development requires the removal of major sources of unfreedom: poverty as well as tyranny, poor economic opportunities as well as intolerance or overactivity of repressive states" (Sen 1999, 3).

Adapting Sen's argument to our own discussion, we can only conclude that decreasing administrative burdens or removing rules in and of themselves is not enough to create a wealth of opportunities for would-be entrepreneurs. If we regard entrepreneurship as something to which everyone should have equal access, we must examine more closely the impediments that prevent particular individuals and groups of individuals from starting successful businesses.

Government should be concerned if the entrepreneurial climate is rife with inequity and social injustice and some groups of people have access to formal economies while other groups do not, because government has an obligation to improve access to formal markets by providing all of its citizens with the tools they need to start businesses.

Why does the government have an obligation to improve access? Let us return to Sen's notion of instrumental freedoms to examine how government can exacerbate economic disentitlement. Per Sen, instrumental freedoms contribute "to the overall freedom people have to live the way they would like to live"; economic facilities "refer to the opportunities that individuals respectively enjoy to utilize economic resources for the purpose of consumption, production or exchange" (Sen 1999, 38–39). Naturally, democratic governments have a responsibility to allow their citizens to employ these economic facilities.

Let us imagine a group of entrepreneurs who all meet the minimum entitlements necessary to enter the market but differ according to their resources. Inequity arises when some of these entrepreneurs cannot open their businesses for economically irrelevant reasons stemming from governmental (in)action. When government fails to supply an individual's entitlements, it denies her economic facilities and indirectly affects her social integration. The remainder of this chapter will focus on economic disentitlement caused by ineffectual governance.

Table 4-1. *Two Perspectives on Improving the Entrepreneurial Climate*

	Problem definition	*Reform agenda*	*Focus*
Economic perspective	Productivity growth lagging behind, unemployment	Regulation and information oriented	Rules Costs Time
Social perspective	Social exclusion, lack of social mobility, deprivation	People and process oriented	Context Mechanisms Motivation

Table 4-1 distinguishes between two perspectives on improving entrepreneurial climates. As previously discussed, recent reform agendas have focused largely on economic aspects by minimizing regulations for nascent entrepreneurs. Their efficacy has mainly been assessed in terms of numbers of rules removed and percentage of administrative burden reduced, with some proven financial success.

If we look at the bottom row of table 4-1 to examine the social perspective on entrepreneurship, we see complementary indicators demonstrating the degree of participation in entrepreneurship by all groups in society, including minorities. This approach focuses on the larger socioeconomic context of the potential entrepreneur and the interplay of factors influencing her business opportunities and motivations (which may very well be more than simply maximizing profits). Certainly, we cannot say that reform agendas have had no eye for the social dimension of entrepreneurship; rather, the choice of instruments for reform implementation has been more consistent with economic perspectives on reform. It is our conjecture that as a consequence, entrepreneurs who are more dependent on their broader social connections have benefited less from regulatory reforms than those who can establish businesses independently.

In the following sections we examine the particular network of problems facing nascent immigrant entrepreneurs. First we present quantitative evidence of possible comparative disadvantage that nascent immigrant entrepreneurs may face. Then we turn to circumstantial evidence and analyze three cases of entrepreneurs in the Netherlands. We uncover the underlying mechanisms at play and make some suggestions for further research. Finally, we discuss some promising international innovations that address the problems under discussion.

Immigrant Entrepreneurs: A Profile

What do we know about immigrant entrepreneurs? Data from local Chambers of Commerce, the Ministry of Economic Affairs, and municipal statistical agencies are not differentiated by ethnicity because of the risk of racial profiling. Furthermore, non-Western immigrants are often treated as one group in the existing literature, despite the importance, in finding facts, of not making unjustified generalizations. In addition, the populations of first-, second-, and third-generation non-Western immigrants are heterogeneous, as many authors have pointed out (EIM 2004; Rabobank Nederland 2006). Despite these pitfalls we consider non-Western immigrants in the Netherlands as a group with more or less shared characteristics, because it is our goal to examine whether non-Western immigrants as a group face difficulties accessing the economy. If this is the case, further research with regard to the specific differences between the members of this group becomes relevant.

Non-Western immigrants encounter many more difficulties in the labor market than do native Dutch people. In 2005 they faced an unemployment rate three times the native unemployment rate, and during the economic recession of 2000 to 2005, unemployment among non-Western immigrants rose at a significantly higher rate than native unemployment rates. Immigrants have, on average, lower levels of education than natives of the Netherlands, and they are often less proficient than natives or not proficient in the Dutch language (Statistics Netherlands and Research and Documentation Center 2007). From a socioeconomic perspective, non-Western immigrants occupy the margins of Dutch society (Kloosterman, van der Leun, and Rath 1999).

Entrepreneurs by Necessity?

It is notable that although unemployment is higher and economic participation lower among non-Western immigrants, the rate of entrepreneurship is growing at a faster rate among immigrants than in other populations. From 1999 to 2002 the number of non-Western entrepreneurs grew 3.1 percent, compared to 0.3 percent for native Dutch entrepreneurs (EIM 2004). The recession may have forced immigrants to choose entrepreneurship as the only alternative to welfare, but it should be noted that higher rates of immigrant entrepreneurship have been consistent over a relatively long period of time. During the period from 1986 to 2000, the rate of immigrant entrepreneurs grew faster than that of native Dutch (Jansen and others 2003, 41). The proportion of immigrant entrepreneurs still lags behind that of native Dutch entrepreneurs (Jansen and others 2003, 7): among 80,700 total starting entrepreneurs in 2005, 14,900 were immigrants (Chamber of Commerce 2006a). However, the percentage of non-Western immigrants who are nascent entrepreneurs, 19 percent, far outpaces their percentage of the Dutch population (10.5 percent).

Geographic Distribution

Non-Western immigrant entrepreneurs operate primarily in the Netherlands' big cities. Sixty-nine percent of non-Western immigrant entrepreneurs do business in the western, more heavily populated part of the Netherlands, alongside smaller majorities of Western immigrant and native Dutch entrepreneurs: 55 percent and 44 percent of their respective entrepreneur populations (EIM 2004, 16). In 2002 the non-Western immigrant portions of the total entrepreneur populations of The Hague and Amsterdam (the two locales of our case studies) were 19 percent and 16 percent, respectively. By 2006 these percentages had risen to 21 percent and 19 percent.

Types of Businesses

As of 2002, despite recent drops in numbers, the hotel, restaurant, and catering business sector, called "horeca" for short, remains the most popular one for non-Western immigrant entrepreneurs, followed closely by trade and the repair business (EIM 2004, 18). When we compare first- and second-generation immigrants, we observe a move away from horeca and toward commercial services and small retail businesses (EIM 2004, 19; Rabobank Nederland 2006, 121). Nevertheless, cafeterias, diners, and snack shops account for a large part of non-Western entrepreneurial activity in the Netherlands.

Immigrant Entrepreneurs' Business Performance

In terms of business survival, non-Western immigrant entrepreneurs tend to perform much worse than their native Dutch counterparts. On average, after five and a half years, only 32 percent of non-Western immigrant businesses were still up and running, as opposed to 53 percent of native-owned businesses (EIM 2004, 43). One of the reasons for their poor performance might be that immigrant entrepreneurs often are emotionally involved in their businesses, and they often start up without drafting a business plan, skip the orientation phase of finding out what licenses are required, and fail to acquire the licenses they need to establish their businesses.[5]

Non-Western Immigrants' Attitudes

One unexpected conflict that has emerged from the government's efforts to guide immigrant entrepreneurs through their business startups is immigrants' strong culturally determined resistance to seeking or accepting assistance from government agencies. In surveys of the three biggest non-Western immigrant populations in the Netherlands, nearly one-half of respondents from North Africa, one-third of respondents from Turkey, and one-third of those from Surinam and the Dutch Antilles considered receiving government aid to be a sign of weakness, compared to just one-tenth of native Dutch entrepreneurs who felt this way (EIM 2006, 17). These convictions raise questions about the government's effectiveness in stimulating entrepreneurship in these populations.

Financial Issues

Immigrants generally have less access to credit and little or no capital of their own. Banks and investors are often reluctant to lend capital to non-Western immigrant entrepreneurs because of their lack of collateral, their higher risks of business failure,

5. Interview with Atalay Celenk at the Institute for New Entrepreneurship, The Hague, April 16, 2007.

and marginal profit rates (EIM 2004, 41; Rettab 2001, 14). The government of the Netherlands, in conjunction with financial institutions, is currently looking at ways to provide microfinancing to immigrant entrepreneurs.

To summarize, non-Western immigrants in the Netherlands, when compared to native Dutch, are
—three times more likely to be or become unemployed
—less likely to be proficient in Dutch
—less likely to receive a higher education
—twice as likely to become an entrepreneur
—more likely to locate a business in an urban area
—more likely to have a business in the horeca sector
—three times more likely not to seek help from the government
—more likely to be ineligible for credit

Behind the Figures on Immigrant Entrepreneurship

The lack of further data of non-Western entrepreneurs posed methodological problems for our research. As discussed previously, we focus on the issue of access to the economy from a social perspective, so data on the following issues are relevant: Who is trying to get access? What are the reasons that some have access and others do not, or give up? In other words, who are the potential entrepreneurs and what are their problems? Are there many non-Western immigrants among these potential entrepreneurs? And if so, do the characteristics enumerated in the previous section impact their ability to get access?

The lack of data means that we do not know who is thinking about starting a business, who's trying, and who's giving up. We cannot analyze the problems of potential entrepreneurs when we only have data on those who have succeeded in starting a business and then either prevailed or failed. In other words, we cannot get access to those who are still trying to get access. Despite the lack of hard data, however, a wealth of anecdotal and circumstantial evidence strongly suggests that many non-Western immigrants, because of their background, encounter many specific barriers to economic participation.

In the Netherlands so-called "racial colorblindness" is often the preferred approach to analysis of society and its issues. However, because "colorblindness masks entrenched racial [and social] inequality," such a perspective will inevitably disguise the fact that ethnic minorities often have a social role analogous to "the miner's canary" (Guinier and Torres 2002, 44, 11): Miners once used to carry canaries with them underground as an early warning sign of the presence of dangerous gases; by analogy, ethnic minorities are among the first to experience the burdens of structural problems damaging society at large. We cannot forget that, though all entrepreneurs are likely to experience some trouble in the license application process, non-Western immigrant entrepreneurs are more commonly and more severely vulnerable to official obstacles, because of their group characteristics.

Imprecise Data

We also cannot rule out the possibility that many non-Western entrepreneurs might be informal entrepreneurs. Hernando de Soto is probably the best-known researcher in the world on the subject of the informal economy. One of the principal arguments in his book *The Other Path* (1989) is that the administrative burden of the formal economy often drives individual entrepreneurs to enter the informal economy. De Soto contends that there are two pivotal moments when businesspeople evaluate their relationships with formal economic activity: first, when they choose to enter the formal economy, and second, when they choose to remain in it. The costs associated with these two moments de Soto calls "costs of access" and "costs of remaining," respectively (132). The costs of access generated by an entrepreneur's initial decision to enter a formal economy might be too high. Informal entrepreneurs, by their nature, cannot be counted in official statistics, leaving the problems they face largely unaddressed by the reform agendas described earlier. Although we consider these informal non-Western entrepreneurs potentially very relevant for our case, the lack of data on this group prevents us from including them fully in our research. To sum up, the lack of data of potential and informal entrepreneurs poses a methodological problem for our research.

Entering the Formal Economy

A second methodological problem we faced is that it is hard to determine an official point of entry to the formal economy. When we take into account the chronology of a standard formal procedure, there are several steps that could be considered a beginning:
   —Gathering information at one of the many points of contact
   —Submitting a business plan for review at the bank
   —Signing a lease contract for a building at the housing corporation
   —Registration at a Chamber of Commerce
   —Registration at the Tax and Revenues Office
   —Applying for licenses at various municipal agencies
   —Official opening of the business at the location
   —Paying taxes (actual proof of turnover)
   From an economic perspective, the first seven stages are essentially irrelevant; the ultimate proof of entry from this point of view is paying taxes. From a social perspective, however, these initial phases are much more important. In the context of non-Western immigrant entrepreneurship, many factors influence an individual's chance of ever starting up. If an individual is functionally illiterate or

does not speak the official language, gathering information is problematic from the outset. In turn, if she knows her chances of being approved for credit are low, she will not put much effort into writing an official business plan. If she does not get credit from a certified bank, she will have difficulty getting a lease contract from a housing corporation. If she wants to register at the local Chamber of Commerce, she will need to produce a lease contract. Finally, if she wants to apply for registration at the Tax and Revenues Office or for the necessary municipal licenses (sometimes more than ten), she will need to submit a certificate of registration from the Chamber of Commerce alongside her application forms. Even the official opening is not a good indicator for entry into the formal economy: most entrepreneurs cannot afford to wait for all of this red tape to be cleared. Our Turkish-Dutch business owner went bankrupt because he wanted to play by the rules.

Redefining the Problem

Lack of data and lack of hard indicators for successful entry make it difficult to produce substantive, quantitative evidence of the comparative disadvantage that nascent immigrant entrepreneurs face. What we do have is substantial circumstantial evidence. We know what is required to start a business. We know that many immigrants are trying to become entrepreneurs, and we know what characteristics they share. What we must now analyze is how these group characteristics influence concrete, individual interactions with the government and other agencies.

To glean this information, our question must become very specific: In what ways and to what degree do governmental regulations and bureaucratic procedures impede access to formal entrepreneurship for nascent immigrant entrepreneurs? We will try to answer this question by analyzing three cases in depth in the horeca sector, one in Amsterdam and two in The Hague.[6] Our answers will provide qualitative insights to enrich our hypotheses regarding access to the formal economy, even if they are inconclusive in regard to the population as a whole.

Cases Studies of Entrepreneurs in the Horeca Sector

One of our entrepreneurs is a first-generation immigrant, one, a second-generation, and one, a third-generation. All of them experienced numerous licensing problems in starting up their businesses (Kafka Brigade 2006; Huijboom and de Jong 2005).

---

6. The case studies were conducted by Jorrit de Jong, assisted by other members of the Kafka Brigade, an action research team that uses qualitative research methods to examine excessive bureaucracy. The research method involves semistructured interviews and structured group interviews based on cases. Cases

The Entrepreneurs' Current Situations

One of the two entrepreneurs in The Hague—let's call him Entrepreneur A—is an experienced Moroccan immigrant entrepreneur. After a year and a half of laborious application for licenses, he started a lunch restaurant. Although the process was long and costly, he admitted he probably would not have started it at all if it had not been for the assistance of some helpful civil servants. The second entrepreneur in The Hague, Entrepreneur B, already owned three branches of a take-out restaurant in several other cities in Holland and wanted to open a branch in The Hague. At the time of our investigation, the branch remained unopened despite two years of trying. The entrepreneur in Amsterdam, Entrepreneur C, is the Turkish-Dutch man whom we introduced at the beginning of this chapter, who wanted to start a sandwich bar in a flourishing part of the city. Although he was accustomed to working for his father's enterprise, a fast-food restaurant, at the time of our interviews, his own business had not yet opened and he had incurred many debts while waiting for the necessary permits. Ironically, his father operates his business informally, without all the required licenses; it was his son's adherence to the law that drove him into debt.

Entrepreneur A

Entrepreneur A's saga with the local government in The Hague started when his application for a license for reconstruction was turned down because it contravened an environmental bylaw. The municipality granted him an exemption from the bylaw, but only after ten months of processing delays, because Entrepreneur A initially applied for the wrong category of horeca permit and then had to supply additional information three times. Although it is burdensome to the entrepreneurs, civil servants at his local municipal office made it clear that they felt that in requiring Entrepreneur A to supply additional information they were doing him a favor—they could simply reject his request out of hand. Entrepreneur A expressed frustration that he could not understand why all of the additional information was needed. The application process for the exemption Entrepreneur A received is highly opaque and also largely unknown to entrepreneurs; the by-law itself regularly comes into conflict with routine zoning plans.

Granting the building license took an additional four months, and was by no means the end of Entrepreneur A's administrative troubles. He was under the misapprehension that the exemption he received also covered an additional "exploitation" license (a license to run a particular kind of business in a particular building), but an inspection soon after the opening of his lunchroom revealed

---

are selected on the basis of criteria growing out of exploratory research. The method is explained at www.kafkabrigade.org.

that he had misunderstood the application form and he had to apply separately for the license. Although the licensing itself went smoothly, Entrepreneur A had to wait an additional six weeks to clear the "BIBOB Procedure,"[7] a process meant to prevent individuals with criminal records from starting a business. Further complicating these applications was a lack of operational transparency: interviews with municipal agencies involved with Entrepreneur A's case showed that some civil servants had no knowledge of the existence of other relevant agencies, let alone their requirements or procedures.

Entrepreneur B

Entrepreneur B's experiences both overlap with and differ from Entrepreneur A's. The zoning plans Entrepreneur B consulted were out of date and nearly incomprehensible. After laboriously choosing a site, Entrepreneur B applied for a building license, which, unusually, was granted without a definitive exemption from environmental bylaws. The local municipal office also took the maximum application time of four and a half months to review his application, without a definitive cause (when asked later, the local agency cited lack of capacity). Like Entrepreneur A, he had to send in additional information twice.

The real stumbling block came when Entrepreneur B applied for a permanent exemption to local environmental ordinances. His initial application was granted, again, after the maximum allowed time of twelve weeks had elapsed. The official application was approved after an additional eight weeks. However, over the course of this five-month wait, the local residents' and entrepreneurs' associations raised objections to the opening of a takeout restaurant, and Entrepreneur B's exemption ended in a lawsuit.

Entrepreneur B faced delays piled on delays. Like Entrepreneur A, he thought that he was applying for his exploitation license at the same time as he was applying for his exemption, whereas in reality each item requires its own application. Although he discovered his mistake in time, the BIBOB procedure slowed his applications further. Moreover, he had not yet established business partnerships for his enterprise in The Hague, leaving him without the necessary affidavits of his character. Instead, he was forced to call upon one of his partners from another business to issue a certificate of moral conduct. Finally, he applied for a certificate of fire safety, but the fire department never processed it. While explaining these many obstacles, Entrepreneur B expressed distress that his local municipal agencies thought he was "bothering" them with his applications while their demands and procedures remained unclear. Yet the civil servants involved in the case commented that if an entrepreneur fails, it is his fault, and he probably caused the trouble himself.

7. Beginning horeca entrepreneurs must provide local agencies with a certificate of moral conduct from all current and previous business partners.

Local policy in The Hague aims to direct entrepreneurs first to the local business desk, a government information desk maintained by the central city government, but in these two cases the entrepreneurs were unaware of this procedure and went to the district office, a government service and information center at the lower district level, first. Even though the district offices could not help these beginning entrepreneurs to the full extent necessary, the would-be entrepreneurs were never directly referred to the appropriate office. These breakdowns in communication extended to the agencies' websites, which, both entrepreneurs commented, had information that was often incorrect and out of date.

Entrepreneur C

Entrepreneur C, in Amsterdam, experienced difficulties of a related nature. First, in order to apply for exploitation and building licenses for his location, he had to register with his municipal Chamber of Commerce. To register, he had to rent a location without knowing whether or not he could actually use it. This posed a huge financial problem to Entrepreneur C, particularly since he lacked the resources of Entrepreneurs A and B. His problems expanded from there. Entrepreneur C found that no agency in Amsterdam, not even the city districts' business desks, could provide a would-be entrepreneur with all the information he or she needed. Rather than full-service offices, he encountered a string of putative "one-stop shops," none of which were actually empowered to take care of any of his needs. In his experience, these small offices only gave information on procedures and referrals to other agencies, without giving substantial or wide-ranging advice on how to open his sandwich shop. These one-stop shops, he felt, only made things less clear.

After Entrepreneur C managed to get his exploitation license, he was forced to apply for a license for reconstruction because he wanted to add a door to his premises. This small alteration incurred three additional months of waiting and an extra 1,200 euros in fees, because the door had to be in keeping with both the appearance of the neighborhood and the regulations of the fire department.

These complications were by no means the last: Entrepreneur C's sandwich bar was treated as a retail store for the purposes of his building license, but as a place for selling food the space was subject to numerous environmental laws and regulations. Because his initial application listed the enterprise as a shop, he failed to consult an environmental agency, leaving him subject later to numerous environmental demands with which he found it almost impossible to comply. These ordinances are so complex that even the desk manager at Entrepreneur C's district business desk has advised entrepreneurs (off the record) to start their businesses directly, without jumping through all the legal hoops, and see what happens. The growing number of rules, coupled with lax enforcement of regulations, frustrated and infuriated Entrepreneur C.

Underlying Obstructive Mechanisms

In all three of these cases, it became clear that the longer the application process, the higher the cost to the applicant. These entrepreneurs have to pay rent on empty storefronts while awaiting official approval for their startups.[8] As they continue to rack up costs during the application process, these entrepreneurs often delay their own applications through their poor understanding of bureaucratic procedure. Unused to the system, they quickly became frustrated with numerous license applications and repeated demands for the same information.

We can distill a number of mechanisms that obstruct access to formal markets from these immigrant entrepreneurs' experiences.

Exacting Application Process

Applying for licenses requires a high level of skill from entrepreneurs. Forms and procedures are often written in official jargon and are difficult to follow, for both applicants and administrators. In our case studies we found that few civil servants are able to understand all of the materials produced by their fellow public officers. The licensing process demands a wide range of additional documentation and information, materials for which the need is often not made clear to the entrepreneurs themselves.

Poor Enforcement of Regulations

This exacting application process stands in sharp contrast to the laxness with which regulatory laws are enforced. Entrepreneurs who choose to start their businesses informally can easily get away without filing for legal documentation. Naturally, they run a risk of being fined, but the advantage of a quick start of their business often outweighs that risk. According to our respondents, this poor law enforcement makes a level playing field impossible.

Lack of Cooperation between Agencies

Registering with the Chamber of Commerce is only the first order of business in starting an enterprise; an entrepreneur cannot open a horeca business formally without holding all relevant licenses. There is a cumulative order to the application process wherein several permits will only be granted once an entrepreneur has received initial documentation. By making license applications dependent on one another, government regulation has made the process of starting a business unnecessarily long and costly. The high costs to the entrepreneur in terms of both time and money make opening a business without some or all required permits seem the only profitable option. To a large extent this is due to a lack of cooper-

8. The original case studies contain appendixes with lengthy flow charts outlining the bureaucratic paths that the entrepreneurs traveled over time. (These are available at www.kafkabrigade.org.)

ation, both among government agencies and between agencies and their clients. Many civil servants openly acknowledge the poor functionality of the current system, yet they are resigned, feeling that there is no alternative to the endless red tape. The result of this apathy is a lack of genuine "one-stop shops" for access to government agencies and a critical absence of appropriate guidance for entrepreneurs regarding regulatory procedures.

Entrepreneurs and Bureaucrats: Different Mind-sets

One thing that becomes clear from the case studies is that entrepreneurs and government agencies have completely opposing perspectives to the same application procedures. Government agencies struggle with a lack of capacity, generally taking the maximum time allowable for any given procedure. Entrepreneurs, by contrast, want to start up their businesses as soon as possible, and they have no understanding of or patience for bureaucrats and their processes.

Civil servants implicitly understand their role to be that of guarantors of public interest, and they often regard markets and businesses as private interests that are not to be trusted. Such bureaucrats generally do not recognize that the workings of government can actually damage public interest by impeding opportunities for citizens and residents, as explored at the beginning of this chapter. At the lower or street levels of bureaucracy, by contrast, we find civil servants who are as frustrated with regulatory bureaucracy as the entrepreneurs they serve, going so far as to recommend not bothering with the licensing process when starting a new enterprise.

Suggestions for Improving Access

We conclude from these three cases that governmental regulations and bureaucratic procedures impede access to the formal economy for nascent immigrant entrepreneurs. The socioeconomic factors affecting these people reduce their opportunities for market entry. Although other entrepreneurs may face the same hurdles, the overall outcome is inequitable, First, because non-Western immigrants have fewer work alternatives, and second, because they are less able to deal with the hurdles. They often have a poorer grasp of the national language, less access to credit or capital, and lower degrees of bureaucratic competency. The cases show that despite numerous policies aimed at helping entrepreneurs, the requirements of government agencies, intermediary organizations such as Chambers of Commerce, and private sector groups (including banks and housing corporations) leave the burden of administration on these entrepreneurs. From an economic perspective the policy reform agendas may make sense, but from a social perspective they leave large groups of entrepreneurs behind. Moreover, the underlying mechanisms show that it is often not the policies, rules, or regulations that are inhibitive to entrepreneurs, but the way these policies are executed (or not), the way the rules are enforced (or not), and the way the regulations are administered through bureaucratic operating procedures.

The government can better understand the problems of non-Western entrepreneurs (and of society at large) by recognizing citizens' ethnicities and taking the problems that derive from that seriously. First, the status of ethnic minority populations often gives warning of structural and far-reaching problems in society. The obstacles impeding the three entrepreneurs we interviewed are likely to pose equally large problems to native Dutch entrepreneurs with lower levels of educational attainment or lower financial means. A second important point is that government guidance of nascent ethnic entrepreneurs tends to be more effective when ethnicity is taken into account in the policymaking and policy implementation processes, an observation that has been made by civil servants and business coaches alike.[9] Of course, we must acknowledge that it can be challenging to take into account ethnicity when formulating general policy. However, in daily administration and executive practice, not doing so may actually be disadvantageous to the interests of all citizens.

Third, governments may want to change some of their administrative policies to make access to the formal economy easier. In doing so they should be guided by their answers to the following questions:

—Can the processing of all of an entrepreneur's licenses be coordinated, say, by assembling teams to facilitate processing, or assigning civil servants as account managers to entrepreneurs' projects?

—How can agencies help entrepreneurs understand why the process must work the way it does, especially applicants who need an extra hand mastering bureaucratic procedures, such as non-Western immigrants who are reluctant to ask for help?

—Can government agencies eliminate complicated jargon in their application forms and communications with entrepreneurs?

—Can entrepreneurs apply for some licenses after initial startup instead of being required to obtain all licenses before startup, to avoid unnecessary bureaucratic procedures that may discourage non-Western immigrants and some natives?

Innovations That Have Improved Access

In search of answers to these questions we can turn to some excellent international examples of better service delivery. We focus here on two overlapping strands: practices that show that, indeed, the license acquisition process can be

9. Business coaches (employees of banks, government agencies, or NGOs) provide guidance to starting entrepreneurs with respect to hiring personnel, setting up a business administration, and marketing products.

made simpler, and those that acknowledge citizen diversity through the development of guidance programs for those who tend to need assistance before even
starting the licensing process. Although we do not discuss here many other types
of innovative practices,[10] naturally, our main point is that it is very possible to improve access to the formal economy for all entrepreneurs, including non-Western
immigrant entrepreneurs. This can be achieved not only by reducing the number
of rules guiding the application process but also by using a social standpoint to
improve the delivery of services and obligations.

Simplifying the License Application Process

Simplification of the license application process can be achieved in many ways.
We will restrict ourselves to two examples.

Singapore operates two projects, the Online Application System for Integrated
Service (OASIS) and the Online Business Licensing Service (OBLS), in order to
simplify applications and minimize paperwork for individual entrepreneurs looking for business licenses. The OASIS project's leaders have eliminated 11 of the
154 licenses required to do business. Of the remaining 143, unnecessary requirements were stripped and internal approving processes streamlined through
interorganizational information sharing. They implemented the OBLS system
and set up an online portal where entrepreneurs apply for relevant licenses using
a single, integrated application form.[11] Information is then passed on to the various pertinent agencies, which in turn notify entrepreneur applicants of the
progress of their applications by e-mail and Short Message Service (a service for
sending text messages on a cellular telephone system). The online portal now
supports sixty-nine types of license applications, and thirty government agencies
are participating in the project (United Nations Public Administration Network
2005). The second example is a recent Dutch initiative called HoReCa1, which
works much like Singapore's OASIS. The HoReCa1 project consists of an Internet portal that allows starting entrepreneurs in the city of Amsterdam's horeca sector to identify which licenses they need for their business through a single questionnaire. Filling out this questionnaire and submitting it also constitutes an
application for all of the necessary licenses, thus unifying information gathering
and application processing into a "one-stop" process for entrepreneurs.

What makes the Singapore and Amsterdam examples so notable is that when
licenses are processed through one centralized application and the client is given
personal attention, we observe significant time and cost reductions for both the
entrepreneurs and the government. In the case of HoReCa1, costs to both the

10. Examples include starting the licensing process only after the enterprise has begun business and
been inspected, or setting maximum time limits on license applications, which if exceeded by local authorities would automatically lead to licenses' being granted (World Bank 2006).

11. See www.business.gov.sg/licenses.

city of Amsterdam and the applying entrepreneurs were cut by 50 percent.[12] By persuading or mandating cooperation among agencies by sharing their already established databases HoReCa1's managers have been able to increase efficiency enormously.

Here we should add a caveat that these innovations in Singapore and Amsterdam are still new, and it remains to be seen whether the back-office operations supporting these "one-stop" solutions operate as efficiently as their front offices do. It has been repeatedly observed in Singapore that cooperation between government agencies is neither automatic nor ensured, and a single website may not improve the situation very much if the value of the project is not acknowledged by individual agencies. A further technical hurdle is Singapore's OASIS promise to its users that they need only use one Web portal. It has been observed in other similar cases that as the program expands to many agencies, the later stages of the process and information from all relevant agencies may not be incorporated into the initial Web portal

Proactive Guidance and Coaching

Ideally, applying for business licenses should be so easy that guidance or coaching is unnecessary. However, most practitioners admit that it is a necessary (though certainly not sufficient) condition for facilitating entrepreneurship. As we have noted before, there is a contradiction at the heart of government programs to coach non-Western immigrant entrepreneurs, because many of the latter regard receiving government help as shameful. Actively trying to stimulate ethnic entrepreneurship has proved to be a difficult and convoluted issue, leading us to the conclusion that additional requirements must be met to make such initiatives useful (Municipality of Haarlem 2002; Municipality of Utrecht 2006).

The added value of the guidance approach is that, in combination with standardized simplified license application systems, coaches can respond to the unique circumstances in which many non-Western immigrant entrepreneurs find themselves. No one will be surprised to learn that different groups require different, culturally sensitive strategies. An anecdote can illustrate what these otherwise often successful entrepreneurs must deal with:

> One day a successful Turkish pizzeria owner in Amsterdam is visited by a public health inspector. The inspector notices the pizzeria owner is not in the possession of the necessary health and safety license and orders him to apply for one. The Turkish entrepreneur is totally unaware of the existence of such a license but complies, and after months of filling out forms and waiting he receives an official document signed by the mayor. Thinking he

12. Royal Horeca Netherlands (Koninklijke Horeca Nederland). "'Horeca1' Amsterdam: Seven Licenses at One Blow" ["'Horeca1' Amsterdam: zeven vergunningen in één klap"], press release, January 23, 2007 (www.horeca.org/smartsite.dws?id=55701&lang=Dutch [accessed June 29, 2007]).

is finally granted the license, he puts it in a frame and proudly hangs it on the wall in a prominent place in the pizzeria. When a regular customer comes by he takes a close look at the document. He notices the pizzeria owner has a rejection of his application hanging on the wall.[13]

Proactive best practices have been implemented in the Dutch municipalities of The Hague and Tilburg and in Leicester, United Kingdom, among many others. In Leicester, an independent social enterprise agency, the nonprofit organization Cooperative and Social Enterprise Development Agency (CaSEda), gives clients personal advice and guidance in starting up their businesses. This agency can tailor its advice to the client's individual needs, taking into account variations in degree of business experience and cultural and linguistic issues. CaSEda's advisers are all members of the Institute of Business Consulting, a nonprofit professional institute for business advisers, mentors, and trainers who specialize in helping small firms.

Leicester's approach stands out in two ways. First, CaSEda has a reputation for working with clients in a fair and democratic way, practicing equal opportunity policies for all clients. They expect their clients to succeed and not to fail, and work with them individually to help them achieve their goals. This might seem logical, and in some countries with a more business-friendly climate, such as the United States, Australia, and Singapore, this attitude can be found in the civil service. Consider, however, that in one of our case studies, the entrepreneur suspected that the local civil servants thought he was bothering them and that it was his own fault if he failed to receive the correct licenses.

A second characteristic of CaSEda is that staff members approach their clients proactively, meeting nascent entrepreneurs not only at their offices but also at venues of the client's choice. They promote their message through unorthodox channels such as mosques, temples, churches, community centers, employment job centers, and other business support organizations. Potential entrepreneurs often feel more at ease approaching someone in these more familiar settings when seeking advice, after which they may be referred to CaSEda directly. Once the initial round of introductions has been conducted in a context familiar to the nascent entrepreneur, the client is generally more at ease in visiting CaSEda's own offices (CaSEda 2005, 2006). In these more familiar environments, starting entrepreneurs, especially non-Western immigrant entrepreneurs, are much more likely to be receptive to the advice they are given. The business environment in Leicester is now so encouraging that a group of Somali immigrants actually decided to move from The Hague to Leicester during the 1990s to take advantage of its beneficial entrepreneurial climate (CaSEda 2006, 6; Municipality of The Hague 2004). In 2003 Leicester won an award for being the European city with

13. Hans Kamps (Dutch Advisory Board on Administrative Burdens, The Hague), author interview, April 19, 2007.

the most successful integration of immigrant and ethnic minorities into its society (Municipality of The Hague 2004). Given what we have observed in case studies throughout this chapter, it is not surprising that in practical terms, successful entrepreneurship stimulates immigrant integration.

Conclusion

Accessing the formal economy is a time-consuming, complicated, and opaque endeavor for most entrepreneurs. These problems are only partly the result of too many rules on the books; in practice, it is service delivery and law enforcement that often make licensing such a difficult and lengthy process. The requirements of government agencies, intermediary organizations such as Chambers of Commerce, and private sector groups (including banks and housing corporations) are out of touch with one another, leaving the burden of administration on entrepreneurs, who often do not know how to navigate these bureaucratic labyrinths. Faced with requirements that are difficult or impossible to meet, even well-intentioned entrepreneurs are forced, or even encouraged by their own civil servants, to break the rules.

Poor client services and tangled red tape work against all nascent entrepreneurs, but some groups are more vulnerable than others. Immigrant (and particularly non-Western) entrepreneurs, who often have a poorer grasp of the national language, less access to credit or capital, and lower degrees of bureaucratic competency, face higher rates of business failure, even though, as a demographic group, they are disproportionately more likely than natives to start enterprises. Government regulation and failures in public management impede access to formal entrepreneurship, implicitly excluding the disadvantaged from access to the formal economy, not through policy but through poor management. Certainly, some barriers to entrepreneurship exist for a reason—the government is justified in wanting to dissuade inexperienced and incompetent entrepreneurs from starting up a business too easily. However, this goal of culling out nonviable applicants should be included as part of policy rather than be a side effect of unnecessarily complex application procedures.

These government-engineered obstacles are by no means facts of life: established best practices around the world demonstrate that improvement is possible. Successful practices work not only to minimize and centralize application procedures but also to acknowledge differences in beneficiary groups that may cause some starting entrepreneurs to struggle more with licensing than others. This social perspective restates the problem of access to the economy as an urgent challenge to social justice, one that all governments have a responsibility to redress. This call to justice demands a more equity-oriented approach to reform agendas.

References

Balkenende, J. P. 2006. "Courage and Pride." [In Dutch.] Letter from Prime Minister Balkenende on the founding of the Federation of Young Entrepreneurs in the Netherlands (www. hogiaf.nl/v2/index.php?option=com_content&task=view&id=13&Itemid=49 [accessed June 29, 2008]).

Cabinet of the Netherlands (Dutch Government). 2002. "Working on Trust: A Matter of Action. Coalition agreement of the cabinet CDA, LPF, VVD." [In Dutch.] July 3 (www. minaz.nl/dsc?c=getobject&s=obj&objectid=93357 [accessed June 12, 2007]).

———. 2003. "Participation, Employment, Deregulation: Coalition Agreement of the Cabinet CDA, VVD, D66." [In Dutch.] May 16 (www.minaz.nl/dsc?c=getobject&s=obj&objectid=93322 [accessed June 12, 2007]).

———. 2007. "Working Together, Living Together: Coalition Agreement of the Cabinet CDA, PvdA and Christenuie." [In Dutch.] February 7 (www.regering.nl/dsc?c=getobject&s=obj&objectid=74638 [accessed June 12, 2007]).

CaSEda. 2005. *Annual Review 2004–2005*. Leicester, U.K.

———. 2006. *Annual Review 2005–2006*. Leicester, U.K.

Chamber of Commerce. 2006. *Profile of Start-ups 2005*. Amsterdam: Chamber of Commerce.

de Soto, H. 1989. *The Other Path*. New York: Harper & Row.

EIM. 2004. *Monitor of Ethnic Entrepreneurship*. [In Dutch.] Zoetermeer.

———. 2006. *Memo on Appropriate Advice: Entrepreneurs, Demand, and Supply of Advice*. [In Dutch.] Zoetermeer.

European Commission. 2003. *Green Paper: Entrepreneurship in Europe. Brussels: European Commission* (http://eur-lex.europa.eu/LexUriServ/site/en/com/2003/com2003_0027en 01.pdf [accessed May 15, 2007]).

Guinier, L., and G. Torres. 2002. *The Miner's Canary: Enlisting Race, Resisting Power, Transforming Democracy*. Harvard University Press.

Huijboom, N., and J. de Jong. 2005. *Belgians Do It Better: Six Reasons to Emigrate Tomorrow*. [In Dutch.] Amsterdam: Meulenhoff-Manteau.

Jansen, M., J. de Kok, J. van Sprongen, and S. Willemsen. 2003. *Immigrant Entrepreneurship in the Netherlands: Demographic Determinants of Entrepreneurship of Immigrants from Non-Western Countries*. Zoetermeer: Scales.

Kafka Brigade. 2006. *Kafkabrigade: Licensing Starting Entrepreneurs: City Government of The Hague*. [In Dutch.] The Hague.

Kloosterman, R. Leun, J. van der Leun, and J. Rath. 1999. *Mixed Embeddedness: (In)formal Economic Activities and Immigrant Businesses in the Netherlands*. Oxford: Blackwell.

Ministries of Finance and Economic Affairs. 2007. *Plan for Reducing Administrative Burdens for Business 2007–2011*. [In Dutch.] Plan submitted to the Dutch Parliament, code 29 515, no. 202. The Hague.

Municipality of Haarlem. 2002. *Analysis and Possible Solutions: Stimulating Ethnic Entrepreneurship in Haarlem*. [In Dutch.] Haarlem.

Municipality of The Hague. 2004. *Report of a Working Visit to Leicester*. [In Dutch.] The Hague.

Municipality of Utrecht. 2006. *New Entrepreneurial Talent in Utrecht: Profile and Program of Action for Ethnic Entrepreneurship*. [In Dutch.] Utrecht: Department of Economic Affairs, Office of City Development.

Rabobank Nederland. 2006. *Vision on Regional Dynamics: Focus on the Potential of Ethnic Minorities in the Netherlands*. [In Dutch.] Utrecht.

Rettab, B. 2001. *The Emergence of Ethnic Entrepreneurship: A Conceptual Framework*. Zoetermeer: EIM Business and Policy Research.

Sen, A. 1999. *Development as Freedom*. New York: Anchor Books.

Statistics Netherlands and Research and Documentation Center. 2007. *Integration Monitor 2006*. [In Dutch.] The Hague.

United Nations Public Administration Network. 2005. "Innovations in the Public Sector Compendium of Best Practices: Winners of the United Nations Public Service Awards (2003 to 2005)" (http://unpan1.un.org/intradoc/groups/public/documents/UN/UNPAN02 2259.pdf [accessed June 29, 2008]).

World Bank. 2006. *Doing Business 2006*. Washington.

5

Appropriate Fit:
Service Delivery beyond Bureaucracy

GUY STUART

Bureaucracies, communities, and individuals are often at odds in standard service-delivery systems. Bureaucratic experts with a mandate from democratically elected legislatures have no time for the input of the varied communities and individuals they serve—the latter have already had their say through the ballot box. As a result, bureaucracies impose their expertly drawn up service-delivery processes on a citizenry that is then forced to comply with their requirements if they are to have a chance of gaining access to services. Or, in Lipsky's version of the same conflict, the bureaucratic experts have no interest in hearing what those they serve have to say because unclear mandates from the legislature make their jobs difficult enough already, and one of their coping strategies is to control their clientele through their use of bureaucratic procedures and the exercise of street-level discretion (Lipsky 1980, 58).

Interest in participatory service-delivery systems is a response to the conflict between bureaucracy, on the one hand, and communities and individuals, on the other. Participatory efforts are designed to tap into the local knowledge of the community and secure residents' commitment to the projects they choose (World Bank 1996, 4–5). As a result, the projects are more likely to be appropriate for the particular conditions of the community and to be maintained by the community in the long run, once the bureaucratic experts have moved on to new projects. But these efforts have their own problems with regard to the ability of bureaucrats to identify and respect the felt needs of individuals within communities (Cleaver 2001, 51–52).

An alternative response to the problems of bureaucracy has been to privilege individual autonomy in the delivery and use of public services. Hence the interest in voucher systems, which allow individuals to choose among public and private sector service providers using public subsidies, and the interest in "right to know" systems that empower individual citizens by giving them accurate, detailed information about the services governments deliver. As a result, citizens act as consumers, choosing the most suitable service delivery provider for their individual needs, and voting with their feet and their dollars when a provider fails to deliver. Of course, these systems have their own problems in that they do not take into account the limited capacity of individual citizens, who are being asked to process large amounts of information in order to make informed decisions. Furthermore, the ability to act as a consumer of public services, with the option of exit, requires that there be more than one provider of such services, which in many cases may not be possible.

In this chapter I argue that the three levels of bureaucracy, communities, and individuals need not be in conflict. Evidence from the field of microfinance—the provision of financial services to the poor—supports this and also suggests that large-scale organizations can be efficient and effective and simultaneously promote equitable access to services. But the evidence also suggests that getting these levels to fit together is not an easy task and requires that close attention be paid to the distribution of three sets of essential elements across the different levels: decision-making authority, information, and capacity (human, physical, and financial). Drawing on the lessons of microfinance, this chapter develops a framework for how to think about effective service-delivery systems. The framework enables a systematic analysis of the distribution of authority, information, and capacity across the three service-delivery levels and forms the basis for problem-driven solutions to service-delivery problems, rather than a priori prescriptions that privilege one service-delivery level over another.

The chapter is structured as follows. In the next section I describe how microfinance institutions (MFIs) have developed service-delivery systems that integrate bureaucracy, communities, and individuals to increase access to financial services. I then provide a case study of a government program in India, the Self-Help Program, as an example of a specific government initiative to expand access. From these data, the following section explores the question of what constitutes an appropriate fit. I conclude with an argument for a problem-driven approach to the solution of distributed service-delivery problems.

Increasing Access to Financial Services

Over the past thirty years Microfinance Institutions (MFIs) have greatly increased access to financial services among the poor. MFIs now provide financial services to roughly 100 million households, whose average per capita income is less than two dollars per day adjusted for purchasing power parity (Daley-Harris 2007, 2). MFIs have achieved this against a backdrop of failed government policies to increase access, the failure of mainstream commercial banks to meet the needs of a viable, profitable market, and the limitations of the informal sector in meeting the financial needs of the poor equitably. As noted, the key to MFIs' achievements has been their ability to engage and fit together three different service-delivery levels. I now look at each level in turn and contrast the success of MFIs with the failures of traditional government programs, commercial banks, and the informal sector.

Bureaucracy: The Benefits of Formalization and Standardization

If you go to the offices of any large MFI you will see a familiar bureaucratic sight: people working at computers entering data, processing paper, and attending meetings to share information or troubleshoot particular problems that have arisen.[1] This familiar sight is not misleading: MFIs *are* large bureaucracies that deal with thousands of people every day and process huge amounts of information and money. In fact, their competitive advantage over informal financial service providers lies in part in their bureaucracies.

MFIs provide financial services to the poor. They do so in a market already populated by a wide variety of indigenous, informal organizations, such as money lenders, deposit collectors, various forms of savings and insurance clubs, and a wide variety of rotating savings and credit associations, called ROSCAs (Rutherford 2004, 31). These last get their name from the fact that the funds deposited into the associations by their members rotate to different members at different times—one week one member takes a turn with the funds, and the next week another does. To understand how MFIs increase access we have to understand the ways these organizations are distinct from existing indigenous financial service providers.

Indigenous providers offer rudimentary financial services such as loans, deposit collection, and insurance to people who are part of their social network (see, for example, Ruthven 2002, 267). This network gives them the information and accountability structures that allow them to extend services to their customers— they are able to enforce the informal contracts on which the provision of their services rests because they know how to track people down and apply the appropriate pressure on them to comply with the contract terms. This has a couple of

---

1. This section draws heavily on Stuart (forthcoming, 2008).

consequences. First, the indigenous provider's market extends only as far as his social network reaches. Second, to gain access to indigenous providers, the poor must be able to tap into an existing social relationship with the provider or someone connected with him.

Microfinance institutions bring the benefits of bureaucracy to this type of market. Two key characteristics of bureaucracies are their formality and the standardization of their service offerings. MFIs that are formal or semiformal have the ability to extend their services beyond the personal networks of an informal individual service provider because they rely on formal procedures and relationships to deliver the services, rather than informal, interpersonal relationships. In practice this manifests itself in the ability of MFIs to provide services to people whom they initially do not know very well, but whom others in the community know.

A direct result of this approach to financial service provision is that the poor gain access to MFI services without the need for a personal relationship with someone in the MFI. They may have to have a personal relationship with other members of their community, but that is a much lower hurdle to participation. More generally, MFIs, by not being confined to limited social networks, can compete throughout the markets they enter.

The largest MFIs in the world reach millions of households, and there is a large number of smaller ones that reach hundreds or tens of thousands of clients. If they have one transaction a week with each of their clients, whether it be the disbursal of a loan, accepting a savings deposit, or the payment of an installment on a loan, a large MFI may handle hundreds of millions of transactions a year. Each one of those transactions is likely to involve the flow of money and the flow and recording of information. To manage this massive flow of information and money an MFI must have formal systems in place to ensure that the money and information flow to the right places and are organized in the right manner.

Formalization establishes the rules for the handling of information to ensure that it is properly recorded and transmitted, and that its accuracy can be verified through crosschecks and audits. Mistakes in the recording of the information or in the handling of the money can have severe consequences for the organization. If an MFI has inadequate systems to record the inflow of savings deposits or loan repayments, it opens itself up to chaos and to fraud. Formalization also establishes the rules for handling money so as to minimize the opportunity for fraud. An MFI's handling of cash must be extremely closely monitored to avoid not only fraud but also the no less dangerous result of client dissatisfaction and a loss of faith in the integrity of the organization, which can result in a mass exodus of clients. Finally, formalization of bureaucratic processes, if done well, can promote an organizational culture that is inimical to fraud and sloppiness.

A challenge for MFIs is that they must accomplish this in an environment that is hostile to these sorts of efforts. Roads are poor, information technology has to be protected against power losses and power surges, information networks are not reliable, security is poor, and the pool of potential employees may not be adequately educated. Furthermore, and critical to this analysis, the environment in which MFIs operate is extremely hostile in another key regard: the availability of standardized, formal financial information that can be readily accessed and used as a basis for credit decisions. MFIs cannot rely on other systems to furnish financial information regarding, for example, potential clients' income and expenditures, assets and liabilities, and credit history, which they need in order to manage risk. They must produce their own information. As a result, MFIs need good systems for gathering information that has not been verified by any other organizations. These systems rely on a systematic data-gathering process, combined with the willingness of the community to share information with them, and their credit officers' ability and experience in judging the veracity of that information (discussed in more detail in the next section). Again, formalization plays an important part in this process of producing information and then making it amenable to analysis so that the MFI can begin to make decisions based on its own experience with its clients.

MFIs standardize their systems and limit the services they provide so that there are fewer standard systems for their employees to manage (Woller 2002, 307–08). This standardization allows them to achieve economies of scale as they expand the volume of their business and decrease their administrative costs to manageable levels. Just as formalization allows them to cut across social networks and reach a broad segment of the poor, so standardization makes it cost-effective to do so.

With respect to service-delivery systems, the large MFIs look very much like any other large, bureaucratic organizations—though ones that may be more focused on keeping systems simple. They have detailed, standardized personnel rules, cash management rules, and information-processing systems. For example, Bank Rakyat Indonesia has a standard set of five performance metrics that each of its 3,000 or so village-level units reports to its local branches in five one-page reports. The branches aggregate the information in these reports and send the consolidated reports to the next level in the organizational hierarchy, and so on. The result is a set of simple, standard reports that managers at different levels of the organization can use in their decisionmaking.

It is common to find MFIs offering just a few standard services. For most of its existence, Grameen Bank offered two basic credit products: a general loan with a one-year term, payable in weekly installments, including a compulsory savings contribution; and a housing loan with a maximum term of ten years (introduced in 1984). The housing loan product has some flexibility in terms of intended use—land purchase, home improvement, or new home construction. The larger size of these loans makes such flexibility more economically feasible than it would be for the smaller loans; also, the housing loans only constituted about 5 percent of Grameen Bank's loan disbursals in 2006 (Grameen Bank 2006). In 1997 Grameen rolled out a higher-education loan, which by April 2006 had reached only 10,200 borrowers (Barua 2006, 58). In September 2000 the Grameen Bank, under its new "Grameen II" strategy, rolled out a variety of new services: flexi-loans, micro-enterprise loans, a pension scheme, and a variety of savings and in-surance options. In 2002 it introduced its beggar loans—officially, the Struggling Members Program, whereby the bank makes no-interest loans with a flexible repayment schedule to beggars to help them finance some sort of business activ-ity (Barua 2006).

In the same way, the microfinance division of Bank Rakyat Indonesia, which has about 3 million borrowers and 30 million savers, offers one basic credit prod-uct, Kredit Umum Pedesan, or KUPEDES, and four basic savings products.[2] As with Grameen Bank, standardization is key, and the dominant credit product is the monthly installment loan for working capital repayable over an eighteen- to twenty-four-month term.[3] But unlike Grameen, there is some flexibility within the constraints of standardization, and the bank offers a mix of standardization and flexibility. KUPEDES is offered with a variety of repayment schedules and terms, thirty-six varieties in all.[4] For example, to meet different cash-flow sched-ules, the bank offers loans to fish farmers that have a term and repayment sched-ule that differs from the schedule for loans offered to agricultural farmers. Among the savings products, SIMPEDES, by far the most popular, requires no mini-mum balance, there are no fees, and unlimited withdrawals are allowed.

A third example of the bias toward standardization among MFIs is Compar-tamos, the fastest-growing MFI in Latin America. It offers three credit products: a village banking loan, a group loan, and an individual loan. The first of these is by far the most commonly used. Until recently Compartamos was unable to offer savings opportunities because it was not a licensed bank, but was operating as "limited objective" credit company. But in June 2006 it converted into a bank and is now able to accept savings deposits.

What makes MFIs different from money lenders and other indigenous providers of financial services is their formality. MFIs take a fundamentally dif-ferent approach to financial services than indigenous providers, in which they seek to build relationships with their clients through the provision of services, rather than only provide services to those with whom they already have a rela-tionship. This enables them to transcend highly localized networks, which in turn gives them the opportunity to scale up. To reap the benefits of economies of scale when they scale up, MFIs must standardize. The results are bureaucracies with a

2. Up until 2006 Bank Rakyat Indonesia offered Simaskot, which was the urban version of its basic rural savings product, Simpedes (literally, "rural savings"), but in 2006 it phased out the former (see Bank Rakyat Indonesia, "Financial Statements with Independent Auditors' Report, December 31, 2006, with Comparative Figures for 2005," at http://library.corporate-ir.net/library/14/148/148820/items/246863/BRI%20Dec%2031,%202006%20&%202005%20_English_Release.pdf).

3. J. Rosengard, personal communication, July 2007.

4. Ibid.

high degree of standardization in policies, procedures, and services that are at the forefront of expanding the poor's access to financial services.

Communities: Leveraging Embeddedness

Though bureaucracy is central to the success of large-scale MFIs, they cannot rely on bureaucracy alone to reach their clients; if they were to do so they would be like any other commercial financial institution. MFIs must rely on the existing social structure of the communities within which their clients are embedded to help them reach out to the poor and manage both parties' credit risk.

By their nature, MFIs do not have direct access to local knowledge about their borrowers. This puts them at a disadvantage relative to indigenous, informal credit providers who are embedded within the communities they serve and have good local knowledge. But MFIs have overcome this disadvantage through the development of service-delivery methodologies, especially with respect to credit, that take advantage of the authority relations and information available within the communities they serve.

It is common for an MFI to insist that its borrowers form peer groups or village banks, which the MFI uses to manage its risk. In a peer-group setting it manages risk by lending to individual members of a group but making the group as a whole liable for the loan. This puts the burden on the group, whose members have good local information, to screen who receives a loan and who does not, to provide each other with support when needed, and to enforce repayment, especially in cases of default. In a village bank setting, an MFI lends to the bank as a whole and the members of the bank decide among themselves who should get a loan and how to enforce its repayment.

In the case of MFIs that make loans to individuals without a peer-group guarantee, the challenge is to understand the existing social structure in which their borrowers are operating and work out the most effective way to extract actionable information from it. For example, in urban settings, MFIs often require that a borrower have been in business for six months or a year in the same location. They verify this by interviewing the neighbors of the prospective borrower before they conduct the application interview with the prospective borrower.

Though MFIs rely on the existing social structure to help them manage risk, they also try, over time, to build relationships with their clients, becoming, essentially, part of the social structure of the borrowers. One important technique is "step-lending." The MFI makes small initial loans and then increases the loan amount as loans are repaid and the MFI gains knowledge about the borrower. The MFIs use this technique whether they do peer lending, village banking, or individual lending. In addition, loan officers spend a lot of time in the field monitoring their clients informally.

On the savings side, the role of the community is less important in terms of managing risk, but it plays a role in helping MFIs to reach out to potential savers and mobilize their deposits. In this context, the role of the community is to provide not the customer but the MFI with a "stamp of approval" that provides potential savers with some assurance that their hard-won savings are safe. For example, in building savings-led cooperatives in Andhra Pradesh, the Cooperative Development Foundation, when it first started out, would hold informational meetings in the home of a high-status family to gain credibility (Stuart, forthcoming, 2008). More recently, as its reputation has grown, the Cooperative Development Foundation has been able to rely on word-of-mouth across villages to give them credibility, enhanced by the fact that they have begun to hire local village women to be outreach workers. As is the case with step-lending, over time MFIs are able to embed themselves into the communities they serve, thus solidifying the trust their clients have in them as financial institutions.

In addition, MFIs can use group methods for collecting savings that lower transactions costs. The Indian government has been promoting self-help groups (SHGs) since about 1995. One of the roles the groups play is to collect the savings of their members and then deposit them in a local bank branch in one account, thus saving the bank the costs of managing a number of small accounts.

Thus, MFIs have succeeded in blurring the boundary between the bureaucracy of the financial institution and the communities they serve. This is in stark contrast to traditional commercial banks, which wait for clients to come to them.

Individual Autonomy

Users of financial services are like other types of consumers in that they can choose to use the services as they see fit. But credit and insurance services come with obligations, compliance with which is important for the survival of the MFI providing these services. As a result, MFI clients are autonomous, but they are still subject to certain accountability mechanisms, especially if they are borrowers or insured. The clients have "accountable autonomy" (Fung 2004). The accountability rests with the formal systems of the MFI and the informal systems of control that stem from the leveraging of community embeddedness. Clients' autonomy lies in the fact that MFIs today do little to try to control the use to which clients put their services.

Client autonomy is one of microfinance's key innovations, when compared to traditional government credit programs. Before the microfinance revolution, governments in the developing world saw the delivery of subsidized rural credit as a way to promote rural development. Their approach was generally to lend money to farmers for specific agricultural inputs such as fertilizer or some sort of agricultural implement. Not trusting the farmer to use the loan for its intended purpose, the credit agencies required farmers to produce evidence of their purchases of the right input or equipment, or even made the purchase themselves. The results were often disastrous, because the borrowers, to gain access to credit, were forced to comply with loan-use requirements that did not fit their needs, and the government bureaucracy was burdened with large loan-use verification costs (Robinson 2001, 146–47).

MFIs have largely rejected this approach. They let the poor choose the tools for their own development and provide them with the financial services to support the use of those tools. The assumption here is that it is the person closest to the problem, the person experiencing the problem, whether it be poverty or a lack of power, who is best equipped to identify the solution. Nevertheless, though it is hotly debated in the field, many MFIs do take the extra step of providing training and support to their clients, in an attempt to enhance the impact that access to financial services brings.

Of course, clients are still accountable, regardless of what use they make of loans. Borrowers who do not use their loans wisely will be less likely to be able to repay them; at this basic level the borrower is accountable. But the borrower is not the only one who is accountable. An MFI's management is also accountable. For the MFI, accountability lies in its ability to demonstrate to its board of directors or external funders that it is having an impact on its clients' lives. As a result, MFIs are in a precarious position—their accountability rests on the actions of thousands, if not millions, of poor individuals (mostly women) with little education, living and trying to make a living in an impoverished context.

Yet there is credible evidence that this approach to the myriad goals that MFIs have set for themselves, or had set for them, works. There is evidence of poverty alleviation, women's empowerment, the creation of sustainable financial institutions and systems, and, in some cases, economic development (see Armendariz and Morduch 2005, 199–229, for an overview of impact studies; Khandker 2005, for a detailed panel study on microfinance clients in Bangladesh; and Snodgrass and Sebstad 2002, for a summary of studies in India, Peru, and Zimbabwe). In addition, there is evidence of improvements in children's school attendance and their health, especially where training and support have been given to clients of microfinance to learn and enact simple procedures to improve the lives of their children (Snodgrass and Sebstad 2002). One way to think about these empirical findings is that though the chain of causation is not necessarily direct, and is often confounded by other variables, the evidence supports the decision of MFIs to grant their clients autonomy and to hold them to account in a very simple fashion, through the loan repayment mechanism.

Summary

In sum, effective MFIs bring the benefits of bureaucracy to the markets they serve. A key component of this bureaucracy is its ability to treat the clients of MFIs fairly—they are all subject to the same policies and procedures, from which the clients themselves benefit. Furthermore, MFIs are better able to provide benefits to their customers when they have good accountability mechanisms in place.

As a result, MFIs are able to offer greater access than the informal providers of financial services.

MFIs' bureaucracies succeed in part because they take advantage of the existing social relations of the community in which their clients are embedded and thus avoid one of the pitfalls of bureaucracy: overreliance on formal knowledge to the neglect of local, informal knowledge. They use the communities' social relations to manage risk, improve outreach, and engender trust. Furthermore, over time, they seek to embed themselves in the communities they serve, so MFIs do not function like traditional bureaucracies but rather blur the boundary between themselves and the communities they serve, in contrast to traditional commercial banks.

Finally, MFIs have successfully mitigated the overly prescriptive tendencies of bureaucracies by granting their clients autonomy in how they use the financial services provided to them. This practice is a radical break from the past, when government programs sought to control borrowers' use of loan proceeds, thus denying individuals any autonomy and authority over financial decisions that had a direct impact on their well-being.

A Case Study of Government's Expanding Access: The National Bank for Agriculture and Rural Development's Self-Help Group Program

The largest MFIs have very different origins and current ownership structures, including member-owned (Grameen), government-owned and then privatized (Bank Rakyat Indonesia), nonprofit (Association for Social Advancement and Bangladesh Rural Advancement Committee), and nonprofit converted to for-profit (Compartamos, Bancosol). Given the focus of this book on the ability of government to improve access to services, it is worth considering a relatively new but rapidly growing player in the microfinance field, India's National Bank for Agriculture, and Rural Development's Self-Help Group (SHG) program.

The National Bank for Agriculture and Rural Development (NABARD) is a subsidiary of the Reserve Bank of India, and it is fair to characterize the SHG program as a government program, though it leverages the authority, capacity, and information of both the private sector and the communities it serves. As of March 31, 2007, NABARD claimed to be serving 58 million women, both as borrowers and savers, making it the largest MFI program in the world. This claim is based on the number of women who were members of self-help groups that had a linkage with a commercial bank, regional rural bank, or cooperative bank—at that time there were over 4.1 million such groups with savings amounting to about $878 million and outstanding loans amounting to about $3 billion (National Bank for Agriculture and Rural Development 2007, 2–3). The SHG program started as a pilot project in 1992 and was implemented on a national scale beginning in 1996. The program promotes the formation of groups of about fifteen women who come together to engage in activities and projects to promote their mutual well-being. The activities and projects can be in any sphere the group chooses, ranging from political activism to business development. An integral part of the SHG program is the development of groups' abilities to access and use financial services offered by existing mainstream financial institutions, whose loans to the groups are then refinanced by NABARD at a rate lower than that being charged to the groups, giving the banks access to more funds and a net gain on the loans they make to the groups. The women in the group are encouraged to save, deposit the group's savings in a bank, lend those savings among themselves, and eventually borrow from a formal financial institution. This last step establishes the SHG's "linkage" to the banking system (Harper 2002, 4). The number of SHGs that have been linked has grown dramatically in recent years. In the first five years of the program, just over 259,000 groups were added. In the five years up to March 2006, over 1.9 million were added. These self-help groups have resulted in a huge expansion of access to financial services.

The SHG program is leveraging the branch network of the formal financial sector in combination with the existing social structure in which rural women are embedded to improve access to financial services. Furthermore, the banks have an incentive to reach out to SHGs because lending to those groups counts toward the quota of credit that the banks must disburse to "priority sectors"(Reserve Bank of India 1996, 2).

NABARD has expended considerable effort to bring the SHGs and the formal financial sector together. As of March 31, 2007, it had cumulatively trained over 1.5 million people, including over 200,000 bankers. Though two-thirds of those trained were members of SHGs, this was only part of NABARD's effort on the SHG side of the equation (National Bank for Agriculture and Rural Development 2007, 68–69). It also spent 161 million rupees (over $3.75 million in 2007 dollars) on payments to self-help promotion institutions, which did the work of directly promoting the SHGs (National Bank for Agriculture and Rural Development 2007, 118).

Despite these efforts there is a concern that the quality of the groups being formed and their ability to sustain themselves beyond the initial startup period is poor. A recent evaluation of the SHGs found that there were both "lights" and "shades" in the track record of the SHGs thus far (Sinha and others 2006; henceforth cited as the "Lights and Shades" study). The "Lights and Shades" study found deficiencies in the formal structures of the SHGs and argued that progress in developing them "will require greater clarity of vision and objectives and a systematic approach to building capacity and providing guidance" (Sinha and others 2006, 137). In particular,

... record keeping at the group level has emerged as a very weak aspect of SHG functioning—with only marginal differences depending on who maintains the records. Complicated records and MIS [management information systems] seem to be part of the problem of poor book-keeping. Good book-keeping is critical for the sustainability of financial operations and continued mutual trust among members. Good quality of book-keeping means completeness, accuracy, up-to-date information and transparency.

The requirement that SHGs keep their own formal financial records to track loans to individuals within the groups (as in the case of village banking) and to track savings deposits raises an interesting challenge to the clear line of demarcation drawn between community and bureaucracy. In essence, the SHG program is requiring groups to take on some bureaucratic functions, and the "Lights and Shades" study is critical of the fact that that bureaucratization at the community level has not been carried out effectively. The study makes two interesting points: the failure of the groups to adopt formal record-keeping procedures may have something to do with the fact that the procedures they are being taught are too complicated; and only formal procedures can ensure accountability (Sinha and others 2006). The study is silent as to whether members of the groups with poor records actually lack information about their financial standing in their group. It may be the case that the records are poor according to formal standards but are perfectly adequate for the purposes of the group, especially as the group is limited in size and has a social structure that takes care of accountability.

The "Lights and Shades" study also highlighted problems relating to the exclusion of the poor because of excessive standardization of the policies and procedures for gaining access to financial services through the SHGs. This problem highlights the fact that community intermediation can only go so far in mitigating the exclusionary nature of overly standardized bureaucratic procedures. The study calls for more training at the group level, presumably to enable groups with poorer members to be more flexible in how they offer access to services (see Sinha and others 2006, pp. 43–44). Again, the problem here may be that the training the groups receive emphasizes strict adherence to methods of mobilizing savings and managing loan repayments that do not suit all group members.

One final point to note is that there has been little recent research on the extent to which banks have been able to adapt their practices to manage their linkages with SHGs in an efficient and effective manner. One area of concern is that the loan recovery rate of many of the banks is low. Of the twenty-two public sector commercial banks reporting their recovery rates, nine reported having recovery rates of between 50 percent and 79 percent in March 2007 (National Bank for Agriculture and Rural Development 2007, 6). Two-thirds of the loan volume outstanding to the SHGs was owed to public sector commercial banks at that time. Overall, 20 percent of all banks report recovery rates of between 50 and 79 percent, and 7 percent report recovery rates of less than 50 percent.

In sum, NABARD's SHG program has reached a massive scale by promoting the formation of groups embedded in the existing social structures of India's villages. Furthermore, these groups have autonomy in deciding their own agendas and, for individuals within the group, deciding how they want to use the services to which they gain access through the groups. NABARD has linked these groups to the formal sector through its linkage program, but has been less successful in ensuring that the groups themselves adopt basic formal practices designed to ensure accountability among members of the group. It remains to be seen whether there are informal accountability mechanisms in place that mitigate the lack of formal mechanisms. Furthermore, the evidence suggests that the nature of the linkage is overly standardized. The concern is that the lack of formality will undermine the long-run viability of the groups, while the standardized nature of the linkage program will exclude the poorest from gaining benefits. Finally, it is unclear whether the banks have adapted their policies and procedures to enhance their ability to serve the SHGs. Their low loan recovery rates suggest that either they have failed to adapt to manage the credit risk of the SHGs or they are treating the program as a government give-away.

The Appropriate Fit

Implicit in the discussion of the way in which MFIs have effectively combined the service-delivery levels of bureaucracy, communities, and individuals is a discussion of the distribution of three elements—authority, information, and capacity—across those three levels. In this section I make the distribution of these three elements across these three levels explicit, as a way to begin to draw out the lessons microfinance has for other distributed service-delivery systems. I use the phrase "appropriate fit" to describe a service-delivery system where the distribution of authority across levels is appropriate for the people working at those levels, given the information and capacity they have, and where there is a good fit across the levels in terms of who is authorized to do what, so that the people working within the service-delivery system can achieve the system's stated intent.

The "authority" column in table 5-1 depicts a typical distribution of authority involved in the delivery of financial services by an MFI. The bureaucracy handles the product design, documentation, and the disbursement and collection of cash, including its accounting. The community handles risk management, and the individual handles the use of the money. These authorized activities fit together to enable an MFI to deliver financial services to the poor.

What is appropriate about the fit across the levels in terms of the authorized activities assigned to each? There is an attempt to match authority with information

Table 5-1. *Creating an Appropriate Fit*

		Authority	Information	Capacity
			ALIGNMENT	
Bureaucracy		1. Best-case scenario: elements are aligned at the appropriate levels, given existing conditions (status quo)		
Community	Determined by status quo			
Individual		2. If there is a mismatch, can a cell be changed to create an alignment?		

Source: Author.

and capacity. Individual autonomy is premised on the idea that individuals know best their own felt needs, and they are in the best position to act to fulfill them, though their capacity to act is limited to their own skills and resources, or those that they can buy, and is circumscribed by their educational attainment and social status. Community responsibility for risk management is based on the idea that the community has the best information about those within it and can best exert pressure on them. MFIs' professional knowledge gives them the confidence to exert authority over the types of services offered and the methods for offering them, and they have the information-processing capacity to manage a large number of small cash transactions that allows them to offer services on a mass scale.

So one aspect of appropriate fit is the alignment of authority, information, and capacity at each level. Those with the right information and capacity should have the authority to act within a service-delivery system. This is a very practical idea because it proposes that the authority to act should be distributed according to the current distribution of information and capacity. It also sounds like a conservative idea because it proposes that the distribution of authority be based on the status quo. But it is only *seemingly* conservative, because an intellectually honest analysis of the distribution of information and capacity would reveal that these elements are distributed widely, and in places where they are currently not recognized. In fact, at the heart of the microfinance revolution is the idea that the poor can make decisions for themselves and effectively manage financial risk. MFIs have recognized that and based their bureaucracies on that recognition. So when designing a distributed service-delivery system, start with the existing distribution of information and capacity and assign authority to act accordingly to create an alignment.

This matching of authority, information, and capacity is an ideal, but the reality is more complicated, and is still the subject of much debate within the field of microfinance. There are many unanswered questions about the autonomy of the individual client served by MFIs. Intra-household dynamics complicate the question of autonomy, especially for women, who are embedded within a household that is in turn embedded in a gendered social structure that, in most societies, circumscribes the decisionmaking authority of women. At a less structural level many MFI practitioners assume that their clients do not have sufficient information or capacity to effectively use their services, so they provide training and other types of educational instruction.

There is also ambiguity about the role peer groups play in risk management. On the one hand are data that show that they can be overly harsh in their treatment of delinquent members (Rahman 1998); on the other hand there is evidence that MFIs do not enforce the joint liability provisions of the peer-group method for fear of an adverse reaction from the rest of the group, who will see it as an overly harsh penalty, and choose to default themselves. Finally, there are many MFIs that are switching to individual lending from peer lending, either relying on their existing relationships with borrowers who graduated from peer-group to individual lending to manage their risk, or simply using alternative methods to manage risk. As a result, it is unclear whether MFIs need the level of embeddedness peer groups provide or whether they can rely on embedding themselves into the community through step-lending and other relationship-building methods.

And there remain the questions about whether MFIs as formal organizations offering standardized services can be truly effective in their outreach. Standardization can be exclusionary because it does not meet the needs of all the poor—especially the poorest of the poor. The poorest are likely to require greater flexibility in terms of when they can deposit money, pay an insurance premium, or repay a loan, because their incomes are more variable. It is unclear whether MFIs have gotten the trade-off between standardization and customization right, and whether, as a result, their overreliance on standardization has limited their capacity to serve the poor. Furthermore, to the extent that credit officers, tellers, and branch managers are rewarded according to the value of the business they do, they may well have a bias against the poorest, who may require more time to service and have smaller transactions that generate less rewards for the MFI employees. Thus, if the goal is to serve all the poor, it is unclear whether the MFI bureaucracy is the most appropriate level at which to manage outreach to clients.

The uncertainty surrounding the fit between the three elements of authority, capacity, and information (across the three levels of bureaucracy, community, and the individual) highlights an essential characteristic of the microfinance experience: the malleability of the three elements. Authority comes in many different guises and can be built up over time—for example, as an MFI gains legitimacy in a community it becomes part of its authority structure. In the same way as relationships within communities and between MFIs, communities, and individual clients change, so do the flows of information. And training and education can increase the capacity of bureaucrats, communities, and individuals, as can new ways to raise money or investments in physical infrastructure. So the challenge the manager of a distributed delivery system faces is not only to work out the distribution of the elements of service delivery across the three levels of service delivery, but also to work out when and how to change the elements available to each level, or to work out how to respond to requests from other players seeking to change the authority, information, and capacity to which they have access.

As a result, a further lesson that microfinance teaches those interested in distributed service-delivery systems is that none of the elements at each level should be taken as given—they are malleable, and there can be mismatches. This is apparent in other spheres where distributed service-delivery systems operate. For example, those working in the field of HIV/AIDS in developing countries have found that the community is an effective partner to professional medical workers in delivering antiretroviral drugs to patients with low education and limited resources. Members of the community can assist the patient in complying with the strict schedule according to which they must take the antiretroviral medication. In this case, medical professionals have taken advantage of the information and authority already extant in the community to assist with compliance; they have had to enhance the capacity of the community to do this work through training programs (Galang and Stuart 2006). The same reasoning can be applied to other mismatches.

As a result, we have a more dynamic framework in which the contents of the cells are not given, but can be actively managed (table 5-1). The question for practitioners and researchers then becomes three-fold: What is the content of the cells in my current service-delivery system? Are authority, information, and capacity aligned at each level to take advantage of the status quo to support an efficient, effective, and equitable service-delivery system? Can one element be altered or enhanced to create a better alignment in the case of a mismatch?

There is no a priori assumption that any one level should be privileged over another in configuring the delivery of services. Nor is there any assumption that all the authority, information, and capacity rest at one level. Rather, the argument here is that these elements are distributed across the three levels; sometimes there is a match between the type of authority and the information and capacity available at one level but not at another, or at none of the levels. The practical problem then is to work out how to create matches at each level in such a way that each level has an appropriate role to play, and the activities at each level fit together is such a way that the system as a whole achieves its intended result. In other words, the distribution of elements across levels should be problem-driven, not prescriptively given to comply with an a priori bias in favor of one level or another.[5] This raises one final question: Under what conditions is it worth investing time and energy to bring elements into alignment, rather than simply working with what you have? This question is beyond the scope of this chapter.

Conclusion

In this chapter I argue that bureaucracies, communities, and individuals need not be at odds in promoting efficient, effective, and equitable distributed service-delivery systems. The lessons from microfinance institutions are that these levels can work together to enable the delivery of services on a massive scale, so long as there is an alignment of authority, information, and capacity at each level, and a recognition that information and capacity exist not only within the bureaucracy but also within the community and within individuals. The challenge for researchers and practitioners is to identify what exists in each of the nine cells that lie at the interface of the three levels and three elements, analyze whether they are in alignment, and decide whether it is worth fixing mismatches. This process should be problem-driven, not based on a priori assumptions that privilege one level over another, and should focus on delivering efficient, effective, and equitable access to services.

References

Armendariz, B., and J. Morduch. 2005. *The Economics of Microfinance*. MIT Press.

Barua, D. C. 2006. "Lessons Learned from Grameen Bank's Experience: Micro-Credit, Insurance, Pension, and Struggling Members' Program." Paper presented at the Regional Workshop on Social Protection as a Resource Person, organized by the World Bank Institute and the South Asia Region. Sri Lanka, May 2006 (http://info.worldbank.org/etools/docs/library/233782/Barua.pdf).

Cleaver, F. 2001. "Institutions, Agency, and the Limitations of Participatory Approaches to Development." In *Participation: The New Tyranny?* edited by B. Cooke and U. Kothari, 36–55. New York: Zed Books.

Daley-Harris, S. 2007. "State of the Microcredit Summit Campaign Report, 2007" (www.microcreditsummit.org/pubs/reports/socr/EngSOCR2007.pdf).

Fung, A. 2004. *Empowered Participation: Reinventing Urban Democracy*. Princeton University Press.

Galang, R., and G. Stuart. 2006. "Emergency Response to a Long-Term Crisis? Médecins Sans Frontières and HIV/AIDS in Ethiopia." Case Study 1851.0. Harvard University, Kennedy School of Government.

Grameen Bank. 2006. *Annual Report 2006* (www.grameen-info.org/index.php?option=com_content&task=view&id=305&Itemid=292).

5. The importance of problem-driven distribution of elements was suggested to me by "Toward a Pragmatic Conception of Democracy," a presentation made by Archon Fung at the Taubman Center Summer Working Series. Kennedy School of Government, Harvard University, Cambridge, Massachusetts, July 12, 2007.

Harper, M. 2002. "Promotion of Self Help Groups under the SHG Bank Linkage Programme in India." Paper presented at a seminar on the SHG-Bank Linkage Program. New Delhi, November 25 and 26.

Khandker, S. 2005. "Microfinance and Poverty: Evidence Using Panel Data from Bangladesh." *World Bank Economic Review* 19, no. 2: 263–86.

Lipsky, M. 1980. *Street-Level Bureaucracy: Dilemmas of the Individual in Public Services.* New York: Russell Sage Foundation.

National Bank for Agriculture and Rural Development. 2007. *Status of Microfinance in India, 2006–07.* Mumbai (available at NABARD website: www.nabard.org).

Rahman, A. 1998. "Microcredit Initiatives for Equitable and Sustainable Development: Who Pays?" *World Development* 26, no. 12.

Reserve Bank of India. 1996. "Linking of Self Help Groups with Banks-Working Group on NGOs and SHGs—Recommendations—Follow-up." Circular RPCD. No. PL.BC.120/04.09.22/95-96.

Robinson, M. 2001. *The Microfinance Revolution: Sustainable Finance for the Poor.* Washington: World Bank.

Rutherford, S. 2004. *Grameen II—At the End of 2003: A "Grounded View" of How Grameen's New Initiative Is Progressing in the Villages.* Dhaka, Bangladesh: MicroSave.

Ruthven, O. 2002. "Money Mosaics: Financial Choice and Strategy in a West Delhi Squatter Settlement." *Journal of International Development* 14: 249–71.

Sinha, F., and others. 2006. "Self Help Groups in India: A Study of the Lights and Shades." Report prepared for CARE, Catholic Relief Services, GTZ, and USAID. Gurgeon: EDA Rural Systems Private Ltd.; Hyderabad: Andhra Pradesh Mahila Abbhivruddhi Society.

Snodgrass, D., and J. Sebstad. 2002. *Clients in Context: The Impacts of Microfinance in Three Countries.* Washington: Management Systems International.

Stuart, G. 2007a. "Organizations, Institutions, and Embeddedness: Caste and Gender in Savings and Credit Cooperatives in Andhra Pradesh, India." *International Public Management Journal* 10, no. 4.

———. 2007b. Microfinance and subsidies: Who pays?" *Ethics and Economics* 5, no. 1.

———. Forthcoming, 2008. "Sustaining Public Value Through Microfinance." In *In Search of Public Value: Beyond Private Choice*, edited by J. Bennington and M. Moore, London: Palgrave Macmillan.

Woller, G. 2002. "From Market Failure to Marketing Failure: Market Orientation as the Key to Deep Outreach in Microfinance." *Journal of International Development* 14: 305–24.

World Bank. 1996. *World Bank Participation Sourcebook, ESD (Environmentally Sustainable Development).* Washington.

PART IV

Access to Public Services

6

Revenues and Access to Public Benefits

MICHAEL LIPSKY

There are no public benefits unless public authorities authorize funds to pay for them. This is the case whether the benefits are provided in cash, as vouchers, or as services. This point seems elementary, but the relationship between providing revenues for public benefits and providing access to public benefits is not straightforward. As I hope to show, the process of enacting revenues for public benefits influences the choices and decisions of administrators of public programs considerably beyond simply authorizing budget levels.

A useful point of departure is the anatomy of the social compact. The social compact may be understood as the set of goods and services that citizens broadly expect to be available to them, and political authorities expect to provide. In a democratic society, citizens understand at some level that they are the authors of the social compact, that they have brought the social compact into being. The social compact, along with patriotism, a sense of history, and other critical elements, shapes citizen loyalties and behaviors toward the state and fellow citizens.

We usually think of the social compact as signifying a relationship between the state and citizens as actual or potential beneficiaries, but it is more than this. It is also an understanding that extends throughout the polity, including people who will never receive public benefits, that certain circumstances will trigger certain state responses. For example, an adult who never expects to have children still expects to live in a society in which children with special needs receive targeted assistance. Such a person benefits indirectly from that assurance, even though he or she does not directly benefit.

At this level, the social compact is fairly stable over time. New programs are introduced as the range of problems deemed to require public action expands, and as new populations are included in the broad consensus of who deserves protection. Although recent decades have witnessed vigorous efforts to cut back the welfare state, the basic composition of the broad social compact has remained intact. The primary exception in the United States has been the transformation of the basic welfare program for dependent children from an entitlement program to a time-limited assistance program emphasizing work effort. But a version of the old program remains in place, and the totality of public benefits provision otherwise has not changed very much (Pierson 2001, 72).

The notion of the social compact summarizes very broadly the relationship of people to the state with respect to the provision of social policies. However, the laws and regulations that help give shape to the social compact only begin to suggest the actual provision of public benefits. This is because public benefits are significantly mediated by government agencies and partner organizations in the private and social sectors. At any given time, the social compact in reality reflects in part decisions made by public managers within their broad discretion to implement policy.

Public managers are governed by three work-related imperatives that have important implications for the distribution of public benefits.

First, to go over familiar ground, they are expected to administer the laws under their jurisdiction fairly, effectively, and efficiently (and, it should go without saying, honestly). This means that, as James Q. Wilson (1967) instructed:

—They strive to treat similarly situated citizens in the same way.

—They seek to administer programs to achieve the best results.

—They try to achieve these objectives at the lowest possible cost consistent with achieving the expected results.[1]

These requirements of public management are often at odds with one another, which is why the conflicts among these objectives are the core challenges of public administration in human services.

Second, public managers are expected to "add value" in their core areas of responsibility. The best public managers, Mark Moore (1995) rightly observes, constantly search for ways to achieve their objectives and manage the conflicts at the heart of their work in new ways that expand the capacity of their agencies, render them more effective, or achieve results at lower cost. Public managers strategize how to extend benefits widely and most efficiently when programs are just starting up or growing, and they strategize how to reduce or limit growth

---

1. Another critical requirement of administrators is that they are expected to act responsively within their range of discretion. This element need not concern us here.

when programs decline in popularity or funds are reduced. Strategic rationing of services is a normal part of organizing public benefits programs.

Third, on the public stage, managers typically are explicitly or implicitly part of an executive team and are expected to support the administration of which they are a part. Managers may advocate for their areas of responsibility while the policies of the executive are being formulated, but once the policies and revenue allocations are decided within a broad governmental policy framework, public managers are expected to defend the policies of the framework and the plans for their implementation.

This defense of the executive's priorities can be harmless and of little consequence. But it can also go so far that public managers actually claim that changes in policy that involve program cutbacks will not cause any harm, when in fact diminished access to services will be the evident result of the changes.

The imperative to be part of the executive team—understandable as it is—sometimes makes public managers collaborators in masking the discrepancy between public expectations of service provision and actual outcomes. Since public managers are the primary source of information about the effectiveness of public programs, this is a critical problem in public perceptions of service provision. (In practice sometimes events conspire to make it impossible for the fiction to be maintained, but on a routine basis public managers end up "fronting" for the policies of the ruling government.)

It is normal and desirable for public managers to look for ways to do more with fewer resources, or to develop innovative ways to maintain some degree of service when funding is reduced. However, other aspects of their role are more problematic.

—Public managers are loath to admit that their adjustments may result in reducing access to services or other benefits of eligible citizens.

—The result is that at times rationing of public benefits reduces access without any acknowledgment that access has been reduced. At times this reduction can even be inconsistent with public laws and popular expectations.

—The mismatch between public expectations and actual service or benefits delivery undermines confidence in government capacity to deliver public benefits and reduces confidence in the public benefits system, broadly conceived.

Public benefits in the broadest sense, once created, tend to be sustained over time, and they are difficult to dislodge once they are put into place. This is probably as it should be. The social compact should be relatively stable; public benefits should not change erratically, subject to the vagaries of election cycles or other temporary influences.

Public benefits also tend to expand over time, as many observers have pointed out. Sometimes, conditions for expansion of public benefits are salutary across the board. In the United States, following World War II, this expansion occurred through an alignment of developments that created an era of "easy finance" shaped by an expanding economy, a "peace dividend," and inflation, which reduced the cost to government of borrowing money and boosted tax revenues from the income tax as a result of "bracket creep" (Steurle 1996).

Sometimes benefits expand because the recipient pool begins modestly but predictably increases as the years go by (this happened with Social Security). The number of recipients or the range of benefits may also increase as a result of the demands of claimants or the actions of politicians responding to constituent preferences. Some programs, such as the Earned Income Tax Credit (EITC) program in the United States, begin modestly but over time expand even without changes in the law as recipients are recruited to them (Howard 1997).

The social compact also has expanded over time as new groups are added to those deemed deserving of social protection and support. In my immediate memory the following have been acknowledged as newly deserving recipients of public benefits in the United States:
—Children with special needs
—Victims of domestic violence
—"Street children" (homeless teenagers)
—so-called gifted children
—School children who don't speak English
—People living with HIV/AIDS

Benefits to new groups and expansions of benefits to traditional clients of the state are typically enacted one at a time. These benefits are added to the obligations of the state rather than substituted for other benefits. In other words, in the broad social compact new claims are not typically subject to a benefits "budget," in which adding social welfare benefits in one place is balanced by reducing them elsewhere.

In contrast to the rhythms of enacting public benefits, the raising and allocation of revenues to support public benefits have entirely different dynamics. Taxes are negotiated and enacted separately from the adoption of welfare state programs, and they are adopted literally in different places than public benefits. The people who legislate about and advocate for public benefits serve on legislative committees responsible for programs (such as a committee on health and human services), while revenues to support public programs are debated in the tax or revenue committees.

Reflecting these fractured dynamics, as I write in the spring of 2008 there are two very different and entirely separate conversations currently taking place in the United States on the future of social provision. One focuses on deficits in the public benefits package—most notably, the inadequacy of health insurance provision (47 million lack health insurance in the United States) and the erosion of employer-provided health insurance (Center on Budget and Policy Priorities 2007). The other conversation focuses on controlling the costs of the large social benefits programs (Social Security, Medicare) in order to bring government obligations in line with long-term prospects for revenues to support them.[2] There is hardly a soul who participates in both conversations, including the people who are offering themselves as presidential candidates.

The important result of this disjuncture between the discourse on programs and the discourse on revenues is that proponents of lower taxes don't attack public benefits programs directly. Instead, they pursue a variety of indirect attacks designed to deprive governments of the ability to fund social programs. They almost never attack the consensus on social provision; instead, they seek to undermine the capacity to provide public benefits. (The exception in the United States was the successful attack on the old public welfare system for encouraging dependency.)

Following are some of the strategies opponents of public benefits use to restrict capacity to pay for them. I focus here on developments at the state level in the United States, since this is where so many allocation decisions are made (consider that in 2005 state and local governments expended two and a half times as much money as the federal government on public policy matters if you exclude national defense and international affairs, interest on the debt, and Social Security and Medicare, the two big federal entitlement programs).[3]

Cutting Taxes in Good Times; Cutting Programs in Bad Times

American states, responsible for the administration of almost all social spending outside of the big federal health-care and Social Security programs, regularly alternate between budget surpluses and budget shortfalls because their tax collections vary with the business cycle, and forecasters are unable to predict economic trends precisely. In healthy economic times a state is likely to find itself with higher-than-expected income and sales tax revenues. In the 1990s, with conservative political forces dominating politics in the states, the occurrence of revenue surpluses provided the opportunity to cut taxes—not on a one-time basis, but permanently. When the inevitable downturn in the business cycle occurred, tax revenues predictably declined as well, and state funds were no longer able to support existing program levels. States then proceeded to cut services.

Cutting taxes in good times and cutting services in bad times is a formula for shrinking the welfare state more or less automatically, without directly challenging the broad social policy consensus. That services are not typically restored, or restored fully, in good times reflects in part the persistent "structural" fiscal deficits of the states. In states with structural deficits, tax collections, for various reasons,

2. L. Montgomery and N. Henderson, "Burden Set to Shift on Balanced Budget; Bush Likely to Force Democrats' Hand," *Washington Post,* January 16, 2007, p. A1.

3. Compare figures at www.census.gov/govs/estimate/0500ussl_1.html and www.census.gov/compendia/statab/tables/08s0459.pdf (accessed March 28, 2008).

do not keep pace with population increases, inflation, and the high cost of providing certain services with high growth levels, such as health care and prisons (Lav, McNichol, and Zahradnik 2005).

Capping Expenditures and Tax Increases

Beyond the politics of taxes and the business cycle, advocates for smaller government have sought to set limits on the rate of government spending. The best-known example of this occurred in the state of Colorado, where a series of constitutional amendments known collectively as the Taxpayer Bill of Rights (or TABOR) among other provisions limited state spending increases to a combination of population growth and inflation. Because program costs can increase at a greater rate than the allowable inflation rate, and some parts of the population (such as school-age children) can increase faster than population growth overall, over time state services declined drastically relative to the need. Under TABOR, Colorado went from being a state widely admired for its public services to being one of the worst performers on such social policy indicators as access to prenatal care and the percentage of children who lack health insurance (Bradley and Lyons 2005).

TABOR-style initiatives and similar measures "cap" expenditures so that state governments must initiate round after round of budget cuts. In the case of TABOR and similar measures, incorporating the caps into state constitutions makes them even more difficult to dislodge.

For a time states can attempt to fund some services through user fees or dedicated sources of funding such as revenues from lotteries. Exempting popular programs, such as public school funding, from the formula for capping expenditures can make these measures more attractive to the general public, while placing even greater pressure on the public services that are not exempted.

Limiting the rate at which states levy taxes can have an effect similar to capping expenditures. Starting with California's famous Proposition 13, enacted in 1978, American states have pursued limits on public services through tax caps of one sort or another. The predictable result has been a decline in public benefits. As Karen Lyons and Iris Lav have pointed out, from 1978 to 2000 California went from spending $600 more per pupil than the national average on public school funding to spending $600 less than the average. Once renowned for student achievement, California now ranks among the lowest of the states on that measure (Lyons and Lav 2007).

Tax caps, like expenditure caps, also limit government capacity without actually requiring criticism of any particular program.

Because the social compact tends to be relatively stable, states subject to limitations on one tax often make up for the resulting gap in revenues by raising taxes elsewhere. For example, state income tax caps may limit a state's ability to provide assistance to local schools, forcing increases in the local property tax and creating the predictable backlash. The reverse happened in California, where the property tax limitations of Proposition 13 shifted substantial responsibilities for schools to the state and created greater reliance on the regressive sales tax.

Tax experts say that revenue stability is best achieved when the three main sources of taxes—income taxes, sales taxes, and property taxes—are more or less in balance and no one part of the population experiences taxes as excessive. Capping one source of revenue has the effect of discrediting the tax system overall by placing an excessive burden on the other sources, creating a cascade of tax revolts (consider the current efforts in Florida to reduce property tax levels).[4]

Encumbering the Legislative Process

A complementary approach to limiting public revenues is making it more difficult to enact tax increases. This has been achieved in many states by increasing the size of the legislative majority necessary to pass tax legislation, or requiring that all tax measures must be subject to a popular vote. Enshrining such requirements in the state constitution, so that they cannot easily be overturned, reduces states' flexibility to fund public benefits programs. These procedural impediments raise the difficulty of increasing revenues for public programs.

Undermining Government as an Instrument of the Common Good

An overarching campaign to undermine public support for government has shaped the environment in which these revenue reduction initiatives have thrived. By now this development is familiar: conservative think tanks and their allies, and sympathetic public officials, since approximately 1980 have relentlessly and successfully promoted a worldview that

—denigrates government as a set of failed institutions inherently incapable of responding to critical social needs,

—emphasizes the interests of the individual over the needs of the society and community,

—idealizes the private sector and an unfettered market economy as instruments of securing the common good (Blumenthal 1988; Rich 2005).

The resulting heightened distrust of government makes it more difficult to raise revenues for public purposes.

For the most part, this ideological onslaught has gone uncontested. Conservatives criticize government; liberals in response tend to defend particular programs, but not the essential role of government as such. At times, liberals have

4. M. E. Klas, "Panel Weighs Caps on Government Revenue," *Miami Herald*, March 26, 2008 (www. miamiherald.com/548/story/470258.html [accessed March 28, 2008]).

joined the chorus of government criticism. President Clinton bowed to the antigovernment critique rather than oppose it when he famously pronounced the end of "big government" and made the centerpiece of his otherwise promising effort to "reinvent government" the elimination of half a million federal jobs.

The American skepticism toward government, always endemic to some degree, will undoubtedly remain part of the landscape for some time, although the most severe expressions of this point of view are perhaps abating. The American public is more ready than it was just a few years ago to accept that government is necessary to achieve certain public purposes, such as protecting the public from hazards and harm, and planning for the future. The Katrina hurricane disaster provided many lessons in why we need a strong and accountable government. Since then a constant barrage of environmental and consumer crises has kept the importance of government strongly in front of the public mind. Nonetheless, the habits of mind developed over decades will continue to skew the public discourse toward preferences skeptical of government capacity and constrained in assuming that the public sector can and should play a vigorous role when critical issues present themselves.

Revenue and Access to Public Benefits

Thus far I have made two general points. First, the social compact in which public benefits are embedded is only partially elaborated in the laws governing public benefits. Although the statutes broadly outline the social compact at any given time, the compact is fully enacted on the government side only when it is mediated by public managers who make the critical decisions as to how benefits will be distributed and who choose among conflicting alternatives in deciding on implementation strategies. Perhaps needless to say, public managers are always making such decisions, both to restrict services but also when there are opportunities to expand them.

Second, because public benefits programs tend to be popular with citizens who receive them and general publics that approve of them, efforts to restrict or limit public benefits do not take place in public debates on the merits or flaws in individual benefit programs. Rather, they tend to take place in an arena that might be described as "generally shrinking the welfare state."[5] Writing broadly about trends in public benefits at the national level, Paul Pierson (2001) similarly observes, "There is a fundamental asymmetry between the organized advocates of public spending, who favor *particular* governmental initiatives, and their opponents,

---

5. It is difficult to find efforts to shrink the welfare state by criticizing specific programs. The exceptions—social policies that come in for specific criticisms—tend to be attacks on benefits to groups of people who are objects of social stigma, such as "welfare recipients," or "illegal aliens." On the transformation of welfare from an entitlement program to one with time-limited benefits subject to congressional appropriations, see Weaver (2000).

who (at least rhetorically) criticize government spending *in general and on principle*" (66; italics added).

Putting these two observations together, we see that shrinking the size and scope of government involves tasks that regularly and inevitably fall on public managers. When public benefits are growing, programs are enacted very specifically and one by one. When public benefits shrink, they do so as reductions in the overall "envelope" of public benefits. When benefits are reduced it is the "pie" that shrinks, not the individual pieces of the pie. Thus, it falls on public managers and other responsible public officials to make the strategic decisions to limit public benefits.

What are the implications of this observation for access to public benefits?

1. The process of limiting access to public benefits is not nearly as transparent as the creation of public benefits. Cuts in services, selective closing of offices, higher caseloads, staff cutbacks—all of the ways managers incrementally reduce services in response to shrinking budgets—take place in the hidden recesses of administrative practice, not in the relatively brighter light of legislative inquiry (Lipsky 1984).

2. Opponents of budget cuts find it difficult to offer effective opposition to service and benefits reductions because

—those reductions for the most part are not systematically reported;

—it is often hard to gauge the effect of incremental decreases in services;

—public managers are programmed to defend their cutbacks and other changes in access and to characterize the changes as relatively harmless. They will not, or cannot by virtue of their position, be helpful to advocates.[6]

In doing this, they are acting "normally." The "normal" experience of public managers is to seek improvements in service delivery either to expand capacity or to provide the best services possible when resources are reduced. It is normal for managers to face rising case loads and budgets that fail to increase with legitimate demand. Public managers, as a normal part of their job, are involved in service and benefits rationing. Sometimes innovation will lead to improved services, as might be the case with the use of the Internet in accessing benefits. At other times, particularly when benefits are delivered through street-level bureaucrats and require human interactions, strategic rationing of services is the norm.

3. Sometimes, even in fiscally difficult times, access to some programs can increase. School readiness programs such as universal kindergarten, for example, have been particularly favored by some U.S. state governors in recent years (National Association for the Education of Young Children 2007). Prisons have been dramatically expanded in the United States since the mid-eighties and are slated to grow by almost 200,000 prisoners by 2011 (Pew Charitable Trusts 2007).

6. To be sure, public managers sometimes may be seen as high-profile advocates seeking to retain the scope and level of services under their purview. However, this advocacy has its limits, and managers who persist may find themselves out of a job, or marginalized in an administration attempting to present a solid face.

But for every well-publicized expansion of public benefits in one agency, managers in other agencies will be expected to cut benefits as they strive to bring their service delivery profiles into balance with the reduced resources available to them.

In accepting the budget realities as the agencies experience them, the advocacy groups ultimately reinforce and give comfort to those who want to limit public benefits. They become the tacit allies of their opponents who want to shrink government. As the apocryphal advocate for smaller government and reduced public spending would say: "I don't really care whether the mental health advocates or the advocates for universal kindergarten prevail. All I want is smaller government." The advocates experience proposed cuts in services as attacks on the agencies that serve their constituents. But in reality, from the point of view I offer here, the cuts are just second-order consequences of the pressures on revenue.

One might draw several conclusions from these observations. First, more attention might be paid to the ways public managers strategize to manage the challenges of shaping public benefits policies and administration when their normal environment is a "structural deficit" in which revenues do not keep up with increases in cost, need, and demand, and do not keep up with changing definitions of best practices.

Second, advocates for public services might spend less energy protesting cutbacks in services and pay more attention to the assumptions underlying tax and budget policies. Citizen groups concerned with human services and benefit agencies need to recognize their mutual interest in expanding the revenue base for public benefits and placing public revenues on a sound footing that is less vulnerable to the ups and downs of the business cycle. To be successful they will have to suppress their (understandable) instincts to compete with one another for short-term gain and find ways to work together for long-term solutions to budget and revenue problems.

Awakenings of these sorts are evident in many places in the United States, where disparate interests are coming together in statewide coalitions to work together to ensure an adequate tax base on which public benefits rely. It is particularly difficult to do in the short run, when the public discourse is controlled by antitax activists and allied interests. The prospects are more promising if the groups take a long-run perspective—always difficult, to be sure—to build support for necessary public programs.

To conclude, and to return to the theme of this chapter, there are no public benefits unless public authorities authorize funds to pay for them. Citizens and scholars interested in public benefits would do well to pay much more attention than they currently do to the resources available for distribution, making sure not to take as "givens" limitations that are said to exist. Without denying that governments face real constraints, to say "resources are limited" is to make a political claim, not a statement about reality. Observers concerned about equity in society typically have congregated around issues of public policies that promise to address significant social problems. The burden of this chapter is to point out the simple and complex ways in which access to benefits significantly depends on the structure and distribution of revenues.

References

Blumenthal, S. 1988. *The Rise of the Counter Establishment*. New York: HarperCollins.

Bradley, D., and K. Lyons. 2005. "A Formula for Decline: Lessons from Colorado for States Considering TABOR." Center on Budget and Policy Priorities, October 19 (www.cbpp. org/10-19-05sfp.pdf [accessed March 24, 2008]).

Center on Budget and Policy Priorities. 2007. "Number and Percentage of Americans Who Are Uninsured Climbs Again" (www.cbpp.org/8-28-07pov.pdf [accessed March 28, 2008]).

Howard, C. 1997. *The Hidden Welfare State: Tax Expenditures and Social Policy in the United States*. Princeton University Press.

Lav, I., E. McNichol, and R. Zahradnik. 2005. "Faulty Foundations: State Structural Budget Problems and How to Fix Them." Center on Budget and Policy Priorities (www.cbpp.org/5-17-05sfp.pdf [accessed March 28, 2008]).

Lipsky, M. 1984. "Bureaucratic Disentitlement in Social Welfare Programs." *Social Service Review* 58: 3–27.

Lyons, K., and I. J. Lav. 2007. "The Problems with Property Tax Revenue Caps." Center on Budget and Policy Priorities, June 21 (www.cbpp.org/6-21-07sfp.htm [accessed March 28, 2008]).

Moore, M. 1995. *Creating Public Value: Strategic Management in Government*. Harvard University Press.

National Association for the Education of Young Children. 2007. "State Early Care and Education Public Policy Developments: Fall 2007" (www.naeyc.org/policy/state/pdf/State%20 ECEPolicyDev.pdf [accessed March 28, 2008]).

Pew Charitable Trusts. 2007. "Public Safety, Public Spending: Forecasting America's Prison Population 2007–2011" (www.pewtrusts.org/uploadedFiles/wwwpewtrustsorg/Reports/ State-based_policy/PSPP_prison_projections_0207.pdf [accessed March 28, 2008]).

Pierson, P. 2001. "From Expansion to Austerity: The New Politics of Taxing and Spending." In *Seeking the Center: Politics and Policymaking at the New Century*, edited by M. Levin, M. Landy, and M. Shapiro, 54–80. Georgetown University Press.

Rich, A. 2005. "War of Ideas: Why Mainstream and Liberal Foundations and the Think Tanks They Support Are Losing in the War of Ideas in American Politics." *Stanford Social Innovations Review* Spring: 18–25.

Steurle, C. E. 1996. "Financing the American State at the Turn of the Century." In *Founding the Modern American State, 1941–1996: The Rise and Fall of the Era of Easy Finance*, edited by W. E. Brownlee, 409–44. Cambridge University Press.

Weaver, R. K. 2000. *Ending Welfare as We Know It*. Brookings.

Wilson, J. Q. 1967. "The Bureaucracy Problem." *Public Interest* 6: 3–97.

7

Bureaucratic Bias and Access to Public Services: The Fight against Non-Take-Up

ARRE ZUURMOND

O ne of the basic questions of political science remains: Who gets what, when, and how (Lasswell 1935)? And who decides? If we abide by a dichotomy between politics and administration, then after the processes of policy development and decisionmaking there should be no politics left in a policy's execution. This is where, ideally, we find the bureaucratic apparatus of the state at work, an apparatus that must function *sine ira et studio* ("without anger or enthusiasm"), that is, without any personal or political preferences. Bureaucrats, like evenhanded Themis, the goddess of justice (who is not blind, only blindfolded), should provide impartial and equal access to all citizens. Adapting the old adage "There is no republican way to build a road," we can say, "There is no republican way to deliver services."

Despite the ideal of evenhandedness, many analyses of public administration have shown convincingly that politics persist even in service delivery. In this chapter we will focus on one pressing political issue: equality of access to public services. Innovators must ask why it is that not all citizens share equal access to the services to which they are entitled. Why do some groups of citizens find it more difficult to obtain their rights than other groups? Why does non-take-up exist and how prevalent is it?

After examining the specific features of non-take-up, we will turn to more general analysis: the theories of Max Weber and Michael Lipsky (on the "street-level bureaucrat") may shed light on these questions. As a social philosopher and idealist, Weber holds that it is unacceptable for political considerations to influence administration. Lipsky (1980) takes the opposing position: that discretion, whether we like it or not, is omnipresent in the crowded offices of policy execution. We will put these theories to the test with two recent innovations that show us how the use of an electronic information infrastructure challenges the role of local bureaucrats in providing public services. Although government reforms in information management can reduce the level of non-take-up, government itself continues to be an instrument limited by political considerations. We shall then end with projections of the future of access in the face of changing organizational structures.

Description of Non-Take-Up and Analysis of Its Origins

Once legislators have agreed to provide benefits to their constituents, it falls to the state bureaucracy to arrange delivery of the promised service. But how successful is the state in executing its duties? The following examples illustrate how difficult it can be to reach all eligible citizens with the services designed for them.

First we turn to the case of public aid offered in all Dutch municipalities. If citizens residing in Holland remain below a certain income level for a number of years, they become entitled to a supplementary welfare benefit. Yet despite long-term implementation of this aid, only a fraction of low-income individuals are aware of their eligibility, and a mere 20 to 40 percent know where to apply for extra financial assistance for the elderly and disabled. Although the Ministry of Social Affairs has begun a campaign for municipalities to publicize the availability of these funds, citizen awareness remains low. Even with the introduction of this initiative, only 40 percent of municipalities are actively seeking eligible beneficiaries, another 30 percent are considering strategies, and the remaining 30 percent have no knowledge of the policy at all. New advertising efforts, data matching, an Internet site, and direct mail campaigns have been introduced, but have had little effect.

A second example can be found in Belgium. In this program of basic energy delivery, certain income groups are entitled to receive gas and electricity at reduced prices. It is estimated that 300,000 people are entitled to these benefits, but only 200,000 actually receive the price reduction.

A third example of pervasive non-take-up can be found in the United Kingdom, where the Inland Revenue allows a tax reduction for people confronted with high health costs. The non-take-up rate for this service among those eligible is 45 percent (Department for Work and Pensions, United Kingdom, 2006a).

These three examples show that access is a serious problem: some services remain largely unknown to their supposed beneficiaries, preventing potential recipients from applying for the full range of services they should receive.

Table 7-1. *Eligibles' and Noneligibles' Use of Inland Revenue Service in the United Kingdom*

Percent

	Citizens say they do not use service	Citizens say they use service	Total
Are noneligible for service	21	5[a]	26
Are eligible for service	45	30	74
Total	65	35	100

Source: Department for Work and Pensions, United Kingdom (2006a).

a. In theory this figure should be zero. The fact that 5 percent of citizens report that they receive services to which they are not entitled may indicate fraud, corruption, incorrect information, or wrongful understanding of the service's intended beneficiaries.

Research conducted in the Netherlands has shown that almost half of the individuals susceptible to non-take-up would no longer be in the lowest income bracket if they were to receive all of their entitlements. Because of non-take-up they remain needlessly caught in the trap of poverty (Netherlands Social and Cultural Planning Office 1997, 158).

This problem of non-take-up is by no means new; it was debated in the United Kingdom in the wake of the Second World War (van Oorschot and Kolkhuis Tanke 1989, 24; van Oorschot 1994, 63). On one side of the debate were the "selectivists," who argued for the application of a means test to guarantee that only the "deserving poor" would be included in the target group of certain policy instruments.[1] On the other side were "universalists," who asserted that means tests not only set poverty traps for citizens, but also raised operation costs and increased the probability of non-take-up (Netherlands Social and Cultural Planning Office 2007, 20).

Targeting Subject Groups: The Hit Rate

For every policy that creates entitlements, be it in health care, education, or social security, policymakers must determine which citizens are eligible to receive benefits and which are not. In other words, there is a target group for every public service. Unfortunately, there are also often mismatches between a policy's intended targets and its actual recipients.

This gives rise to four different groups. The first are citizens who neither are eligible for nor receive a given service. In the second are individuals who are entitled to and are receiving a certain benefit. A policy instrument can be said to be 100 percent effective when these first two categories form 100 percent of the total

1. A means test means that citizens' finances are scrutinized to ascertain whether or not they are eligible for a certain benefit.

population: there is a 100 percent "hit rate" when all those targeted by a policy benefit from it and all those who are not targeted do not.

In practice, however, this almost never occurs, because of the existence of two other categories. In the third category are individuals who are entitled to benefits but who do not receive them, called eligible nonrecipients (ENRs). This phenomenon is called non-take-up. In the fourth group are those who receive benefits to which they are not entitled, called noneligible recipients (NERs). The disjuncture represented by the latter groups can occur not only as a result of fraud or corruption but also because a policy or its categories either are unclear or are altered by decisions made during implementation. Incorrect information can also cause misdirection of aid: data on citizens used to calculate entitlement are not always correct. Finally, in some cases the exclusion of noneligible recipients is too difficult—in terms of time, money, or capacity—to be carried out. It is accepted that certain citizens receive benefits they are not entitled to; this is called spillover (see figure 7-1 on the next page).

Reasons for Low Take-Up Levels

There is much research with respect to non-take-up (Netherlands Social and Cultural Planning Office 2007). Kerr (1983, 16–17) identifies six obstacles to receiving services:
—The conviction that the individual is not needy
—A lack of knowledge regarding the existence of possible entitlements
—The belief that the individual is not eligible
—The perception that potential benefits are too small to meet the need
—Fears that entitlement has negative consequences or implies negative conditions
—Concerns about instability of a personal situation that may make an individual ineligible to receive benefits in the future.

Several case studies have demonstrated that non-take-up is higher when public perception is that the level of compensation is low (Netherlands Social and Cultural Planning Office 2007, 26). We also know that the social network of the potential recipient is an important factor in take-up rates. If an individual's friends or colleagues inform her of a certain public service, she is both more likely to pursue the benefits in question and less likely to feel stigmatized for applying for them (Currie 2003).

Proactive communication about services can also improve take-up rates. Researchers working in four different Dutch cities found that three of the four had a non-take-up-rate of around 24 percent. In one city, however, Nijmegen, the rate of non-take-up was only 8 percent. The researchers identified the role of the municipality's civil servants in seeking out potential recipients as the cause of these comparatively low non-take-up rates (van Oorschot 1994, 286). By contrast, there

Figure 7-1. *Finding the Target Group for a Policy*

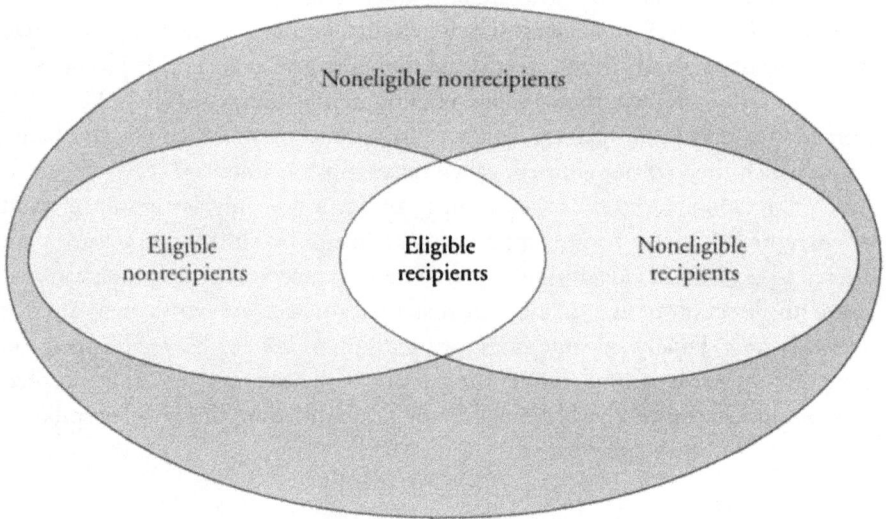

is evidence that higher levels of non-take-up result when potentially eligible recipients must initiate transactions with local government (Netherlands Social and Cultural Planning Office 2007, 37).

A study conducted by the Department for Work and Pensions (DWP) in the United Kingdom explains why some citizens are unwilling to ask for services to which they are entitled. Table 7-2 presents rates of non-take-up for different services. It shows general levels of take-up between 50 and 94 percent, while making an important distinction between caseload non-take-up and expenditure non-take-up. The first indicator focuses on the *number* of recipients per service, whereas the second identifies *the total amount* of money claimed. The two indicators point to unexpected results: citizens eligible for fewer benefits tend not to apply for any public relief. The more individuals are entitled to receive, the more likely they are to apply for benefits.

To analyze non-take-up further, the DWP commissioned additional research focusing specifically on ENRs of pension credit, an allowance for people with income or pensions under a certain threshold. According to this report, "One reason for non-take-up may be because pensioners are unaware of Pension Credit eligibility rules, and are not fully familiar with the circumstances in which they can claim. Of pensioners most likely to be ENRs, 13 percent believed (wrongly) that if you live with your adult children, you cannot apply for Pension Credit. Also, 17 percent thought that owning their own home would also make them ineligible for Pension Credit. Additionally, 14 percent believed that those who receive finan-

Table 7-2. *Take-Up, by Type of Public Service*

Percent

Public service	Take-up by caseload	Take-up by expenditure
Income support	83–94	90–97
Pension credit	61–69	72–97
Housing benefit	84–91	87–93
Council tax benefit	62–68	65–71
Job seeker's allowance	50–59	55–66

Source: Department for Work and Pensions, United Kingdom (2006a).

cial help from their families would be barred from claiming Pension Credit" (Department for Work and Pensions, United Kingdom, 2006b).

What can we discern from these findings about barriers to take-up? What explains the lower level of access to these services? The DWP's researchers conclude that the difficulty is not ignorance of Pension Credit program per se but rather widespread assumed ineligibility and concern over the program's effect on their other benefits. Many ENRs fear that claiming Pension Credit will actually worsen their living conditions because they may forfeit rights to other government services. In addition to these two primary barriers to take-up, according to the DWP research, a number of secondary obstacles also discourage PC participation, particularly the perceived complex and intrusive nature of the application process (see figure 7-2 on the next page).

Statistical Analysis of Subgroups within ENRs

Now that we have established that levels of non-take-up are high, indicating that access to government services is uneven, the next question arises: Is access or lack of access equally distributed across all citizens? Is the distribution of take-up and non-take-up random, or can we find a pattern?

Turning again to research conducted in the Netherlands, we can identify several answers to this question. As early as 1981, the Netherlands Social and Cultural Planning Office (SCP) had already begun to investigate which citizens were getting the most out of government. In the earliest reports, the conclusions were clear: the higher individuals' socioeconomic status, the greater the benefits they received from the state. Although public housing and social security funds were allocated to people with lower incomes, other services more than compensated for this. Wealthier families were able to send their children to secondary school and then to university whereas the children of poorer families had to begin work at sixteen. Because the Dutch state pays a large portion of each student's costs, a preponderant percentage of education funds went to higher-class families. Furthermore,

Figurre 7-2. *Map of Barriers to Claiming Pension Credit*

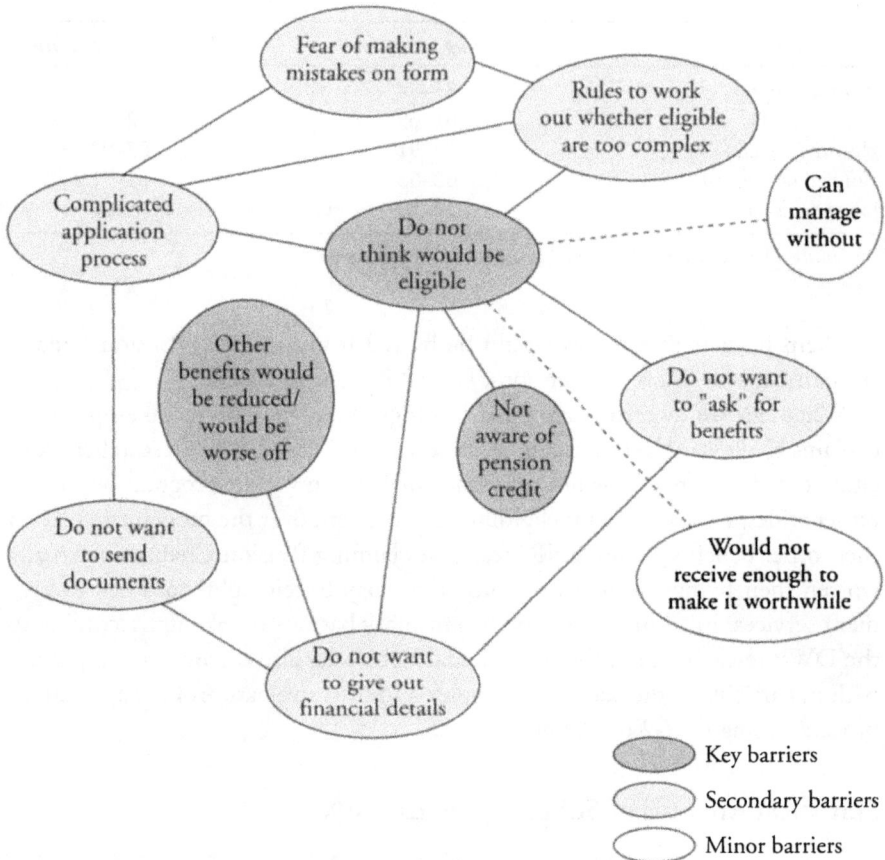

because interest paid on mortgages is tax deductible in Holland, individuals who owned their homes received substantial subsidies from the government—the larger the home, the larger the subsidy. The state spent half as much on public housing in 1981 as the amount it lost on tax deductions and subsidies for mortgages for private homes (Netherlands Social and Cultural Planning Office 1981).

In recent years this picture has been changing, partly because of new policies more explicitly directed at lower-income brackets, but also partly because of revised demographic definitions that make it difficult to gauge whether education funds are benefiting the poor or not. Students used to be included in the households of their parents for statistical purposes, but they are now calculated as separate entities. Because student incomes tend to be low across the board, it appears that the majority of the government's funds for education are going to less-advantaged individuals. In fact, however, most students continue to be from higher-income families, and their comparative poverty as students is a temporary

Table 7-3. *Relation between Demographic Characteristics and Non-Take-Up*

	Eligible NonRecipients (ENRs) (percent)	Recipients (percent)	Statistical significance (Kramer's V)
Sex			.006 (not significant)
Male	37	36	
Female	63	64	
Age			.07 (.003)
25–44	14	11	
45–64	44	41	
65 and older	42	48	
Educational level			.12 (.000)
Very low	52	43	
Low	18	21	
Medium	15	14	
Medium to high	5	8	
High	10	15	

exception in a lifetime of relatively high socioeconomic status. Analysis from the perspective of lifelong income would give quite a different picture.

Further research in the Netherlands examines non-take-up on the part of citizens who are handicapped or chronically ill. In cases when citizens spend above a given percentage of their income on medical expenses, these costs become tax-deductible. This service is not well known and carries a relatively high administrative burden. Let us consider how the non-take-up is distributed in this case. Table 7-3 shows the main demographic differences in non-take-up, with ENRs divided into different subgroups.

We can see from table 7-3 that non-take-up, as one aspect of lack of access, is not equally distributed across all demographics. Age is an important factor. Younger people have a lower level of access than expected, and older people enjoy greater access. Of course, the specific nature of the public service being studied (tax deduction to compensate for high health-related expenditures) may skew these conclusions, because younger people tend to be healthier and more highly educated. Nevertheless, according to these data, the inverse correlation between age and access is clear, as is the correlation between lower socioeconomic status and poorer access to services. The difference in access between men and women is statistically insignificant.

Other studies have generated contrary evidence. In a study on non-take-up of a rent subsidy conducted by the SCP in 2007, statisticians found that lower income corresponded with higher degrees of take-up, possibly because the program was a

Table 7-4. *Level of Non-Take-Up in Relation to Level of Income*
Percent

Level of non-take-up	Level of income (relative to minimum income)
18	Lower than 105
31	Between 105 and 130
41	Above 130

Source: SCP (2007).

widely known, heavily communicated, and actively delivered public service (see table 7-4).

Again, however, this difference can be explained in the context of the service being studied. We have already seen that smaller benefits reduce the chance that individuals will take advantage of the benefit. In the case of the rent subsidy, higher total income translates to a proportionally smaller benefit that does not provide enough incentive for many people in this demographic to apply for it.

Theories of Public Administration and Non-Take-Up?

We have established that non-take-up exists and that non-take-up is not randomly distributed. Now, a third question arises: What can public administration tell us about this problem? The two main themes within administration are public policy and organization. Policy must determine the initial parameters of "who gets what, when, and how," while organizations are required for the implementation of the policy. For the purposes of this chapter, the policy is clear: those who are entitled to a public service should receive it. There is (or should be) no explicit policy creating unequal access. Instead, we must turn to organizations for explanations, because if there is unequal access, it arises either at the level of organizational implementation or from the recipients themselves.

Max Weber and the Rational Legal Bureaucracy

For the exercise of power, an apparatus is needed. According to Max Weber, policymakers require organizations with monocratic (centralized) leadership in order to become effective. The organization characterizing modern Western democracies for Weber is the rational legal bureaucracy, which is strictly hierarchical, standardized, centralized, specialized, and formalized. Its political leaders are responsible for the bureaucracy's substantial rationality—the "what," the political and ideological choices to be made. Its managers are responsible for the organization's functional rationality—the "how," the means by which political goals can be achieved, tactics identified, and policy executed; in other words, operations.

Weber (1920/1972) argues that rational legal bureaucracy in its purest form is by far the most precise, continuous, disciplined, strict, trustworthy, and multipurpose organizational form to realize political goals (128). More specifically, he claims that management through such bureaucracies means that services will be delivered irrespective of the personal convictions of the bureaucrats delivering them. As Weber puts it, *sine ira et studio*—"without anger or enthusiasm" (129).

In its most extreme and purified form, the task of the civil servant is the dutiful execution of policy, regardless of personal belief. The fundamental characteristic of Weber's civil servants, then, much like workers in private enterprise according to Marx, is that they do not possess the means of production. Rather, the tools of government are in the hands of democratically elected political powers. In a state employing rational legal bureaucracy as a model, the civil servant works "more or less like a 'paragraph machine.' Inputs are the law, the facts, the costs and the taxes. Outputs are authoritative decisions and the explication of the legal arguments on which the decisions are based" (Weber 1920/1972, 824–25). Weber stresses the bureaucrat's rational, formalistic reasoning.

Civil servants base their decisions on two types of knowledge: *Dienstwissen* ("service knowledge," gained within the bureaucracy) and *Fachwissen* (technical knowledge or expertise in a subject area). For Weber, the development of a highly trained corps of bureaucrats was necessary in the process of modernization (see Jacobi 1969). As nations developed out of centralized monarchies, this professionalization permitted knowledgeable government workers to appropriate the tools of governance from the landed aristocracy to create democratic, unified states with a "caged king" as a figurehead. As the bureaucratic class developed, further measures curtailing the power of the king and his court emerged, including civil rights and the rule of law. Finally, liberal revolutions reduced the political powers of the military, police, and the legal system. Thus, the nation-state and the modern citizen were born.

In theory, these developments freed the citizenry from the despotic powers of the king and aristocracy, which were so characteristic of absolutist periods of state formation (the ancien régime). In the wake of these reforms and liberal revolutions, citizens could ostensibly speak out freely, start their own businesses, or even begin their own political movement. Yet anyone who has read Franz Kafka's novel *The Trial (Der Prozess)* will recognize the risks inherent in a bureaucracy without a division of powers or mechanisms to protect the individual against red tape and judicial abuse. The protagonist, Josef K., is arrested, but never receives a formal indictment. He goes to court, but does not know how to defend himself. His lawyers' mystifying assertions that he is influencing people in "the right places" lead nowhere, and the protagonist himself is powerless before layer upon layer of opaque procedures. Every move he makes leads inexorably to his own conviction and ultimate execution. Even though Kafka's work is largely metaphorical, the genuine real-life desperation of being caught in an unending and threatening bureaucracy resonates with individuals across the world. Despite Weber's idealistic interpretation, large-scale bureaucracies can lead to loss of personal freedom and can even be life–threatening, for example, if a dictator takes political control of a state's bureaucratic apparatus.

Weber's Normative View vs. Empirical Reality

If the story in Kafka's *The Trial* can be true, then Weber's theory cannot be. In the empirical material we presented on non-take-up we uncovered some interesting indicators of bureaucratic malfunction: ENRs fear paperwork, yes, but even more, they worry that new entitlements may interfere with their existing rights. They do not want to change their current positions because they are afraid of Kafkaesque entanglements springing from the will of individual bureaucrats, all coming from different organizations with their own sets of rules. This prospect becomes all the more daunting when an individual's own bureaucratic competence is low, as is the case with those from lower socioeconomic backgrounds. They do not trust that they can win out in battles with public servants (Scheepers 1990), so they refrain from applying at all. Getting access to benefits appears to them to be too risky.

Max Weber is a proponent of formal, rationalist organizations, but other writers advocate different perspectives. More recent thinking—for example, the Human Relations School, focusing on informal group processes (Roethlisberger and Dickson 1934)—have introduced more empirical approaches to the study of organizations and have found that formal hierarchical structures are not key to organizational performance.

In the traditional debate on organizational structure, a key variable is the strength of central control throughout an organization. Joan Woodward (1965) first studied the relationship between organizational structure and technology, discovering that structure shifted from nonhierarchical to hierarchical and back to nonhierarchical, depending on the degree and intensity of an organization's use of technology. When organizations produce customized units such as a house, a ship, or a hand-manufactured car, simple informal structures with lots of horizontal communication tend to evolve. Such organizations also tend to be relatively low-tech. By contrast, organizations that produce "batches" of a product—say, 100,000 units of a specific model of car—are more likely to develop strict, vertical, mechanistic bureaucracies. Naturally these organizations must use some degree of technology to produce their products. A third type of organization, the process-technology organization, produces goods not by unit but by quantity (for example, gallons of milk or gasoline, pounds of sugar and so on); they also employ a maximum level of technology. Here Woodward once again found informal and nonhierarchical organizational structures, but of a very different nature than in the first type of organization. In this case, highly specialized professionals run the machines that in turn manage a continuous flow of production by maintaining a connection with one another. These professionals generally share backgrounds (for example, chemistry), and the machines store their collective knowledge. Production protocols are a part of the shared, consolidated knowledge infrastructure. Thus, horizontal and informal communication becomes more important than hierarchical positions and vertical communication. In such an organization, we find a more or less organic structure with a high level of central control brought about by the organization's technology.

Lawrence and Lorsch (1967) argue that performance depends on the ability of an organization to cope with its environment. Each organizational subsystem adapts to the part of its environment that is most relevant to the subsystem in question, meaning that the degree of differentiation among subsystems is a function of the organization's context. Thus, if an organizational environment is complex, dynamic, and highly interdependent, the organization tends to decentralize its decisionmaking power by introducing boundary spanners and other coordination mechanisms. From a structural point of view, such an organization resembles Mintzberg's (1979) professional bureaucracy, with an informal, organic structure and little central control. By contrast, organizations with simple, steady, and noninterdependent environments give rise to structures reminiscent of Mintzberg's machine bureaucracy.[2]

So, perhaps we can apply Weber's theories to organizations with static and noninterdependent environments, whereas Mintzberg's professional bureaucracy model becomes more applicable to organizations operating in dynamic, complex, and interdependent environments. In such cases the strategic apex of the organization cannot oversee and direct everything and must delegate formal power (the power to decide who gets what, when, and how). As trained professionals become responsible for the execution of increasingly complex tasks, the organization develops a horizontal and decentralized structure. Vocational training and the ability to assess rapidly changing situations (*Fachwissen* and *Dienstwissen*) help these professionals perform their tasks.

Lipsky: The Street-Level Bureaucrat

Michael Lipsky describes precisely this latter type of organization, formulating the notion of a street-level bureaucracy staffed by public servants who must work in an environment of complexity, dynamism, and interdependency. Street-level

---

2. Mintzberg integrates many insights in the relation between organizational environment and organizational structure. Two important configurations are the machine bureaucracy in a stable, noncomplex, and noninterdependent environment, and the professional bureaucracy in a dynamic, complex, and interdependent environment.

bureaucrats face more needs than they can meet and more demands than they have resources to fill, so they need to develop coping strategies. They retain discretionary powers, which are in essence political powers and should not be allotted to bureaucrats (at least in Weber's view). It is uncertain that they will use this discretion as the political powers intended. There is endless negotiation with policymakers, as street-level bureaucrats can make it appear that they are meeting targets while they in fact maintain a fair degree of license in interpreting policy. As confirmed by an American study conducted by Steven Maynard-Moody and Michael Musheno (2003), street-level workers "actually make policy choices rather than simply implement the decisions of elected officials." On the basis of a study of forty-eight street-level state employees in two states, investigators concluded that street-level bureaucrats' beliefs and prejudices about the people with whom they interact continually influence both their execution of policies and rules and their treatment of citizens.

The Street-Level Bureaucrat and Non-Take-Up

Can we depend on street-level bureaucrats to solve the problem of non-take-up? On the one hand, they might argue that the norms of their vocation would incline them to show solidarity with their clientele, especially that part of the clientele that is also trustworthy and in need. On the other hand, the prevalence of coping strategies and the continuous negotiations with management could lead to goal displacement as street-level bureaucrats try to operate successfully between management and clients. Such pressures can lead the street-level bureaucrat to help only clients who are easiest to assist, which almost by definition excludes eligible nonrecipients. ENRs are precisely the clients who will not come to the street-level bureaucrat on their own initiative; they are the clients who do not know where to go for help or who are anxious about seeking out more aid. Once they do arrive, their situations are generally complex, with many potentially conflicting eligibilities, none of which may be particularly financially valuable. For the street-level bureaucrat, the ENRs' cases present a difficult challenge, sometimes with little result for either the beneficiary or the bureaucrat. Add to these factors the low level of bureaucratic competence many lower-socioeconomic-class ENRs exhibit, and we can see that helping ENRs may not coincide with the interests of many street-level bureaucrats. To summarize our findings so far, there is a high level of non-take-up, distributed unevenly across social classes, leaving individuals with lower socioeconomic status and low bureaucratic competence less able to access public services. Classic bureaucracy theory does not acknowledge this problem, and modern organization theory leaves its solution to the discretion and personal ethics of professional public servants. However, empirical studies of street-level bureaucrat capacities indicate that they will not be responsive to the problem of non-take-up, a challenge that remains unsolved.

In Search of a Solution to Non-Take-Up

If innovators want to establish effective policies with high levels of take-up but they cannot count on either formal organizations or street-level bureaucrats to achieve their goals, what can be done? Two case studies of new efforts to fight non-take-up are suggestive.

Innovation 1: Using IT Infrastructure to Facilitate Parking Permits for the Handicapped (Belgium)

In Belgium, disabled persons must apply for a special parking permit once every ten years to be allowed to park in designated parking lots in the vicinity of shops, museums, schools, and so on. It is estimated that about 40,000 applications are processed annually and that 200,000 of these special permits are currently in use. The administrative procedure can be complex, and the amount of time it takes depends on the reason of the application:

—Five weeks if the applicant has lost his or her original permit

—Five weeks if the applicant is renewing a permit

—Five months for a new permit, because of extensive, labor-intensive information-gathering procedures

To apply, clients must fill out a set of forms, file a dossier, and procure a special declaration determining the status of their handicaps.

Belgium maintains the Crossroads Bank, an organization that connects all the data of 2,000 public organizations involved in at least one of 182 public service-delivery products. The bank does not itself collect personal data, but it can find and collect dossiers from its affiliated organizations on any and all public service beneficiaries if requested to do so by another institution in its network. To protect the security of service recipients, the bank only delivers these data if the organization has a legal mandate to gain access to a client's data.

All disabled people with driver's licenses who also own cars can be traced through the Crossroads Bank's network, and innovators realized that non-take-up could be avoided by using data already available from other service agencies. The state apparatus decreed that all 25,000 eligible disabled individuals would receive their parking permits automatically. This case typifies a proactive form of service delivery, in which individuals get a service without having to ask for it. Beneficiaries do not need to be aware of their rights nor fill in lengthy forms nor visit crowded offices. The street-level bureaucrat's discretion and resistance never become an issue in this form of service provision because it entirely obviates the necessity for client-bureaucrat interaction. It provides maximum accessibility and efficiency without employing a large number of civil employees. Moreover, to further reduce the administrative burden of issuing parking permits to disabled drivers, Belgian policymakers resolved that everyone with a permanent disability would receive a lifelong parking permit, one that would not expire after a term of ten years. Clearly it is very unlikely that a person who has had the misfortune to lose her legs will grow them back again!

Innovation 2: Lower Energy Prices for People with Low Socioeconomic Status (Belgium)

A second initiative, also from Belgium, has not yet been completely implemented at this time. It will also employ the Crossroads Bank network to provide reductions in energy and gas prices for low-income Belgians who are eligible to receive this cost relief; of 300,000 who are eligible only 200,000 are currently taking advantage of it—a 33 percent non-take-up rate. (The subsidies are paid out of a central fund to which all users of gas and electricity contribute and from which companies can reclaim their reductions.) As in the case of parking permits for the disabled, the solution is simple: gas and electricity companies will send their user lists (clients will be identifiable only by number) to the Crossroads Bank, which will return the lists with an indicator showing eligible nonrecipients who should be getting the price reductions.

Although this solution appears simple, implementation of the service has been delayed by the intervention of politics into policy. Non-take-up is cheaper for the government than full service provision, and if the number of claimants for this reduction goes up, an extra 100 million euros may be needed to defray the cost, leading to higher fees of all Belgian clients of the energy companies. Currently the issue is the subject of intense political debate, but during an election season, no politician will dare to demand extra expenditures. A compromise has been reached whereby ENRs have been identified and will receive notifications by mail requesting that they file a form for their gas and electricity reductions at a local government office. Yet as long as bureaucrats insist on paper forms and office visits for this service, the level of non-take-up will stay high. This leads to a perverse impasse: the policy pretends to help those in need, but street-level bureaucrats and their requirement of paper forms obstruct and prevent people from accessing their rights. Bureaucrats are cheaper than the subsidies or entitlements they grant (Dumortier and others 2006).

Innovation 3: Expansion of the Tax Administration (Netherlands)

The Dutch equivalent of Belgium's Crossroads Bank is the Tax Administration, which has a high level of "*Dienstwissen*": it knows everything about all the taxpayers! Until recently, public service policy implementation was under the jurisdiction of various government organizations, but in recent years all services have been brought together under the Tax Administration. In the first year of this new situation, the Tax Administration suffered high levels of non-take-up for its new services. Reformers in both chambers of parliament decided to use records of past service applications to identify individuals with rights to benefits they were not getting. One such search generated over 6 million names of potential recipients of a benefit. They all received a form in the mail that they had only to sign and return to the government. In the following year, if their circumstances had not changed, they did not have to submit a second form to receive the grant again. The Tax Administration received 5,200,000 forms back and approved 4,200,000 new beneficiaries for the grant.

Although the details of this case study remain incomplete, what is clear is that the level of non-take-up is dropping thanks to this kind of proactive service delivery. By providing fully automated services, administrators can also eliminate excessive paperwork and lengthy office visits for clients. The state has been able to raise take-up rates by using available client information and by redesigning its apparatus for service delivery. In this case, parliament will pay the extra costs of more efficient and widespread service provision.

Analysis

These innovations provide evidence that non-take-up rates can be reduced. Introducing automatic service delivery without using too much paper or personnel has proved to be very effective. Such initiatives can be implemented by using information available from other service organizations to identify potentially eligible clients. Since interoperability (the ability to exchange data electronically) has already been enhanced by the increasing numbers of government forms available online, the execution of public policy no longer needs to depend on professional bureaucrats—what Lipsky calls street-level bureaucrats. These street-level bureaucracies are being replaced by what we can call *infocracies* (see Zuurmond 1994; Zuurmond and Snellen 1997), which base their decisions on previously collected information and which work impartially, characterized by Weber as "*sine ira et studio.*" Computers are by nature as impartial as the ideal bureaucrat aspires to be: they neither produce coping strategies nor do they bring their own prejudices to the implementation of policy.

Introducing an efficient information infrastructure and redesigning an organization's work processes does, however, require increased expenditures for program costs as a greater proportion of eligible clients receive their benefits. High levels of non-take-up mean low costs for the public organization involved. One way to cover such expenditures is the automation of service delivery: as fewer bureaucrats are required, operation costs drop. If fully automated, most of the procedures discussed in these case studies require scarcely any personnel. There is one caveat to the automation of service delivery, which is that individual program designers become very important to the interpretation of policy in such models. In translating the rules of the law into algorithms, they exercise discretion much as street-level bureaucrats used to do. Because of these designers' power, some writers call them "system-level bureaucrats"—they decide who gets what, when, and how (Bovens and Zouridis 2002).

Enhancement of access cannot be achieved within existing budgets, and this places policy execution back into the realm of political debate. In some cases there will not be sufficient funds for new initiatives, leading politicians to continue to rely on paper forms and leading street-level bureaucrats to obstruct full access to services and accepting non-take-up. As long as bureaucrats are cheaper than maximum accessibility to public services, ENRs of low socioeconomic status will not receive the full extent of aid available to them.

Conclusions

We can draw several conclusions from these analyses. First, non-take-up is not a negligible problem; in fact, in some cases 30 percent to 50 percent of eligible service recipients do not benefit from their rights. Lack of access is a serious challenge primarily affecting citizens with lower socioeconomic class backgrounds.

Second, non-take-up rates and demographics vary according to the kind of service involved and the perceived obstacles to the service that prevent ENRs from applying for benefits. The greatest difficulty is not lack of knowledge of a program's existence but lack of a clear overview of the consequences of accessing services. ENRs often feel uncomfortable with large bureaucracies and fear Kafkaesque entanglements and red tape, so they avoid as many interactions with service providers as they can. We have found that services with proactive communication strategies such as in the city of Nijmegen can reduce non-take-up dramatically.

Classic theories of bureaucracy do not acknowledge the problem of non-take-up, since these theories presuppose that individual discretion plays no part in policy execution. We have seen, however, that street-level bureaucrats have discretion, and that in some cases they are neither able nor willing to help all clients asking for assistance. To deal with the problem of insufficient time and resources and in order to survive, they develop coping strategies and interpret policy. We cannot rely on street-level bureaucrats to solve the problem of non-take-up because they are not institutionally positioned to address the issue. Indeed, it seems likely that many citizens with genuine needs never even reach the stage of seeking out such a bureaucrat, further exacerbating the problem of non-take-up.

In the case studies presented in this chapter, we witnessed a new approach to access that makes use of interorganizational information sharing to locate eligible citizens and grant rights directly and automatically to them. This is called proactive service delivery. Successful initiatives in Belgium and the Netherlands have demonstrated that reusing information already available to public organizations makes it possible to identify whole target groups for service delivery. Using these infrastructures, administrators can reduce non-take-up to 0 percent, excluding no one who is eligible for benefits and ensuring that lower-class status and lack of bureaucratic competence do not snare individuals in the poverty trap.

Nonetheless, this goal of eliminating non-take-up generates its own problems. Such programs need fewer employees and more money. If politicians cannot find extra funds to provide for ENRs coming into the system, street-level bureaucrats persist in reducing access to services to maintain the budgetary status quo. If supplementary funds can be made available, procedures for service delivery can be redesigned to reduce the number of bureaucrats involved and maximize take-up.

By redesigning organizational processes, innovators are creating new models for service-delivery apparatuses called infocracies. These infocracies are process-oriented organizations working in interorganizational value chains and using shared information infrastructures. They are reminiscent of Woodward's process-technology organizations, but they deal in public service, not heavy chemistry,

These infocracies are making street-level bureaucrats and their crowded offices obsolete as they are replaced with system- or even sector-level bureaucrats whose discretion lies in the design of systems for policy execution. This hidden discretion at the level of implementation creates a new frontier for necessary political debate, which has yet to begin.

Finally, perhaps we can consider the difference between Weber's and Lipsky's philosophies of administration to be a result of their different perspectives. Weber is normative: he describes how bureaucracies should work. Lipsky is empirical, describing how a bureaucracy actually works. Of course, Weber knows that reality does not bear out his narrative, but he is less interested in how administration does work and more in how it should work. He does not entrust decisionmaking power to bureaucrats, insisting that they might not be utterly impartial nor untouched by political concerns. Lipsky demonstrates the validity of Weber's concerns by uncovering the problematic aspects of the high degrees of discretion enjoyed by traditional street-level bureaucrats.

If we understand organizational structures as answers to certain societal problems such as lack of access, perhaps we can discern why this completely new organizational form, the infocracy, is emerging now. The infocracy is cheaper, more effective, and more obedient to its political masters than rational legal bureaucracies. It can implement responsive and efficient strategies in the face of complex, dynamic, and interdependent organizational environments. The infocracy gives higher degrees of access to a wider range of citizens across economic and social classes. Still, it is not a panacea: the infocracy offers fewer jobs and is more costly than traditional bureaucracy in that it engages more clients: with full take-up, the amount of budget claimed can be much higher than when there is a clear level of non-take-up. Its development should therefore be a matter of political, rather than administrative, debate.

References

Bovens, M., and S. Zouridis. 2002. "From Street-Level to System-Level Bureaucracies: How Information and Communication Technology Is Transforming Administrative Discretion and Constitutional Control." *Public Administration Review* 62, no. 2: 174–84.

Currie, J. 2003. "The Take-Up of Social Benefits." Paper presented at the conference in honor of Eugene Smolensky, held at Berkeley, December 12 and 13. Los Angeles: UCLA.

Department for Work and Pensions (United Kingdom). 2006a. *Pension Credit Estimates of Take-Up in 2005–2005.* London.

———. 2006b. *Understanding the Relationship between the Barriers and the Triggers to Claiming Pension Credit.* DWP Research Report 336. London.

Dumortier, C., S. Meyer, B. Demeyer, and K. Bacchus. 2006. *Comparative Study of Energy Policies and Instruments.* [In Dutch.] Brussel/Leuven: Centre d'Études Économiques et Sociales de l'Environnement and Higher Institute for Labour Studies.

Jacobi, H. 1969. *Die Bürokratisierung der Welt: Ein Beitrag zur Problemgeschichte.* [The bureaucratization of the world: A contribution to the history of the problem.] Neuwied: Luchterhand.

Kerr, S. 1983. *Making Ends Meet: An Investigation into the Non-Claiming of Supplementary Pensions.* London: Bedford Square Press.

Lasswell, H. D. 1935. *Politics: Who Gets What, When, How.* New York: McGraw-Hill.

Lawrence, P., and J. Lorsch. 1967. "Differentiation and Integration in Complex Organisations." *Administrative Science Quarterly* 12: 1–30.

Lipsky, M. 1980. *Street-Level Bureaucracy: The Dilemmas of the Individual in Public Services.* New York: Russell Sage Foundation.

Maynard-Moody, S., and M. Musheno. 2003. *Cops, Teachers, Counselors: Stories from the Front Lines of Public Service.* University of Michigan Press.

Mintzberg, H. 1979. *The Structuring of Organizations.* Englewood Cliffs, N.J.: Prentice-Hall.

Netherlands Social and Cultural Planning Office. 1981. *Profiting from Government.* [In Dutch.] The Hague.

———. 1997. *Poverty Monitor 1997.* [In Dutch.] The Hague.

———. 2007. *Money on the Shelf.* [In Dutch.] The Hague.

Roethlisberger, F. J., and W. J. Dickson. 1934. *Management and the Worker: Technical vs. Social Organization in an Industrial Plant.* Harvard University Press.

Scheepers. 1990. *Informatization and the Bureaucratic Competence of the Citizen.* [In Dutch.] Tilburg.

van Oorschot, W. J. H. 1994. *Take It or Leave It: A Study of Non-Take-Up of Social Security Benefits.* Tilburg: Tilburg University Press.

van Oorschot, W. J. H., and P. Kolkhuis Tanke. 1989. Non-take-up and Social Security—Fact, Theories, Research Methods: An Overview of the State of Affairs in Netherlands and Abroad. [In Dutch.] The Hague: Ministry of Social Affairs.

Weber, M. 1972. *Wirtschaft und Gesellschaft: Grundriß der Verstehenden Soziologie.* [Economy and society: Foundations of interpretive sociology.] Tübingen.

Woodward, J. 1965. *Industrial Organization: Theory and Practice.* Oxford University Press.

Zuurmond, A. 1994. "The Infocracy: A Theoretical and Empirical Reorientation on Max Weber's Ideal Type in the Information Age." [In Dutch.] Erasmus University, Rotterdam.

Zuurmond, A., and I. Th. M. Snellen. 1997. "From Bureaucracy to Infocracy." In *Beyond BPR in Public Administration: Institutional Transformation in an Information Age,* edited by J. A. Taylor, I. Th. M. Snellen, and A. Zuurmond, 205–24. Amsterdam: IOS Press.

8

Providing Services to the Marginalized: Anatomy of an Access Paradox

ALBERT JAN KRUITER AND JORRIT DE JONG

> To understand street-level bureaucracy one must study the routines and
> subjective responses street-level bureaucrats develop in order to cope
> with the difficulties and ambiguities of their jobs.
>
> —Michael Lipsky,
> *Street Level Bureaucracy: Dilemmas of the Individual in Public Services*

Bureaucracies have problems with marginalized people, and vice versa. Even when assisted by adequately funded, well-intentioned programs with eager social workers, marginalized individuals typically have a hard time escaping from poverty and societal disenfranchisement. Quite often their situations deteriorate precisely because of the misdirected "help" offered by social or human services. The design, delivery, management, and accountability of these services are not compatible with the multiple, complex, and interrelated structural problems facing the marginalized. Families with behavioral problems, the homeless, the mentally ill,

This chapter is based on research that was conducted in the Netherlands by Albert Jan Kruiter, J. de Jong, J. van Niel, and C. Hijzen, and published in 2008 as *De Rotonde van Hamed; Maatwerk voor mensen met meerdere problemen* (*Hamed's roundabout: Customized solutions for people with multiple problems*). This research was funded by G27, an association of twenty-seven medium-large cities in the Netherlands. An earlier version of the chapter was presented to the Network of Innovators in the Mediterranean Region (InnovMed) convened by the United Nations Department of Economic and Social Affairs, Division of Public Administration, in Dubrovnik, April 25, 2008.

drug addicts, and unemployed and underage school dropouts all share at least one problem in common: they don't fit into the service-provision molds of standardized bureaucracies. Professionals working with these clients often feel that they are victims of an access paradox: there are plenty of resources to help the marginalized, but rules and regulations often inhibit the provision of adequate care. Many professionals fear that they have become part of the problem instead of part of the solution. In this chapter we examine the nature of this access paradox. We will also draw lessons from successful attempts to create tailor-made solutions for marginalized people based on research we did in thirteen Dutch cities.[1]

Many Problems, Many Agencies

Maurice is not fit enough to work, and he and his wife, Alice, have five children to support. Maurice and Alice are in serious debt. Because they owe the tax authority a great deal of money, they have enrolled in a debt rehabilitation scheme that allows them to spend only one euro a day per person. A financial coach monitors their expenses and decides how much their allowance for the month should be. Alice works one day a week as a cleaning lady and Maurice is on welfare. The law stipulates that welfare recipients must apply for work while accepting benefits, forcing Maurice to seek employment even though his physician has recommended that he stay home and rest. In an effort to resolve these conflicts, a social worker suggests that Maurice start volunteer employment in order to practice working regular hours.

Whatever Maurice does, he cannot satisfy the demands of all the people trying to help him. In fact, he is always violating at least some of the rules to which he is subject simply because the programs and policies that apply to his situation are not in sync with one another. In his own words, Maurice has "his back against the wall."[2]

Maurice's story is typical of people with multiple problems in the Netherlands. It is hard to find the exact number of individuals living under circumstances like these, because there are no reliable statistics for this category. "Marginalized people with multiple problems" inherently show up in multiple-policy categories and derivative statistics. Agencies rarely combine and filter their statistics for this "category," but experts estimate that between 35,000 and 70,000 Dutch families (or between 160,000 and 170,000 people) deal with multiple structural problems in their daily lives.[3] Furthermore, these difficulties are almost always interrelated. To

1. The cities are Leeuwarden, Groningen, Zwolle, Deventer, Enschede, Hengelo, Arnhem, Heerlen, Eindhoven, Nijmegen, Dordrecht, Zaanstad, and Leiden.
2. We interviewed over twenty-five people in situations similar to Maurice's. Maurice's story has been simplified for the sake of brevity, and the names have been changed in order to protect the privacy of the people involved.
3. Dutch National Parliament, Second Chamber (2006). In *The Social State of the Netherlands, 2007,* the Netherlands Social and Cultural Planning Office (2007, 284) examines the relationship between

take an extreme example, drug addicts who need a lot of money may get into debt and lose their jobs, their homes, their belongings, and, finally, the underlying structure and rhythm governing their lives. Less serious problems often follow similar patterns: someone who drops out of school without a diploma will have fewer opportunities in the job market and may apply for social benefits earlier than someone who decides to stay in school. Individuals can be unfortunate and they can create their own difficulties; often, with marginalized people, it is a combination of both. Nonetheless, those already facing uncertainty on the edges of society tend to be magnets for even more challenges.

This cycle of structural challenges is not only a problem for those directly affected. Their environments also suffer: families with behavioral problems are often nuisances to their neighbors. Drug addicts engage in criminal behavior. School dropouts do not realize their full societal and economic potential. Thus, providing public services to the marginalized is not only an act of solidarity, humanity, and benevolence, but it is also a way to maintain community order and to invest in society (Figueira-McDonough 2007, 15).

The problems of marginalized individuals may be interrelated, but the remedies provided by the welfare state's organizations often are not. Many agencies operate strictly within the politically or bureaucratically constructed boundaries of their policy domains or jurisdictions. Organizations that are most often involved in assisting marginalized people with multiple problems can be listed by domain. Health-care service providers include autonomous general practitioners, municipal health-care services, mental health services, hospitals, drug addict care centers, social rehabilitation centers, crisis intervention teams, homeless shelters, parent coaching organizations, youth care agencies, youth care administration agencies, insurance companies, assessment agencies, home care agencies, and many other local and regional organizations and initiatives. In the domain of housing and neighborhood policy, key organizations include housing corporations, municipal housing services, crisis relocation services, mediators, neighborhood social work initiatives, and numerous other entities charged with preventing or resolving neighborhood conflict and tensions in the social sphere. Marginalized people also interact regularly with agencies of labor and social security, such as the Department of Public Benefits, debt rehabilitation agencies, special social benefits agencies, the Centers for Labor and Income, the Social Security Administration Agency, national and local tax authorities, and several one-stop shops serving special target groups. Specialized human and social service organizations include groups promoting social and cultural participation in neighborhoods, traditional social workers, youth social workers, women's social workers, and services for seniors, disabled, or traumatized people. The educational domain offers a range of services:

income, education, and labor-market position. One of the conclusions it reaches is that 2 percent of the Dutch population under sixty-five years of age faces a cumulative-problem situation in all three areas.

schools for primary, secondary, special, adult, and vocational education, remedial teaching services, municipal initiatives against truancy, regional centers for coordination of anti-truancy and anti-dropout policies, and public and private programs for the motivation, training, and reintegration of school dropouts, the unemployed, and those in special categories such as immigrants, former inmates, and so on. Law enforcement agencies encompass police departments, public prosecutors, bureaus for alternative penalties, child-protective services, parole officers, bailiffs, and neighborhood surveillance offices. We also must not overlook private initiatives by charity organizations or religious groups that offer services to the marginalized in many of these fields, including the Salvation Army, food banks, and immigrant advocacy groups.

This list of organizations is far from comprehensive, and in every city the catalogue will look different, but the vast range of services canvassed gives us an impression of the sheer number of agencies faced by those with difficulties in multiple domains. An individual who has run away from home because of domestic violence, who left school without a diploma, and who wants to apply for social benefits may easily wind up doing intake interviews at three or more offices. If this individual also has a criminal record, children, health problems, and debts, soon fifteen or twenty organizations will be involved in one way or another. The complexity of the client's situation is reflected in the involvement of numerous specialized agencies and professionals. In one of the cities in which we conducted research, we interviewed a man who had been in contact with forty-two different organizations in a period of five years. None of these organizations was aware of this profusion, but all agreed that it was not in the best interest of the client.

It is hard to calculate accurately what the efforts of these organizations cost overall. On the basis of our previously quoted population figure of 160,000 to 170,000 people with multiple problems and of case studies of the direct costs of helping such individuals, we estimate that the Dutch government spends 3.3 billion euros annually on this group (20,000 euros per capita). In terms of results and policy outcomes, though, none of the respondents in our research who worked for these agencies could argue decisively that the money led to structural improvement for their clients.

The dilemma facing service providers in the Netherlands is this: there is much help available, but very few services are effective, which wastes both public funds and professional energies. This is one important reason to scrutinize the service-delivery system. But there is another reason. People with problems in multiple domains may present extraordinary challenges for the delivery system at large, but situations that are less complex and serious frequently encounter similar obstacles in terms of lack of cooperation and coordination between organizations. Cases of marginalized people with multiple problems, extreme though they may be, can also expose mechanisms impeding public managers and professionals from delivering adequate services to average clients, those with much simpler problems.

Mismatch of Problems and Responses

The Dutch welfare state is both highly institutionalized and highly specialized (de Swaan 1988). Many organizations are responsible for various subcategories of social problems and human needs. Very few organizations focus on the *relations between* these needs and problems. As a consequence, the challenges facing marginalized people with multiple difficulties are managed separately. Every agency has its own domain of expertise and its professional staff act accordingly. People with relatively few problems or special needs tend to benefit from this specialization, since specialization and standardization of procedures improve agency efficiency and customer orientation in public service. However, those with more numerous problems suffer disadvantages from these very same features. They fit into neither one category nor another, they deviate from bureaucratic standards, and they often demand exceptions to institutional rules.

Pol Ghesquière's research (1993) on individuals with multiple public service needs shows that the bureaucracy associated with institutional solutions often presents a problem in its own right for beneficiaries (5). Our research provided many corroborations for these findings: for example, we interviewed a man with psychological problems and an addiction to drugs who was told he could not see a psychiatrist until he quit abusing substances. However, he also could not enroll in a rehab center until he dealt with his psychological problems. This Catch-22 situation became an additional source of anxiety for the addict, aggravating his fears and making it harder for him to quit using drugs.

We also spoke with a sixteen-year-old boy who dropped out of school but wanted to go back. He had neither an income of his own nor parents who could help him, so he applied for public benefits. When he began school again, he lost his right to welfare because he was no longer available for the labor market. Desperate for money, the boy dropped out of school again. A second teenager whom we interviewed was caught in a similar trap. He had racked up serious debts several years ago and was living on the streets as a result, incurring several tickets for loitering and sleeping in public places. After two years he got back on track, found a place to live, and even sought to attend school again. Social workers, schoolteachers, and welfare officers all supported his plans, but the unpaid tickets followed him, and charges were finally brought against him for delinquency of payment. He was convicted and sentenced to house arrest and had to drop out of school again.

An Access Paradox

Despite a range of efforts at coordination by public service agencies and extensive communication between individual professionals, people with service needs in multiple domains typically lack access to adequate care and assistance. We call this "the access paradox." The structural mismatch between the nature of such a person's problems and the institutional capacity to deal with them inhibits both people with multiple difficulties and the professionals trying to help them. Instead of alleviating their situations, bureaucratic rules and regulations seem to add to their problems. To better understand this access paradox and to explore the potential for improvement, we spoke with over four hundred people involved in social services, including a sample of the clients they are attempting to serve. We conducted policy analysis, workflow analysis, case studies, semistructured interviews, and case-based group interviews in thirteen Dutch cities. We found that the group interviews, so-called "pressure-cooker sessions," provided much insight into the workings of individual agencies and their professionals. In many cases, the street-level workers, managers, policymakers, and politicians who convened in these sessions were exchanging concerns, views, and ideas in a systematic way for the first time.[4] The pressure-cooker meetings functioned as laboratories in which the anatomy of an exemplary case was dissected and discussed. One of the recurring analyses by participants in all thirteen cities was that deviant cases were often forced by "the system" to fit into a preconceived mold. The uniqueness of each situation had to be ignored to make such complex cases fit the standard. In the process, agencies and professionals may increase the accountability of their actions, but they also reduce their own effectiveness. Indeed, many of them acknowledge fully that making an exception for exceptional cases would better serve the purpose of their work. To escape from this access paradox, many of them strongly advocate tailor-made solutions for people with multiple needs. However, tailor-made solutions typically require a creative use of resources and a departure from standard operating procedures, creating tensions for caseworkers, managers, policymakers, and politicians concerned with legitimating their actions.

Tailor-made Solutions

Tailor-made solutions for people with multiple problems are hard to implement if professionals and managers insist on going by the book. The law and agency handbooks available to service providers are by no means the only guidelines they can turn to: discretion is an important feature of professional work. Ronald Dworkin (1977) defines discretion as follows: "The concept of discretion is at home in only one sort of context; when someone is in general charged with making decisions subject to standards set by a particular authority. . . . Discretion, like the hole in a doughnut, does not exist except as an area left open by a sur-

---

4. This action research method is documented at length in Kruiter and de Jong (2007). A similar approach is presented in English on the website www.kafkabrigade.org.

rounding belt of restriction" (31). Thus, professionals do not operate in a regulatory vacuum; rather, they work in an open space that permits them to adhere to the spirit rather than the letter of the law, to deviate from standard policies and operating procedures to develop tailor-made solutions for clients. One social worker told us that he allowed a man enrolled in a debt rehabilitation program to keep a little money every week to buy cigarettes. Strictly speaking, the policies of his program should not allow for cigarette purchases, but the social worker knew that his decision to bend the rules would increase the likelihood of compliance with overall program goals. It was his professional decision to use his discretionary authority.

The use of discretion is neither necessarily nor always in the best interests of the client or of society at large. Michael Lipsky (1980, 1984) has pointed out that street-level bureaucrats sometimes use discretion to accomplish organizational targets instead of really solving problems or serving clients. They may also use their discretion to make priorities of easy cases and disregard more difficult clients. Although professional autonomy may have its upsides and its downsides, one must acknowledge that all professionals enjoy some degree of discretion. The question we must pose, then, is this: How can or should professionals use this discretion in order to advance public value (Sossin 2005)?[5] As Ann Forsyth (1999) puts it, "Discretion has a number of potential problems: lack of accountability, manipulation, unpredictability, intrusiveness and poor decision making. Yet, discretion is unavoidable in areas in which bureaucracies or other working groups deal with complex problems" (5).

Prior to the bureaucratization of public welfare, the system could be loosely described as discretionary, professional, and decentralized. With the development of the welfare state, demand for public services grew, and with it the number of regulations and standard routines multiplied. The goal of controlled spending led to rationalization, standardization, and centralization at the expense of customized solutions informed by professional judgment (Handler 1983, 1270). Joel Handler argues that the pendulum now has to swing back from this extreme of routinization to a *mixed system* of both regulation and discretion (Handler 1983, 1277–86).

The emphasis on standards, rules, routines, and centralized control in the current welfare state is likely to serve the bulk of the clients in a cost-effective way. However, as we have discussed, people with special needs and more complex situations are better served by a system that allows professionals to exercise a larger degree of discretion. The more "special cases" there are, the more motivated deviation under consultation becomes a crucial element of the work of service professionals.

---

5. See also Sparrow (2000, 238–54) for an interesting discussion of forms of discretion in regulatory enforcement.

Barriers to Tailor-Made Solutions

An important question emerges: Which cases require the use of discretion and which do not (Handler 1983, 1277)? One of the conclusions of our research is that professionals distinguish fairly easily between the two in practice. They know a tough case when they see one. They know when a case calls for a standard response and when a tailor-made solution makes more sense. The real problem here is that professionals often find the barriers between standard and tailor-made solutions, between rules and exceptions, between policy and discretion, to be too high.

Anxieties of Professionals in Social Services

In 2007 a family coach working for Child Protective Services in the Netherlands was sued because she failed to prevent the death of a toddler neglected by her mother (Inspectorate for Youth Care, Utrecht 2005). The case caused enormous turmoil in the professional community of child-protective officers. Eventually charges against the coach were dropped, but the trial has had an immense impact on regulations. The office of Child Protective Services immediately announced stricter procedures to guide and monitor officers. Yet officers working in this field make decisions with far-reaching consequences every day. Even when a service professional follows the rules of her agency to the letter, individual choice continues to be a key factor in any intervention. In the wake of sensational cases such as this one, child service managers and caseworkers often share anxieties over the public outcry, legal charges, and political interventions that can result from high-profile failures in judgment. They want to reduce the risks associated with making difficult decisions in a complex environment closely monitored by the public. Professionals under such intense scrutiny may prefer clear guidelines and routines, even at the expense of freedom to tailor solutions to meet the needs of clients more accurately (Crozier 1964). As a consequence, policymakers, managers, and professionals attempt to fill the hole in the donut, "because now we do not know if we have done something wrong or not," as the director of the child-protective agency involved in the trial remarked.[6] Limiting discretion will not necessarily help the children they serve, but it will protect the professionals working to defend children. Professionals in child-protective services often prefer the security provided by the constraints of more detailed regulation over the paralyzing anxiety they experience in regulatory vacuums. The primary factors underlying our access paradox in all thirteen cities were, first, reluctance to use the leeway afforded by discretion to design targeted solutions for clients with particular needs, and, second, demands from service providers themselves to limit the flexibility of professional decisionmaking.

---

6. M. Beek and M. Ruepert, "Oversight for Child Protective Services [Jeugdzorg krijgt tuchtraad]" [in Dutch], *Algemeen Dagblad,* November 5, 2007.

Self-Regulation and Organizational Behavior

Another mechanism shaping service delivery in most of the thirteen cities we studied was organizational behavior and the informal rules that guide it. Here, we define organizational behavior loosely as a set of institutions that guide the actions of the members of an organization. We found that these institutions (for example, work-flow processes, standard operating procedures, routines, norms, social codes, and so forth) have become major impediments to creating tailor-made solutions for clients with complex needs. In many cases, both national policies and the law allow plenty of room to accommodate complex multidomain situations, but professionals have not experienced this freedom in practice because they understand institutionalized practices to be "ordered by law." When asked why certain agency procedures could not be altered, recurring responses included "That's just the way it is here," "We have always done things this way," "We can't make exceptions just like that!," "If we make an exception for this case now, we have to make exceptions for others in the future as well," "The alderman would never approve of this," and "That's not our call." But when we checked legal statutes, policies, and organizational mandates for corroboration, it always turned out that it *was* their call.

Two examples are illustrative. First, many social workers told us that making exceptions for some cases and not others was against the first article of the Dutch constitution, which states that equal cases must be treated equally. They contended that special measures for individual clients meant inequity in service provision. For some reason, however, no one has mentioned the important, widely known administrative legal clause that says that unequal cases are to be treated unequally in proportion to the degree to which they are unequal (van Ballengooij and others 1999, 72). A second example of regulatory confusion: Almost all social workers are strongly convinced that the law forbids them to share case information under any circumstances. However, the Dutch Information Privacy Act in fact demands that social workers actively share case information if and when it improves accessibility and quality of services in the best interest of the client (Dutch National Council on the Protection of Confidential Personal Information 2007). The perceived regulatory limitations on professional discretion were all imposed by organizational norms and not by external authorities. In other words, most of those interviewed were unaware that constraints on designing individualized services were self-imposed.

So why do professionals and their managers come up with rules that impede their work, have no legal basis, and prevent them from creating the very tailor-made solutions they themselves advocate? One answer to this question is that these "rules" are a kind of coping mechanism for making tough decisions. In precarious situations where human lives are at stake and individual judgments may have drastic consequences, many professionals feel more comfortable making their calls if they are covered by external rules and regulations. It follows from this that if legislators and policymakers fail to furnish service professionals with sufficient guidelines, standards, and routines to protect them, they may invent such measures themselves. Over time, in a more or less conscious process of institutionalization, customs and norms evolve to become recognized organizational behavior. Organizational behavior then becomes formally entrenched in operating procedures and rules that legitimize some actions and sanction others. The hole in the donut becomes smaller, and it becomes harder to deal with the complexities of people with multiple problems. The irony is that these protective mechanisms, as we learned in group interviews, do not reduce professional anxiety, but change it: instead of feeling anxious about acting on their own behalf, social workers now worry about not being able to act in the best interest of their clients. These conflicting drives (the demand both for more regulation and for more individual latitude) reveal a deep discomfort with the use of discretionary authority.

Fragmentation and Discretion

The literature on discretion addresses the issue primarily in the context of a single organization. In the case of people with multiple needs, many organizations can be involved (for example, in the thirteen case studies we conducted, the number of organizations working with each individual ranged between fifteen and twenty). These organizations operate under different legal frameworks, with different political mandates, and with different missions, strategies, and tools. Sometimes they even compete with each other for a share of the "care" market. Some of the organizations are 100 percent public sector, others 100 percent private sector, and still others are hybrids. From the perspective of the client, though, they have one thing in common: they all control one piece of the puzzle. They all have part of the information, the resources, the authority, and the expertise needed to deal with a case. With this fragmentation arises the problem of coordination. One or two organizations may be willing to treat a complex case as an exception to rules, but this does not guarantee that others will do the same. Who defines what an exception is and how? Who is responsible for coordinating subsequent efforts to create a tailor-made solution? And what does this cooperation mean in terms of accountability? Without exception, the social workers and managers with whom we spoke indicated that the problems associated with coordination are seriously limiting their capacity to help clients. Professionals willing to use their discretionary authority often find themselves "trespassing" on the domains of colleagues in other organizations. One agency's hole is another agency's donut, so to speak. An illustration (see figure 8-1) may help to show the interference on different levels caused by the shape of the problem (that is,

Figure 8-1. *Fragmentation and Discretion in a Complex Case*

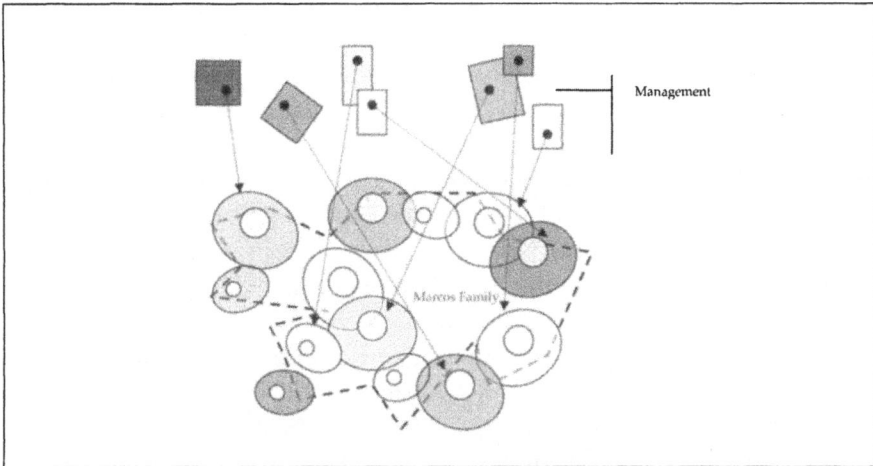

its complexities), the scope of organizational mandates, and the latitude for discretion (that is, donuts and holes).

Figure 8-1, being an imperfect schematic impression of the concepts discussed, may function as a visual aide for the following observations:

—People with multiple problems must interact with multiple organizations.

—These organizations provide services, enforce laws, or do both.

—No single organization covers all dimensions of such cases.

—Even together, all the organizations involved do not address every aspect of complex cases (some problems are still undiscovered or unaddressed).

—Organizational mandates overlap or exclude one another. In instances of overlap, organizations may not conflict, but they may not work in harmony, either. In instances of exclusion, organizations may work in harmony, but they may also conflict.

—Professionals using discretionary latitude in the context of their own organizational mandates must also confront the mandates of other organizations.

—The possibility of a tailor-made solution may exist in the context of one organization's mandate, but almost never in the context of all mandates (that is, there is not enough overlap of the donut holes).

—Fragmentation exists on both the management and work-floor levels.

—From a management perspective, it is hard to analyze such cases in their entirety.

—From a professional's perspective, it is hard to see the total authorizing environment.

—Coordination among agencies to engineer an individualized solution for one case will probably take a lot of effort.

The Challenge

These circumstances may explain why creating tailor-made solutions is not standard practice in the case of people with difficulties in multiple domains. Professionals are often reluctant to use their discretionary latitude, and if they are not, they may run into problems with the norms of other organizations. Using discretion to create individualized service provision therefore remains largely a theoretical possibility. In practice, the access paradox persists: people with multiple problems encounter a range of organizations, each of which deals with a part of the problem. The lack of a coherent, cross-agency strategy to deal with such cases leaves clients with more bureaucracy and professionals with less confidence than they need. To break this vicious cycle, it is important to revisit the role of professionals and public managers in the institutional context of their work.

Innovations in Social Services in the Netherlands

In thirteen Dutch cities, we have seen how public managers are doing just that. Their methods and remedies differ, but their strategies to create tailor-made solutions for people with multiple problems exhibit similar basic elements. We have isolated twenty principles that these innovative professionals and managers have introduced in their work.[7] These principles, applied in whatever configuration, have helped them to escape from the access paradox. All of these principles refer to the work that people do, in whatever capacity, to create public value. In some cities, service professionals were the initiators of change, whereas in other cities managers took the lead. In some cities, innovators came from the public sector, whereas in other cities they came from the private or voluntary sectors. What is most important is the fact that these innovators all perceived their work to be a balancing act between the demands and needs of marginalized people on the one hand and the policies and regulations of the institutional world on the other. Their challenge was to create a better match between the two.

To examine the strategies of these public managers more closely, we will use an analytical model developed and taught by Mark Moore at the John F. Kennedy school of Government (Moore 1995). This model, known as the "strategic triangle," introduces the element of public value into the discourse of public management. The basic assumption is that, to some extent, all public managers face the same challenge: to create public value through generating support for the use of public resources. There is no single best way to meet this challenge: the variables are highly dynamic, making strategic public management a continuous cycle

---

7. Some of these principles were being followed in all thirteen cities, whereas others were followed in just a few. These particular twenty principles emerged after we coded the results of the semistructured interviews and tested an initial list by means of group interviews. This list is not limitative and may be refined with further research and analysis.

Figure 8-2. *The Innovator Located in Moore's Strategic Triangle*

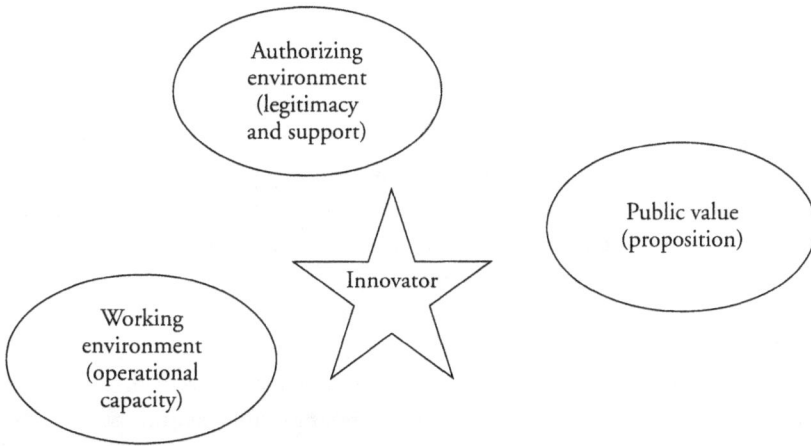

of adjustment and readjustment. This balancing act can be extremely demanding, especially for managers who follow the higher purpose implicit in their mandates beyond mere operational allocation of budget resources. To survive and succeed in such an environment, managers need to understand that their job is an entrepreneurial one. Just as an entrepreneur in the private sector generates private value by identifying and realizing opportunities, a public manager must create value for the public by pinpointing and capitalizing on chances that come her way. This redefinition of public value may very well mean that the operational capacity needs to change, either qualitatively or quantitatively, or that the scope of the mandate or authority structure must evolve, or both. Hence, the balancing acts.

Public-Value Propositions

Successful innovators are always aware of the three elements illustrated in figure 8-2 and work continuously to stabilize them. The professionals and public managers involved in innovations in the thirteen Dutch cities we studied were all in the business of realigning the authorizing environment and the operational capacity in order to accommodate the implementation of public-value propositions. To use the terms of this chapter, they were rearranging institutional responses to meet the needs of people with multiple problems. In this next section we list their working principles and place them in all three corners of Moore's strategic triangle (see figure 8-2).

Principle 1: Approach Clients as Individuals

Successful approaches treat people with multiple problems as individuals, not as cases, targets, or subjects of a specific policy. The uniqueness of their situations prevails over the institutional tendency to categorize and simplify. The central question becomes "What is needed?" instead of "What is our policy or my job?"

Principle 2: No Selection Criteria

Many people with multiple problems are excluded from services because they do not match specific program criteria. They are too old, too young, too poor or not poor enough, have too few or too many kids, too many diplomas or too few, and so forth. An important principle in many successful programs is the radical reduction of admission criteria to one simple question: *Do you have problems that you feel you are not able to solve by yourself?*

Principle 3: Restoring Trust

Marginalized people often lose their trust in government and in the workers acting on its behalf early on in the process of seeking public assistance. They have dealt with too many organizations that have done too little for them. Successful approaches have focused on restoring trust by asking clients to tell their stories rather than having them fill out a standard intake questionnaire.

Principle 4: Taking Clients Seriously

Marginalized people often are themselves the best sources of information and expertise on their own problems. Too often, however, they are not involved in discussing potential solutions; social workers may treat the marginalized as clients in need of help, rather than as people with their own ideas about the directions they want to go. Successful approaches operate by the rule *talk with clients and not about them.*

Principle 5: Small Steps

A tailor-made solution does not necessarily have to be an all-encompassing care concept or rehabilitation plan. Very often, well-chosen, feasible first steps determine the positive outcome of a program. Successful approaches have involved clients in defining the first small steps that will eventually lead to structural improvement. Such initial steps might include assistance with job applications, finding a new place to live, sorting out paper work, or any other action that will get a client back on track. Needless to say, such small steps are hardly ever listed as part of standard programs, but a little guidance at the outset can trigger a chain of changes that empower individuals to regain control over their lives.

Principle 6: Proactive Attitude and Endurance

Successful service professionals typically don't wait for people to come to visit them. They work proactively to identify the people who have fallen between the cracks. After they have helped their clients get back on track, they do not forget them. Professionals keep in touch and make sure their clients are continuing to thrive.

Authorizing Environment: Legitimacy and Support

Creating tailor-made solutions requires both flexibility with respect to standard procedures and willingness to make exceptions to rules. It also demands a degree of strategic maneuvering in the authorizing environment. The following principles are drawn from the various ways that innovative professionals and managers have dealt with accountability issues.

Principal 7: Flexible Accountability Structure

Administrators in charge of innovative programs supported alternative accountability mechanisms in cases of people with multiple problems. As soon as professionals labeled a case "complex," they were allowed greater degrees of discretion. This meant that they could focus on the challenges at hand, instead of being forced to comply by rote with standard procedures. One alderman in the city of Arnhem stated in the group interview: "Targets are not just simple performance indicators; they are points for discussion. They are never set in stone, but are intended to start a conversation among politicians, managers, and professionals about what is desirable and feasible." This kind of flexibility in management and in structures of accountability appeared to be highly important in most of the cities studied. Some interviewees told us that it is a necessary condition for empowering professionals to create tailor-made solutions.

Principle 8: Sense of Purpose

As we have seen, the practice of social services has become highly elaborate. Some politicians respond to this increasing complexity by leaving it all to the professionals to sort out. Another response is to intervene without knowing enough about the nuts and bolts of practice. The responsible politicians and administrators we interviewed typically chose a third option: they took an interest in the complexities of the work, but did not allow themselves to intervene and micromanage nor to be paralyzed as decisionmakers. Through repeated interactions with workers at all levels from different organizations, these leaders facilitated the emergence of a sense of direction, a sense of purpose for the agencies involved. Only then would they make decisions to formalize the mission and strategy developed from the bottom up.

Principle 9: Administrative Law

Whether consciously or not, many managers we interviewed expressed themselves in terms of the principles of administrative law. Some of these principles have been codified over the past decades to guide administrative behavior. They complement material laws, as for example in circumstances when laws conflict with other laws, with common sense, or with natural justice. As we have seen earlier in this chapter, managers and professionals are often unfamiliar with their legal rights to use their discretion, or they can be reluctant to use it for one reason or another. The innovators whom we interviewed, however, based their policies on the principles of administrative law to justify the exceptions they made. By emphasizing the regulatory legitimacy of applying their own principles to difficult cases, managers can reassure professionals worried about accountability. More important, administrators can send a message that it is the duty of service professionals to consider making exceptions to agency policy if the situation so warrants. Administrative law requires from all government officials that they respect the vulnerability of the citizen vis-à-vis the state, and its demands that they take responsibility in situations where individuals have gotten lost in society. The language of these administrative laws also allows managers to converse with their colleagues and counterparts in other organizations. They may have different political bosses, policy objectives, and operating procedures, but these managers do share their public identities as members of a government body. In that capacity, they must act not only in compliance with material laws but also in compliance with administrative law. These innovators found that administrative law could be used as a lever to encourage interagency cooperation.

Principal 10: Entrepreneurship

We found that successful innovators all displayed entrepreneurial qualities and attitudes. Had they not had room for discretion in their work, they would have created it. They define their work as the identification of opportunities to serve their people. Their most important weapon in their struggle with traditional authorizing environments is the positive outcomes of their initiatives. With the confidence that comes from success, these innovators show the higher-ups the results of their work and then inform them that they have used a bit more discretion than they are allowed. In doing so, they are gradually expanding the hole in the donut.

Principle 11: Shift of Coordinating Authority

The traditional hierarchical structure of public sector organizations does not always meet the need of service professionals to cooperate horizontally between organizations. This was particularly true of the kind of coordination required to make the innovations in these thirteen cities successful. Instead of investing decisionmaking authority in higher management, these programs placed the coordinating leadership as close to the clients as possible. This decision shifts a great deal of authority from upper management to individual caseworkers. Depending on the situation and nature of a client's problems, a specific caseworker is assigned to the coordination of all efforts and services across agencies, in which role she has a considerable degree of discretion. Nonetheless, she is expected to consult with all the other involved organizations and professionals regularly. Decentralization of decisionmaking power within the organization is combined with centralization of decisionmaking power across organizations.

Working Environment: Operational Capacity

Now that we have discussed the principles that have guided innovators in approaches to people with problems in more than one area and in their relations with the authorizing environment, we turn to the principles that have guided the design and management of their operational capacity.

Principle 12: Mediator Role

A first step for many of the programs we encountered was to establish a mediator between an individual or family seeking public assistance on the one hand and all of organizations involved on the other. This mediator acts on behalf of both, making sure that clients have access to benefits while complying with rules and regulations. The mediator's role is to unify the client's demands with the organizations' offerings at one point of contact for both parties.

Principle 13: Sharing Information

Fragmentation of public services has led to fragmentation of information. Without accurate and up-to-date information, it is hard to diagnose and remedy clients' difficulties in a coherent and sustained way. Many successful programs have therefore made information sharing the new norm. Some organizations have collectively established new rules and routines for the exchange of crucial data, acknowledging that materials that may be irrelevant to one party may be essential for another. Proactive sharing of information in the newly established legal framework for confidentiality enables all organizations to act more adequately and efficiently.

Principle 14: Assign Responsibility

Successful projects feature designated social workers who are assigned the responsibility of coordinating all government interactions and interventions. This case manager takes the lead in establishing common goals, streamlining interventions, allocating services and obligations, monitoring progress, reporting back to the involved agencies, and continuously evaluating the whole process.

Principle 15: Recombination of Functional Units

In most cities, the delivery of services and the practice of law enforcement are organized along functional lines. We have already discussed the fact that the problems of marginalized people are highly interrelated. To improve government capacity to deal with this interrelatedness, special units have been created in various cities. These units combine different government functions, such as administration of public benefits, guidance from welfare to work, and advice on educational programs. We have also seen units that brought together a specific mix of government functions on a neighborhood level. This recombination dramatically reduced fragmentation of public services and made them much more accessible for the target group. The restructuring of front offices did not involve mergers or other fundamental changes of the standing organization. However, information and experiences at these consolidated front offices were reported back to policymaking and management levels much more easily and forcefully.

Principle 16: Joint Assessments

Even when professionals are willing to join forces, and their managers are willing to let them, they are often inhibited by rigid financial accountability procedures. Even if a coordinated effort to alleviate a problematic situation would save money, it may be hard to defend spending money that has been earmarked for slightly different purposes. Professionals and managers in some of the thirteen cities we studied have created "emergency budgets," which are used for exceptional situations. They have observed that quick interventions can often prevent bad situations from getting worse. Emergency budgets enable professionals to allocate funds without lengthy assessment procedures. The only stipulation is that involved professionals must agree with the use of emergency monies for a specific case. Of course, these budgets can only be used in exceptional situations. But the idea of joint assessments to speed up the process of resource allocation is being further developed in various cities.

Principle 17: Human Resource Management

It is by no means a coincidence that the results of the programs in these thirteen Dutch cities have been positive. For many of them, specific recruitment and selection strategies were employed to ensure a good outcome. Job descriptions and interview questions were rewritten and reworded to attract applicants with the ingenuity, courage, and strategic skills required to provide services successfully to the marginalized. Previously, social workers were hired to work for "their" organizations; now, they are hired by organizations to work for "their target group." Their performance is also evaluated according to criteria that are relevant to the nature of their employment.

Principle 18: Solutions Outside the Box

In many cities we have observed civil-society organizations or private sector entities implementing successful service programs. According to the innovators with whom we spoke, starting initiatives outside of the rule-driven public sector, with its political dynamic, has huge advantages. Operating outside of traditional government agencies simplifies accountability structures and makes hiring and firing less difficult; it also makes it easier to take risks and to experiment with new approaches. In some cities, these initiatives have intentionally been held at a distance from government, while in other cities, government organizations have joined or adopted the initiative once it became a success.

Principle 19: Differentiated Delivery System

As we have discussed, public services are standardized for a reason. Most clients encounter the government through fairly straightforward interactions and transactions. Standardization and process optimization just makes sense in terms of cost efficiency for the bulk of the cases. Tailor-made solutions, as we have argued, are much more effective and efficient for people with multiple problems, the exceptional cases. One major dilemma for innovators has been to determine the correct ratio between standard procedure and tailor-made solutions. When is a situation "complex," when are exceptions justified, and when can clients be trusted to support themselves again? Programs in these thirteen cities have shown that there is a third category, *between* standard procedure and exception. Part of the programs' success lies in the fact that they have developed ways to deal with a substantial number of complex cases on a regular basis. The amount of effort and resources invested in this group may vary from city to city and from time to time. What is important is that public service organizations must provide for a differentiated system of service delivery and law enforcement.

Principle 20: Feedback Loops

Most programs we visited were the result of professional and managerial dissatisfaction with current practice. There has been a major disjuncture between policies (aspirations) and implementation (value created). The innovators whom we interviewed did not perceive themselves as such; rather, they described themselves as public managers drawing lessons from the past and translating them into consequences for the future. The fact that their initiatives have been perceived as innovative indicates that inferring lessons and implementing them is not a habit of public service providers. Feedback loops enabling public managers to adjust policy and practice in response to information about "reality" are not commonly in place. And this is exactly what the innovators say they are doing: managing a process of continuous adjustment to the complex realities of their work. Nearly all the innovators emphasized that their programs are not one-size-fits-all solutions to an assortment of problems. They are works in progress. In practice, professionals and managers continue to monitor, analyze, report back, discuss, and strategize, both horizontally and vertically.

The twenty principles enumerated here were not found to be practiced in one place at one time. Some innovative programs featured only one or two of the principles, while others employed as many as ten or fifteen. The challenges facing our innovators also varied from city to city. Some cities have accomplished much in restructuring the operational capacity, but haven't quite succeeded in securing structural support from their authorizing environments. Others are working hard to create public value for clients and the community at large with the support of politicians, but they haven't been able to realign their new approaches with their operational capacity. Nevertheless, taken together the case studies of the thirteen cities provide the elements of a more or less coherent strategy to improve the quality and accessibility of services to the marginalized.

Conclusion

People with multiple problems are often those most dependent on public services but least capable of dealing with all the bureaucracy associated with the vast range of organizations and procedures involved. Specialization and standardization appear to have made service delivery and law enforcement more cost-efficient. If this is true at all, then it is only true for clients with relatively simple demands. Clients with more complex needs typically fail to benefit from their entitlements, despite all the well-intentioned efforts of professionals trying to help them. The paradox lies in the fact that they have access to the system, but not the kind of access that creates value for them or for society. Obtaining and maintaining access to benefits and assistance indeed becomes an issue in its own right, distracting clients and professional workers from dealing with the core problems.

We have seen that the root causes of this access paradox lie in the fact that custom-designed solutions are difficult to implement. We have argued that the use of discretion is essential to creating individualized support, but many professionals and managers are reluctant to exercise the latitude for professional judgment that the law provides. If they do use the discretionary authority at their disposal, they immediately run into boundary problems with other organizations and their respective professionals. Even if they are willing to make exceptions with respect to their own policies and rules, the scope of influence of any one organization is too limited to deal adequately with a complex case in its entirety. Because of this, professionals are likely to retreat to standard procedure. Instead of doing what is necessary, they are doing what is possible, given the constraints of their authorizing environment and operational capacity.

Case studies from thirteen Dutch cities have shown that innovations in the delivery of social services to the marginalized have successfully responded to the access paradox. The essence of these innovations was to make possible, on a regular basis, the development of tailor-made solutions for clients with complex demands. Professionals were encouraged and empowered to use their discretionary authority in the best interests of their clients and of the community at large. Managers redefined their jobs in terms of horizontal coordination across agencies to balance the obligation of public accountability with the need for exceptions to rules for clients facing wide-ranging challenges. Creating tailor-made solutions has become the new model for dealing with such cases. We have isolated and described here twenty principles that have guided innovators as they realign their authorizing environments and operational capacity with this new approach.

References

Crozier, M. 1964. *The Bureaucratic Phenomenon*. London: Tavistock.

de Swaan, A. 1988. *In Care of the State: Health Care, Education and Welfare in Europe and the USA in the Modern Era*. Cambridge and New York: Polity Press/Oxford University Press.

Dutch National Council on the Protection of Confidential Information. 2007. Personal Information Bulletin 31A. Oktober (www.cbpweb.nl/downloads_inf/inf_va_samenwerkingsver banden.pdf?refer=true&theme=purple [accessed June 30, 2007]).

Dutch National Parliament, Second Chamber. 2006. Parliamentary Proceedings. *Kamerstuk* 29815, no. 47 (January 26).

Dworkin, R. 1977. *Taking Rights Seriously*. Harvard University Press.

Figueira-McDonough, J. 2007. *The Welfare State and Social Work: Pursuing Social Justice*. Thousand Oaks, Calif.: Sage.

Forsyth, A. 1999. "Administrative Discretion and Urban and Regional Planners Values." *Journal of Planning Literature* 14, no. 1: 5–15.

Ghesquière, P. 1993. *Families with Multiple Problems. Problematic Social Care Situations in Perspective*. [In Dutch.] Leuven and Apeldoorn: Garant Uitgevers.

Handler, J. F. 1983. "Discretion in Social Welfare: The Uneasy Position in the Rule of Law." *Yale Law Journal* 92, no. 7: 1270–86.

Inspectorate for Youth Care, Utrecht. 2005. *Report on the Quality of Processes in Youth Care*. [In Dutch.] (www.minvws.nl/rapporten/djb/2005/rapport-inspectie-jeugdbeleid-utrecht.asp [accessed October 15, 2007]).

Kruiter, A. J., and J. de Jong. 2007. *View from the Front Line*. [In Dutch.] The Hague: Nicis Institute.

Kruiter, A. J., J. de Jong, J. van Niel, and C. Hijzen. 2008. *Hamed's Roundabout: Custom-Designed Solutions for People with Multiple Problems*. [In Dutch.] The Hague: Nicis Institute.

Lipsky, M. 1980. *Street Level Bureaucracy: Dilemmas of the Individual in Public Services*. New York: Russell Sage Foundation.

———. 1984. "Bureaucratic Disentitlement in Social Welfare Programs." *Social Service Review* 58, no. 1: 3–27.

Moore, M. H. 1995. *Creating Public Value: Strategic Management in Government*. Harvard University Press.

Netherlands Social and Cultural Planning Office. 2007. *The Social State of the Netherlands, 2007*. [In Dutch.] The Hague: SCP.

Sossin, L. 2005. "From Neutrality to Compassion: The Place of Civil Service Values and Legal Norms in the Exercise of Administrative Discretion." *University of Toronto Law Journal* 55: 427–47.

Sparrow, M. 2000. *The Regulatory Craft: Controlling Risks, Solving Problems and Managing Compliance*. Brookings.

van Ballegooij, G.A.C.M., D. W. Bruil, G. P. Kleijn, and A. E. Schilder. 1999. *Administrative Law in the Era of the AWB Act*. [In Dutch.] Deventer: Kluwer.

PART V

Access to Accountable Government

9

Calling 311:
Citizen Relationship Management
in Miami-Dade County

ALEXANDER SCHELLONG

In this chapter I show how Miami-Dade County, Florida (called Dade County prior to 1967), managed to make its vast array of services available to its highly heterogeneous residents and at the same time ensured a sustainable transformation toward a more citizen-centric government. I argue that a well-functioning system for citizen-initiated contacts with the government plays a crucial role in realizing citizens' access to government services. These contacts provide governments with valuable information about citizens' concerns and government performance. Citizen-initiated contacts to public administration are more than just requests for public services. They are a valuable mode of public participation, if properly utilized. Thus, the Miami-Dade case provides lessons not only about the specific innovations undertaken but also about improving the relationship between citizens and the government at large.

Much has changed in the last few decades with regard to public service delivery. Particularly on the local and county level, government obligations and challenges have become increasingly complex (Benton, Byers, and Cigler 2007). Accommodating diverse populations, governments have had to reconsider how they provide their services. The one-size-fits-all approach did not acknowledge

I would like to thank all the administrative members of Miami-Dade County under the leadership of George Burgess for their valuable feedback and for their providing access to data from the 311 initiative. In particular, the case study would not have been completed without the immense help of Judı Zito, Mary Trujillo, Becky Jo Glover, and Loretta Cronk.

this diversity and failed to provide the level of access to government information and services that both citizens and governments desired. In search of efficiency and effectiveness public managers and policymakers drew from a broad range of measures—mostly private sector management concepts and new organizational forms, business models, and technology. Yet, in contrast to the rhetoric, real transformations toward citizen-centric government have been scarce. Miami-Dade County is one of the exceptions. Its utilization of contact centers accessible via the number 311 has made a significant contribution to improving access to the government for citizens. In this chapter I examine some of the key factors that made the innovation successful, but before focusing on the solution I describe the barriers that impeded access for certain groups of citizens in the past.

Understanding Citizen-Initiated Contact

Citizens contacting administrators generally takes place at the municipal or county level (Milakovich 2003). Up to three-fifths of the population is believed to contact administrators in any given year on the local level; this rate of participation is unsurpassed by any other form of citizen participation (Sharp 1986). Many citizens interact with public administration rarely (every three to five years) and perceive these interactions as a waste of time, causing them unnecessary monetary expense and sometimes even anxiety (Daum 2002; Pippke 1990).

Citizen-initiated contacts differ most clearly from other types of participation in government in that their roots are in citizens' needs for government services. Models to explain citizen-initiated contacts vary and are conflicting. The discourse has mostly focused on the factors inducing contacting, but not the consequences (Thomas and Melkers 1999). There is considerably less agreement on which of those factors are important, as well as on when and why they are important. Some researchers believe that contacting is related to the same factors that affect other forms of political participation, such as voting (Leighley 1995; Verba and Nie 1972). Therefore, contacting would be inversely related to socioeconomic status, civic orientation, and skills. Indeed, members of ethnic and racial minority groups in Colorado Springs were much less likely to contact government than whites (Hero 1986).

Others have proposed the needs-awareness model, according to which some need and some awareness must be present for a citizen to initiate a contact (Jones and others 1977). Need is mostly created through negative externalities produced by citizens' or government's actions. Awareness means that the citizen knows that government is legally responsible; that the government entity will act when contacted; and that the citizen has access to a channel of influence.

Contacting has six dimensions:[1]

---

1. Adapted from Coulter (1988).

1. Nature of contact
2. Substantive content of contact communication
3. Referent (recipient of government action)
4. Level of government contacted
5. Channel of contact and communication
6. Target of citizen contact

First, the nature of the contact can be a request, an opinion, or information. Second, the content of citizens' calls—the information or opinions they passing on to a government entity—is of a virtually infinite variety. The third dimension, the referent, is the entity that is the direct recipient of government action: an individual, a family, a group, or the community at large. The level of government contacting can also increase the probability of cross-boundary issues. The channel determines the mode (synchronous, asynchronous) and communication behavior. Finally, the target that receives a citizen contact may be an elected official or a public servant.

It is easy to see that administrative contacting is a complex but important part of the citizen-government relationship. There are many opportunities to improve it, but it would be unrealistic to think that one solution can fix every problem inherent in citizen contacting.

Why Citizen-Initiated Contact with Government Is Important

Citizen-initiated contacting of public administration to request or complain about a service is a critically important mode of public participation in the urban political system (Coulter 1988). The citizens' opinions offer policymakers information to "(1) understand and establish public needs; (2) develop, communicate and distribute public services; and (3) assess the degree of public service satisfaction" (Vigoda 2000). Participation also offers citizens intrinsic rewards that result from the feeling of increased control, greater discretion, opportunities to make choices, sociality, and the presence of expressive values (Alford 2002; Lengnick-Hall 1996). Citizens have also demonstrated the capability of participating more fully in the political, technical, and administrative decisions that affect them, when they have been given the chance (Roberts 2004). Therefore, citizen-initiated contacts are as much a linkage between political elites and the masses as is voting in elections, because citizen-initiated contacts support four democratic elements: participation, representation, responsiveness, and distributional equity (Velditz, Dyer, and Durand 1980). Citizen-initiated contacts with the government are expressions of the desire to get access to those in authority. Sometimes it is not clear from the outset, to either the citizen or the government official, what kind of authority is being asked for in a contact. Is the citizen calling the government in its capacity as representative democratic body, as executive body, as enforcer of the rule of law, or as service provider? The reason why citizen-initiated contacts are so crucial in terms of access is that both citizen and government need to establish what kind of contact is wanted, and how adequate access to the proper official, body, or service may be realized for both sides.

The Paradox of New Public Management and Citizen Orientation

Citizen orientation, as we have argued, is far more ambiguous than some of the dominant management trends would have us believe. In the 1980s, public administrators responded to the critique to "steer rather than row," and to be entrepreneurs of a new, leaner, and increasingly privatized government (Denhart and Denhart 2003). Market-based reform movements such as New Public Management (NPM) sought to optimize agency operations and create a more citizen-oriented government (Frederickson and Smith 2003). As a consequence, government has been fragmented and composed of partially autonomous agencies and semi-independent departmental units that all have their own cultures and norms. Moreover, arrangements with private and nongovernmental organizations increased and blurred the boundaries of government. This did not necessarily help to improve access for citizens. Researchers, therefore, wondered: "In our rush to steer, are we forgetting who owns the boat? Government belongs to the citizens" (Denhart and Denhart 2000). Accordingly, public administrators should focus on their responsibility to serve and empower citizens as they manage public organizations and implement public policy. In other words, with citizens at the forefront, the emphasis should not be placed on either steering or rowing the governmental boat, but rather on building public institutions marked by integrity and responsiveness. Moreover, public institutions should communicate with citizens and not merely to citizens. With the beginning of the new century, advances in information and communication technology (ICT) promised what New Public Management had failed to achieve: the creation a citizen-centric government.

The Promise of all things E

New technologies did not turn out to be the magic wand that could solve all problems. Concepts and discussions of what some call "eGovernment"—broadly, the use of ICT for internal and external government processes, obligations, and activities—have paid particular attention to notions of citizen choice, satisfaction, orientation, and building a new relationship with the citizenry (Schellong 2008).[2] In this chapter, the term "eGovernment" refers to the role of government

2. There is still no commonly accepted definition of eGovernment, and variations in the definition depend on the context (Allan and others 2006) and its degree of broadness. Many researchers limit eGovernment to public information and service provision over the Internet (Dawes 2002). Broader definitions of eGovernment underline the change of internal and external government operations through technology, electronic public services, and electronic participation (Grönlund 2002). In some cases, the terms "eGovernment"

in regulating and facilitating growth of the information society and ICT (König and Adam 2001; Gisler and Spahni 2001). An example of regulating would be adjusting property rights laws to fight illegal downloading from the Internet; an example of facilitating would be funding schools' purchase of IT equipment.

In practice, eGovernment visions and concepts expected ICT, in particular the Internet, to improve access to electronic public services and government information anytime and anywhere (Fountain 2001). Governments throughout the world tend to stress and communicate the citizen-oriented character of their eGovernment programs (Stoltzfus 2005). When the first phase of their eGovernment programs ended in 2005, governments around the world reported them to be highly successful.

Although there certainly are many noteworthy success stories to be told, such as that of online tax filing, a recent study on the progress of eGovernment in the United States concluded that overall "the eGovernment offerings reported are limited, relatively unsophisticated, and primarily involve information and non-transactional services. . . . In recent years, the adoption of eGovernment services has slowed considerably and, in some areas, seems to have halted" (Coursey and Norris 2008). Moreover, instead of infusing organizational and institutional change, most eGovernment projects represent the simple reproduction of existing institutional patterns and structural relations among agencies (United Nations 2003). Therefore, public administration is still constrained in the provision of seamless and unified services by jurisdictional and budgetary boundaries.

Overall, the expected radical transformation of government has not happened. It is now clear that the challenge for government is not the implementation of technologies but organizational change (Fountain 2007). User uptake also falls short of expectations. One of the core reasons for this is the digital divide: the major disparities in society in terms of information technology ownership, access, and use (Organization for Economic Cooperation and Development 2001). Possibly half of the adult population remains outside the digital world, which includes digital government (West 2005). The rate of access to a computer and the Internet among demographic subgroups varies by sex, age, education, income, ethnicity and race, household structure, physical capacity, and geographic location (Hargittai 2003). Those who have access tend to be male, younger, and better educated and have higher incomes than the public as a whole (West 2005). Older individuals make less use of the Internet and prefer other ways of taking up contact with government. Interestingly, minorities are more likely to access websites at the local level if they feel they have content that is relevant to their need (Council for Excellence in Government 2000).

---

and "eGovernance" are used synonymously or within the context of eDemocracy. See Peri (2001), for instance, described eGovernance as "digital support for policy making; decision making; group work between ministers and their juniors, senior civil servants working on policy formulation, development and management," which could instead be associated with the term eDemocracy within eGovernment.

Governments worldwide have to acknowledge that neither New Public Management nor eGovernment developments have significantly improved government's capacity to interact with citizens. Where eGovernment has been successful, it has optimized existing organizations and procedures and has improved access for those who already knew how to access government information and services. Just like administrative contacting, access to government is a complex issue, which needs to be structured before a solution can be created. What kind of framework can provide that structure?

A Framework for Digital and Nondigital Access Barriers

Policymakers often fall into the trap of choosing a monotopical approach to solving administrative problems, instead of first investing effort in systematically conceptualizing the issue of access. The framework presented here synthesizes findings of recent research in public management, public policy, and sociology. Table 9-1 gives an overview of the complex barriers within the citizen–government domain. Starting with the macro-level and moving down to the micro-level, we can group these barriers on four levels: the system, the organization, the service or information, and the individual. Even though this framework does not permit us to explore causes, it can improve the discussion and strategies of improving access.

First, access to technology or a service does not imply use. For example, many citizens own a computer and an Internet connection, yet they still prefer visiting an agency to make contact with government. Direct interaction gives citizens greater comfort, especially in connection with complex issues. Citizens' preferences also depend on the stage in the transaction process, the nature of the service, and processing the citizen's inquiry. Along these lines, low usage statistics might reflect the existence of barriers or a period of low demand, or, since many services are required to be part of the public service spectrum by legislation, they might target only very specific groups or rare life events.

Second, the existence of information, services, and other methods of public participation does not guarantee public knowledge about such opportunities. Governments fail at outreach and educating the public about their offerings because they lack either the resources or capabilities for marketing. It is hard for government to justify diverting taxpayers' money to these kinds of activities.

Third, we need to look at the objective of access, that is, we need to understand information and services within their respective contexts and their impact on the overall system. For example, when the U.S. Environmental Protection Agency started the Toxic Release Inventory, some environmentalists claimed it would divert the agency's limited resources from effective regulatory action (Rosegrant 1992). Others criticized the type and value of the information provided. Industry representatives were concerned about revealing proprietary busi-

Table 9-1. *Framework of Access Barriers to Government Information and Services*

	System	Organization	Service and information	Individual
Government	political system, lack of ICT and general infrastructure, legislative changes or technological developments	structure, public outreach capacity, budget	design, usability, language, wording, timeliness of content, perceived impact of information	language, lack of citizen-oriented behavior, understanding of the role of the citizen, experience with citizen participa- and interaction
Citizen	geographic loca-tion; lack of: ownership and citizenship, economic and technological development			income, gender, age, education, lit-eracy, ethnicity, race, physical capacity, knowl-edge, general and past experience, self-efficacy, interest, social support, trust in government

ICT = information and communication technology.

ness information or provoking unnecessary public alarm. They were aware of how released information would reshape the regulatory and legislative debate on environmental, health, and safety issues. In fact, media coverage and environ-mentalists' initiatives increased once data were publicly available.

Finally, it is important to establish a commonly understood and accepted goal and result of access. What level of access is acceptable and how do we measure it? How is any information gathered from citizens used to create public value? And what are our criteria for "public value"? These questions can only be answered on the political level. For example, a municipal government in Europe or the United States that operates various service centers throughout a city might be considered a successful example of improved access, whereas a single service point using out-dated infrastructure in a developing country might not be considered an improve-ment of access, from a developed-country perspective. Yet it is quite possible that the latter could have had greater impact in making government relatively more accessible than the former. Also, improved access through so-called "one-stop" service centers, whose purpose is to eliminate the need for citizens to interact with multiple government entities to accomplish one goal, may successfully disguise the fact that the organizational structure and processes in the background have not been changed (see chapter 10 for an example of this issue). In short, it depends on the perspective.

The Importance of the Contact Center for Public Service Delivery

Public services can be provided through various channels: at the agency head-quarters, at a contact center, via the Internet, and by mail. Trends in Internet and phone penetration underline the importance of the contact center, such as the 311 phone number, as access channel for citizens.

Today's society is increasingly mobile, with citizens spending many hours at work or on the move. Consequently, the mobile citizen uses both landlines and mobile phones. Mobile phones show a penetration rate of around three times that of the Internet (about 1.1 billion users) or fixed lines. Mobile phones are likely to replace the computer as the primary device for getting online and access to public services offered via the Internet.[3] Thus, mobile phones allow bridging some access barriers, as illustrated in the following example. It was recently reported in a newspaper that a homeless man who awoke inside a garbage truck that was about to compact its load in Oak Park, Michigan, was rescued after he made a mobile phone call to the police.[4] This anecdote is evidence that mobile phones allow affordable access to government for individuals belonging to the lowest socioeconomic level.[5] Cities that have started the 311 initiatives second this assessment.

311 and Citizen Relationship Management

On July 23, 1996, President Bill Clinton called for a national community polic-ing number to help alleviate the abundance of nonemergency calls that were bur-dening 911 emergency systems. The Federal Communications Commission (FCC) reserved 311 as a telephone number for nonemergency police and other government services in 1996. In 2000 the FCC assigned another three-digit num-ber (211) for the exclusive use of community social and health services. In order to fulfill the FCC's mandate to provide nationwide public access by 2005, the national 211 initiative was started. Municipal, state, and federal leadership, along with nonprofit organizations and telecommunication providers, came together to ensure that the implementation of the 211 service would incorporate a shared vision, a commitment to the standards, and collaboration of all parties. As a

3. "Nomads at Last," *The Economist,* October 4, 2008.
4. "Man Rescued from Garbage Truck," *Detroit Free Press*, December 30, 2006.
5. "Call to Give Homeless Broadband," *BBC News*, 2005 (http://news.bbc.co.uk/1/hi/uk_politics/4396372.stm [March 2007]); "Cell-Phone Use Growing More Popular among the Homeless," *Raleigh News & Observer*, March 27, 2006.

result, 211 can be reached in almost any state, whereas 311 is used by just about eighty municipalities and counties scattered throughout the United States.

The City of Baltimore was the first municipality to implement 311. Although there was a general seven-digit government information phone channel available, citizens were not aware of it and dialed 911 instead. The city's decision to implement 311 resulted in a 50 percent reduction of nonemergency calls to 911. The City of Chicago, in 1999, was the first to use the contact center number in a new way to deliver services to utilize the data the contact center gathered for city management and performance management. Other municipalities, such as Houston, Denver, and New York, and counties such as Miami-Dade followed Chicago's lead.

The 311 contact centers have two primary functions. The first is to respond to standard inquiries; the second is to gather service requests and information from citizens. The degree to which these two factors come into play depends on the number of services available through the contact center and the knowledge of citizens about those services. The majority (up to 80 percent) of contact center interactions are one-time information inquiries that do not require any follow-up or the gathering of detailed information about the caller.[6] Unlike in a commercial calling center, the geographic location of reported issues is more important than information about the caller. Most calls are handled by call takers who are commonly referred to as customer service representatives (CSRs). They are trained to develop a customer-friendly attitude, an attitude of caring and helpfulness to callers. They act as mediators between citizens and departments and are able to use software tools to resolve citizen inquiries for multiple organizational entities. Over time, CSRs build a unique knowledge about organizational cross-boundary issues, individual department processes, and customer service. This makes them valuable human resource assets for many of those departments. However, the work of CSRs is only as good as the support they receive from departments. Therefore, 311 projects have an influence not only on the coordination of the flow of information but also on the processes of taking action in departments.

The 311 initiatives are sometimes referred to as citizen relationship management, or CiRM (Schellong 2008), a term derived from "customer relationship management," or CRM (Peppers and Rogers 2004). In the private sector, CRM is a widely applied concept used in building and managing relationships between firms, suppliers, and customers. It typically includes information technology and a variety of channels for interacting with customers. In addition, holistic CRM initiatives require a customer-centric business philosophy, effective business processes, and often dramatic cultural and organizational transformation (Zablah, Bellenger, and Johnston 2004). Although CRM has been researched and applied in private enterprises for years, it has only recently gained attention as a concept

6. Figure based on reviews of contact center data in the United States and Germany.

for government. Many articles on eGovernment briefly touch on CRM directly or indirectly when referring to aspects such as one-stop service centers or a multichannel environment (Marche and McNiven 2003; von Lucke 2003; Beers 1999; Brown 2005), but CiRM currently lacks a common definition and conceptualization. The term CiRM is still applied in a blanket fashion to any and all citizen-focused initiatives—online portals, electronic case management, 311 contact centers, physical one-stop service centers, or the use CRM software.

Improving Access in Miami-Dade County

"You have reached Miami-Dade 311. How may I provide you with excellent service?"

Miami-Dade County covers more than 2,000 square miles and has a population of around 2.3 million. About 1.3 million people live in its thirty-five incorporated municipalities and more than 1 million people live in the unincorporated areas of the county. The county operates as a two-tier federation, meaning that the municipalities and the county are separate jurisdictions, all with their own responsibilities. Public services such as police and zoning or code enforcement are provided by the municipalities and paid for by municipal taxes. The county delivers services such as public housing or transportation as well as police and fire rescue, paid for by county taxes, to those living in unincorporated areas.

Miami-Dade's efforts to become more citizen-centric were the result of a long-term strategic plan that was developed by an internal task force in 1999. Until that time, the county neither had a strategic plan nor did it own the number 311, which was already in use by the government of the City of Miami for its call center. The county did operate eleven contact centers, but some of those experienced "abandoned call" rates—callers giving up and hanging up as a result of long waiting times—of up to 40 percent. This stemmed from limited staff resources in peak times or poor agent utilization rates, meaning that agents did not handle calls efficiently enough to keep up with the incoming volume. In addition, case management systems were either nonexistent or outmoded. Citizens were often bounced around between departments, put on hold, or forced to navigate a maze of over 1,600 agency phone numbers by themselves. Not surprisingly, service levels and access varied significantly, and many citizens were frustrated. According to a resident survey conducted in 2003, 69 percent of the respondents felt they knew only a little about county services, and overall satisfaction with quality of service was rated at 37 percent.

George Burgess, the county manager, recalls how initiating 311 in 2002 became a way to improve the ease at which the public interacts and communicates with its government. He also realized the value of 311 in the data that could be generated, which could help his department better manage and deploy resources and better understand what was important to different geographic areas

in the county. In fact, during and after Hurricane Wilma, in 2005, the county's
311 contact center was able to provide decisionmakers, including FEMA officials,
with real-time situation reports based on input from citizens and county employees acting as "eyes-and-ears on the ground" (Schellong and Langenberg 2007).
Assistance and supply points were organized on the basis of recognizable patterns
and hotspots.

The 311 project with its multijurisdictional customer contact center was not
the county's first attempt to centralize and streamline contact from residents. In
2001 the county launched its Web portal. Judi Zito, then chief information officer and now director of the county's Web-based Government Information Center (launched in 2006), was able to transfer many valuable lessons from Miami-
Dade's portal project to the 311 implementation. Judi Zito remembered that
switching from the "Internet to the phone was like the same thing over again."
Departments were reluctant to adapt their intake processes to the new channel.
Moreover, citizens' channel preferences depended largely on the target group
and the type of service. The building industry wanted to do as much online as
possible, whereas older people preferred the phone or direct contact in a service
center. Of course, from a cost perspective the county would prefer the citizens to
do everything online, but Zito noted that this would be tantamount to denying
access for many citizens: "There will be certain parts of the population that will
never use the Internet channel. Some do not own a computer. [Even if]
you . . . give a computer to a certain population . . . they will never use [it].
Some people are caught in their own 'digital divide' because they just don't want
to use it."

To those who lack access to a computer, the county is offering over 1,200 computers and free wireless Internet access in public libraries. In addition, Team
Metro, a Miami-Dade County department, provides many services—including
passport applications, various permit applications, code-compliance forms—
through fifteen physical over-the-counter one-stop government service centers and
a mobile "Government on the Go" bus unit. Team Metro also offers a thirteen-
week citizen's academy program several times a year, which provides citizens with
information, resources, and tools they need to become knowledgeable community
members. Further access to government information is provided through Miami-
Dade TV. On the state level, Florida recently instituted the Open Government Initiative, which provides citizens with information on legislative processes, the state
budget, and details of Florida's public record laws.

The "Telephone Reassurance Program," an outreach initiative by the 311 project team, aims at improved inclusion of the elderly in the community. Call takers and supervisors call participating senior citizens every other day to determine
their well-being. One of the participants who lives alone and has no family said
that this program "gives me peace of mind." In case of an emergency involving
participating citizens, the 311 team will inform the listed emergency contact.

Generally the 311 program follows a similar proactive strategy in all of its activities. Call takers try to follow up with citizens whose requests couldn't be answered immediately. Getting such a call from the contact center frequently astonishes citizens who are still under the impression that "call takers are just sweeping it under the rug" and that "no one's gonna call me back on this."

According to an internal survey, the largest proportion of people who know about 311 and take advantage of it are welfare recipients and Hispanics aged fifty and older living on a fixed income. Predicting citizen demand for a channel or service in advance is difficult. With regard to 311, it was also very hard to make projections about the effects of consolidating government calls to one entry point. In fact, studies of other 311 projects reported a 70 percent increase in calls within one year (Solomon and Uchida 2003).

While many public managers and elected officials in Miami-Dade would like to improve public service even more, they caution that there are limits to what they can do to improve citizens' orientation toward government. As service levels increase, so do citizens' expectations, which are then harder to meet. Furthermore, budget resources and citizens' willingness to provide these resources through taxes act as a barrier. As one county executive stated, "The expectation of government has gotten so low that when something positive happens they are taken aback by it. You know that won't last for long. You passed our honeymoon period and essentially all these great things that you did are fuelling the demand for more great things."

Miami-Dade County was a founding member of the Florida 311 Coalition, which was established in 2004 to facilitate coordination and collaboration among state, county, and municipal governments in developing 311 systems. In fact, it is the county's long-term goal to collaborate with all of its thirty-five towns and cities in a single 311 system, to further improve access to government for its citizenry. At the moment, though, the focus of the 311 project is still on integrating all county departments within three to six years.

One of the early departments to join the 311 program was Animal Services, and its operations and accessibility were influenced by the collaboration. The monthly reports from the 311 team helped Animal Services to better understand citizen demand and the internal changes needed to meet that demand. Complaints and request intake times expanded along with the operating hours of the 311 contact center. In addition, field officers were equipped with mobile devices that allowed tracking and responding to service requests in close to real time. Since 2006, a Web-enabled reporting system, called "ServiceStat," has been established. ServiceStat combines performance data (for example, whether service requests are still "open" or are closed), GIS mapping, and 311 call information. It is available for decisionmakers within departments and elected officials, and at some point in the future will be accessible by the public for accountability and management. (Provision of data to elected officials and the public is delayed by two weeks, to prevent short-term-oriented management.) To manage the cross-departmental collaboration, implement service improvements, and analyze citizen data, the 311 program managers created a customer service advocacy (CSA) unit. The CSA can be compared to an internal consulting unit whose underlying goal is to improve the citizen's experience. CSA unit members are responsible for the performance and integration of a group of departments.

Since May of 2006, CSA functions and various outreach and citizen service responsibilities have been centralized in the Government Information Center (GIC). The GIC coordinates the multichannel environment such as the Web portal, the 311 program, and kiosks and physical locations, and incorporates analytical services through its reporting unit. For example, a secret shopper program was used to provide citizen perspectives on county services. A three-month analysis with Miami-Dade Transit revealed, among other things, that citizens expected higher visibility of train-cleaning crews. Miami-Dade Transit responded by introducing roving cleaning crews inside Metrorail trains instead of placing them at the hub points at the end of the tracks. Another study showed that there were deficiencies in how the county served the hearing-impaired community.

These measures are just the beginning of GIC's plans to fully capture and use the data across all channels (311, portal, in person) that can provide valuable information for policy making, management, and a consistent level of customer service in the county.

Conclusion

Miami-Dade's innovative practices have generally led to improved access for a broad group of citizens, an improvement partially but not totally attributable to the 311 initiative. There are several aspects to the problem of access to government services and the efforts to deal with it.

We started out with the assumption that the people living in Miami-Dade County had an access problem. The county already offered the public the choice of different channels to interact with government, but these options only directed people to specific departments of the government. Each department was mainly concerned with its own "customer focus." Process alignment on the intra- and interdepartmental level was poor—that is, departments followed the silo structure of bureaucracy and didn't communicate well or coordinate their activities. Since many citizens, especially those with less experience in dealing with the bureaucracy, did not know where to go in the first place to get their problems solved, the so-called customer focus did not result in a genuine citizen-oriented government. In fact, a portion of Miami Dade's population even chose to not contact government at all. Easy access did not lead to quality service, and quality service was not easily accessible. The county had neither a single strategy nor a coordinated approach to customer service. This has changed. The technology used for Miami's 311 may have been a necessary condition, but it was not a sufficient condition. What made the difference was organizational alignment based on a genuine accommodation to citizens' characteristics and their varying ability to access different parts of the government. The county optimized access by using appropriate old and new technology. In particular, 311 manages to bridge the gap between technology utilization and the need for flexibility to deal with human variety. It also serves the needs of an evolving and ever more mobile society. In addition, the 311 program mediates individual access barriers such as literacy, gender, income, or citizenship. Increasing call volume and positive media coverage show that 311 was able to eliminate some of the latent organizational, service, and individual barriers on the government's side as well as on the citizens' side that were presented in the case study. Members of groups such as seniors and lower socioeconomic groups who tend to be excluded from the digital revolution now can gain access by different means—the 311 contact center. Thus, Miami-Dade improved access to government for all citizens. Access in Miami-Dade is mutually beneficial. Government bodies also get real-time feedback and insights into the public's changing needs. The GIC provides the routines to analyze, process, interpret, and understand the knowledge acquired from citizens. Furthermore, the GIC ensures a holistic approach to citizen centricity in a multijurisdictional environment.

Of course, Miami-Dade's initiatives did not solve all access barriers to government mentioned here, but the real focus on citizens' needs and capabilities and the smart combination of technology and organizational alignment of departmental efforts shows the potential of citizen-oriented government. If more governments follow Miami-Dade's example, it could result in what scholars have referred to as the "collaborative mutual value era" (Fox and Miller 1995): administrators and citizens understand the citizen–government relationship as one that is determined by mutual interest in increasing public value. In the new era, the public agency setting becomes a polis, a true public space (Smith and Huntsman 1997), a state that Aristotle called "active citizenship" (Vigoda 2002). The active citizen is one who, exercising practical wisdom in the public interest, joins in rendering decisive judgment about some aspect of governance.

References

Alford, J. 2002. "Why Do Public-Sector Clients Coproduce? Toward a Contingency Theory." *Administration & Society* 34, no. 1: 32–56.

Allan, D. O. J., and others. 2006. "The eGovernment Concept: A Systematic Review of Research and Practitioner Literature." Innovations in Information Technology, November 1–5.

Beers, V. J. J. M. 1999. "Electronic Service Delivery in Public Administration: Some Trends and Issues." *International Review of Administrative Sciences* 65, no. 6: 183–95.

Benton, J. E., J. Byers, and B. A. Cigler. 2007. "Conducting Research on Counties in the 21st Century: A New Agenda and Database Considerations." *Public Administration Review* 67, no. 6: 968–83.

Brown, D. 2005. "Electronic Government and Public Administration." *International Review of Administrative Sciences* 71, no. 2: 241–54.

Coulter, P. B. 1988. *Political Voice—Citizen Demand for Urban Public Services.* University of Alabama Press.

Council for Excellence in Government. 2000. "E-Government: The Next American Revolution" (www.excelgov.org/index.php?keyword=a432c10480be99).

Coursey, D., and D. F. Norris. 2008. "Models of E-Government: Are They Correct? An Empirical Assessment." *Public Administration Review* 68, no. 3: 523–36.

Daum, R. 2002. *Integration of Information and Communications Technology in Local Administration.* [In German.] Baden-Baden: Nomos.

Dawes, S. 2002. "The Future of e-Government." Center for Technology in Government, State University of New York, Albany.

Denhart, J. V., and R. B. Denhart. 2000. "The New Public Service: Serving Rather Than Steering." *Public Administration Review* 60, no. 6: 549–59.

————. 2003. *The New Public Service: Serving, Not Steering.* Armonk, N.Y.: M. E. Sharpe.

Fountain, J.E. 2001. *Building the Virtual State—Information Technology and Institutional Change.* Brookings.

————. 2007. "Challenges to Organizational Change: Multi-Level Integrated Information Structures (Miis)." In *Governance and Information Technology*, edited by V. Mayer-Schoenberger and D. Lazer, 63–93. MIT Press.

Fox, C., and H. T. Miller. 1995. *Postmodern Public Administration: Towards a Discourse.* Thousand Oaks, Calif.: Sage.

Frederickson, H. G., and K. B. Smith. 2003. *The Public Administration Theory Primer.* Boulder: Westview.

Gisler, M., and D. Spahni. 2002. *eGovernment—Eine Standortbestimmung* [in German]. Bern, Stuttgart, Wien: Paul Haupt.

Grönlund, A., ed. 2002. *Electronic Government: Design, Applications, and Management.* London: Idea Group.

Hargittai, E. 2003. "The Digital Divide and What to Do about It." In *New Economy Handbook*, edited by D. C. Jones. San Diego: Academic Press.

Hero, R. E. 1986. "Explaining Citizen-Initiated Contacting of Government Officials: Socioeconomic Status, Perceived Need, or Something Else?" *Social Science Quarterly* 67: 626–35.

Jones, B. D., S. Greenberg, C. Kaufman, and J. Drew. 1977. "Bureaucratic Response to Citizen Initiated Contacts: Environmental Enforcement in Detroit." *American Political Science Review* 72, no. 1: 148–65.

Konig, K., and M. Adam. 2001. *Governance als entwicklungspolitischer Ansatz*, No. 219 [in German]. Speyer: Speyerer Forschungsberichte, Deutsche Hochschule für Verwaltungswissenschaften Speyer.

Leighley, J. E. 1995. "Attitudes, Opportunities, and Incentives: A Field Essay on Political Participation." *Political Research Quarterly* 48, no. 1: 181–209.

Lengnick-Hall, C. A. 1996. "Customer Contributions to Quality: A Different View of the Customer-Oriented Firm." *Academy of Management Review* 21, no. 3: 791–823.

Marche, S., and J. D. McNiven. 2003. "E-Government and E-Governance: The Future Isn't What It Used to Be." *Canadian Journal of Administrative Sciences* 20, no. 1: 74–86.

Milakovich, M. E. 2003. "Balancing Customer Service, Empowerment and Performance with Citizenship, Responsiveness and Political Accountability." *International Journal of Public Management Review* 4, no. 1: 61–82.

Organization for Economic Cooperation and Development. 2001. *Understanding the Digital Divide.* Paris: OECD Publications.

Peppers, D., and M. Rogers. 2004. *Managing Customer Relationships*. Hoboken: Wiley.

Pippke, W. 1990. "Consultation Design in Computer-Aided Administration." [In German.] In *New Information Services in Relation to Citizens and Administration* [in German], edited by K. Lenk, 79–95. Heidelberg: Decker & Müller.

Roberts, N. 2004. "Public Deliberation in an Age of Direct Citizen Participation." *American Review of Public Administration* 34, no. 4: 315–53.

Rosegrant, S. 1992. *The Toxics Release Inventory: Sharing Government Information with the Public*. Harvard University, John F. Kennedy School of Government.

Schellong, A. 2008. *Citizen Relationship Management: A Study of Customer Relationship Management in Government*. New York: Peter Lang.

Schellong, A., and T. Langenberg. 2007. "Managing Citizen Relationships in Disasters: Hurricane Wilma, 311 and Miami-Dade County." Paper presented at the Hawaii International Conference on System Sciences (HICSS-40). Waikoloa, Hawaii, January 3–6.

Sharp, E. B. 1986. *Citizen Demand Making in the Urban Context*. University of Alabama Press.

6, Peri. 2001. "E-governance: Do Digital Aids Make a Difference in Policy Making?" In *Designing E-Government: On the Crossroads of Technological Innovation and Institutional Change*, pp. 7–27. The Hague: Kluwer.

Smith, G. E., and C. A. Huntsman.1997. "Reframing the Metaphor of the Citizen-Government Relationship: A Value-Centered Perspective." *Public Administration Review* 57, no. 4: 309–18.

Solomon, S. E., and C. D. Uchida. 2003. *Building a 3-1-1 System for Police Non-Emergency Calls*. Austin, Texas: Austin Police Department and Greater Austin Crime Commission.

Stoltzfus, K. 2005. "Motivations for Implementing E-Government: An Investigation of the Global Phenomenon." Paper presented at the dg.O2005, Sixth Annual National Conference on Digital Government Research: Emerging Trends. Atlanta, May 15–18.

Thomas, J. C., and J. Melkers. 1999. "Explaining Citizen-Initiated Contact with Municipal Bureaucrats: Lessons from the Atlanta Experience." *Urban Affairs Review* 34, no. 5: 667–90.

United Nations. 2003. *World Public Sector Report 2003: E-Government at the Crossroads*. New York.

Velditz, A., J. A. Dyer, and R. Durand. 1980. "Citizen Contacts with Local Governments: A Comparative View." *American Journal of Political Science* 24: 50–67.

Verba, S., and N. H. Nie. 1972. *Participation in America*. New York: Harper and Row.

Vigoda, E. 2000. "Are You Being Served? The Responsiveness of Public Administration to Citizens' Demands: An Empirical Examination in Israel." *Public Administration* 78, no. 1: 91–165.

———. 2002. "From Responsiveness to Collaboration: Governance, Citizens, and the Next Generation of Public Administration." *Public Administration Review* 62, no. 5: 527–40.

von Lucke, J. 2003. Governance and Administration in the Information Age. [In German.] Final report of the research project Governance and Administration in the Information Age, Research Institute for Public Administration, German Institute for Administrative Sciences, Speyer. Berlin: Duncker & Humblot.

West, D. M. 2005. *Digital Government. Technology and Public Sector Performance*. Princeton University Press.

Zablah, A. R., D. N. Bellenger, and W. J. Johnston. 2004. "An Evaluation of Divergent Perspectives on Customer Relationship Management: Towards a Common Understanding of an Emerging Phenomenon." *Industrial Marketing Management* 33: 475–89.

10

Demanding to Be Served: Holding Governments to Account for Improved Access

ANWAR SHAH

Despite significant progress on improving access to government services since the mid-twentieth century, access to basic services in developing countries, especially by the poor and other disadvantaged members of society, requires further concerted efforts. A few governments in developing countries may see service provision as an act of benevolence rather than of responsive and accountable governance. Adam Smith wrote in *The Wealth of Nations*, "It is not from the benevolence of the butcher, the brewer or the banker that we expect our service, but from the regard to their own interest." Taking this analogy to the public sector, how do we ensure that citizens in developing countries have the right to be served by their governments rather than to be (ruthlessly) ruled? In this chapter I discuss operational approaches to make this dream a reality. The overall thrust of such approaches is citizens' empowerment to hold their governments to account for service delivery through an institutional framework with justiceable rights (liable to trial in a court of justice) to public services and redress and an accountability framework to deal with government failures.

An earlier version of this chapter was presented at an invited seminar at the Kennedy School of Government, Harvard University, in April 2007. The author is grateful to the seminar participants and Jorrit de Jong and Gowher Rizvi for comments and to Nahida Ahmadova and Kiran Choudhry for comments and contributions. The views expressed in this chapter are those of the author alone and should not be attributed to the World Bank Group and its executive directors.

Access to Basic Services in Developing Countries: Promise and Actual Results

Developing countries have set lofty goals for constitutional rights to basic services. Table 10-1 provides a summary view of such rights in large countries. In most countries, access to free primary and secondary education is guaranteed to all. Most governments also promise to provide universal and almost free access to health care. Nearly half of the countries examined promise welfare assistance to mothers, children, and needy persons, assistance to those out of work, protection for seniors, equal economic opportunity, and safeguards for minorities and disadvantaged groups. In September 2000, in New York, world leaders agreed to establish eight millennium development goals (MDGs) to be achieved by the year 2015. These included halving poverty and hunger, achieving universal access to primary education, reducing child mortality rates by two-thirds and maternal mortality rates by three-fourths, arresting the spread of HIV/AIDS and malaria, improving access to safe water and sanitation by 50 percent, and improving housing for at least 100 million slum dwellers.

What is the record of achieving these goals? In some developing countries, the constitutional mandate for rights to basic services is not fulfilled in practice. Governments may strive to provide these basic services, but there is no accountability if the promised access is not delivered. In fact, in a majority of cases, access to basic services such as education and health remains highly constrained for disadvantaged groups such as women, the poor, the needy, and rural residents. Residents in most countries in South Asia and sub-Saharan Africa do not have any access to social protection and social safety nets in spite of their countries' lofty constitutional promises.

As far as the MDGs are concerned, there has been remarkable progress in recent years in dealing with poverty and hunger, partly attributable to the economic success of China and India. The goal of universal primary education appears achievable in East Asian and Pacific Rim countries, eastern Europe, and Latin America, but sub-Saharan Africa and South Asia are still lagging behind. Some progress has been made to meet the goals of reducing child and maternal mortality, but they are unlikely to be achieved by 2015; in any event, reliable statistics are not available to monitor progress. Similarly, no reliable statistics are available to monitor progress in arresting HIV/AIDS and malaria. Most regions have made excellent progress in improving access to safe water, but progress has been slower in providing sanitation, especially in sub-Saharan Africa. Improving the housing conditions for slum dwellers also remains an unmet challenge.

Approaches to Improving Access That Have Not Met High Expectations

The development literature is replete with cases where high expectations were not realized in improving access to basic services over the five decades since 1960 (Naim 1999; see also Osborne and Plastrik 1997 for popular myths on public sector reform).

Provide More and More External Assistance

The foremost advocates of this approach are some leading academics (see United Nations Millennium Project 2005). The basic argument in support of such higher volume of assistance is that developing countries lack the technical know-how and finance to deal with issues confronting their development and an infusion of foreign capital and know-how will solve this problem. These arguments have some merit, but the past history of external assistance provides only a mixed record of success. Most studies confirm that external assistance has not been as productive as anticipated (Broad and Cavanagh 2006; Rodrik 2006), and only some projects show successful sustainable outcomes; moreover, policy reforms may be either postponed or delayed in anticipation of qualifying for higher assistance in the absence of reform (Huther, Roberts, and Shah 1997).

Spend More and Do More

This approach derives from the perception that the government's lack of adequate revenues contributes to less-than-adequate service delivery. Government performance could be improved by allowing a government greater access to revenues to promote higher public spending. Evidence of developing-country experiences does not substantiate the view that higher spending always leads to improved and better quality of public services. In fact, the evidence indicates that there is not always a one-to-one relationship between spending and service delivery in developing countries. Instead, in a few cases, higher spending has led to reduced access to basic public services because of dysfunctional governance (see World Bank 2004).

Spend Less and Do Less

This approach rests on a view of government as a leviathan with bureaucracies that may be too large; therefore downsizing and outsourcing government functions may improve government efficiency (Gangl 2007). This approach may be helpful up to a point, but there are some critical functions, such as unemployment insurance, social welfare assistance, and environmental protection, that the private sector may not be able to perform, or at least not adequately without government oversight (Kitchen 2005).

Table 10-1. *Constitutional Rights of Access to Basic Services in Developing Countries with 2005 Population over 75 million*

Country (2005 population in millions)	Primary and secondary education	Public health care	Water	Sanitation	Shelter	Social welfare	Social protection	Equal opportunity	Protection of disadvantaged groups
Bangladesh (142)	Free up to high school	Yes				Yes	Yes	Yes	Yes
Brazil (186)	Free	Yes				Yes	Yes	Yes	Yes
China (1,304)	Only primary free	Yes			Yes	Yes	Yes	Yes	Yes
India (1,095)	Free	Yes						Yes	Yes
Indonesia (221)	Free								
Mexico (103)	Free					Yes	Yes		
Nigeria (132)	Free including university	Yes			Yes		Yes		Yes
Pakistan (156)	Free				Yes	Yes	Yes	Yes	Yes
Philippines (83)	Free	Yes							Yes
Vietnam (83)	Free	Yes				Yes			

Source: Constitutions of countries.

Run Government like a Private Business

There is some merit in applying business principles to managing government operations (Dickinson 1996), but the lack of a bottom line for governments makes the application of such an approach difficult. The government has the power of extortion and can carry out taxation in perpetuity to finance its deficits. Government managers therefore may have the luxury of consistently making bad decisions without facing the fiscal consequences of these decisions, whereas in the private sector, poor managerial decisions affect the profitability of the firm and a multitude of such decisions may put the firm out of business.

Hire Better People and Find an Enlightened Leader

This approach rests on the view that government operations could be improved by introducing meritocracy in civil service and by seeking enlightened leaders. In fact, developing-country experiences show that some countries with merit-based civil services performed quite poorly in service delivery, as the problem was not the people but the governmental system that failed to provide incentives for results-based accountability. As for the enlightened leader, it is difficult to envisage a democratic political process to identify and install such leadership.

Reform Government by Strengthening Internal Top-Down Processes

Strengthening vertical hierarchical accountability and streamlining managerial oversight are desirable goals, but developing-country experiences do not provide support for the view that simply strengthening top-down processes improves government's service delivery performance (Jenkins 2007; Veron and others 2006).

Combat Corruption through Anticorruption Agencies

An important reason for failed access to basic public services is that public resources are siphoned off as a result of corruption and malfeasance. Anticorruption, or "watchdog," agencies have often been advocated as an antidote to corruption, but in countries with endemic corruption, these agencies have been shown to compound the incidence of corruption. Their effectiveness depends on the "governance-corruption nexus": where there is good governance, anticorruption agencies can be effective, but where governance is weak, they often add to the existing corruption and can be abused as tools for victimization of political opponents (Shah 2007, 246; Pope and Vogl 2000).

Improve Fiscal Transparency and Financial Accountability

These are desirable reform measures and can be expected to have major positive impacts on government integrity and accountability, though impact will be limited in countries with a high incidence of corruption and absence of rule of law. There is also the usual perception in developing countries that measures to strengthen financial accountability simply allow corrupt officials to maintain a consistent set of accounts without curtailing their corrupt acts (see Khan 2007; Dye 2007; De Mello 2000). Recent experiences of member countries of the Organization for Economic Cooperation and Development suggest that such measures improve government performance if there is good governance in the first place. In OECD countries, the success of fiscal transparency initiatives depends upon the following (see Wright 2008):

—Simple and relevant information being provided to citizens in a user-friendly manner

—Citizens have the opportunity to engage without being overtaxed by excessive consultation requirements

—The citizens trust government's resolve regarding transparency and integrity
These conditions are often not satisfied in transparency initiatives undertaken by governments in countries with a high incidence of corruption.

Build Technical Capacity

Building technical capacity can be helpful in most countries (except in cases where there is some evidence that a lack of technical capacity does not contribute to dysfunctional governance). A few developing countries with technically competent bureaucracies may fail to serve their citizens in the absence of an incentive regime that reinforces results-based accountability.

Implement Participatory Approaches to Budgeting and Decisionmaking

Participatory budgeting represents a direct-democracy approach to budgeting. Done right, it has the potential to make governments more responsive to citizens' needs and more accountable to them for performance in resource allocation and service delivery. It nevertheless comes with significant risks. Participatory processes can potentially be captured by interest groups; the undemocratic, exclusive, or elite nature of public decisionmaking can then be masked and an appearance created of broader participation and inclusive governance, while in fact public funds are used to advance the interests of powerful elites (Banerjee and others 2008; Cooke and Kothari 2001). To prevent such abuses, participatory process should be coupled with an emphasis on good governance and must fully recognize local politics and the formal and informal power relations that exist, so that the process yields outcomes desired by the median voter.

Treat Citizens as Clients and Strengthen Social Accountability

The main argument is that treating citizens as clients and consumers will help government improve service-delivery performance because citizen feedback would serve as an important influence in overcoming deficiencies in service-delivery systems. The social-accountability movement takes this idea further by emphasizing the importance of civic engagement in serving clients better (Ackerman 2005). These approaches provide a public sector analogue to consumer sovereignty in the marketplace. This view is very helpful and worth pursuing with vigor, but its strong positive impact remains to be documented (see Caddy, Peixoto and McNeil, 2007 for a few examples). A note of caution may be in order: some corrupt regimes and interest groups may abuse so-called participatory approaches to advance the interests of the elite (Cooke and Kothari 2001).

Thus, although the development literature is replete with technocratic ideas, in practice such ideas have not yielded desired demonstrable improvements in government performance uniformly. In the next section, we revisit a few ideas that have shown some, albeit limited, promise of success.

Approaches That Have Shown Some Promise of Success in Practice

A number of innovations in government during the last two decades have demonstrated some potential for success.

Sunshine Provisions

Enlarging the sphere of information on government operations available to citizens creates an enabling environment for government accountability. One important example is the Citizens' Report Card program in Bangalore, India, where an independent citizens' right-to-information advocacy group publicizes the service-delivery performance of state and local governments and demands action to overcome bottlenecks (see Paul 1998). Another approach, practiced in Uganda with some success, was the expenditure tracking surveys, which tracked government finances and its leakages, but this program no longer exists (Reinikka and Svenson 2004).

Subsidiarity

The subsidiarity principle means assigning responsibility to the lowest order of government unless a convincing case can be made for higher-order assignment. The European Union adopted this principle as a framework for jurisdictional design. Conceptually, this principle strengthens bottom-up accountability by moving public decisionmaking closer to citizens. In practice, some form of democratic governance is required for such accountability to work. Therefore, the success of programs resting on this principle depends on comprehensive political, administrative, and fiscal decentralization. Most developing countries are prepared to implement political decentralization but show reluctance in shifting fiscal and administrative powers to local governments (Shah 2002).

Results-Based Accountability

Results-based accountability requires erecting a framework to hold government to account for service-delivery performance. Such approaches, characterized as New Public Management, have the following features:

—Contracts or work program agreements based on prespecified outputs, performance targets, and budgetary allocations

—Managerial flexibility, coupled with accountability for results

—Use of the subsidiarity principle in assigning responsibility to different levels of government

—Competitive public service provision

Two approaches to results-based accountability have been implemented by a select group of countries, one relying on market-like arrangements and the other relying on managerial norms and competence (see table 10-2). The former strategy, "making managers manage," used by New Zealand, mandates the incorporation of budgetary allocations and competitive pressures in contracts. The "letting managers manage" approach is practiced in Australia, Sweden, and the United States. The contract-based approach relies on incentives and competitive market mechanisms to enforce accountability of public managers. The empowerment approach simply hopes that managers will be ethically and professionally motivated to deliver good performance. Both strategies provide the flexibility public managers need to improve performance. The critical differences between them are the reliance on incentives and competitive spirit in the first and the centrality of goodwill and trust in the latter. Accordingly, the two approaches represent different perspectives on how to reward public servants. The performance-based contracts reward the chief executive financially if the organization achieves its performance targets. The "let managers manage" approach holds that public servants are more motivated by the intrinsic rewards of effective public service than by material benefits.

It is important to stress that managerial accountability must be based on outputs rather than outcomes, as the latter are beyond managers' direct control, are difficult to define and quantify, and are impossible to use as a costing basis. There are other good reasons for instituting output-based accountability.

1. It is difficult or implausible to link outcomes directly with managerial actions and decisions, as outcomes are remote in time and space from the program's activities and interactions with other factors. The extent of a manager's direct control over outputs is usually much more substantial than over outcomes.

2. Outcomes are immensely difficult to identify, and certainly difficult to quantify. The time frame for measuring outcomes normally includes time after the program intervention and is generally not in sync with the budgeting cycle.

3. Calculating the cost of the effort to achieve outcomes can be more difficult than costing outputs. Outcomes are typically achieved by the interaction of a

Table 10-2. *Comparison of Two Alternate Results-Based Accountability Approaches*

Theoretical models	"Make the managers manage"	"Let the managers manage"
Strategies	Market-like arrangements	Managerial norms and competence
Mechanism	Contracts	Empowerment
Commonality	Give public managers the flexibility they need to improve performance	
Differences	Use specific, narrowly written performance contracts that leave little room for trust	Implicitly trust public managers to exercise their judgment intelligently
	Motivate improvements with extrinsic rewards	Motivate primarily by the intrinsic rewards of public service
Examples	New Zealand	Australia, Sweden, United States

Source: Shah and Shen (2007).

number of different planned/unplanned factors and interventions, not as the result of a single intervention by one program in isolation. Hence, it is inappropriate and unrealistic to hold public managers accountable for outcomes. The focus on outputs as practiced in New Zealand and Malaysia offers greater potential for accountability for results. Outcomes should, however, be monitored and could be the basis for cabinet accountability for promised outcomes. An exclusive emphasis on quantitative output measures without some attention paid to outcomes can distort attention in delivery agencies and runs the risk of elected officials' losing sight of the bigger picture regarding the impact of their programs on citizens and society.

To foster output-based accountability it is essential to increase managerial flexibility by relaxing central input controls. Relaxing central input controls operates at two levels: first, the consolidation of various budget lines into a single appropriation for all operating costs (salaries, travel, supplies, and so on); second, the relaxation of central management rules that inhibit managerial flexibility, particularly the personnel management function, which is where most central rules exist. The personnel cost is generally the largest component of operating expenditures, and it has little effect to consolidate budget lines if central rules in this area prevent any flexibility.

Alternative Service-Delivery Framework

The alternative service-delivery (ASD) framework represents a dynamic consultative and participatory process of public sector restructuring that improves the delivery of services to clients by sharing governance functions with other government entities, individuals, community groups, and the private sector, and introducing competitive pressures into public service provision. The implementation of this approach requires subjecting government operations to seven sequential tests:

1. *Public-interest test.* Does the program area or activity serve a public interest?

2. *Role-of-government test.* Is there a legitimate and necessary role for the government in this program area or activity?

3. *Jurisdictional-design-test.* Applying the subsidiarity principle, what would be the appropriate roles of various levels of government?

4. *Partnership test.* What activities or programs should or could be transferred in whole or in part to the private or voluntary sector?

5. *Competition test.* Are public providers subject to competitive pressures from nongovernment providers? How should financing be structured to foster competition in provision of public services?

6. *Efficiency test.* If the program or activity is continued, how could its efficiency be improved?

7. *Affordability test.* Does the resultant package of programs and activities fall within the fiscal constraints? If not, what programs or activities should be abandoned?

This ASD framework can help rationalize government operations and subject government provision to competitive pressures from nongovernment providers. Since the 1990s, federal and provincial governments in Canada have had significant success in improving service-delivery performance through the use of this framework (Shah 2005; McDavid 2000).

Benchmarking

Benchmarking means comparing one's performance to appropriate analogous entities. With enhanced focus on government accountability, especially at the local level, local governments in North America use neighboring jurisdictions to get a handle on their relative efficiency and performance. This introduces a sense of competition to deliver services more cost-effectively. Benchmarking is also used to compare one jurisdiction's performance against its own performance historically. Such a comparison can reveal trends of government efficiency and productivity.

Direct Democracy

Direct-democracy provisions aim to give citizens an opportunity to participate directly in important public decisions that may have a significant bearing on their quality of life. Switzerland requires public referenda for all major projects and policy changes, and questions of national importance have also been decided in this way in Canada. Provisions for direct democracy help to introduce responsive and accountable government.

Citizens' Charter

A citizens' charter is defined as a constitutional or legal enactment by which the government commits itself to delivering a specified standard and quality of public services and being held accountable for nondelivery. In Malaysia a "clients' charter" was established in 1993 that required specifying standards of services to form the basis of public accountability of government agencies and departments. This charter requires all government agencies and departments to identify their customers, establish what their needs are, and notify clients about the standards of services available. Public agencies are required to report and publish, annually, in print and on the Web, both service improvements and compliance failures. Corrective action is required to deal with compliance failures. Clients also have a right to redress through the Public Complaints Bureau (see Chiu 1997; Siddiquee 2002, 2006).

A similar approach has been undertaken by the local government in Naga City, Philippines. For all local public services delivered by the city, citizens are advised on the service standards and how they could obtain access to such services (see Naga City Government 2003).

Why Access Remains a Nagging Problem: Conceptual Perspectives

Why does access to basic services by the poor remains a field of dreams? Recent thinking from two different conceptual directions may answer this question. The first perspective is a reinterpretation of the New Public Management (NPM) literature by Mark Moore and others (see Moore 1996; Shah 2005). The second is an attempt to answer the question by using newer ideas from the neo-institutional economics (NIE) literature.

New Public Management Perspectives

A simple way to see why the public sector is dysfunctional, does not deliver much in developing countries, and yet is difficult to reform, is to take a closer look at the public sector's mission and values, its authorizing environment, and its operational capacity (Moore 1996).

PUBLIC SECTOR'S MISSION AND VALUES. Societal values and norms, as embodied in the constitution or in annual budget policy statements, may be useful points of reference for public sector mandates and the values inherent in these mandates. Unwritten societal norms that are widely shared or acknowledged should also be taken into consideration. In industrialized countries, the mission and values of the public sector are spelled out by means of a medium-term policy framework. For example, there is a formal requirement in Canada and New Zealand that a policy statement of this type be tabled in the parliament by March 31 (about two to three months in advance of the budget statement). Public sector values in developing countries are rarely set forth clearly in this way because the orientation of the public sector remains toward "command and control" rather than toward serving the citizenry. To an official trained in "command and control," the need to develop a code of conduct with a client orientation may appear frivolous.

AUTHORIZING ENVIRONMENT. The authorizing environment includes formal (budgetary processes and institutions) and informal institutions of participation and accountability. Do these institutions and processes work as intended in providing an enabling environment for the public sector to meet its goals? Do various levels of government act in the spirit of the constitution in exercising their responsibilities? What are the checks and balances against deviant behavior? In industrialized countries, institutional norms are strictly adhered to, and there are severe moral, legal, voter, and market sanctions against noncompliance. In a developing-country environment, noncompliance is often neither monitored nor subject to any sanctions.

OPERATIONAL CAPACITY AND CONSTRAINTS. If the available operational capacity is not consistent with the task at hand, what is authorized is not necessarily what will get done. Furthermore, the operational capacity that is available may be circumvented by the bureaucratic culture or incentives that reward rent seeking, command and control, corruption, and patronage, all with little concern for responsiveness to citizen preferences in service delivery and almost a total lack of accountability to citizen voters.

Figure 10-1 shows that discordance among mission, authorizing environment, and operational capacity contributes to a dismal public sector performance in the delivery of public services. Furthermore, what is delivered in terms of outputs and outcomes is typically inconsistent with citizens' preferences. Consequently, the challenge of public sector reform in any developing country is to harmonize the public sector's mission and values, its authorizing environment, and its operational capacity so that there is a close, if not perfect, correspondence among these three aspects of governance. Such a task is daunting for many developing countries, since they often have lofty goals yet lack an authorizing environment that is capable of translating these goals into a policy framework. This problem is often compounded further by bureaucratic incentives that make any available operational capacity to implement such a framework rather dysfunctional.

Table 10-3 presents a stylized comparison of the institutional environment in a primitive society, a developing country, and an industrialized country. It is interesting to note that although technical capacity in the modern sense was nonexistent in a traditional society (small community or group governance), nevertheless public sector outcomes were consistent with member preferences as a result of harmonization of the society's goals, its authorizing environment, and its operational capacity. The cultures of such societies more often than not focused on accountability regarding results. The system of rewards and punishments was credible and swift, and much of the business relations were based on informality and trust. Thus, although per capita GDP in such societies was quite low, member satisfaction with collective action was observed to be high and quite possibly not too far behind the degree of satisfaction with public sector experience in today's industrial societies.

Figure 10-1. *Public Sector Institutional Environment in Developing Countries*

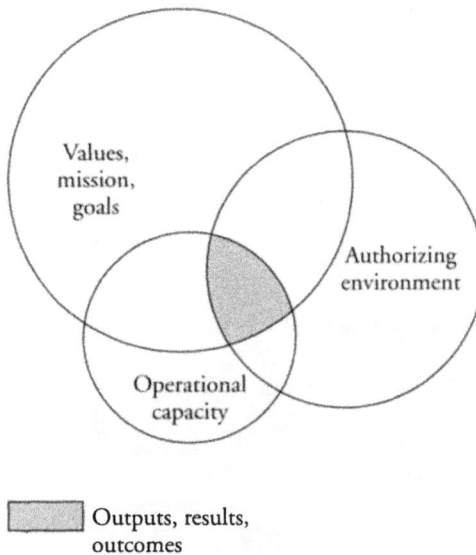

Outputs, results, outcomes

Source: Adapted by the author from Moore (1996).

This contrasts with the picture that we have of typical developing countries. In such countries there is discordance among the society's goals, authorizing environment, and operational capacity, so that not much gets accomplished and citizens' expectations are unmet. Lack of accountability and the evaluation culture leads to a systemic malaise, blunting any self-correcting mechanisms that may exist. Semiformality imposes additional costs on doing business and does not lead to any benefits in business relations because they lead to a lack of respect for the law. Contracts may not be honored and therefore carry little value. In view of the dysfunctional nature of the public sector in many developing countries, it is important for these to leapfrog forward (or even backward) to a public sector culture that puts a premium on client orientation and accountability for results.

Neo-Institutional Economics (NIE) Perspectives

Neo-institutional economics sees the lack of access to public services in developing countries as a problem of transaction costs being too high for citizens to hold the government to account. NIE treats citizens as principals and public officials as agents. The principals have bounded rationality, meaning that they act rationally on the basis of the incomplete information they have. To gain a more informed perspective on public sector operations, they face high *transaction costs*

Table 10-3. *Features of Public Sector Institutional Environment, by Type of Society*

Feature	Traditional society	Developing country	Industrial country
Goals	Clear and realistic	Vague and grandiose	Clear and realistic
Authorizing environment	Strong	Weak	Strong
Operational capacity	Consistent and functional	Dysfunctional	Consistent and functional
Evaluation capacity	Strong	Weak	Strong
Public sector orientation	Ouput	Input controls, command and control	Input, output, and outcome monitoring
Public sector decisionmaking	Decentralized	Centralized	Decentralized
Private sector environment	Informality and trust	Semiformality but lack of trust and disregard for rule of law	Formal and legal
Accountability culture	Rewards and punishment	Victimization of adversaries	Learning and improving

Source: Shah (2005).

in acquiring and processing the information. The agents (public officials) are better informed than the principals, and this asymmetry of information allows agents to indulge in opportunistic behavior that goes unchecked as a result of the high *transaction costs* faced by the principals and the lack or inadequacy of countervailing institutions to enforce accountable governance. Thus, corrupt countries lack transparency in governance and have inadequate mechanisms for contract enforcement, weak judicial systems, and inadequate provisions for public safety. This raises the transaction costs in the economy, further raising the cost of private capital and the cost of public service provision. The problem is further compounded by path dependency: a major break with the past is difficult to achieve as any major reforms are likely to be blocked by influential interest groups. Other obstacles are cultural and historical factors and mental models whereby those who are victimized by corruption feel that attempts to deal with corruption will lead to further victimization, with little hope of corrupt actors' being brought to justice. These considerations lead principals to the conclusion that any attempt on their part to constrain corrupt behaviors will invite strong retaliation from powerful interests. Therefore, citizen empowerment—through devolution, fiscal transparency, citizens' charter, bill of rights, elections, and other forms of civic engagement—assumes critical importance in combating corruption because it may have a significant impact on the incentives faced by public officials to be responsive to public interest (see Shah 2007).

A Synthesis: Citizen-Centric Governance as an Approach to Access

I have reviewed ideas emerging from the literature on political science, economics, public administration, law, federalism, and the NIE with a view to developing an integrated analytical framework use for improving access to public services. The dominant concern in this literature is that the incentives and accountability framework operative on various levels of government are not conducive to service delivery consistent with citizens' preferences. As a result, corruption, waste, and inefficiencies permeate public governance. Top-down hierarchical controls are ineffective, and there is little accountability because citizens are not empowered to hold governments accountable (Shah 2005; Andrews and Shah 2005).

Fiscal federalism practices around the world focus on structures and processes, with little regard for outputs and outcomes. These practices support top-down structures in which federal legislation is preeminent (federal legislation overrides any subnational legislation). The central government is at the apex, exercising direct control and micromanaging the system. Hierarchical controls exercised by various layers of government have an internal, rule-based focus and there is little concern for mandates. Government competencies are determined on the basis of technical and administrative capacity, and almost no regard is shown for client orientation, bottom-up accountability, and lowering of transaction costs for citizens. At various levels, government indulges in uncooperative zero-sum games for control.

This tug of war leads to large swings in the balance of power. Shared rule is a source of much confusion and conflict, especially in federal systems. Local governments are typically the handmaidens of states and are given straitjacket mandates and limited home rule in their competencies, so that citizens have only a limited role in deciding what local governments should do. In short, in this system of "federalism for the governments, by the governments, and of the governments," local governments get crushed under a regime of intrusive controls emanating from higher levels of government.

The governance implications of such a system are quite obvious. Various orders of government suffer from agency problems associated with incomplete contracts and undefined property rights, as the assignment of taxing, spending, and regulating remains to be clarified—especially in areas of shared rule. Intergovernmental bargaining leads to high transaction costs for citizens due to a lack of clarity about which level of government bears responsibility. Pork-barrel politics results in a tragedy of the commons, as various levels of government compete to claim a greater share of common resources. Under this system of governance, citizens are treated as agents—as subjects or clients—rather than as principals, or governors (see Shah and Shah 2006; Shah 2007).

The dominant themes emphasized in the literature on reversing this trend and making governments responsive and accountable to citizens are the subsidiarity principle, the principle of fiscal equivalency, the creation of public value, results-based accountability, and the minimization of transaction costs for citizens. These themes are useful but should be integrated into a broader framework of citizen-centered governance, to create an incentive environment in the public sector that is compatible with a public sector focus on service delivery and bottom-up accountability. Such integration is expected to deal with the commitment problem in various levels of government by empowering citizens and by limiting their agents' ability to indulge in opportunistic behavior.

Such integration takes as its starting point the neo-institutional perspective that various levels of government (agents) are created to serve, preserve, protect, and promote public interest on the basis of the values and expectations of the citizens of a state (principals). The underlying assumption is that there is a widely shared notion of the public interest. Governments are given coercive powers to carry out their mandates. A stylized view of this public interest comprises four dimensions of governance outcomes that embody the spirit and substance of citizen-centric governance.

1. *Responsive governance.* The fundamental task of governing is to promote and pursue the collective interest while respecting formal (rule-of-law) and informal norms. This is done by government's creating an enabling environment to do the right things—in other words, government promotes and delivers services consistent with citizen preferences. Further, the government carries out only the tasks that it is authorized to do; it follows the compact authorized by the citizens at large.

2. *Fair (equitable) governance.* For peace, order, and good government, the government ensures protection of the poor, minorities, and disadvantaged members of the society.

3. *Responsible governance.* Governmental authority is carried out according to the precepts of due process, with integrity (absence of corruption), fiscal prudence, concern for providing the best value for money, and a view to earning the trust of the people.

4. *Accountable governance.* Citizens can hold the government to account for all its actions. This requires that the government be transparent in its operations and work to strengthen voice and exit options for principals. It also means that government truly respects the role of formal and informal institutions of accountability in governance.

Table 10-4 presents some preliminary ideas for discussion on how to operationalize these concepts in reforming public governance in developing countries.

The distinguishing features of citizen-centered governance are:

—Citizen empowerment through a rights-based approach (direct democracy provisions, citizens' charter)

—Bottom-up accountability for results

—Subsidiarity principle and home rule

Table 10-4. *Criteria for Assessing Citizen-Centric Governance, by Outcome*

Governance outcome	Relevant considerations
Responsive governance	Public services consistent with citizen preferences
	Direct, possibly interactive, democracy
	Safety of life, liberty, and property
	Peace, order, rule of law
	Freedom of choice and expression
	Improvements in economic and social outcomes
	Improvements in quantity, quality, and access to public services
	Improvements in quality of life
Fair governance	Fulfillment of citizens' values and expectations in relation to social justice and due process
	Access of the poor, minorities, and disadvantaged groups to basic public services
	Nondiscriminatory laws and enforcement
	Egalitarian income distribution
	Equal opportunity for all
Responsible governance	Open, transparent, and prudent economic, fiscal, and financial management
	Working better and costing less
	Ensuring integrity of government operations
	Earning trust
	Managing risks
	Competitive service delivery
	Focus on results
Accountable governance	Justiceable rights and due process
	Access to justice and information
	Judicial integrity and independence
	Effective legislature and civil-society oversight
	Recall of officials and rollbacks of program possible
	Effective limits to government intervention
	Effective restraints to capture by special interests

Source: Author.

—Evaluation of government performance as the facilitator of a network of providers by citizens as governors, taxpayers, and consumers of public services

The framework of citizen-centered governance emphasizes reforms that strengthen the role of citizens as the principals and create incentives for government agents to comply with their mandates. The commitment problem may be mitigated by creating citizen-centered local governance—by having direct-democracy provisions, introducing governing for results in government operations, and reforming the structure of governance, thus shifting decisionmaking closer to the people. Direct-democracy provisions require referenda on major issues and large projects and require that citizens have the right to veto any legislation or government program (International Council on Human Rights Policy 2005). A "governing for results" framework requires government accountability to citizens for service-delivery performance. Hence, citizens have a charter defining their basic rights as well as their rights of access to a specific standard of public services. Output-based intergovernmental transfers strengthen compliance with such standards and strengthen accountability and citizen empowerment (Shah and Shah 2006).

Implementing the Framework: Potentials and Pitfalls

I have here argued that disparate technocratic approaches to public sector reforms in the past were doomed because they failed to empower people to demand access to basic services from their governments. To overcome this, I have presented a framework for citizen empowerment that if implemented could serve to create a responsive, responsible, fair, and accountable governance in developing countries. But how can this cat be belled, and who will do it? I have provided a few simple principles and practical ideas to overcome formidable obstacles to such fundamental reform.

Nevertheless, it is recognized that implementing the suggested framework is the fundamental challenge of development. In principle such a framework is easy to implement, but putting it into practice on the ground is another matter. Under current circumstances, it would be nearly impossible to implement such a framework in some developing countries because of the confluence of opposing factors. Entities potentially blocking such reforms include powerful political and bureaucratic elites in developing countries who are stakeholders in the status quo.

But all is not lost. The confluence of globalization, the information revolution, and recent concerted efforts by the international development assistance community are bringing about citizen empowerment by allowing the sun to shine in on government operations and empowering citizens to hold government to account through the instantaneous expansion of their knowledge and information base. These are powerful influences in moving governments to accept, albeit reluctantly, rights-based accountability and provide a flicker of hope for moving this fundamental reform agenda forward. The intent of this chapter is to motivate reformers within and beyond government and to assist citizens who would like to see their governments reformed and government leaders who seek to serve their people and earn their trust.

References

Ackerman, J. M. 2005. "Human Rights and Social Accountability." World Bank Social Development Paper 86, Participation and Civic Engagement. Washington: World Bank.

Andrews, M., and A. Shah. 2005. "Citizen-Centered Governance: A New Approach to Public Sector Reform." In *Public Expenditure Analysis*, edited by A. Shah, 153–82. Washington: World Bank.

Banerjee, A. V., B. Rukmini, E. Duflo, R. Glennerster, and S. Khemani. 2008. "Pitfalls of Participatory Programs: Evidence from a Randomized Evaluation in Education in India."

Unpublished paper. Washington: World Bank Development Research Group Human Development and Public Services Team.

Broad, R., and J. Cavanagh. 2006. "The Hijacking of the Development Debate: How Friedman and Sachs Got It Wrong." *World Policy Journal* 23, no. 2: 21–30.

Caddy, J., T. Peixoto, and M. McNeil. 2007. "Beyond Public Scrutiny: Stocktaking of Social Accountability in OECD Countries." WBI Working Paper Series. Washington: World Bank.

Chiu, N. K. 1997. "Service Targets and Methods of Redress: The Impact of Accountability in Malaysia." *Public Administration and Development* 17: 175–80.

Cooke, B., and U. Kothari. 2001. *Participation: The New Tyranny?* London: Zed Books.

De Mello, L. R., Jr. 2000. "Fiscal Decentralization and Intergovernmental Fiscal Relations: A Cross-Country Analysis." *World Development* 28, no. 2: 365–80.

Dickinson, R. 1996. "The Rush to Sell Off Government." *American Demographics* 18: 41.

Dye, K. 2007. "Corruption and Fraud Detection by Supreme Audit Institutions." In *Performance Accountability and Combating Corruption*, edited by A. Shah, 303–22. Washington: World Bank.

Gangl, A. 2007. "Examining Citizens' Beliefs That Government Should Be Run like a Business." *Public Opinion Quarterly* 71, no. 4: 661–70.

Huther, J., S. Roberts, and A. Shah. 1997. *Public Expenditure Reform under Adjustment Lending: Lessons from World Bank Experience.* Washington: World Bank.

International Council on Human Rights Policy. 2005. *Local Governments and Human Rights: Doing Good Service.* Vernier, Switzerland: ATAR Roto Press.

Jenkins, R. 2007. "The Role of Political Institutions in Promoting Accountability." In *Public Sector Governance and Accountability Series: Performance Accountability and Combating Corruption*, edited by A. Shah, 135–82. Washington: World Bank.

Khan, M. A. 2007. "Auditing to Detect Corruption." Unpublished paper. Washington: World Bank.

Kitchen, H. 2005. "Delivering Local/Municipal Services." In *Public Sector Governance and Accountability Series: Public Services Delivery*, edited by A. Shah, 117–52. Washington: World Bank.

McDavid, J. C. 2000. "Alternative Service Delivery in Canadian Local Governments: The Costs of Producing Solid Waste." *Canadian Journal of Regional Science* 23: 157–74.

Moore, M. 1996. *Creating Public Value.* Harvard University Press.

Naga City Government. 2003. The Naga City Citizens Charter. Manila, Philippines.

Naim, M. 1999. "Fads and Fashion in Economic Reforms: Washington Consensus or Washington Confusion?" Paper presented at the IMF Conference on Second Generation Reforms. Washington, November 8–9 (www.imf.org/external/pubs/ft/seminar/1999/reforms/index.htm).

Osborne, David, and Peter Plastrik. 1997. *Banishing Bureaucracy.* New York: Penguin.

Paul, Samuel. 1998. "Making Voice Work: The Report Card on Bangalore's Public Services." World Bank Policy Research Working Paper 1921. Washington.

Pope, J., and F. Vogl. 2000. "Making Anti-Corruption Agencies More Effective." *Finance & Development* 37, no. 2: 6–9.

Reinikka, Ritva, and Jakob Svensson. 2004. "The Power of Information: Evidence from Public Expenditure Tracking Surveys." In *Global Corruption Report*, 326-29. Berlin: Transparency International.

Rodrik, D. 2006. "Goodbye Washington Consensus, Hello Washington Confusion? A Review of the World Bank's Economic Growth in the 1990s: Learning from a Decade of Reform." *Journal of Economic Literature* 44: 973–87.

Shah, A. 2002. "Fiscal Decentralization in Transition Economies and Developing Countries: Progress, Problems and the Promise." In *Federalism in a Changing World—Learning from Each Other,* edited by R. Blindenbacher and A. Koller, 432–60. McGill-Queen's University Press.

———. 2005. "On Getting the Giant to Kneel: Approaches to a Change in the Bureaucratic Culture." In *Fiscal Management,* edited by A. Shah, 211–28. Washington: World Bank.

———. 2007. "Tailoring the Fight against Corruption to Country Circumstances." In *Performance Accountability and Combating Corruption,* edited by A. Shah, 233–54. Washington: World Bank.

Shah, A., and F. Shah. 2007. "Citizen Centered Local Governance: Strategies to Combat Democratic Deficits." *Development* 57: 72–80.

Shah, A., and S. Shah. 2006. "The New Vision of Local Governance and Evolving Roles of Local Governments." In *Local Governance in Developing Countries,* edited by A. Shah, 1–46. Washington: World Bank.

Shah, A., and C. Shen. 2007. "A Primer on Performance Budgeting." In *Budgeting and Budgetary Institutions,* edited by A. Shah, 137–76. Washington: World Bank.

Siddiquee, N. A. 2002. "Administrative Reforms in Malaysia: Recent Trends and Developments." *Asian Journal of Political Science* 10, no. 1: 105–30.

———. 2006. "Public Management Reforms in Malaysia: Recent Initiatives and Experience." *International Journal of Public Sector Management* 19, no. 4: 339–58.

United Nations Millennium Project. 2005. *Investing in Development: A Practical Plan to Achieve Millennium Development Goals.* New York: United Nations.

Veron, R., G. Williams, S. Corbridge, and M. Srivastava. 2006. "Decentralized Corruption or Corrupt Decentralization? Community Monitoring of Poverty-Alleviation Schemes in Eastern India." *World Development* 34, no. 11: 1922–41.

World Bank. 2004. *Making Services Work for Poor People. World Development Report 2004.* Washington.

Wright, J. 2008. "Access to Information: The Role of Fiscal Transparency: The Experience of Canadian Provincial Governments." Unpublished paper. Washington: World Bank.

PART VI

Access to Justice

11

Access to Justice in the United States: Narrowing the Gap between Principle and Practice

DEBORAH L. RHODE

"Equal justice under law" is one of the United States' most proudly proclaimed and widely violated legal principles. It embellishes courthouse entries, ceremonial occasions, and constitutional decisions, but it comes nowhere close to describing the American legal system in practice. Millions of individuals lack any access at all to justice, let alone equal access. According to most estimates, about four-fifths of the civil legal needs of the poor and two- to three-fifths of the needs of middle-income individuals remain unmet. Government legal aid and criminal defense budgets are capped at ludicrous levels, which make effective assistance of counsel a statistical impossibility for most low-income litigants. We tolerate a system in which money often matters more than merit, and equal protection principles are routinely subverted in practice (Rhode 2004; Houseman 1998, 369, 402; Rhudy 1994, 223).

This is not the only legal context in which rhetoric outruns reality, but it is one of the most disturbing, given the fundamental rights at issue. A commitment to equal justice is central to the legitimacy of democratic processes; many nations come far closer than the United States to realizing this ideal in practice. It is a shameful irony that the country with the world's most lawyers has one of the least adequate systems for legal assistance. It is more shameful still that the inequities attract so little concern. Over the last two decades, American legislatures have cut spending on legal aid by about a third and placed increasing restrictions on the clients and causes that government-funded programs can represent. Although indigent criminal defendants are legally entitled to "effective assistance of counsel," few actually receive it. Over 90 percent of cases are resolved by guilty pleas, generally without any factual investigation. Court-appointed lawyers' preparation is often minimal, sometimes taking less time than the average American spends showering before work. In the small minority of cases that go to trial, convictions have been upheld where defense counsel were asleep, high on drugs, suffering from mental illness, or parking their cars during key parts of the prosecution's case (Rhode 2004, 4, 15).

Part of the problem is the lack of public recognition that there is a serious problem. Although most Americans agree that the wealthy have advantages in the U.S. justice system, about four-fifths believe that it is still the "best in the world" (American Bar Association 1999, 59). About the same number also believe, incorrectly, that the poor are entitled to counsel in civil cases. Only a third of Americans think that low-income individuals would have difficulty finding legal assistance, a perception wildly out of touch with reality (American Bar Association 1999, 63, 65; Johnson 1994, 199). Fewer than 1 percent of lawyers are in legal aid practice, which works out to about one lawyer for every 1,400 poor or near-poor persons in the United States (Galanter 1999, 1113; Access to Justice Working Group 1996, 4–6; Tremblay 1999, 2481).

The criminal justice system reflects an even wider gap between public perceptions and daily realities. Americans generally believe that the process coddles criminals, whose lawyers routinely get them off on technicalities. Such assumptions come largely from movies, television, and certain highly publicized trials in which zealous advocacy is the norm. Counsel in celebrated cases leave no stones unturned—but they are charging by the stone. Most defense counsel cannot, and no media glare is available to encourage adequate preparation. Few Americans have any clear appreciation of what passes for justice among the have-nots, and those who do are not necessarily motivated to respond to the crisis. The groups most in need of legal assistance have the least access to political leverage that could secure it. A common attitude, expressed with uncommon candor by one chair of a state legislative budget committee, is that he did not really "care whether [poor defendants were] represented or not" (Ostroff 1981, 2).

But all of us *should* care about access to justice. It is not only the poor who are priced out of the current system. Millions of Americans, including those of moderate income, suffer untold misery because legal protections that are available in principle are inaccessible in practice. Domestic violence victims cannot obtain orders of protection, elderly medical patients cannot collect health benefits, disabled children are denied educational services, defrauded consumers lack affordable remedies. The list is long and the costs, incalculable. Moreover, those who attempt to navigate the system unassisted confront unnecessary obstacles at every turn. In most family, housing, bankruptcy, and small claims courts, the majority of litigants lack lawyers. Yet the system has been designed by and for lawyers, and too little effort has been made to ensure that it is fair or even comprehensible to the average claimant. Given the increasing centrality of law in American life, we can no longer afford a system that most citizens cannot themselves afford.

Defining the Goal: Access for Whom? For What? How Much? And Who Should Decide?

In theory, it is difficult to disagree with "equal justice under law." In practice, however, the concept begins to unravel at key points, beginning with what we mean by "justice." In most discussions, "equal justice" implies equal access to the justice system. The underlying assumption is that social justice is available through procedural justice, but that is a dubious proposition. Those who receive their "day in court" do not always feel that "justice has been done," and with reason. The role that money plays in legal, legislative, and judicial selection processes often skews the law in predictable directions. Even those who win in court can lose in life. Formal rights can be prohibitively expensive to enforce, successful plaintiffs can be informally blacklisted, and legislatures may overturn legal rulings that lack political support.

These difficulties are seldom acknowledged in discussions of access to justice, which assume that more is better, and that the trick is to achieve it. But even from a purely procedural standpoint, that assumption leaves a host of conceptual complexities unaddressed. What constitutes a "legal need"? A vast array of conflicts and concerns could give rise to legal action. How much claiming and blaming is our society prepared to subsidize? As a practical matter, does access to the legal system also require access to legal assistance, and if so, how much is enough? For what, for whom, from whom? Should government support go only to the officially poor, or to all those who cannot realistically afford lawyers? Under what circumstances do individuals need full-blown representation by attorneys, as opposed to other less expensive forms of assistance? How do legal needs compare with other claims on our collective resources? And, most important, who should decide?

The complexities are compounded if we also think seriously about what would make justice truly "equal." Equal to what? Although there is broad agreement that the quality of justice should not depend on the ability to pay, there is little corresponding consensus on an alternative. How do we deal with disparities in incentives, resources, and legal ability? True equality in legal assistance would presumably require not only massive public expenditures but also the restriction of private expenditures. And, as the theorist R. H. Tawney (1964) once noted about equal opportunity generally, it is not clear what would prove most problematic: "the denial of the principle or the attempt to apply it" (103). If cost were no constraint, what would prevent excessive resort to expensive procedural processes? Our ideal world is surely not one in which all disputes are fully adjudicated. How, then, can we develop more equitable limiting principles than ability to pay?

These questions cannot be resolved in the abstract, but a few general observations can help put them into broader context. By virtually any measure, the United States falls well short of providing even minimal, let alone equal, access to justice for those of limited means. Unlike most other industrialized nations, the United States recognizes no right to legal assistance for civil matters, and courts have exercised their discretion to appoint counsel in only a narrow category of cases. Legislative budgets have been equally restrictive. The federal government, which provides about two-thirds of the funding for civil legal aid, now spends only about $8 per year for those living in poverty. Less than 1 percent of the nation's total expenditures on lawyers goes to help the seventh of the population that is poor enough to qualify for legal assistance (Rhode 2004; Houseman 2002, 1233; Rhudy 1994, 236–38). The inadequacies in criminal defense for indigents are of similar magnitude. On average, court-appointed lawyers receive only about an eighth of the resources available to prosecutors. Moreover, millions of Americans who are above poverty thresholds are also priced out of the legal process for the vast majority of their legal concerns.

These inequities are particularly appalling for a nation that considers itself a global leader in human rights. Equal justice may be an implausible aspiration, but more accessible legal institutions are within our reach. Many nations with comparable justice systems and far fewer lawyers than the United States do much better at making basic legal rights available. These countries typically provide more sources of low-cost legal assistance, and more substantial government subsidies for low-income residents. For example, according to the most recent comparative research available, the United States allocates only about a sixteenth of what Great Britain budgets for civil legal assistance, a sixth of what New Zealand provides, and a third of what some Canadian provinces guarantee (Brennan Center for Justice 2003, 5; Johnson 2000, S195). Realistic reforms in the delivery of legal services could go a long way toward ensuring that more Americans can assert their most fundamental rights. To make that possible, the public needs a clearer sense of its own stake in the reform agenda.

The Growing Role of Law and the Rationale for Legal Assistance

As commentators since Alexis de Tocqueville have noted, law and lawyers occupy a distinctively central role in the United States. The importance that Americans attach to legal institutions has deep ideological and structural roots. It is not surprising that a nation founded by individuals escaping from governmental persecution should be wary of state power and protective of individual rights. Cross-national studies find that Americans are less willing than citizens of other nations to trust a centralized government to deal with social problems and to meet social welfare needs (Burke 2000, 179). This distrust is reflected and reinforced by political institutions that give courts a crucial role in constraining state power, safeguarding individual rights, and shaping public policy. The United States relies on legal institutions to protect fundamental values such as freedom of speech, due process, and equal opportunity that are central to its cultural heritage and constitutional traditions. This nation also finds privately financed lawsuits to be a fiscally attractive way of enforcing statutory requirements without spending taxpayer dollars on legal costs. Much of this country's environmental, health, safety, consumer, and antidiscrimination regulation occurs through litigation (Burke 2000, 179; Kagan 2001).

Moreover, despite policymakers' frequent laments about litigiousness, the role and reach of law is increasing, a trend that reflects broader global forces. As patterns of life become more complex and interdependent, the need for legal regulation becomes correspondingly greater. In Western industrialized countries, improvements in the standard of living have also led to increased expectations about the functions of law in maintaining that standard. Throughout the last half century, many societies have come to expect what the American legal historian Lawrence Friedman (1994) labels "total justice." Unsafe conditions, abusive marriages, discriminatory conduct, and inadequacies in social services that were once accepted as a matter of course now prompt demands for legal remedies and for assistance in obtaining them. More and more of our everyday life is hedged about by law. Family, work, and commercial relationships are subject to a growing array of legal obligations and protections. As law becomes increasingly crucial and complex, access to legal assistance also becomes increasingly critical.

That fact has not been entirely lost on American judicial and legislative decisionmakers, but neither have they taken the steps necessary to ensure accessible legal services. In 1932 the United States Supreme Court offered the commonsense observation that an individual's "right to be heard [in legal proceedings] would be, in many cases, of little avail if it did not comprehend the right to be heard by counsel" (*Powell* v. *Alabama* 1932). In the years that followed, courts gradually built on that recognition to find a constitutional right to legal representation for indigent criminal defendants (*Alabama* v. *Shelton* 2002; *Argersinger* v. *Hamlin* 1972; *Gideon* v. *Wainwright* 1963), but courts have largely failed to extend guarantees of legal assistance to civil contexts, even where crucial interests are at issue. In the leading decision on this point, *Lassiter* v. *Department of Social Services* (1981), the Supreme Court interpreted the due process clause to require appointment of counsel in civil cases only if the proceeding would otherwise prove fundamentally unfair. In making that determination, courts must consider three basic factors: "the private interests at stake, the government's interest, and the risk that [lack of counsel] will lead to an erroneous decision."

Although that standard is not unreasonable on its face, courts have applied it in such restrictive fashion that counsel is almost never required in civil cases. This reluctance is problematic on several grounds. Some civil proceedings implicate interests as significant as those involved in many minor criminal proceedings where counsel is required. It is, for example, a cruel irony that in cases involving protective orders for victims of domestic violence, defendants who face little risk of significant sanctions are entitled to lawyers, but victims whose lives are in jeopardy are not. The rationale for subsidized representation seems particularly strong in cases like *Lassiter,* where parental rights were at issue, legal standards were imprecise and subjective, proceedings were formal and adversarial, and resources between the parties were grossly imbalanced. Under such circumstances, opportunities for legal assistance are crucial to maintain the legitimacy of the justice system. As the United States Supreme Court has recognized in other contexts, the "right to sue and defend" is a right "conservative of all other rights, and lies at the foundation of an orderly government" (*Chambers* v. *Baltimore & Ohio R.R.* 1907). Providing representation necessary to make those rights meaningful fosters values central to the rule of law and social justice. For many individuals, legal aid is equally critical in legislative and administrative contexts. Such assistance is the only way that millions of Americans can participate in these governance processes. Not only does access to legal services help prevent erroneous decisions, it also affirms a respect for human dignity and procedural fairness that are core democratic ideals.

Courts' reluctance to extend the right to legal assistance has more to do with pragmatic than principled considerations. As the law professor Geoffrey Hazard has noted, no "politically sober judge, however anguished by injustice unfolding before her eyes," could welcome the battles involved in trying to establish some broadly enforceable right to counsel (Hazard 1999). Given legislatures' repeated refusal to fund legal assistance at anything close to realistic levels, courts are understandably wary about stepping into the breach.

Political opposition to guaranteed legal services builds on several longstanding concerns. The first is that the assistance that poverty lawyers provide may sometimes worsen the plight of the poor. One commonly cited example involves representation of "deadbeat" tenants or consumers. Landlords and merchants forced to litigate such matters allegedly pass on their costs in rents or prices to other, equally impoverished but more deserving tenants and customers who manage to honor their financial obligations. A further objection is that even if some legal services do help the poor, it is inefficient to provide those services in kind rather than through cash transfers. Any broad-based entitlement to legal aid assuredly would encourage overinvestments in law, as opposed to other purchases that the poor might value more, such as food, medicine, education, or housing. Critics note that poor people with unmet legal needs rarely spend their discretionary income on lawyers. And it is by no means clear that clients, if given the choice, would invest in the kinds of broad public interest litigation that legal services attorneys often prefer (Macey 1992, 1115, 1117; Besharov 1990, 329–36; Boehm 1998; Posner 1998, 513–14; Silver and Cross 2000, 1481–484).

These claims raise several difficulties that do not emerge clearly in public debate. To begin with, the value of legal assistance cannot be gauged by what the poor are willing and able to pay. Those who cannot meet their most basic subsistence needs often are unable to make purchases that would prove cost-effective in the longer term. That is part of what traps them in poverty. Yet even for those individuals, legal services may be a highly efficient use of resources. A few hours of legal work can result in benefits far exceeding their costs. Review of legal services programs reveal countless examples, such as brain-damaged children and elderly citizens on fixed incomes who receive essential medical treatment, or impoverished nursing mothers who gain protection from dangerous pesticides. For many forms of legal assistance, it would be difficult, if not impossible, to attach a precise dollar value, but the benefits may be enormous and enduring. Government-subsidized assistance makes it possible for millions of poor people to leave violent marriages, avoid homelessness, and obtain crucial health, education, and vocational services (Brennan Center for Justice 1999a, 2; Brennan Center for Justice 1999b, 9–10, 13).

Moreover, law is a public good. Protecting legal rights often has value beyond what those rights are worth to any single client. So, for example, holding employers of migrant farm workers accountable for unsafe field conditions, making landlords liable for violations of housing codes, or imposing penalties for consumer fraud can provide an essential deterrent against future abuse. Contrary to critics' claims, it is by no means clear that the costs of defending such lawsuits will all be passed on to other poor people, or that those costs are excessive in light of the deterrent value that they serve. Understaffed legal services offices have little reason to spend scarce resources litigating meritless cases that critics endlessly invoke. This is not to suggest that society in general or the poor in particular would benefit if every potential claim were fully litigated. But neither is ability to pay an effective way of screening out frivolous claims. America's gross inequalities in access to justice are an embarrassment to a nation that considers its legal system a model for the civilized world.

The Inadequacy of Legal Assistance

A half century ago, the United States Supreme Court observed, "There can be no equal justice where the kind of trial a man gets depends on the amount of money he has" (*Griffin et al.* v. *Illinois* 1956). Both criminal and civil cases bear daily witness to the truth of that observation, yet our nation's judicial and legislative decisionmakers have repeatedly failed to address it.

In criminal cases, over three-quarters of American defendants facing felony charges are poor enough to qualify for court-appointed counsel. Legal assistance for these defendants takes three main forms: competitive contracts, individual case assignments, and public defender programs. As with Tolstoy's unhappy families, each of these systems breeds unhappiness in its own way.

Under competitive bidding systems, lawyers offer to provide representation for all, or a specified percentage, of a jurisdiction's criminal cases in exchange for a fixed price, irrespective of the number or complexity of matters involved. Such systems discourage effective representation by selecting attorneys who are willing to turn over high volumes of cases at low cost. Caseloads can climb as high as 900 felony matters or several thousand misdemeanors. Rarely can these attorneys afford to do adequate investigation, file necessary motions, or take a matter to trial. "Meet 'em, greet 'em, and plead 'em" is standard practice among contract attorneys. In one all too typical example, a lawyer who agreed to handle a county's entire criminal caseload for $25,000 filed only three motions in five years (Berlow 2000, 28).

Similar disincentives for effective representation occur under other systems. Private practitioners may be assigned to handle matters on a case-by-case basis. These lawyers receive minimal flat fees or hourly rates, coupled with a ceiling on total compensation. Limits of $1,000 are common for felony cases, and some states allow less than half that amount. Teenagers selling sodas on the beach make higher rates than these attorneys. Low ceilings apply even for defendants facing the death penalty, and attorneys subject to such compensation caps have ended up with hourly rates below $4. For most court-appointed lawyers, thorough preparation is a quick route to financial ruin. Analogous problems often arise in the remaining jurisdictions, which rely on public defender offices. Although the quality of representation in some of these offices is quite high, others operate with crushing caseloads (Jaksic 2007, 7; American Bar Association, Standing Committee on Legal Aid and Indigent Defense 2004; Dwyer, Neufeld, and Sheck 2000; Cole 1999, 83–85).

Under all of these systems, the vast majority of court-appointed counsel lack sufficient resources to hire the experts and investigators who are often essential to an effective defense. The same is true for defendants who hire their own counsel. Most of these individuals are just over the line of indigence and cannot afford substantial legal expenses. Their lawyers typically charge a flat fee, payable in advance, which creates obvious disincentives to prepare thoroughly or proceed to trial.

Many defense counsels also face nonfinancial pressures to curtail their representation. A quick plea spares lawyers the strain and potential humiliation of an unsuccessful trial. Such bargains also preserve good working relationships with judges and prosecutors, who confront their own, often overwhelming caseload demands. Indeed, a reputation for thorough representation on behalf of the accused is unlikely to work to counsel's advantage among the judiciary who control appointments. Judges coping with already unmanageable caseloads have been reluctant to appoint "obstructionist" lawyers who routinely raise technical defenses or demand lengthy trials (Burnett, Moore, and Butcher 2001, 597, 622, 641). Taken together, these financial and nonfinancial pressures help explain why over 90 percent of defendants plead guilty, often before their counsel does any factual investigation (McConville and Mersky 1995, 216).

The problem is compounded by the lack of accountability for inadequate performance. Neither market forces nor judicial and bar oversight structures provide a significant check on shoddy representation. Defendants typically lack sufficient information to second-guess lawyers' plea recommendations and trial strategies. Even if clients doubt the adequacy of their counsel, they can seldom do much about it. Indigent defendants have no right to select their attorneys, and court-appointed lawyers do not depend for their livelihood on the satisfaction of clients.

Nor is "mere negligence" enough to trigger bar disciplinary action, establish malpractice liability, or overturn convictions resulting from ineffective assistance of counsel. Convicted criminals are generally unsympathetic litigants. To establish their lawyer's civil liability, they must also establish their own innocence. To obtain a reversal of a conviction, they must show specific errors falling below "prevailing professional norms" and a "reasonable probability" that "but for counsel's unprofessional errors, the results would have been different" (Leubsdorf 1995, 111–19; Mallen and Smith 1996, paragraph 25.3, 234–43). That burden is almost impossible to meet. In one representative survey, over 99 percent of ineffective assistance claims were unsuccessful (Flango and McKenna 1995, 259–60). Tolerance for ineptitude and inexperience runs even to capital cases. Defendants have been executed despite their lawyers' lack of any prior trial experience, ignorance of all relevant death penalty precedents, or failure to present any mitigating evidence (Cole 1999, 87; Green 1993, 499–501). As one expert puts it, too many capital cases end up in the hands of lawyers who have "never tried a case before and never should again" (Bright 1999).

Many low-income civil litigants fare no better. As noted earlier, legal services offices can handle less than a fifth of the needs of eligible clients and often are able to offer only brief advice, not the full range of assistance that is necessary. Americans do not believe that justice should be for sale, but neither do they want to pay for an adequate alternative. Less than 1 percent of the nation's expenditures on legal services goes to civil legal assistance for the poor. America spends only about $2.25 per capita on civil legal aid for the one-seventh of its population that is eligible. That funding level is one-sixth to one-fifteenth of that of other countries with comparable legal systems such as Canada, Australia, and Great Britain (Rhode 2004, 112–13). In some jurisdictions, poor people must wait over two years before seeing a lawyer for matters, like divorce, that are not considered emergencies, and other offices exclude such matters entirely.

Legal aid programs that accept federal funds may not accept entire categories of clients who have nowhere else to go. Groups that are the most politically vulnerable are now the most legally vulnerable as well. Federally funded programs may not take cases involving the "unworthy" poor, defined expansively to include prisoners, undocumented aliens, women seeking abortions, and school desegregation plaintiffs. Unrealistic income eligibility ceilings also exclude many individuals who are just over the poverty line and who also cannot afford counsel (Pickering 1999, 57–58; Legal Services Project 1998; U.S. Government Printing Office 1999, paragraph 1611.3). The result is that millions of Americans lack access to the legal system. Millions more attempt to represent themselves in a process stacked against them.

Self-Representation and Nonlawyer Assistance

The last quarter century has witnessed a rapid growth in self-representation and in related materials and services. Kits, manuals, interactive computer programs, online information, form-processing services, and courthouse facilitators have emerged to assist those priced out of the market for lawyers. But especially for the individuals who need help most, those of limited income and education, such forms of assistance fall far short. Much of the difficulty lies with judicial and bar leaders who have resisted the concept of access to law without lawyers. On issues such as procedural simplification and lay services, the legal profession has often contributed more to the problem than the solution.

In courts that handle housing, bankruptcy, small claims, and family matters, parties without lawyers are less the exception than the rule. Cases in which at least one side is unrepresented are far more common than those in which both sides have counsel. In some jurisdictions, over four-fifths of these matters involve self-represented "pro se" litigants. Yet a majority of surveyed courts have no formal pro se assistance services, such as facilitators who can advise parties, or interactive computer kiosks that can help them complete legal forms. Many of the services that are available are unusable by those who need help most, namely, low-income litigants with limited computer competence and English language skills (Engler 1999, 2047; Goldschmidt 1998, 20).

All too often, parties without lawyers confront procedures of excessive and bewildering complexity, and forms with archaic jargon left over from medieval England. Court clerks and mediators are instructed not to give legal "advice," since that would constitute "unauthorized practice of law." Even courts that have pro se facilitators caution them against answering any "should" questions, such as "Which form should I file?" The result is that many parties with valid claims are unable to advance them. Pro se litigants in family and housing courts are less likely to prevail or to do as well as litigants with lawyers who raise similar issues (Kaye and Lippman

1997, 2; Engler 1999, 2056, 2060, 2064; Greacen 1995, 10–12; Kurtzberg and Henikoff 1997, 90; Maryland, Office of Attorney General 1995; Legal Services Project 1998, 3; Engler 1997, 107–08, 154–55).

Some courts are openly hostile to unrepresented parties, whom they view as tying up the system or attempting to gain tactical advantages. Even the most sympathetic judges often have been unwilling to push for reforms that will antagonize lawyers whose economic interests are threatened by pro se assistance. Particularly for elected judges, support from the organized bar is critical to their reputation, election campaigns, and advancement; encouraging parties to dispense with lawyers wins few friends in the circles that matter most (Engler 1997; State Bar of California 1996, 47).

Similar considerations have worked against other efforts to broaden access to nonlawyer providers of legal services. Almost all of the scholarly experts and commissions that have studied the issue have recommended increased opportunities for such lay assistance (Rhode 1996, 701; American Bar Association, Commission on Nonlawyer Practice 1995). Almost all of the major decisions by judges and bar associations have ignored those recommendations. Nonlawyers who engage in law-related activities are subject to criminal prohibitions that are inconsistently interpreted, unevenly enforced, and inappropriately applied. The dominant approach is to prohibit individuals who are not members of the state bar from providing personalized legal advice (American Bar Association 1983; see also California Business and Professional Code 2008). For example, independent paralegals generally may type documents but may not answer even simple legal questions or correct obvious errors. The American Bar Association (2000) has recently taken actions to strengthen enforcement of these prohibitions, and many state and local bars have launched similar efforts. Yet research concerning nonlawyer specialists in other countries and in American administrative tribunals suggests that these individuals are generally at least as qualified as lawyers to provide assistance on routine matters where legal needs are greatest. Concerns about unqualified or unethical lay assistance could be met through more narrowly drawn prohibitions and licensing structures for nonlawyer providers (Rhode and Luban 2009; Baker 1999a, 54; Citron 1989; Kritzer 1998, 198–203).

The same is true of multidisciplinary partnerships between lawyers and other service providers such as health professionals, real estate agents, insurance agents, accountants, and financial advisers. Most European nations permit such partnerships, and no evidence suggests a significant problem. Legitimate concerns about conflicts of interest and professional independence could be addressed through regulation, not prohibition.

A profession truly committed to access to justice would not only support such reforms, it would also rethink the rules governing lawyers' dealings with unrepresented parties. In response to massive opposition from attorneys, the American

Bar Association rejected a proposed ethical standard that would have prevented lawyers from "unfairly exploiting" pro se litigants' ignorance of the law and from "procur[ing] an unconscionable result." According to opponents, "parties 'too cheap to hire a lawyer' should not be 'coddled' by special treatment" (Rhode 1985, 611). Under the rule ultimately approved in 2008 (American Bar Association 2008, Model Rule 4.3), lawyers' sole responsibilities are to avoid implying that they are disinterested, to refrain from giving advice that is not disinterested, and to make "reasonable efforts" to correct misunderstandings concerning their role. Such minimal obligations have proved totally inadequate to curb overreaching behavior. Counsel for more powerful litigants in landlord-tenant, consumer, and family law disputes have often misled weaker unrepresented parties into waiving important rights and accepting inadequate settlements. Since these individuals typically do not know, cannot prove, or cannot afford lawsuits to prove that they were misinformed by opposing counsel, such conduct has rarely resulted in any disciplinary sanctions or legal remedies (Engler 1997, 133–37).

Further problems arise in the small number of civil cases where courts or legislatures have mandated appointment of counsel for indigent litigants. As in criminal matters, ludicrously inadequate compensation discourages effective representation. Even where legal assistance is adequate, court time is not. Overcrowded caseloads lead to rubber stamp review in matters that most affect ordinary Americans. Judges who spend weeks presiding over minor commercial disputes may have less than five minutes available to decide the future of an abused or neglected child (Forer 1984, 99, 132–33).

The Limitations of Lawyers' Pro Bono Service

A final context in which rhetoric outruns reality involves lawyers' charitable "pro bono" service. American bar associations' ethical codes and judicial decisions have long maintained that lawyers have a responsibility to assist those who cannot afford counsel (see American Bar Association 2008, Model Rule 6.1; American Bar Association 1981, Ec 2-25 and 8-3). Leaders of the profession have endlessly applauded the "quiet heroism" of their colleagues in discharging that responsibility. A constant refrain in bar publications is that "no other profession . . . is as charitable with its time and money" (Haig 1993, 2).

Such claims suggest more about the profession's capacity for self-delusion than for self-sacrifice. Pro bono service has never addressed more than a tiny fraction of the public's needs for assistance, and neither courts nor bar associations have been willing to require significant levels of pro bono participation. The scope of judicial power to compel lawyers to provide unpaid legal assistance remains unsettled, largely because the power has so rarely been exercised. The Supreme Court has never definitively resolved the issue, although some of its language and summary rulings imply that the judiciary has inherent authority to require such assistance at least in criminal cases (*Sparks* v. *Parker* 1979). Lower court decisions are mixed, but most have upheld mandatory court appointments as long as the required amount of service is not "unreasonable." Yet in the face of strong resistance and inadequate performance by many lawyers, courts have been reluctant to exercise their appointment power. They have been even less willing to adopt ethical rules requiring a minimum amount of pro bono service. State codes of conduct include only aspirational standards, which typically call for twenty to fifty hours a year of unpaid assistance (or the financial equivalent) to persons of limited means or to other charitable causes (Rhode 2005).

How many lawyers meet these aspirational standards and how much service they actually provide to the poor is impossible to determine with any precision. Information is spotty because only three states mandate reporting of contribution levels, and because many lawyers take liberties with the definition of "pro bono" and include any uncompensated or undercompensated work, including services for deadbeat clients. However, the best available research suggests that the American legal profession averages less than half an hour a week and under half a dollar a day in pro bono contributions, little of which goes to the poor. Most goes to assist family, friends, and charitable causes that largely benefit middle- and upper-income groups. Fewer than 10 percent of lawyers accept referrals from legal aid or bar-sponsored poverty-related programs. Pro bono participation by the profession's most affluent members reflects a particularly dispiriting distance between the bar's idealized image and actual practices (Seron 1996, 129–33; Rhode 1999, 2423). Only a third of the nation's large law firms have committed themselves to meet the ABA's Pro Bono Challenge, which requires contributions equivalent to 3 to 5 percent of gross revenues, but even of these, fewer still meet that goal. Only about two-fifths of lawyers in the nation's 200 most profitable firms have contributed at least twenty hours a year (Rhode 2005, 20; American Bar Association, Standing Commission on Pro Bono and Public Service 2005; Press 2005, 2007).

Efforts to increase the profession's public service commitments have met with both moral and practical objections. As a matter of principle, many attorneys believe that compulsory charity is a contradiction in terms and that requiring service would infringe on their own rights. From their perspective, if equal justice under law is a societal value, then society as a whole should bear its cost. The poor have fundamental needs for food and medical care, but we do not demand that grocers or doctors donate their help in meeting those needs. Why should lawyers' responsibilities be greater (Lardent 1990, 97–99; Baker 1999b, 22)?

There are several problems with this line of argument, beginning with its assumption that pro bono service is "charity." Lawyers have special powers and privileges that entail special obligations. Attorneys in this nation have a much more extensive and exclusive right to provide crucial services than attorneys in other countries or members of other professions (Boon and Levin 1999, 402; Citron 1989; Parker 1999, 1–9). The American bar has jealously guarded those prerogatives, and its success in restricting lay competition has helped to price services out of reach for many consumers. Under these circumstances, it is not unreasonable to expect lawyers to make some pro bono contributions in return for their privileged status. The standards set forth in bar ethical codes calling for under an hour a week of service hardly justify the overblown descriptions that many lawyers attach: "latent fascism," "economic slavery," and "involuntary servitude" (Rhode 2000, 136–37; Eldred and Schoenherr 1993–94, 391 n.97; Mazzone 1990, 22).

A further objection to pro bono obligations is pragmatic. According to critics, having reluctant dilettantes dabble in poverty law is an expensive and often ineffective way of providing services of unverifiable quality (Kraw, 1999, 4; Macey 1992, 4; Sackett 1998, 22). But the question is always, "Compared to what?" For many low-income groups, some assistance will be better than none, which is their current only option. Concerns of cost-effectiveness could be readily addressed by two strategies. One is to offer lawyers a broad range of service opportunities coupled with educational programs and support structures to equip private practitioners to offer assistance outside their normal expertise where legal needs are greatest. Another is to allow private practitioners who are unwilling or unqualified to assist low-income or public interest clients the option of substituting cash assistance to legal aid providers (Rhode 2005).

Moreover, critics often overlook or undervalue the extent to which pro bono activities serve professional as well as societal interests. For many lawyers, public service offers ways to gain additional skills, trial experience, and community contacts. Such career development opportunities, in the context of causes to which attorneys are committed, are often their most rewarding professional experiences. Many lawyers report that they would like to do more pro bono work but are in institutions that do not support it. Public service can reconnect many lawyers to the social justice concerns that prompted many of them to study law in the first place. And exposing all members of the bar to how the justice system functions, or fails to function, for the have-nots may also broaden support for reform (Lubet and Steward 1997, 1299; Rhode 2005, 44–46; Rhode 1999, 2420).

A similar point could be made about increasing pro bono service by law students. Fewer than 10 percent of American law schools now require such service, and most students graduate without pro bono legal experience (Law School Survey of Student Engagement 2004, 8). Issues concerning access to justice and public service have been missing or marginal in core law school curricula, and bar accreditation standards have failed to make such concerns an educational priority. These oversights represent a missed opportunity for both the profession and the public. Pro bono programs can offer students, no less than lawyers, invaluable skills training and a window on what passes for justice among low-income communities. If we want lawyers to see public service as a professional responsibility, that message must start in law school (Rhode 2005; Rhode 1999, 2433–43).

An Agenda for Reform

No issue presents a more dispiriting distance between America's core principles and actual practices than access to justice. But rather than addressing the tension, we retreat into platitudes. We embrace equal justice as a social ideal, but fail to make even minimal access a social priority. The reasons reflect both ignorance and self-interest. Most Americans are not well informed about access to justice, nor do they have adequate incentives to mobilize for reform. Unlike health care, which is a crucial and continuing need, the demand for legal assistance is much more episodic and is more readily met, however imperfectly, by self-help. So, too, the obstacles to reform are especially formidable, given the organized bar's incentives and capacity for resistance. No other occupation enjoys such prominence in all three branches of government, and it has traditionally been well positioned to block changes that might benefit the public at the profession's financial expense.

Yet a number of forces are now coalescing to improve the prospects for reform. Americans want a legal system that is fair, efficient, and affordable. For most individuals, the current system falls far short. Unmet needs are growing. As noted earlier, federal funding for civil legal aid has been cut by almost a third in real dollars over the last two decades, and most cash-strapped states and localities have been unable to make up the difference. Nor have their criminal defense budgets kept pace with escalating demands. The injustices resulting from shoddy representation have also attracted greater notice among the press and public, partly as a result of the increasing numbers of defendants who are exonerated by DNA evidence. Moreover, the growing market in self-help materials, fueled by escalating technological innovation, has encouraged more individuals to represent themselves and to demand more accessible dispute resolution services. In the face of such pressures, almost all states have created new access to justice organizations and initiatives. A growing constituency within the legal profession also has come to recognize the need for greater support of these efforts. Leaders of state bar associations are increasingly aware that if they do not become more responsive to public needs, others will. Unless lawyers develop the necessary reforms, reforms will be forced upon them.

Despite the conceptual difficulties in defining what precisely we mean by access to justice and how much is enough, several core principles should command broad agreement. First, equal access to justice may be an unattainable ideal, but adequate access should be a social priority. To that end, courts, bar associations, law schools, legal aid providers, and community organizations must work together to coordinate comprehensive systems for the resolution of disputes and the delivery of legal services. Second, these systems should maximize individuals' opportunities to handle law-related problems themselves, without expensive representation by attorneys. Third, those who need legal services but cannot realistically afford them should have access to competent assistance. Opportunities for help should be available for all individuals of limited means, not just the "worthy poor" now eligible for federally funded civil legal aid.

Needs for legal services range across a spectrum, from basic information to full-service representation by an attorney. Reforms that minimized the need for costly representation could enable many individuals to more effectively address their law-related problems. Strategies include simplifying laws; making self-help materials and document preparation assistance readily accessible; better protecting unrepresented parties; providing greater access to nonlawyer providers; and expanding opportunities for informal dispute resolution. All jurisdictions should have comprehensive pro se assistance programs and less restrictive rules governing unauthorized lay practice and multidisciplinary partnerships. An appropriate regulatory structure should take account of the ability of nonlawyer specialists to provide effective assistance, the risks of consumer injury if their assistance is inadequate, and the ability of consumers to evaluate providers' qualifications and to remedy problems resulting from ineffective performance or conflicts of interest. Sweeping prohibitions on lay practitioners should be replaced with licensing and certification systems that impose competence qualifications, ethical standards, and effective malpractice remedies (American Bar Association, Commission on Nonlawyer Practice 1995, 137; Rhode 2000, 136–37; Rhode 1996, 714–15).

Americans would also benefit from more effective channels for informal dispute resolution, not only in courthouses but also in neighborhood, workplace, and commercial settings. Considerable evidence suggests that well-designed employee and consumer grievance procedures benefit both businesses and individual participants, and that most people prefer to resolve disputes through informal, out-of-court processes (Parker 1999; Zander 2000, 29–32; Genn 1999, 217–18). Promoting fair internal remedies will generally prove more cost-effective than relying on less accessible judicial intervention. In fact, alternative dispute resolution procedures for certain civil and minor criminal matters can often enable participants to craft outcomes that better address their underlying problems than more formal adversarial processes.

Finally, effective legal assistance must be available to all who need but cannot realistically afford it. What constitutes "effectiveness," "need," and "affordability" are, of course, somewhat subjective determinations. But by almost any standard, the United States' current system comes nowhere close. Both judicial and legislative decisionmakers must do more to ensure competent performance of lawyers in criminal cases, and opportunities for legal representation in civil cases. Courts should strengthen standards governing malpractice and ineffective assistance of counsel and require states to allocate sufficient resources for indigent defense. Statutory fees should permit a reasonable hourly rate for adequate preparation, and caseloads should not exceed guidelines for competent representation. Criminal defendants should not have to prove their innocence to show malpractice. It should be enough to establish the likelihood that minimal competent representation would have yielded a better outcome. In civil contexts, the judiciary should be more willing to appoint lawyers and to strike down funding restrictions that prevent adequate representation.

Other eligibility restrictions also require rethinking. Most European nations guarantee legal assistance for a much broader category of individuals than those entitled to legal aid in the American system. For example, the European Court of Human Rights has extended the guarantee of appointed counsel to cases with important interests at stake where an unrepresented litigant cannot represent himself or herself effectively (*Airey* v. *Ireland* 1979, 305; Richardson and Reynolds 1994, 360; Cooper 1994, 253; *Quail* v. *Municipal Court* 1985). Under the legal aid eligibility structures of most European countries, relevant considerations include the following: Does the claim have a reasonable possibility of success? What would be the benefits of legal assistance or the harms if it is unavailable? Would a reasonable lawyer, advising a reasonable client, suggest that the client use his or her own money to pursue the issue? In assessing financial eligibility, these systems typically operate with sliding scales. Such an approach permits at least partial coverage for a broader range of clients than American legal aid offices, which serve only those below or just over the poverty line (U.S. Government Printing Office 1999). These more liberal eligibility structures avoid a major limitation of the United States model, which excludes many individuals who have urgent problems and no realistic means of addressing them (Houseman 1998, 431).

To be sure, expanding access in this country will pose substantial challenges. In a political climate that has been reducing entitlements for the poor, any proposal for increased legal aid will face an uphill battle. But a legal services program that included a wider spectrum of the public would have broader appeal than the current program, which benefits only low-income communities. Moreover, subsidies for an expanded system could come from a variety of sources likely to command greater support than general funds. Examples include a tax on law-related revenues; a surcharge on court filing fees based on the amount in controversy; increased opportunities for fee awards to prevailing parties; and pro bono requirements for lawyers that could be satisfied by a minimum amount of annual service, such as fifty hours, or the financial equivalent. In a nation that spends over $90 billion every year on private legal fees, a modest 2 percent tax would substantially increase the capacity of civil legal aid programs. So would more significant pro bono contributions by close to a million attorneys.[1]

Resistance to such requirements might be reduced by providing a broad array of service opportunities, along with training and backup assistance, and by allowing financial contributions as a substitute for direct assistance. Even if skeptics were correct that rules mandating pro bono work would be difficult to

1. Johnson (1994); E. Cummins, "Novel Proposal Would Privatize Legal Services for Poor," *San Francisco Daily Journal,* August 22, 2001; W. Carlson, "San Francisco Lawyers Propose Tax on Lawyers," *San Francisco Chronicle,* February 7, 1989, A7.

enforce, the benefits might still be substantial. At the very least, these requirements would support the many lawyers who would like more pro bono involvement, but who are in workplaces that fail to provide adequate resources or credit for such work. A less controversial alternative would be to require that lawyers report the contributions that they make to legal aid and public interest causes. Experience to date indicates that such reporting rules have led to modest increases in the resources available to poverty law organizations. Further improvements might result if contribution rates were widely publicized and if clients, colleagues, and job candidates began paying more visible attention to employers' pro bono records.

At last count Google revealed some 800,000 lawyer humor sites, and their largely unflattering content highlights the extent of public disaffection with the legal profession and the legal system. That dissatisfaction is not without basis. It is a national disgrace that civil legal aid programs now reflect less than 1 percent of the nation's legal expenditures, and that a majority of Americans cannot afford to use their justice system. It is a professional disgrace that pro bono service occupies less than 1 percent of lawyers' working hours, and that the organized bar has so often put its own economic interests in restricting access ahead of the public's. We can and must do better. Engraved on the entrance of the United States Supreme Court, "Equal justice under law" should remain our aspiration, and it should not just decorate our courthouse doors. It should guide what happens inside them.

References

Access to Justice Working Group. 1996. *Access to All: Fulfilling the Promise of Access to Civil Justice in California.* San Francisco: State Bar of California, Office of Legal Services.
Alabama v. *Shelton.* 2002. 535 U.S. 654.
American Bar Association. 1981. *Model Code of Professional Responsibility.* Chicago.
———. 1999. *Perception of the U.S. Justice System.* Chicago.
———. 2000. "Select Committee Report on the 2000 Midyear Meeting" (www.abanet.org/leadership/2000hous.html).
———. 2008. *Model Rules of Professional Conduct.* Chicago.
American Bar Association, Commission on Nonlawyer Practice. 1995. *Nonlawyer Activity in Law-Related Situations.* Chicago.
American Bar Association, Standing Commission on Pro Bono and Public Service. 2005. *Supporting Justice: A Report on the Pro Bono Work of America's Lawyers.* Chicago.
American Bar Association, Standing Commission on Legal Aid and Indigent Defense. 2004. *Gideon's Broken Promise: America's Continuing Quest for Equal Justice.* Chicago.
Argersinger v. *Hamlin.* 1972. 407 U.S. 25.
Baker, D. 1999a. "Is This Woman a Threat to Lawyers?" *ABA Journal* 85 (June): 54–57.
———. 1999b. "Mandating Good Works: Colorado Proposal Requiring Pro Bono Draws Fire from Most Lawyers. *ABA Journal* (March): 22.
Berlow, A. 2000. "Requiem for a Public Defender." *American Prospect* 85 (June): 32.

Besharov, D. J., ed. 1990. *Legal Services for the Poor: Time for Reform*. Washington: American Enterprise Institute.

Boehm, K. F. 1998. "The Legal Services Program: Unaccountable, Political, Anti-Poor—Beyond Reform and Unnecessary." *Saint Louis University Public Law Review* 17: 321–51.

Boon, A., and J. Levin. 1999. *The Ethics and Conduct of Lawyers in England and Wales*. Oxford: Hart.

Brennan Center for Justice. 1999a. *Legal Services Clients Tell Their Story*. New York.

———. 1999b. *Restricting Legal Services: How Congress Left the Poor with Only Half a Lawyer*. New York.

———. 2003. *Struggling to Meet the Need: Communities Confront Gaps in Federal Legal Aid*. New York.

Bright, S. 1999. "Keep the Dream of Equal Justice Alive." Commencement Address, Yale Law School (http://schr.org/reports/docs/commence.pdf).

Burke, T. 2000. *Lawyers, Lawsuits, and Legal Rights*. University of California Press.

Burnett, C. G., M. K. Moore, and A. K. Butcher. 2001. "In Pursuit of Independent, Qualified and Effective Counsel: The Past and Future of Indigent Criminal Defense in Texas." *South Texas Law Review* 42: 595–694.

California Business and Professions Code. 2008 Section 6126. San Francisco (http://law.one cle.com/california/business/6126.html).

Chambers v. *Baltimore & Ohio R.R.* 1907. 207 U.S. 142.

Citron, J. 1989. *The Citizens' Advice Bureau: For the Community, by the Community*. London: Pluto Press.

Cole, D. 1999. *No Equal Justice: Race and Class in the American Criminal Justice System*. New York: New Press.

Cooper, J. 1994. "English Legal Services: A Tale of Diminishing Returns." *Maryland Journal of Contemporary Legal Issues* 5: 247–69.

Dwyer, J., P. Neufeld, and B. Sheck. 2000. *Actual Innocence*. New York: Doubleday.

Eldred, T. W., and T. Schoenherr. 1993–94. "The Lawyer's Duty of Public Service: More Than Charity?" *West Virginia Law Review* 96: 367–403.

Engler, R. 1997. "Out of Sight and Out of Line: The Need for Regulation of Lawyers' Negotiations with Unrepresented Poor Persons." *California Law Review* 85: 79–158.

———. 1999. "And Justice for All—Including the Unrepresented Poor: Revisiting the Roles of the Judges, Mediators and Clerks." *Fordham Law Review* 67 (April): 1987–2070.

Flango, V. E., and P. McKenna. 1995. "Federal Habeas Corpus: Review of State Court—Convictions." *California Western Law Review* 31: 237–75.

Forer, L. G. 1984. *Money and Justice: Who Owns the Courts?* New York: Norton.

Friedman, L. M. 1994. *Total Justice*. New York: Russell Sage Foundation.

Galanter, M. 1999. "Farther Along." *Law and Society Review* 33: 1113–23.

Genn, H. G. 1999. *What People Do and Think about Going to Law*. Oxford: Hart.

Gideon v. *Wainwright*. 1963. 372 U.S. 335.

Goldschmidt, J. 1998. "How Are Courts Handling Pro Se Litigants?" *Judicature* 82: 13–22.

Greacen, J. M. 1995. "No Legal Advice from Court Personnel: What Does That Mean?" *Judges' Journal* 34: 10.

Green, B. A. 1993. "Lethal Fiction: The Meaning of 'Counsel' in the Sixth Amendment." *Iowa Law Review* 78: 433–516.

Griffin et al. v. *Illinois*. 1956. 351 U.S. 12.

Haig, R. L. 1993. "Lawyer-Bashing: Have We Earned It?" *New York Law Journal* 210: 2 (November).

Hazard, G. C., Jr. 1999. "After Legal Aid Is Abolished." *Journal of the Institute for the Study of Legal Ethics* 2: 375–86.

Houseman, A. W. 1998. "Civil Legal Assistance for the Twenty-First Century: Achieving Equal Justice for All." *Yale Law and Policy Review* 17: 369–433.

———. 2002. "Civil Legal Assistance for Low-Income Persons: Looking Back and Looking Forward." *Fordham Urban Law Journal* 29: 1213–243.

Jaksic, V. 2007. "A Crisis in Funding." *National Law Journal,* March 27, 1.

Johnson, E., Jr. 1994. "Toward Equal Justice: Where the United States Stands Two Decades Later." *Maryland Journal of Contemporary Legal Issues* 5: 199–221.

———. 2000. "Equal Access to Justice: Comparing Access to Justice in the United States and Other Industrial Democracies." *Fordham International Law Journal* 24: S83–S110.

Kagan, R. A. 2001. *Adversarial Legalism: The American Way of Law.* Harvard University Press.

Kaye, J. S., and J. Lippman. 1997. *The Housing Court Program: Breaking New Ground.* New York: New York State Unified Court System.

Kraw, G. M. 1999."Pro Malo Publico." *San Francisco Recorder,* August 25.

Kritzer, H. 1998. *Legal Advocacy.* University of Michigan Press.

Kurtzberg, J., and J. Henikoff. 1997. "Freeing the Parties from the Law: Designing an Interest and Rights Focused Model of Landlord/Tenant Mediation." *Journal Dispute Resolution* 1: 53.

Lardent, E. F. 1990. "Mandatory Pro Bono in Civil Cases: The Wrong Answer to the Right Question." *Maryland Law Review* 49: 78–102.

Lassiter v. *Department of Social Services.* 1981. 452 U.S. 18.

Law School Survey of Student Engagement, 2004. *Student Engagement in Law Schools .*

Legal Services Project. 1998. *Funding Civil Legal Services for the Poor: Report to the Chief Judge.* New York: State Unified Court System.

Leubsdorf, J. 1995. "Legal Malpractice and Professional Responsibility." *Rutgers Law Review* 48: 101–59.

Lubet, S., and C. Stewart. 1997. "A 'Public Assets' Theory of Lawyers' Pro Bono Obligations." *University of Pennsylvania Law Review* 145: 1245–307.

Macey, J. R. 1992. "Mandatory Pro Bono: Comfort for the Poor or Welfare for the Rich." *Cornell Law Review* 77: 1115–23.

Mallen, R. E., and J. M. Smith. 1996. *Legal Malpractice.* New York: West Group.

Maryland, Office of Attorney General. 1995. "Opinion of the Attorney General of the State of Maryland no. 95-056 (December 19, 1995)" (www.divorcelawinfo.com/agopinio.htm).

Mazzone, M. J. 1990. "Mandatory Pro Bono: Slavery in Disguise." *Texas Lawyer,* (October): 22.

McConville, M., and C. Mersky. 1995. "Guilty Plea Courts: A Social Disciplinary Model of the Criminal Justice State." *Social Problems* 42: 216–34.

Ostroff, R. 1981. "Missouri Remains Unable to Pay Indigents' Counsel: Pro Bono Revolt Grows." *National Law Journal,* May 11, 2.

Parker, C. 1999. *Just Lawyers: Regulation and Access to Justice.* Oxford University Press.

Pickering, J. 1999. Testimony on Legal Services Corporation, Subcommittee on Commercial and Administrative Law of the House Committee on the Judiciary, 106 Congress, 1 sess., September 29 (http://judiciary.house.gov/legacy/pick0929.htm).

Powell v. *Alabama.* 1932. 287 U.S. 45.

Posner, R. 1998. *Economic Analysis of Law.* New York: Aspen Law & Business Publishers.

Press, A. 2005. "Brother, Can You Spare 20 Hours?" *American Lawyer,* September 1 (www.law.com/jsp/PubArticle.jsp?id=900005435978).

———. 2007. "In House." *American Lawyer,* July.

Rhode, D. L. 1985. "Ethical Perspectives on Legal Practice." *Stanford Law Review* 37: 589–652.

———. 1996. "Professionalism in Perspective: Alternative Approaches to Nonlawyer Practice." *New York University Review of Law and Social Change* 22: 701–16.

———. 1999. "Cultures of Commitment: Pro Bono for Lawyers and Law Students." *Fordham Law Review* 67: 2415–47.

———. 2000. *In the Interests of Justice: Refining the Legal Profession*. Oxford University Press.

———. 2004. *Access to Justice*. Stanford University Press.

———. 2005. *Pro Bono in Principle and in Practice*. Stanford University Press.

Rhode, D. L., and D. Luban. 2009. *Legal Ethics*. New York: Foundation Press.

Rhudy, R. J. 1994. "Comparing Legal Services to the Poor in the United States with Other Western Countries: Some Preliminary Lessons." *Maryland Journal of Contemporary Legal Issues* 5: 223–46.

Richardson, M., and S. Reynolds. 1994. "The Shrinking Public Purse: Civil Legal Aid in New South Wales, Australia." *Maryland Journal of Contemporary Legal Issues* 5: 349–69.

Sackett, G. G. 1998. "Dear Access to Justice Task Force." *Utah Bar Journal* 11 (February): 22–23.

Seron, C. 1996. *The Business of Practicing Law: The Work Lives of Solo and Small Firm Attorneys*. Temple University Press.

Silver, C., and F. B. Cross. 2000. "What's Not to Like about Being a Lawyer?" *Yale Law Journal* 109, no. 6: 1443–503.

Sparks v. *Parker*. 1979. 368 Southern 2d 528 (Alabama).

State Bar of California. 1996. *And Justice for All: Fulfilling the Promise of Access to Civil Justice in California*. San Francisco.

Tawney, R. H., ed. 1964. *Equality*. London: Unwin.

Tremblay, P. R. 1999. "Aiding a Very Moral Type of God: Triage among Poor Clients." *Fordham Law Review* 67: 2475–532.

U.S. Government Printing Office. 1999. Code of Federal Regulation. Volume 45, paragraph 1611.3. Washington.

Zander, M. 2000. *The State of Justice*. London: Sweet & Maxwell.

12

Legal Empowerment of the Poor: Innovating Access to Justice

MAAIKE DE LANGEN AND MAURITS BARENDRECHT

The relationship between law and development is both promising and troubling. In the early seventies a famous article declared the field of law and development studies to be in crisis (Trubek and Galanter 1974). Two decades later, after fresh experiences with bringing the rule of law to ex-communist countries, some claimed that this crisis was continuing (Adelman and Paliwala 1993). At the same time however, from the late 1980s onward, attention to the role of governance in development increased, and as a consequence the functioning of the legal system in developing countries drew fresh interest. Economists started to uncover promising relationships between economic growth and the quality of legal institutions (Rodrik, Subramanian, and Trebbi 2004). In this context the focus was initially on promoting the rule of law and the reform of the formal institutions of the justice sector such as the judiciary and the legal profession. Partly in response to these top-down, state-centric reforms, "access to justice" as a bottom-up approach has been adopted by numerous organizations and experts over the past decade or so (van Rooij 2007). In the process, the meaning of access to justice has broadened from gaining access to the formal legal system to a more general emphasis on obtaining

The authors would like to thank Nina Berg and Veronique Verbruggen for detailed comments on an earlier version of this chapter. The views expressed here are those of the authors and do not necessarily represent those of the United Nations or the United Nations Development Program.

just remedies for rightful grievances, as well as achieving personal security and the protection of property rights (UNDP 2004).

These days, legal empowerment of the poor is gaining steam as a new approach more relevant to poor people's daily struggle for survival, one that links more directly to poverty reduction and human development than traditional rule-of-law promotion and law and development (Golub 2006). It shares many of the goals of these approaches, but chooses different strategies to achieve these goals. It overlaps with the "access to justice" approach, but prioritizes three domains that are crucial to the livelihoods of the poor: their property, their labor, and their business undertakings. In this chapter we consider the legal empowerment approach as a new agenda for access, exploring whether it takes a more realistic approach to improving the poor's access to justice.

Currently, one prominent advocate for this new approach is the Commission on Legal Empowerment of the Poor, an independent global commission, with its report "Making the Law work for Everyone" (Commission on Legal Empowerment of the Poor 2008a). This commission was co-chaired by Madeleine Albright and Hernando de Soto and hosted by the United Nations Development Program (UNDP). The commission's starting point was the observation that around the world, the poorest and most disadvantaged groups in society conduct the majority of their social, economic, and even political transactions and interactions in what is called the "informal sector," the "informal economy," "outside the rule of law," or the "extralegal economy." In the words of Co-chair Albright (2006, 10):

> These citizens do not own the houses or apartments in which they live, have no title to the land they till, cannot prove that the livestock they feed and care for are their own, do not qualify for credit, and have no legal license to sell what they produce. Many do not possess any legal documents, even a birth certificate or proof of identity. . . . Constantly vulnerable, they may be exploited by all who wield power, including criminals, predatory government officials, unscrupulous employers, and single-minded developers who may want to move the poor out of the way.

In this chapter we begin with some general observations on the state of access to justice around the world. Because access to justice is hard to measure and data on such access are scarce, we will give a description of the barriers to justice and mechanisms of exclusion and analyze how these work out for the poor in developing countries. Next we describe various strategies to improve access to justice, focusing on the innovative bottom-up approaches highlighted by the Commission on Legal Empowerment of the Poor. We will then discuss the agenda for access to justice in terms of what we know and what we do not know yet. We conclude by stressing the need for an innovative approach to the delivery of justice:

combining insights from academic research, smart innovation processes, sustainable "business models," and know-how from practical experience.

The State of Access to Justice

Some people may know justice when they see it. Most people have a keen idea about injustice. But we know very little about the extent to which the demand for justice is fulfilled—what share of people's legal needs is being met. Laws and legal systems can be designed on paper by legislatures building civil codes, criminal law, and court procedures. Justice, on the other hand, is delivered piecemeal, case by case, person by person. Whether a system works for groups of people with similar problems is hard to establish. It is much easier to survey people about the way they access water than to ask them whether they have access to personal security, to protection of their property, or to fair redress of their grievances in relation to other people. Justice needs are context-specific: they emerge in particular situations when people's interests are threatened by others, and the services required to serve these needs are highly variable.

In a recent paper, one of the authors of this chapter tried to identify the most urgent justice needs on the basis of legal needs surveys carried out in a number of countries (Barendrecht, Kamminga, and Verdonschot 2008). Arguably, many of the most urgent needs are related, first, to basic personal security against aggression from outsiders as well as members of the community; second, to protection of property rights, particularly rights to land and housing; and third, to legal issues that arise in connection with the two most important forms of relationships in which people invest their time and effort: their families and their work. Investments in these relationships may lead to mutual dependency, and sometimes to power imbalances. This interdependency can in turn engender conflict, making it hard to arrive at reasonable results in negotiations among those involved in the relationship. Thus, a need emerges for mechanisms that ensure that such relationships can be terminated on fair terms. For example, women often invest more time, effort, and even assets into their families than their husbands do. These investments will be lost if they end their relationships, making it difficult for them to choose to do so. This then leaves them vulnerable to exploitation. Other justice needs relate to neighbor conflicts, access to water, business relationships, and access to public services.

Legal need surveys consistently demonstrate that individuals employ a range of strategies to deal with these problems besides the official legal system. Fences and other landmarks mark off territory people consider theirs. Problems in relationships may be tackled with the help of priests, local leaders, friends, peer groups, clans, or the occasional police officer. Business relationships may be kept on track by means of reputation mechanisms that have little to do with the official legal system. In Latin America, *tramitadores* ("transactors"), local service providers without formal legal training, help people, for a fee, to deal with the paperwork that the bureaucracy requires. Sometimes these social processes work well, and sometimes they do not.

What we know is that many people live and interact outside the official legal and economic system. The Commission on Legal Empowerment of the Poor presents some interesting figures in this regard. In Bolivia, an estimated 25 percent of the population has no official documents proving their identity and their status as a citizen. In sub-Saharan Africa, 90 percent of all rural landholding is unregistered (Commission on Legal Empowerment of the Poor 2008b, 91). Customary rights may be recognized, but in practice such rights often do not have validity beyond supporting conflicting claims to ownership by farmers, the local community, and village leaders. Cities in developing economies show a similar pattern: 60 to 80 percent of urban dwellings are outside the official property registration system. Informal employment is very common for the poor. In Latin America, 58 percent of women and 48 percent of men who work are employed informally (ibid., 144). Similar patterns of up to 60 percent nonregistration can be found for businesses.

No comparable data exist for the degree of access to justice in situations where someone has a grievance or there is interpersonal conflict. It is safe to assume, however, that access to official judicial procedures in the case of personal conflict is even more limited than access to identity documents and registrations. Even in developed countries, for the poorest 25 percent of the population most court procedures are only accessible if the claimants have access to subsidized legal aid or if they have a claim that is so valuable and likely to succeed that they can sell part of it to a professional lawyer, who works on commission. A legal needs survey conducted in the Netherlands (a country with a reasonably accessible court system and one of the most sophisticated legal aid schemes available) shows that around 45 percent of legal problems remain unresolved, and around half of these can be attributed to the high costs, time demands, and emotional strain of legal proceedings (van Velthoven and ter Voert 2004).

However, interpreting these estimates of exclusion from access to formal legal identity, access to formal employment, access to formal business rights, access to formal property rights, and access to formal courts is difficult. The percentages cited, ranging from 25 to 90 percent of the population, at the very least underline the importance of focusing on the problem of lack of access. Whether or not a person chooses to, or can, access the formal legal system is likely to depend on a variety of factors. Registering as a citizen, property owner, or businessperson has costs: there may be fees or other expenses, and dealing with the bureaucracy takes time. Registration may also have disadvantages, for example, taxes that would otherwise be avoided. Where services connected with public status are of low quality or are equally available to unofficial enterprises, an individual, entrepreneur, or owner of property may decide that official registration is not worth it.

Moreover, an informal system may exist that offers similar benefits at lower cost. These factors may differ from individual to individual, depending on the extent of that person's interests, the local alternatives to official governance structures, and the accessibility of the official system.

When we combine the information on legal needs with the figures about informality, we can safely conclude that for a large proportion of the population in developing countries, the costs of accessing official procedures are higher than the benefits. Since lowering these costs will give more people more choices, a more detailed analysis of the structure of these costs is warranted.

Barriers to Justice

Access to justice is the rule of law as it works out in practice for individuals. A country may have a functioning legal system, but the system may not serve all citizens, or it may only engage in a limited range of cases. The barriers that people face in obtaining access to justice are well known and have been analyzed by academics and practitioners alike (UNDP 2004; Commission on Legal Empowerment of the Poor 2008b, 12–15). Six of the most visible barriers to access to the formal justice system are already insurmountable for many people in developing countries: geographical barriers, financial barriers, language problems, complexity, cultural norms, and delay.

One of the most obvious barriers is the *geographical distance* from courts. In most developing countries, there are too few judges, lawyers, and courts, and those that exist are generally concentrated in the capital or larger cities. Traveling to the courts takes a lot of time and is too expensive for most poor people. This effect is obviously stronger in vast, thinly populated countries lacking modern transportation systems and infrastructure.

Financial barriers can hinder access as well. Court fees can be high and are frequently an obstacle for people even to begin legal proceedings. In addition to official court fees, there are all kinds of additional costs, particularly for poor people. If they cannot read or write they will have to find or pay someone to write their documents. If they do not have an identity document they will have to obtain one first, which costs money; for poor people even the cost of an ID picture is substantial. The legal services of lawyers, advocates, and notaries are expensive anywhere in the world. In many cases there is the obligation for representation by a legal professional, and the market for legal services is often highly restricted. Legal aid systems, if they exist at all, are severely inadequate, even in rich countries (see chapter 11, this volume), but even more so in developing countries. If they exist, they often have to focus their efforts and budgets on criminal defense, and have little left for helping the poor with other legal problems.

The third barrier is *language*. Norms and procedures have to be understandable. Laws are generally drafted and courts operate in the national language(s) of the country, an automatic barrier to all who have not mastered that language. In almost all African countries, the official language is that of the former colonial power, but almost the entire population has a different language as its mother tongue. Even if there is a shared language that all or most people speak, the official language for legislation and court procedures remains that of the former colonial power.[1] An even higher barrier is illiteracy; those who cannot read and write are at a huge disadvantage in modern legal systems, which are strongly based on written documents, in the form of laws, regulations, and legal documents. Even when testimony can be oral, almost every step of a legal procedure requires the submission of written documents. It is easy to understand the impact of these requirements in countries with high illiteracy rates.

Related to language is the *complexity* of laws and court procedures. Because laws are intended to be unequivocal, those who draft laws often resort to highly technical language and sophisticated analytical distinctions. Lawyers the world over are known for their extravagant language and often are accused of unnecessarily complicating things. This is no different in developing countries, though the impact of this complexity is obviously more substantial when the average education level is lower. In addition, drafting laws costs money and better drafting costs more money, so the quality of drafting may be lower in developing countries. The quality of drafting suffers further from lack of institutional capacity, faltering relations between technical ministries and a country's justice ministry, and a general dearth of drafting capacity of national parliaments. Finally, in most developing countries there are different layers of law, which can be analytically separated into four ideal types. The first layer is local norms, and the second is religious norms; some would call these law, but others would not. The third layer is the legislative legacies from colonial periods, and the fourth is legislation adopted since independence, often including fairly recent and sometimes state-of-the-art constitutions (Otto 1991). Thus, there may be a profusion of regulations dating from different periods and arising from varying traditions that can be applicable to one single issue. Lack of rules that establish a hierarchy, as well as fundamental incompatibilities between these different layers, add to the general uncertainty about which rules apply (de Langen 2001). The barriers of language and complexity obviously reinforce one another when one is obliged to decipher complex laws in a language that is not one's mother tongue.

Another barrier is the existence of *cultural norms* that lead to social pressure against pursuing remedies for grievances in court—for example, because taking a conflict to court is seen as dishonorable. Sometimes such pressures arise because taking a case to court is perceived as an embarrassment to community leaders or as a sign that the community cannot handle its own problems (Bappenas, United

---

1. Even in the Netherlands it was not until January 1, 2003, that the last piece of legislation in the French language was abolished. Until that day, the Mining Law of April 21, 1810, promulgated by Napoleon, was still in force, though French rule over the Netherlands ended in 1813!

Nations Development Program Indonesia, and Center for Rural and Regional Development Studies 2007). In yet other cases, the court system is seen as something solely for criminals, and hence to be avoided altogether (UNDP 2004). The common denominator of these cultural norms is that the legal system is seen as external to the small-scale community in which the majority of poor people live their lives.

These are barriers to justice that are encountered mainly when a case is started. But legal proceedings also must end. As the saying goes: Justice delayed is justice denied. Courts in developing countries often have impressive backlogs, and these *delays* form barriers of their own. As the report of the Commission on Legal Empowerment of the Poor indicates, in India over 20 million legal cases are pending, and some civil cases take over twenty years to reach court. Around a million cases are pending in Kenya, and the average judge in the Philippines has a backlog of 1,479 cases (Commission on Legal Empowerment of the Poor 2008a, 32).

Mechanisms of Exclusion from Access to Justice

In addition to these relatively straightforward barriers, there are less visible mechanisms at play that create unequal access. Such mechanisms of exclusion operate differently from country to country and understanding them requires detailed inquiry into the local context. Some examples from Mali can serve to illustrate how such mechanisms operate.

In a small dusty town in the north of Mali, Ousmane, a farmer who was born and raised here, has a conflict with one of his neighbors over who owns a particular piece of land.[2] How can Ousmane find out what the law is? There are no bookstores or even libraries in this town, and Ousmane, like most people here, cannot read. But he does know that there is a justice of the peace. His courthouse is one of the few concrete buildings in the town, so everyone knows it. One day, Ousmane musters up his courage and goes to the courthouse. When he gets to the compound, the first person he runs into is the guard, who tells Ousmane either to come in or when to come back. Ousmane shyly walks toward the building, where he meets a second person, the janitor, who tells him to wait on a small wooden bench on the porch of the courthouse. So Ousmane waits. If he is lucky, he might eventually be able to talk to the official interpreter of the court. The interpreter is the one who de facto grants access to the court clerk. Or not. The clerk, of course, is not always there, does not always have time, and may not feel like helping Ousmane, who is visibly a poor man. Yet if the clerk does not tell

2. This example is fictitious; it is based on observations and combines characteristics of multiple cases studied and persons interviewed during field research conducted by Maaike de Langen from January through April 2001 and from January through April 2002, in Douentza, a small town in Mali about 125 miles south of Timbuktu (see de Langen 2005 for the results of this research).

Ousmane how to submit the papers to start a case, or even that there are papers to submit, how will Ousmane move his case forward? Obviously, the four people mentioned could be very friendly and competent and help Ousmane start his case. Sometimes they are—but sometimes they are not. Ousmane is entirely dependent on these people to show him how the process works, how the court works, and what he has to do.

Since the guard, the janitor, the translator, and the clerk are all poor people themselves, scraping to get by on meager government salaries that are often paid months behind schedule, the knowledge and access that they have can easily be turned into a source for supplementing their salaries. Perhaps not when it is their brother or neighbor looking for help, but when it is someone whom they do not particularly like or do not know at all, what is to prevent them from making a little money on the side? Or when it is not Ousmane, but his wife who comes to the courthouse? They might feel that a woman should not even be able to start a court case. It is easy to see how petty corruption as well as racial or ethnic and gender discrimination can creep into relatively casual daily interactions. The sum of these interactions nevertheless has a strong influence on de facto access to justice. In practice, these people become gatekeepers because of a profound lack of transparency in the institutions and tremendous difficulties in obtaining even the most basic legal information. These factors combine with the fact that there is no functioning mechanism to hold these gatekeepers accountable when they create or become obstacles to access.

Another mechanism of exclusion is the inability of the legal system to distribute information about the law. Many legal systems, particularly in the poorest countries, are dysfunctional to the point that it is impossible to know the laws, rules, and regulations that are in force (Barron, Smith and Woolcock 2004). This is often hard to imagine for lawyers trained in Western countries, where the process of law-making is sophisticated, rules for the publication of laws are clear, and the state has the financial and human resources to sustain the channels of publication and communication necessary for the flow of legal information. In developing—particularly the least developed—countries, this is very often not the case and it may simply be impossible to know the law.

Research in the same town in Mali provides some examples of this unavailability of legal texts. The objective of this study was to look at the effects of national decentralization policy at the local level through a case study of a particular land parcellation and distribution process, called *lotissement*. For four months in early 2002, everyone involved in land issues at the local level was interviewed: the justice of the peace and his assessors, the mayor and his deputies, the village chief and his advisers, local bureaucrats and businessmen, and a judge of the regional court of appeals. All these people used and referred to the law that determines land relations, the *code foncier*, of 1986. The problem was that this law was no longer applicable; it had been replaced by new legislation eighteen months earlier. Yet because the text of that new law had not yet been distributed in northern Mali and no one knew of its existence, it was not being applied (de Langen 2005).

The Malian Penal Code was, similarly, unavailable in this town. In 2001 the judge proudly showed a copy of the French Penal Code, which he was using in his courtroom.[3] It had been easier for him to obtain through his networks a commercially available and annotated version of the French Penal Code than an edition of the Malian Penal Code, which it was his official responsibility to apply. Even though the Malian code is derived from the French one, the French Penal Code is still a foreign piece of legislation. But simply because the text was available, the judge applied it to the cases he had to decide. This problem of the unavailability and inaccessibility of legal texts is widespread, not just in African countries.

Unequal Access to Justice

We have identified six main barriers (geographical, financial, and language barriers, complexity, cultural norms, and delays) and two mechanisms of exclusion (gatekeepers and uncertainty about the law) and this analysis is not exhaustive. The question is how, then, these factors affect people. The law is almost always neutral in theory; nearly all legal systems recognize the principle that all people are equal before the law.[4] However, barriers are far from being neutral. It is a truism that financial barriers impact poor people differently than they do rich people. But the same holds for other kinds of obstacles. If the closest court is fifty miles from your home, it makes a huge difference whether you own a car, can afford public transport, or have to walk. In poor and rich countries alike, it is typically the most vulnerable groups, those with fewer resources, lower levels of education, and less social capital, that have the most difficulty surmounting barriers of language and complexity. The effect of cultural norms that stop people from turning to the formal legal system may be harder to pin down, but it would be an acceptable hypothesis that such cultural norms affect the poor more than the elites. With regard to delays, poor people typically have fewer resources to weather long periods of uncertainty about the outcome of a case. And though we might imagine that delays apply equally to rich and poor, in practice, for the rich there are frequently both formal and informal ways to obtain "expedited" service—thus, even delays in the court system are unlikely to affect rich people as badly as they do poor people. Analytically, all barriers to justice can be seen as factors that increase the costs of achieving redress for grievances and protection of assets.

---

3. Author interview, April 10, 2001, Douentza, Mali. (Interviews were done on the condition of anonymity.)

4. See Article 7 of the Universal Declaration of Human Rights: "All are equal before the law and are entitled without any discrimination to equal protection of the law." Despite this widely shared principle, it has to be recognized that upon closer inspection, discrimination persists in many legal systems, particularly against women.

The two mechanisms of exclusion, the existence of gatekeepers, and uncertainty about the law also hit poor people harder than rich. Those who are responsible for delivering justice have fewer incentives to help the poor than to help the rich. Generally, the rich get better teachers, psychologists, and doctors because they can give more in return. There is no reason why justice would be an exception. Uncertainty about the law can actually become a powerful tool in the hands of those with resources, since they can spend time, or hire a lawyer to spend time, researching the law and selectively using what laws they manage to get their hands on. Furthermore, because the texts of laws and decrees often circulate mostly in government circles, those who have networks that extend into these circles have a greater chance of obtaining photocopies of particular pieces of legislation that support their case.

Deeper power relations cannot be ignored in the analysis of access to justice. For example, the gatekeepers themselves are often poor and relatively powerless. Their behavior may be only a symptom of a larger dysfunctional system, in which some interests may purposely or inadvertently perpetuate inaccessibility for the have-nots. Barron, Smith, and Woolcock (2004) describe how conflicts are also an opportunity for groups to define themselves. Rallying around a cause or refusing to use group pressure to redress grievances are both mechanisms around which extended families, clans, communities, or work-related groups can organize, making it more attractive for members to belong to said group. These strategies make the group (and its leaders) more powerful. Individual grievances and interests may thus be transformed into (or strategically excluded from) group interests, sometimes getting deformed along the way. What starts as a particular problem about payment of salary with an individual employer may end up as a rally against employers in general about working conditions. In environments where group pressure and protection are much more easily accessible than a neutral intervention, the rights and interests of individuals are more likely to become part of a complicated package deal. The group grants protection and informally regulates access to essential goods and services among group members. The individual sees some of his interests and rights protected, and has to submit to the norms and wishes of the group in other matters.

The well-being of the collective may thus become relatively more important than that of the individual. Formal legal systems tend to take the individual as the unit of protection, and thus have difficulty dealing with this social reality. This becomes apparent when legal institutions have to deal with customary land law, which often assigns rights to communities instead of individuals. One of the possible outcomes of these "dynamics of difference," as Barron, Smith, and Woolcock (2004) call them, is that local, customary norms come to be seen as unjust when viewed through the lens of Western human rights lawyers. Because these norms are more or less the result of a trade-off between protection and other interests, they often discriminate against individuals who are disadvantaged within these relationships: women, subsistence farmers, or the poor more generally. Unjust norms at the local level may even migrate upward into the formal legal system.

Because barriers to justice and mechanisms of exclusion affect some people more than others, de facto equality before the law is not achieved and the law then becomes a resource to those who have the knowledge, the networks, and the means to use it.[5] The better-off can use the law to strengthen their positions, while the poor have a much harder time asserting themselves and claiming their rights. Typically, preexisting inequalities will be reinforced or even exacerbated when some people can make use of the law when it benefits them and ignore it when it does not.

Rule-of-Law Reform and Access to Justice Programs

The promotion of the rule of law, which often comprises, but is broader than, technical assistance to law reform, remains very high on the international agenda. Traditional rule of law promotion is dubbed the "rule-of-law orthodoxy" by Thomas Carothers (2006) in his sobering analysis of the lack of success of this "industry" so far. He mentions three types of rule-of-law reform: "Revising laws or whole codes to weed out antiquated provisions[;] . . . the strengthening of law-related institutions, usually to make them more competent, efficient, and accountable[; and] . . . reforms aimed at the deeper goal of increasing government's compliance with law. A key step is achieving genuine judicial independence" (7).

An increasing volume of literature is suggesting, without disputing the importance of the rule of law, that there are still large gaps in our knowledge about how the rule of law develops and what can be done to support or stimulate this process in a way that delivers tangible results for poor people (Carothers 2003, 3). In providing support to justice sector reform, the vast majority of donor efforts focus on the formal legal system, neglecting informal justice systems (Wojkowska 2006). Frequently, such legal development cooperation starts with an analysis of the system. It compares the legal system of a given developing country to functioning systems, mostly in Western countries. This especially happens in areas such as commercial law and the functioning of the financial system, but is also still a prominent aspect of civil justice reform. Based on this comparison, reformers identify what needs to be fixed and (theoretically) how these changes can be achieved, in a process called "attempting to reproduce institutional endpoints" (Carothers 2006, 21).

Does this work? Carothers and his colleagues seriously doubt that such top-down approaches do much good. In particular, it is difficult to see how they can

5. For a groundbreaking discussion see Galanter (1974).

improve access to justice for the majority of the population deprived of the ability to use the formal legal system. Redrafting laws in the economic domain will not do much to help small and medium-size enterprises to protect their business interests, though it may remove some red tape. Training and paying judges will have little effect on the geographical, financial, linguistic, and complexity barriers that individuals face. Fighting court delays and the cultural norms that inhibit taking legal action seem to require something other than fostering legal education and professional standards for lawyers.

Expanding access to courts by setting up local branches or alternative dispute resolution systems with sufficient capacity to serve the justice needs of the poor is expensive. The Council of Europe countries, most of which are stable and lack the conflict triggers that beset developing countries, tend to employ twenty to forty professional judges and ten to forty nonprofessional judges per 100,000 inhabitants (European Commission for the Efficiency of Justice 2006, 77). Court clerks, lawyers, experts, and many other professionals are also required to deal with disputes and crimes satisfactorily. Thus, an average developing country of 20 million inhabitants needs to select, pay, train, manage, and supervise at least 10,000 (semi)professionals to make the legal system work. Given the numerous competing development priorities, developing country governments are unlikely to be able to free up the necessary resources for such a large-scale, long-term investment.

Moreover, a functioning legal system requires a delicate interplay among these professions. Judges cannot work without clerks and access to legal information. Lawyers cannot help their clients without judges. Even finding a path leading to institutional equilibrium on a countrywide level is likely to take many years. In the meantime, the poor will still have problems with local gatekeepers and uncertainty about the law. Not one rule-of-law reform program has originated a really comprehensive or sustainable solution to the challenge of funding and supporting the various interlocking parts of the legal system at the same time.

The best that may be expected from these top-down rule-of-law approaches is that they can gradually spread legal access to larger portions of the population once a nation's economy can support more extensive and better legal institutions. According to one strand of literature, economic development is likely to increase the reach of the rule of law because stronger suppliers of goods and services become interested in bigger consumer markets, and thus need richer customers, which they can only get by guaranteeing them more legal protection. Still, this is not exactly the type of shortcut the law and development world is looking for.

A New Agenda for Access: The Legal Empowerment Approach

The term "legal empowerment" has been around for some time. The concept, as it is used in a number of publications, brings together a range of alternative approaches to promoting access to justice that have been developed largely in response to discontent with traditional rule-of-law and law-and-development approaches. Though certainly not mainstream, the activities and underlying ideas that have been grouped under the concept of legal empowerment are now fairly common throughout the world, and have been applied by many different organizations, in particular by NGOs, at local, national, and international levels. Stephen Golub is the author of a number of texts on legal empowerment, published in reports for the Asian Development Bank, the Carnegie Endowment, and the World Bank (Asian Development Bank 2001; Golub 2003, 2005, 2006).

In these publications, legal empowerment is defined as "the use of legal services and related development activities to increase disadvantaged populations' control over their lives" (Golub 2003, 25). It is seen as both a process and a goal. Golub sees legal empowerment as a strategy combining a number of activities that can be grouped into two main categories, one focusing on access to information and awareness raising and the second on direct support for meeting the legal needs of the target group. In the first category, the activities mentioned include using accessible printed media and broadcast media, performing arts, popular entertainment, community law libraries, and the Internet to deliver legal information. Other activities are different kinds of training, such as community-based training, distance education, youth education, and training of trainers. The second category comprises the use of paralegals, alternative dispute resolution, legal aid, public-interest litigation, administrative advocacy and education, and training for government officials (Asian Development Bank 2001, 41–49).

Legal empowerment as advocated by Golub can be seen as a collection of interventions in the field of law and development that have proved successful in practice. More recent writings have identified five common elements as typical of legal empowerment strategy. These include strengthening the capacities and power of the disadvantaged; selecting issues on the basis of the needs and preferences of the poor; focusing on broader societal, political, legal, and administrative actors, and not only the justice sector; supporting civil society; and relying on domestic ideas and initiatives (Golub 2006, 164). Finally, an important characteristic is the rejection of the traditional, state-centric, justice-sector-focused, and lawyer-dominated "rule-of-law orthodoxy."

The Commission on Legal Empowerment of the Poor takes a somewhat different approach to legal empowerment because the main problems that the commission focuses on are poverty and exclusion, which, it argues, are intimately related. The rallying cry of the Commission on Legal Empowerment of the Poor is that 4 billion people in the world are excluded from the rule of law. This indicates that the agenda of the commission is broader than access to justice alone, because it looks at exclusion from the rule of law more broadly and draws particular attention to the property, the labor, and the business undertakings of the poor. Three shifts of emphasis distinguish the legal empowerment approach:

1. Adopting a legal perspective on the economy at the micro-level
2. Adopting an economic perspective to supplying law at the micro-level
3. Taking a realistic approach to the law and the economy

A Legal Perspective on the Economy at the Micro-Level

The Commission on Legal Empowerment of the Poor (2008a, 3) states, "No modern market economy can function without the law." Inclusive economic growth can only be achieved if the necessary legal framework is in place. The law is seen as a fundamental underpinning of the economy: the invisible hand of the market can only function if there is also the visible hand of the law to organize economic interactions, not only on the level of macro-economic institutions but also on the micro-level of economic interactions.[6] This shift impacts the analytical starting point of the commission: the livelihoods of the poor, livelihoods that are composed of their assets and the activities they undertake. The domain of property rights is relevant to their assets; the domains of labor and business rights are relevant to their activities. The poor need effective legal tools and protection in these areas in order to have a fair chance to improve their lives. Access to justice is the necessary underpinning of these three substantive areas of law.

Legal empowerment is a dual approach based on both protection and opportunity: protection of what poor people have and hold, and opportunity to increase the productivity of their assets and activities. A focus on protection is fairly common when the law in developing countries is assessed, which is often undertaken under the rubric of human rights, especially civil and political rights. Protection of people and of their property is the first step to any kind of development, and for this reason legal empowerment starts with protecting what people have. Yet legal empowerment focuses on the law not only as a means of protection but also as a means of creating opportunity. Access to justice from this perspective implies equal access to remedies against injustices suffered—protection—but also equal access to participation in society and the economy—opportunity.

Particularly in relation to opportunity, the idea of legal empowerment is broader than strict access to justice. In both the access-to-justice approach and the protection dimension of legal empowerment there tends to be a focus on finding resolutions to situations of conflict, but in the opportunity dimension of legal empowerment the focus is more on the institutions that the law creates and the economic transactions that the law facilitates, even when conflict never emerges. The fact that the law organizes behavior and expectation without ever explicitly coming into play is called the shadow function of the law. This shadow function exists only when the possibility of recourse to legal proceedings is genuine—when there is access to justice.

6. Credit for this metaphor of the law as the "visible hand" goes to Jens Chr. Wandel.

In a way, the notion of legal empowerment is a more instrumental perspective on the law, a way of seeing how the legal system as a whole underpins the functioning of society and the workings of the economy. The focus is therefore on law and legal tools as one of the crucial elements that people need to make their economic agency more productive, thereby improving their standard of living. When we look at the law through this lens our attention shifts from the more traditional focus on criminal law, commercial law, and some areas of civil law such as family law to administrative law and other areas of civil law, most notably the domain of property rights.

Where traditional access to justice programs often focus on training judges, building more courts, raising legal awareness, and revising legislation to implement international human rights treaties, legal empowerment programs are more likely to focus on helping people obtain a legal identity, a recognized street address, and an enforceable and protected title to land; increasing the accessibility of business registration; mending dysfunctional permit systems; protecting street vendors; and improving access to financing. Other important elements are enabling multinationals and micro-entrepreneurs alike to enter into and realistically enforce contracts.

An Economic Perspective to Supplying Law at the Micro-Level

We believe that legal empowerment also demands a different way of thinking about access to justice. It does not deny the fundamental importance of access to justice nor the right of all people to be treated equally before the law—on the contrary—but argues that the use of supply-and-demand analysis and the adoption of more pragmatic economic approaches to implementation can be beneficial in making access to justice a reality.

One of the problems of an analysis in terms of barriers to justice is that it focuses on the formal legal system as the sole locus of the "justice" that people want to access. The reality of access to goods and services is that many different types are on offer, of different qualities and fitting different needs. They must also be measured against higher or lower costs of access. Justice is no exception to this rule. From the perspective of the poor, the formal legal system, with its lawyers and courts, is often out of reach, but as we have seen, the poor may have access to informal justice systems to settle their grievances, to local authorities, to religious authorities acting as intermediaries, to groups of the similarly disadvantaged that can take collective action, and to other local routines and ad hoc ways of solving disputes and protecting rights. Therefore, legal empowerment focuses on broader societal, political, legal, and administrative actors, and not only the justice sector.

When we adopt an economic perspective on access to justice, the question becomes, which goods or services have to be supplied by this range of actors?

Law and development literature has not yet produced a convincing definition of the "justice" that should be provided, at least not one that is independent of any particular justice system. We may, however, tentatively list the following elements that should be accessible:

—A setting in which a dispute or a need for protection can be discussed and solutions can be negotiated

—Principles, rules, criteria, or schedules that guide the outcomes of discussion

—A (neutral) person who can decide on outcomes, particularly if the disputants are not able to settle their differences

—Sufficient incentives for the disputants to live up to the outcome that is reached through settlement or neutral decision

These four elements do not fit every need for justice in the same way. Access to justice is not only a matter of norms and processes that enable the settlement of disputes, as the Commission on Legal Empowerment for the Poor has stressed, but also an approach that supplies other goods and services. An inclusive legal system gives access to smoothly functioning legal norms and institutions and allows citizen participation in government law making, as well as providing more tangible services such as birth registrations, identity documents, personal security, and well-defined and secure property rights.

Another consequence of this shift in thinking is that it draws attention to the demand side of justice. This is particularly relevant for states that have very limited budgets for the justice sector but that nonetheless wish to improve their justice systems. By focusing on finding solutions to the needs of the people that are within the means of both the government and the poor, legal empowerment can lead to focused interventions that have a disproportionately large impact. Legal empowerment is context-specific, so the best way to achieve this impact is to base any reforms or programs on an initial analysis of the justice needs of the poor as they themselves perceive them.

Thus, there is a strong emphasis on participation in the legal empowerment approach when it comes to defining problems and designing solutions. Though this approach is not new, there are very few programs that truly take the needs of poor people as a starting point for reforms in the justice sector. One such recent (and impressive) example is research conducted in a project for the Indonesian government and executed with support of UNDP Indonesia (Bappenas, United Nations Development Program Indonesia, and Center for Rural and Regional Development Studies 2007). Extensive research underlying this report focused on identifying the key justice-related issues affecting citizens at the village level, especially the poor and disadvantaged.

The next step is to determine the capacity of the poor to cope with their justice needs and to develop ways to incorporate these findings in planning services. One way of doing this is to follow the base-of-the-pyramid method for developing products and services tailored to the needs of the poor, as proposed by proponents for developing microjustice as the next form of microservice.[7] This method adapts first world technology, management processes, and product development techniques to third world circumstances. It aims to develop products and services that are affordable for the poor, yet sustainable to deliver for legal entrepreneurs on a for-profit basis.[8] One element of microjustice is the idea that justice should be provided by local labor, abundantly available within the communities where the poor live. Microjustice facilitators could provide neutral assistance with communicating and negotiating conflicts, extending local conflict management capacities. These neutral, problem-solving legal services can be provided with information about essential rules of thumb for dealing with the most common legal problems; these rules would correspond to the most urgent legal needs identified at the outset of the program. This information could in some situations be delivered by a Web interface, which would supply both local rules regarding these problems and similar rules for the corresponding problems in other locations. Transparency of informal and formal rules of thumb—for example, on how to calculate indemnities when someone is fired, what a reasonable compensation is for ending a lease, or how to arrive at acceptable amounts for alimony in the case of divorce—could establish "the going rates of justice." This would not only lead to lower costs for dispute resolution but also, it is to be hoped, would enhance the possibility of comparison between locations and jurisdictions, which would also lead to a gradual adjustment of unfair rules in the direction of international standards.

Taking a Realistic Approach to the Law and the Economy

Perhaps it is surprising that taking a realistic approach should constitute a shift in thinking about access to justice, but it is a shift. Lawyers, who generally make up the majority of practitioners in law and development projects, are trained to look at things not as they are but as they ought to be. If a lawyer is in a different country and wants to understand how the law there works, he or she will generally read the country's statutes and laws. Only socio-legal scholars would think to observe actual court sessions and conduct interviews to find out what really happens. Public policymakers often fall into the same trap. They base their policies on assumptions about how the economy works or how society is organized.

Legal empowerment, by contrast, focuses on the economy as it really is, not as models describe it, and on the law as it really works in practice, not as it appears on the books. The informal economy and informal justice systems must be taken into account and should form an integral part of the context analysis. In real life, formal and informal are not opposites, but are two extremes on a continuum. People use a mix of formal and informal institutions, depending on the attrac-

---

7. See Barendrecht and van Nispen (2008) and other papers available at www.microjustice.org.
8. For more information, see the Base of the Pyramid protocol website (http://bop-protocol.org).

tiveness of the alternatives they see in their particular situation. Legal empowerment is about explicitly recognizing the informal sphere and proposing solutions based on a thorough understanding of the informal and the formal spheres and the interplay between the two.

Thus, legal information is a matter not only of learning the law but also of learning how to cope with disputes through negotiation techniques and appropriate communication. Legal services and justice goods not only can be provided by professional lawyers but also can be delivered by forming peer groups that press local power interests gently, or by paralegals who coach clients in dealing with their opponents. Microjustice facilitators may intervene on behalf of clients while maintaining a generally neutral stance, but also may have to create incentives for solving the problem in a mutually satisfactory manner.

Revisiting the Barriers and Mechanisms of Exclusion

Legal empowerment addresses the issue of access to justice in a much broader and more realistic manner than has otherwise been attempted, by looking at linkages that can be created between the informal mechanisms that exist at the local or community level and the formal legal mechanisms that operate at the level of the state. Because local informal mechanisms for dispute resolution are taken into account as an integral way of handling conflicts, the question of access to justice becomes inverted. Are those mechanisms that are accessible just? Legal empowerment starts to work with mechanisms at the local level with three objectives. The first is to create local interaction and discussion about how these mechanisms work and how they compare with similar rules elsewhere, with broader principles of human rights law, with the constitution, and with national legislation. The second objective is to use these local mechanisms as building blocks for improved functioning of the formal legal system and state courts. Third, reformers can create a workable interface between local, informal practices and the formal national legal system through recognition, incorporation, and standardization of elements of these informal practices where appropriate.

In terms of geography, a legal empowerment approach emphasizes local solutions and builds on local mechanisms. Financial barriers to justice will also be reduced: informal mechanisms for dispute resolution have a fee level set to accommodate what the market will bear—in fact, there may be no fees at all. If court proceedings are necessary only in exceptional cases, courts and legal aid will become easier to fund. A hierarchical system of appeal with recognition for lower-level judgments is one option, but there may be other ways to monitor performance of local systems and to make them answer to client needs. Informal mechanisms typically operate more quickly, without formal procedural complexities that tend to delay court proceedings. There may also be a deescalating effect, which is a central element of alternative dispute resolution mechanisms. Whereas court procedures tend to exacerbate conflict by encouraging parties to take extreme positions in a winner-takes-all situation, local mechanisms may be more geared to facilitating settlements and finding solutions acceptable to both sides. The language barrier is easier to deal with at the local level, and procedural and substantive complexity can be significantly reduced. Paralegals and legal clinics can operate in the local language(s). Simplification of all kinds of administrative and licensing procedures will lower barriers of complexity, language, time, and costs. As in all things, however, much depends on the execution. Dispute systems have a natural tendency to become more complex and formalized over time, and the conflicting interests of both clients make them poor guardians of the quality and costs of the justice products they receive.

Cultural norms that prevent people from using the legal system may not operate in the same way for informal justice mechanisms. Of course, other cultural norms will continue to prevent people from meeting some of their justice needs, such as women who dare not speak up against abusive husbands, but resistance can perhaps be reduced. If the dispute system is more accessible and in greater sync with the realities in which people live and organize their economic transactions, it is less likely to be perceived as alien. Involving communities in processes through which nonstate and formal institutions are linked will be crucial. One of the challenges, however, remains to see how local justice reformers can cope with unjust local norms and existing power relations that are often the result of the very institutions that offer the poor some degree of economic and social protection.

Reducing exclusion is what the legal empowerment approach is all about. There are several ways in which legal empowerment removes the obstacles to access enumerated earlier. If legal knowledge is available and shared, gatekeepers will no longer be able to exclude disadvantaged parties with their monopolies on procedural knowledge. There is, of course, the risk that paralegals, microjustice facilitators, or other new legal service providers will themselves become new gatekeepers; mechanisms of accountability and transparency will have to be built in to avert this. Increased transparency of legal information also makes it easier for clients to monitor the quality of legal professionals and increases choice, just as medical information available through the Internet makes it easier for patients to monitor health care providers or to choose less costly self-help medication. Increased transparency of ground-level mediation and negotiation may also prove to be an antidote to power relationships that go awry.

Conclusion: An Access Agenda under Construction

Legal empowerment has the potential to address both obstacles to access and mechanisms of exclusion, thus contributing to a more inclusive rule of law. Making the law work for everyone is a very ambitious target, but bottom-up processes may be able to usher in real progress toward this goal. Legal empowerment employs preexisting mechanisms inducing the market to deliver justice services; it also takes as its starting point the justice needs that are most clearly linked to participation in the economy and to other processes that are essential for human development. Legal empowerment means more than safeguarding certain human rights against government intervention. We must emphasize its focus on the informal economy and informal justice systems, its work with civil society and paralegals, its privileging of legal needs of the poor, its insistence on mediating between local and national legal processes, and its commitment to lowering costs.

However, a promising approach does not yet constitute a feasible strategy. Translating the approach into concrete programs and getting the implementation right will be crucial. It is also difficult, because of weak incentives in a setting of conflicting interests (Barendrecht and de Vries 2004). Before legal empowerment can be made to work wholesale, we need to investigate further the delivery of the four crucial elements of a dispute system. How can reformers create a neutral setting for discussing disputes? How can practitioners ensure that applicable norms and other knowledge they need to solve disputes are made available? Support by information technology may be a solution, but who will publicize the information? Why does the multi-billion-dollar legal information market only seem to serve the legal profession, and not the clients themselves? Making a qualified neutral person accessible to resolve disputes is still a huge challenge. Even developed countries suffer from court delays and high costs of access to justice, so it is hard to find examples of a working technology that can be scaled up for mass production of justice goods. Such advances can only be made in the long run through determined efforts at standardization, cost reduction, and making good use of available best practices. Incentives to live up to outcomes also deserve much more attention. Sanctions provided by the formal legal system may be much more expensive to organize than informal triggers to live up to norms and outcomes of dispute resolution processes. Examples, rewards, reputation mechanisms, and according to one author even limited forms of harassing may be much more effective (Fafchamps 1996). At the same time there is always the danger that these may lead to new inequalities.

Perfect justice is as unlikely to exist as any other perfect service. Implementing perfect justice from above seems to be an impossible mission. Improving justice from the bottom up by empowering clients and by stimulating justice entrepreneurs to innovate legal services is a more realistic approach. Making it happen will be a matter of hard work and of smartly organized trial and error processes, informed by the social sciences. That is the innovation that we think the legal empowerment approach can bring.

References

Adelman, S., and A. Paliwala, eds. 1993. *Law and Crisis in the Third World.* London: Hans Zell.

Albright, M. 2006. "It's Time for Empowerment." In *Legal Empowerment: A Way Out of Poverty.*" Norwegian Ministry of Foreign Affairs, no. 2, p. 10.

Asian Development Bank. 2001. "Law and Policy Reform at the Asian Development Bank" (www.adb.org/documents/others/law_adb/lpr_2001.pdf).

Bappenas, United Nations Development Program Indonesia, and Center for Rural and Regional Development Studies. 2007. "Justice for All? An Assessment of Access to Justice in Five Provinces of Indonesia" (www.undp.or.id/pubs/docs/Justicepercent20forpercent 20All_.pdf).

Barendrecht, M., and B. R. de Vries. 2004. "Fitting the Forum to the Fuss with Sticky Defaults: Failure on the Market for Dispute Resolution Services?" (http://ssrn.com/abstract=572042).

Barendrecht, M., P. Kamminga, and J. H. Verdonschot. 2008. "Priorities for the Justice System: Responding to the Most Urgent Legal Problems of Individuals." TISCO Working Paper No. 001/2008. Tilburg Institute for Interdisciplinary Studies of Civil Law and Conflict Resolution Systems (http://ssrn.com/abstract=1090885).

Barendrecht, M., and P. van Nispen. 2008. "Microjustice TILEC Discussion Paper 2008-010." Tilburg University, Tilburg Law and Economics Center (http://ssrn.com/abstract= 1022936).

Barron, P., C. Q. Smith, and M. Woolcock. 2004. "Understanding Local Level Conflict in Developing Countries: Theory, Evidence and Implications from Indonesia." World Bank Social Development Papers 31018. Washington: World Bank (December).

Carothers, T. 2003. "Promoting the Rule of Law Abroad: The Problem of Knowledge." Carnegie Endowment Working Paper 34, Rule of Law Series. Washington: Carnegie Endowment for International Peace, Democracy and Rule of Law Project (January).

————. 2006. "The Rule-of-Law Revival." In *Promoting the Rule of Law Abroad, In Search of Knowledge,* edited by T. Carothers. Washington: Carnegie Endowment for International Peace.

Commission on Legal Empowerment of the Poor. 2008a. *Making the Law Work for Everyone.* Volume 1 (http://www.undp.org/legalempowerment/report/Making_the_Law_Work_for_ Everyone.pdf).

————. 2008b. *Making the Law Work for Everyone.* Volume 2. *Working Group Reports* (http:// www.undp.org/legalempowerment/docs/ReportVolumeII/making_the_law_work_II.pdf).

de Langen, M. 2001. *Assessors and justice: Configurations of law and custom in conflicts over land in Douentza, Mali.* [In French.] Leiden: Coopération Juridique Malienne-Néerlandaise.

————. 2005. "Complementary answers to one and the same question: Decentralisation in Mali and the experience of the parcellation and distribution of land in Dountza." [In French.] In *Law in Africa: Local experiences and state law in Mali* [in French], edited by G.S.C.M. Hesseling, M. Djiré, and B. Oomen, 118–19. Paris: Editions Karthala.

European Commission for the Efficiency of Justice. 2006. "European Judicial Systems" (www. coe.int/T/DG1/LegalCooperation/CEPEJ/evaluation/2006/CEPEJ_2006_eng.pdf).

Fafchamps, M. 1996. The Enforcement of Commercial Contracts in Ghana. *World Development* 24, no. 3: 427–48.

Galanter, M. 1974. "Why the 'Haves' Come Out Ahead: Speculations on the Limits of Legal Change." *Law & Society Review* 9: 95–160. Also in *In Litigation, Do the "Haves" Still Come Out Ahead?* edited by H. M. Kritzer and S. S. Silbey. Stanford University Press.

Golub, S. 2003. "Beyond Rule of Law Orthodoxy: The Legal Empowerment Alternative." Working Paper 41. Washington: Carnegie Endowment for International Peace (www. carnegieendowment.org/files/wp41.pdf).

————. 2005. "The Legal Empowerment Alternative: Impact and Implications for the Rule of Law and Social Development Programs." Draft working paper produced for the World Bank Legal Forum, "Law, Equity, and Development," session on Legal Empowerment and Justice for the Poor. Washington, December 1–2.

————. 2006. "The Legal Empowerment Alternative." In *Promoting the Rule of Law Abroad: In Search of Knowledge*, edited by T. Carothers. Washington: Carnegie Endowment for International Peace.

Otto, J. M. 1991. "Law in Developing Countries: Object and Approaches." [In Dutch.] In *Eruditia Ignorantia*, edited by the Societas Iuridica Grotius, 95–119. Arnhem: Gouda Quint.

Rodrik, D., A. Subramanian, and F. Trebbi. 2004. "Institutions Rule: The Primacy of Institutions over Geography and Integration in Economic Development." *Journal of Economic Growth* 9, no. 2: 131–65.

Trubek, D. M., and M. Galanter. 1974. "Scholars in Self-Estrangement: Some Reflections on the Crisis in Law and Development Studies in the United States." *Wisconsin Law Review* 4: 1062–102.

United Nations Development Program (UNDP). 2004. "Access to Justice: Practice Note" (www.undp.org/governance/docs/Justice_PN_En.pdf).

van Rooij, B. 2007. "Bringing Justice to the Poor: Bottom-up Legal Development Cooperation." Paper presented at the annual meeting of the Law and Society Association, Berlin, July 24 (http://siteresources.worldbank.org/INTJUSFORPOOR/Resources/VanRooij BringingJusticetothePoor.pdf).

van Velthoven, B. C. J., and M. J. ter Voert. 2004. *Delta of Conflict Resolution.* [In Dutch.] The Hague: Ministry of Justice, Research and Documentation Center.

Wojkowska, E. 2006. *Doing Justice: How Informal Justice Systems Can Contribute.*" UNDP Paper. New York: United Nations Development Program (December) (www.undp.org/oslo centre/docs07/DoingJusticeEwaWojkowska130307.pdf).

PART VII

The Access Agenda

13

The Dynamics of Access: Understanding "the Mismatch"

JORRIT DE JONG AND GOWHER RIZVI

This book is an exploratory attempt to develop a better understanding of mechanisms that impede access to government and public services and programs and innovative solutions that have improved it. In the introductory chapter we defined access as a "match between the societal commitment and institutional capacity to deliver rights and services and people's capacity to benefit from those rights and services." This definition describes an ideal situation—"a perfect match"—that may actually never occur. After all, both society and its institutions are continuously changing. Getting the access match "right" would require a *ceteris paribus* condition that cannot be realistically expected. Therefore, 100 percent access may be understood as one extreme of a continuum whose other extreme is a complete lack of access. Access analysis focuses on situations in between, in which access is problematic to a larger or lesser degree. The studies in this volume show that obstructions to access come in all shapes and sizes. Each chapter examines the gap between the promise and practice of inclusive democratic governance. Chapters on holding governments accountable for basic services (chapters 9 and 10) discuss similar problem areas but present different analyses or solutions. Some chapters deal with the access issues in very different domains or countries, but reach strikingly similar analyses or solutions (for example, the discussions of service delivery systems in chapters 5 and 8 and the discussions of access to justice and legal empowerment in chapters 11 and 12). In this chapter we try to draw some general crosscutting lessons, using the Bureaucrat-Agency-System-Context

(BASC) framework we introduced in chapter 1. Clearly, a single volume cannot come close to covering the vast range of issues that are relevant to access research and analysis; the design and methods of these studies are also far too heterogeneous to allow us to draw conclusions for systematic comparative analysis. But such comprehensiveness was not our purpose. Our goal was to understand better the nature of "the mismatch." The materials presented here are just a few examples of how that mismatch manifests itself. The analyses in the chapters are examples of ways to research and interpret problems of access, as well as to develop practical remedies to improve it. Our conceptualization of access emphasizes that although political ideology and the exercise of power almost always play their roles, the fundamental variables in access analysis are *institutional capacity* (supported by society) on the one hand and *people's capacity* on the other hand.

Institutional Capacity and Societal Commitment

Concerning the delivery of basic services in developing countries (chapter 10), the administration of legal assistance in the United States (chapter 11), and licensing practices for small businesses in the Netherlands (chapter 4), we see that the institutional capacity of the state is inadequate. Underperforming providers of public services cannot be held accountable by the people, funding and oversight of pro bono litigation falls short, and regulatory systems impose huge administrative burdens on small businesses. For a variety of reasons, institutional arrangements, public organizations, officials, and professionals fail to perform. Either they are not doing the right thing, or they are not doing it right. The net effect is the exclusion of certain social groups—usually the least advantaged, weakest groups in society.

We also see that overall societal commitment to the work of the state has a more or less direct influence on the degree of match or mismatch. In chapter 6 it is argued that a general decline of commitment to the social compact and a separation between the discourse on programs and the discourse on revenues have led public managers to balance their books strategically by limiting access to public benefits. Societal commitment and institutional capacity are intimately linked in many ways. Failing institutions are more than a mere institutional, managerial, or technical problem. It is important to note that government dysfunction does not occur in a social, political, or ideological vacuum. For example, the poor representation of women in community forestry groups in South Asia has translated into inequitable decisions over the use of natural resources, with significant losses in efficiency and effectiveness (see chapter 2). These dynamics of exclusion and marginalization may be neglected or even fueled by the functioning of institutions. Institutions, however, are expressions, to at least some extent, of political will and societal commitment to social change. This is why improving access at the level of institutional capacity transcends the technocratic discourse of effective and efficient public management to become an avenue to social justice. If improving access requires institutional, organizational, or managerial reform, it is insufficient to explore merely the level of institutions, organizations, and management. There has to be a willingness to look at the broader picture, the broader context of values, norms, and perceptions in which exclusionary mechanisms have meaning.

People's Capacity and Responsibility

The second variable in our definition of access is "people's capacity to benefit from rights and services"—a variable that is both extremely important and very difficult to make operational. One of the basic assumptions of this book that we discussed early on is, to put it boldly, that it takes two to tango. Exclusion and marginalization do not occur only because governments neglect the needs of citizens or public sector organizations fail to perform. Social groups and individuals—for example, the eligible nonrecipients of social benefits discussed in chapter 7—have characteristics that may inherently or occasionally limit their ability to access democratic processes, economic activity, public services, or justice. Research shows that certain social groups (members of lower socioeconomic classes, elderly and illiterate people) do not apply for benefits because they are ill informed, uncertain, or scared of dealing with the government. The immigrant entrepreneurs portrayed in chapter 4 have similar problems: Are they sufficiently capable of dealing with the authorities while starting up their business? The Malinese man named Ousmane, whose story of seeking justice is presented in chapter 12, basically lacked the time, money, skills, and social capital to accomplish what he set out to do in court. The institutions in place may have worked just fine for these people if only they had had the capacity to make contact with them and interact with them properly.

In workshops, conferences, and classes, the cases presented in this book typically elicit three kinds of reactions to the problem of people's capacity to realize their rights and the services to which they are entitled: (1) "Government should definitely do more to reach out to them, help them, accommodate them"; (2) "People have their own responsibility; government can open doors, but people would still need to walk through the door by themselves"; and (3) "Hmm . . . Don't know . . . That's a hard call . . . A little bit of both, maybe?" Although clearcut, robust answers represented by the former two reactions are always tempting, we felt that the agnostic third reaction was practically and academically most appealing: morally, because it leaves room for a pragmatic approach, taking specific contexts and circumstances into account. We say practically because a complete outreach to all citizens would be just as impossible as entirely neglecting the disabilities of certain citizens. In practice, a middle road will have to be found, and that is exactly what is happening in many places, as the empirical evidence in this book shows. Academically, the agnostic response is most appealing because it allows us to approach each access problem flexibly. Leaving open the options that either institutional or people's capacity or a combination of both may be inadequate enables us to focus on the obstructing mechanisms without framing them ideologically. After all, as we have said before, we are interested in the proper functioning of democratic governance, which should serve advocates on the left, on the right, and in the middle of the political spectrum.

Third Parties for Improved Access

There is another reason to be reluctant to point in one direction or the other. Problems with access of one kind or another may be caused by a dysfunctional relationship between governments and clients, or the state and the citizen, but this does not necessarily mean that the solution will emerge from either side. Third parties may come to the rescue. Organizations or initiatives in the voluntary sector and the private sector, at the international level, the grass roots, and anywhere in between have played important roles in improving access. In many countries civil-society organizations help people fill out tax forms, defend themselves in court, apply for permits or other legal documents, start up businesses, quit drugs, find shelter, and so on and so forth. Microfinance schemes were initiated by nonprofit organizations and other financial institutions. Watchdog organizations such as Transparency International and Human Rights Watch have scrutinized and held governments accountable on behalf of people who were not able to organize protest or defend their rights effectively. In other words, the mismatch between institutional capacity and people's capacity may be the problem of states on the one hand and citizens on the other, but the solutions may come from any platform for social change. And indeed, many of the authors in this volume make recommendations that are not primarily directed at the state or at the citizens, but rather at organizations or initiatives in between. Group formation and education for women in South Asia may be facilitated by external NGOs (see chapter 3). Legal empowerment of rural African citizens may be a task for paralegal professionals (chapter 12). Nonstate mediators may carry forward alternative dispute resolution in the United States (chapter 11). Facilitation of immigrant entrepreneurs may be organized through community-based organizations (chapter 4). In short, many of the successful innovations described in this book have been initiatives by nonstate actors.

This does not mean that states and individual citizens have no important role to play. On the contrary! As we have seen in the case of access to government policymaking (chapter 3), states have an important role in creating institutional frameworks in which civil-society organizations can operate legally and effectively. And states also need to be willing to work with third parties to improve access for citizens. On the other hand, we have learned from the discussion on citizen charters (chapter 10) that community members need to organize themselves actively to ensure that institutional provisions for better access actually work. It takes many individual efforts of citizens to organize themselves. Only in the interaction between collectively articulated demands and institutionally established facilities does the process of improving access become meaningful and significant.

Impediments to Access

In table 13-1 we list some of the obstructionist mechanisms that are discussed in this book, using the analytical framework that we developed in chapter 1, the bureaucrat-agency-system-context, or BASC, framework, to collect and arrange the research represented here. The framework does not catch the full richness of analysis and discussion in each of the chapters, and the BASC model, like any model, forces the material into a specific shape—but it is one that we think is useful to the analysis of access problems. However, we want to emphasize that the authors of the individual chapters—and the readers as well—may or may not completely agree with our interpretation of their work. It is impossible to do full justice to each study presented in this volume, and that is not what we intend to do in table 13-1, but such a table can be helpful in identifying patterns and mechanisms that impede access.

Measures to Improve Access

Most of the contributors to this volume discuss successful innovations that have provided either partial or total solutions to access problems. Some contributors provide recommendations for improved access that have yet to give evidence of success. In table 13-2 we group both proposed and already implemented solutions along the lines of the BASC framework. (Again, these solutions represent the editors' interpretations of the findings presented in this study; the individual authors may not necessarily share either our phraseology or our categorization of these remedies.) Our purpose here is to create a fairly systematic overview of the variety of interventions that may improve access.

The Dynamics of Access

We have examined the state of access to specific services and benefits, for specific social groups, at a specific moment in time, and in specific locations. The result is a patchwork of images with a common theme: the gap between the promise and practice of democratic governance. Scholars from different disciplines and professional backgrounds have investigated access-related inequalities using a common lens: that of access. This lens has helped us see more clearly what the nature and scope of exclusionary mechanisms in democratic governance are. The multilayered, outcome-oriented approach to analyzing the institutional capacity

Table 13-1. *Impediments to Access, in Terms of the BASC Framework*

	Level of analysis—Unit of analysis			
Topics discussed in this volume	*Bureaucrat behavior— Individual and professional*	*Agency performance— Single organization*	*System dynamics— Institutional arrangement*	*Contextual factors— Community and society*
Access to government policy-making in eastern Europe	Higher officials do not invite smaller NGOs (weaker voices) to participate in the consultation process.	Government information is not disclosed fully or on a timely basis to the public at large	The legal framework for civil-society organizations does not help smaller organizations.	People are not easily motivated to rally around environ-mental issues
Access to decision-making about natural resources in South Asia	Men dominate the de-cisionmaking process and implicitly in-timidate women.	Community forestry groups that effectively exclude women have a negative effect on distributional equity.	The bargaining power of women vis-à-vis the state and their communities is weak.	Social norms and perceptions, as well as other factors, act to keep women out of the decisionmaking process.
Access to the formal economy for immigrant entrepreneurs	Rule-abiding behavior and reactive attitude of officials discourage certain groups of entrepreneurs.	Silo orientation; selective enforcement of rules; inadequate provision of information and assistance.	Lack of coordination between agencies and lack of coopera-tion between sectors.	Immigrants are often entre-preneurs by necessity, lack certified qualifications, and typically have an unclear financial status.
Access to financial services for the poor	(Not applicable)	Transaction costs are per-ceived to be too high for most commercial banks.	Financial sector is reluctant to provide financial services to poor people because of per-ceived lack of creditworthiness of those without collateral.	Poor people are reluctant to enroll in schemes not tailored to their needs and abilities.

Access to public benefits in times of budget cuts and a "shrinking" welfare state	Street-level bureaucrats develop "coping strategies" to deal with the mismatch between capacity and caseloads.	Underfunded agencies ration services and benefits by limiting benefits, eligibility, or service levels ("bureaucratic disentitlement").	(Intended) mismatch between creating public benefits and sustaining the means to provide them.	General decline of support for the welfare state.
Access to benefits for eligible nonrecipients	Reactive attitude of street-level bureaucrats.	No incentives created to target eligible nonrecipients; no strategies in place.	Lack of information exchange and infrastructural cooperation among organizations.	Misleading perceptions, fear, lack of information among eligible nonrecipients.
Access to social services for the marginalized	Cautious or risk-averse professionals are reluctant to use their own discretion.	Organizations create norms, rules, and procedures to guide professionals that in fact impede effective action.	Lack of coordination across organizational boundaries, sectors, and policy fields creates impediments.	Clients with problems in multiple domains often are least capable of dealing with the bureaucracy.
Access to government information and assistance	Frontline officers have difficulties "reading" and "translating" requests.	Complaints and service requests are not used as feedback to inform policy.	Lack of inter- and intradepartment process alignment.	Cultural diversity, illiteracy, poorly articulated requests, and concerns.
Access to accountability mechanisms in developing countries	Corruption is widespread among frontline officials in developing countries.	Agencies cannot be held accountable for poor service levels ("they just manage; they don't set policy").	Politicians can be held accountable by means of elections.	Citizens are rarely sufficiently organized to exercise pressure on failing service-delivery systems.
Access to justice in the United States	Pro bono lawyers lack incentives to perform well.	Institutions of justice are backlogged, caseloads are heavy, time per case is limited.	Budgets for legal aid are capped. Legal profession has a strong lobby, which is not working in favor of poor clients.	Defendants are often not aware of their limited access or are not able to voice their complaints.
Access to justice in developing countries	Many "gatekeepers" are corrupt or prone to arbitrary treatment of citizens seeking access to the justice system.	Malfunctioning institutions of justice cause delays. Incompetence at the higher levels of organizations results in low-quality legal information.	Legal framework and institutions are not in line with the legal needs of poor people. Legal information is often unavailable or poorly distributed.	Geographical, financial, cultural, intellectual, and language barriers keep poor people outside the legal framework.

Source: Authors' compilation.

Table 13-2. *Measures for Improved Access, in Terms of BASC Framework*

	Level of analysis—Unit of analysis			
Topics discussed in this volume	*Bureaucrat behavior— Individual and professional*	*Agency performance— Single organization*	*System dynamics— Institutional arrangement*	*Contextual factors— Community and society*
Access to government policy-making in eastern Europe	(Not applicable)	Lower entry barriers for NGOs to participate in consultation processes.	Empower civil society through legal frameworks.	(Not applicable)
Access to decision-making about natural resources in South Asia	(Not applicable)	(Not applicable)	Pass more gender-sensitive laws.	Empower group cohesiveness through external agents, group formation, and education.
Access to the formal economy for immigrant entrepreneurs	(Not applicable)	Shift strategy from law enforcement to compliance assistance.	Simplify the administration of licenses; expand the economic policy focus with the "social" dimension.	(Not applicable)
Access to financial services for the poor	(Not applicable)	Involve communities in managing information and risks.	Rethink and redesign the elements of the delivery system: decision-making authority, information, and capacity.	Create ownership and responsibility for the delivery system within communities.
Access to public benefits in times of budget cuts and a "shrinking" welfare state	(Not applicable)	Pay more (public) attention to the ways agencies and managers shape and ration benefits.	Reconnect the discourse on programs and the discourse on revenues.	(Not applicable)

Access to benefits for eligible nonrecipients	(Not applicable)	Automate detection of non-take-up and proactively provide benefits and services.	Invest in cross-agency information infrastructure (infocracies).	(Not applicable)
Access to social services for the marginalized	Empower professionals to use their discretionary authority in the interest of the client.	Redesign processes so as to facilitate horizontal coordination and tailor-made solutions.	Balance the obligation of public accountability with equity and effectiveness.	Make clients part of the solution instead of part of the problem.
Access to government information and assistance	Create different channels to contact government and staff them with qualified personnel.	Connect complaints management with policy development; make use of citizens' calls.	Realign departments on the basis of citizen orientation instead of functional boundaries.	(Not applicable)
Access to accountability mechanisms in developing countries	(Not applicable)	Create specific output-based accountability frameworks per service; involve citizens in evaluation.	Establish citizen charters defining the basic rights of access to services. Make these rights justiceable through forms of direct democracy.	Mobilize citizens' awareness of their chartered access rights and their responsibility to monitor government performance.
Access to justice in the United States	Create better incentives and peer review for quality pro bono assistance.	Simplify legal procedures and administration.	Simplify law and legal information; develop alternative forms of dispute resolution.	(Not applicable)
Access to justice in developing countries	Assist people dealing with officials, legal documents, and bureaucratic procedures.	Improve the functioning of courts.	Develop alternative dispute resolution mechanisms; involve the private and voluntary sectors and paralegals.	Legal empowerment of citizens is a leading approach: focus on participation rather than justice alone.

Source: Authors' compilation.

of the state can indeed be revealing: in many cases social inequalities look even more systemic and insurmountable than they did before. On a more positive note, these exclusionary mechanisms, once revealed, can be examined and dealt with. Although some impediments may seem immutable and impossible to eliminate, successful innovations have shown that the state of access actually can be changed or at least improved. Elaborating on our BASC framework, we have tried to connect some of the dots to draw some crosscutting inferences.

Perhaps our most important conclusion is that achieving a complete match between the institutional capacity to deliver and people's capacity to benefit from their entitlement will always remain a formidable challenge. The "state of access" is not a static condition but rather an ongoing project, one with both a long history and a robust future. Students of history know that we have come a long way. The Industrial Revolution, which started in England in the eighteenth century and later elsewhere in western Europe, dramatically increased the gross national product, aggregate income, and total supply of goods, but for nearly a hundred years after industrialization, few benefits filtered to the masses. The reason for this is easily explained: the majority of the population had no political rights and hence no capability of enforcing their entitlements. It took the French Revolution, the revolutions of 1830 and 1848, and in Britain the great Reform Acts of 1832 and 1867 to broaden political participation through the gradual extension of the franchise. Only through the exercise of their new political muscle were British and western European workers gradually able to secure a welfare state that distributed some of the benefits of economic growth to them, and from this volume we have learned that these welfare states still struggle to adequately deliver the benefits and services their citizens are entitled to. In most other parts of the world, such entitlements have not even been created and access to basic services such as clean water, sanitation, and electricity is still not secure. Development, understood as a gradual process leading to an expansion of people's freedom to realize their potential, requires a permanent concern for improving access to political decisionmaking, economic participation, public services, and justice. We have argued that access is an issue that cuts across these domains.

Improving access is the process of gradually removing the unfreedoms in all these domains, as Amartya Sen put it in *Development as Freedom* (1999). But even if such a state is possible, it surely will require constant renewal, for situations change, contexts alter, people move, and problems emerge, vanish, and reappear at a much faster rate than institutions do. Therefore, even a hypothetical state of full access could only last so long. Each generation must reassess the state of access to reflect the changing realities and the needs of the citizens.

It is probably more helpful to speak about the *dynamics* of access. Improving access can be understood as a continuous process of alignment between institutions and society. Institutions take time to adapt to new demands made on them by their authorizers as well as by the communities they serve. People take time to adapt to new challenges in their worlds and to articulate new problems, needs, and desires. Societies take time to develop a more or less coherent system of values and some consensus on ambitions with respect to social change or conservation. In any case, access as a match between the societal commitment and institutional capacity on the one hand and people's capacity to take advantage of them on the other depends on the dynamics of that process of alignment.

A major question remains: Who will take responsibility for guiding this process? One answer is that any entity can, but at the very least, the state should do so. Although states are far from able to solve all access-related problems in society and are unable to solve them entirely, they should be cognizant of their responsibility continuously to check whether they are delivering on their promises to their citizens and indeed whether they are fulfilling the duties of inclusive democratic governance. By looking at real-world outcomes, involving citizens and organizations from other sectors in remedying broken institutions and practices, and accepting that improving access is fundamentally a challenge of coproduced governance, states will be able to reassert responsibility as guarantors of social justice in the twenty-first century.

Contributors

BINA AGARWAL is professor of economics at the Institute of Economic Growth, Delhi University. Currently she serves on the UN Committee for Development Policy and the Indian Prime Minister's National Council for Land Reforms. Her publications include nine books and seventy professional papers on a range of subjects: land, livelihoods and property rights; environment and development; the political economy of gender; poverty and inequality; law; and agriculture and technological change. She has been visiting professor at Harvard University, the universities of Michigan and Minnesota, and New York University, and lectured worldwide. Recently she was awarded the Padma Shri by the president of India.

MAURITS BARENDRECHT is professor of private law at Tilburg University's Tilburg Law and Economics Centre (Tilec) and a member of the Government Advisory Council on Social Infrastructure. Previously he was attorney at law with De Brauw Blackstone Westbroek in The Hague. His research focus is on legal conflict resolution from an interdisciplinary perspective. He is currently working on improving access to justice (www.measuringaccesstojustice.com and www. microjustice.org).

JORRIT DE JONG is a research fellow at the Ash Institute for Democratic Governance and Innovation at Harvard's John F. Kennedy School of Government. His research, teaching, and consultancy work focuses on innovations in governance.

De Jong is the former director of the Centre for Government Studies, at Leiden University, the Netherlands. He is cofounder of the Kafka Brigade, an action research organization investigating excessive bureaucracy. De Jong has consulted with governments and NGOs, including the United Nations. A specialist in simulations games, he has taught in many executive education programs.

PETER KASBERGEN holds BA degrees in public administration and political science from Leiden University. As a freelance researcher he has worked among other organizations for the United Nations Population Fund and the Organization for Economic Cooperation and Development. His current academic research involves the viability of microfinance in the Netherlands. As the founder of Public Cinema, he produces short video clips for organizations in the public sector to communicate problems in governance issues, as well as their solutions.

ALBERT JAN KRUITER studied public administration at Leiden University and was senior consultant at the Centre for Government Studies (CGS) there. Before joining the CGS he worked for the Netherlands School of Public Administration where he developed several education programs. In recent years he has been consulting with a variety of public sector organizations including ministries, NGOs, and local governments on innovation, evaluation, and governance-based issues. He published extensively on democracy in a networked society, which is also the main focus of his dissertation research. As of 2008 he continues his research in India.

MAAIKE DE LANGEN is a policy specialist on legal empowerment of the poor for the United Nations Development Program. Previous functions with UNDP include business analyst in New York and program officer for governance and human rights in Chad. She has been a researcher at the Van Vollenhoven Institute for Law, Governance, and Development (Leiden University), where she worked on a legal cooperation project between the Netherlands and Mali and did sociolegal research on local courts and on the effects of decentralization on land governance.

MICHAEL LIPSKY is a visiting professor at Georgetown University's Public Policy Institute. He is also a senior program director at Demos, a public policy and advocacy organization based in New York, where he is primarily associated with Public Works: The Demos Center for the Public Sector. Lipsky is the author of many journal articles and several books, including *Protest in City Politics* (1970), the prize-winning *Street Level Bureaucracy: Dilemmas of the Individual in Public Services* (1980), and *Nonprofits for Hire: The Welfare State in the Age of Contracting* (1993, with S. R. Smith).

DEBORAH L. RHODE is one of the nation's leading scholars in the fields of legal ethics and gender, law, and public policy. An author of twenty books, she is the most frequently cited scholar in legal ethics. She heads Stanford Law School's Center on the Legal Profession and is the founding director of Stanford University's Center on Ethics. Professor Rhode has served as president of the Association of American Law Schools, chair of the American Bar Association Commission on Women and the Profession, and director of Stanford University's Institute for Research on Women and Gender.

GOWHER RIZVI is vice provost for international programs at the University of Virginia and professor at the McIntire School of Commerce. From 2002 to 2008, he was director of the Ash Institute for Democratic Governance and Innovation at Harvard's John F. Kennedy School of Government. Rizvi is the author of several books including *South Asia in a Changing International Order* (1993) and *Bangladesh: The Struggle for Democracy* (1985). He is the founder and editor of *Contemporary South Asia*, an academic and policy studies journal.

SUSAN ROSE-ACKERMAN is the Henry R. Luce Professor of Jurisprudence with a joint appointment between the Yale Law School and Yale's Department of Political Science. She has taught and written widely on corruption, law and development, administrative law, law and regulatory policy, the nonprofit sector, and federalism. Rose-Ackerman has been a fellow at the Center for Advanced Study in the Behavioral Sciences and at Collegium Budapest. Her current research foci are corruption and economic development, and comparative administrative law.

ALEXANDER SCHELLONG is a specialist on Citizen Relationship Management (CiRM) and eGovernment. His studies focus on the impact of information and communication technology on organizational and societal issues. He is a fellow at Harvard University's Program for Networked Governance. Schellong also was a research scholar at the University of Tokyo, working on networked governance and web 2.0. He teaches and consults on these and other topics internationally. Among others, he serves as an expert to the European Commission DG INFSO. Alexander received his PhD from the Johann Wolfgang Goethe-University, Frankfurt am Main.

ANWAR SHAH is lead economist and program leader, Public Sector Governance Program at the World Bank Institute, Washington, D.C., member of the Executive Board of the International Institute of Public Finance, Munich, Germany, and a fellow of the Institute for Public Economics, Edmonton, Alberta, Canada. He has previously served the governments of the province of Alberta and of Canada, the U.S. Agency for International Development, and the UN Intergovernmental Panel on Climate Change (as the lead author). He has published more than two dozen books and numerous articles in leading economic journals on governance, federalism, and climate change issues. His most recent book, *Fiscal Federalism* (with Robin Boadway), is forthcoming from Cambridge University Press.

GUY STUART is a lecturer in public policy at Harvard University's Kennedy School of Government. He received his PhD from the University of Chicago and then worked in Chicago in the field of community economic development. During this time he served as the director of the FaithCorp Fund, a nonprofit community loan fund. At the Kennedy School he teaches courses on management and microfinance. He is currently conducting research on microfinance in India, Mexico, and Malawi, and on developing country distributed service delivery systems.

ARRE ZUURMOND is associate professor of public administration at Delft University of Management and Technology and founder and CEO of Zenc Consultancy in The Hague. Previously he was managing consultant with Roccade Civility and professor of information and communication technology (ICT) and the future of public administration at Leiden University. Zuurmond is a leading specialist in the field of the information society, ICT, and innovation and improvement of operations in the public sector. He is cofounder of the Kafka Brigade, an action research organization investigating excessive bureaucracy.

Index

Abed, Fazle, 25

Access, generally: analytical framework, 20, 21*t*, 275–76; concept of power and, 12–14; definition, 4, 5, 275; to delivery system, 6, 25–27; dynamics of, 18–19, 279–85; economic contexts, 23–25; legal vs. illegal, 14; people's capacity and responsibility, 19, 277–78, 284; process conceptualization, 284–85; quality of services and, 7; research issues, 11, 275; rights to, 5, 6–7; role of third parties in improving, 278–79; scope of access needs in democracy, 5–6; social justice conceptualization, 8–11; state role in promoting, 285; strategies for improving, 31, 279. *See also* Delivery of government goods and services; Exclusionary systems; Improving access, strategies for

Accountability for legal representation, 237

Accountability of governance: access issues, 7–8, 28–29; citizen access to appeal and redress, 7–8; citizen empowerment and, 29, 207; degree of citizen access and influence, 72; in democratic systems, 28, 71; government-citizen communication systems, 28–29; idealized model, 73; legal empowerment approach to dispute resolution, 268; in legal system, 30; mechanisms, 73–74; in public service delivery, 29; rationale, 28, 71–72; results-based, 214–15; role of public advocacy, 74; in service delivery in developing countries, 211–12, 213, 214–15; in service delivery to multi-problem client, 181; strategies for improving, 72–73, 86–89; transaction costs, 219–20; in transition to democracy, 72. *See also* Citizen relationship management; Three-one-one systems

Accountable autonomy, 124

Affirmative action, 10

Agencies: BASC framework for analysis of access, 20, 21*t*; coordination of social service delivery in complex cases, 182–84; determinants of access, 17–18; domains of service for people with multiple problems, 169–70; intragovernmental coordination of regulation, 108–9, 111–12; models of accountability in governance, 74; public manager's response to revenue reductions, 144–46. *See also* Bureaucracies

Akgün, Tamer, 95

www.ingramcontent.com/pod-product-compliance
Lightning Source LLC
Chambersburg PA
CBHW030642270326
41929CB00007B/174